Sociology of "Developing Societies"
South Asia

Sociology of "Developing Societies"
General Editor: Teodor Shanin

THEMATIC VOLUMES

INTRODUCTION TO THE SOCIOLOGY OF "DEVELOPING SOCIETIES"
Hamza Alavi and Teodor Shanin

SOCIALIST "DEVELOPING SOCIETIES"?
(in preparation)

THEORIES OF SOCIAL TRANSFORMATION
(in preparation)

REGIONAL VOLUMES

SOUTH ASIA
Hamza Alavi and John Harriss

SUB-SAHARAN AFRICA
Chris Allen and Gavin Williams

LATIN AMERICA
Eduardo P. Archetti, Paul Cammack and Bryan R. Roberts

THE MIDDLE EAST
Talal Asad and Roger Owen

CENTRAL AMERICA
Jan L. Flora and Edelberto Torres-Rivas

SOUTHEAST ASIA
John G. Taylor and Andrew Turton

Series Standing Order

If you would like to receive future titles in this series as they are published, you can make use of our standing order facility. To place a standing order please contact your bookseller or, in case of difficulty, write to us at the address below with your name and address and the name of the series. Please state with which title you wish to begin your standing order. (If you live outside the UK we may not have the rights for your area, in which case we will forward your order to the publisher concerned.)

Standing Order Service, Macmillan Distribution Ltd, Houndmills, Basingstoke, Hampshire, RG21 2XS, England.

Sociology of "Developing Societies" South Asia

edited by Hamza Alavi and John Harriss

MACMILLAN

First published 1989

Published by
MACMILLAN EDUCATION LTD
Houndmills, Basingstoke, Hampshire RG21 2XS
and London
Companies and representatives throughout the world

Typeset by Wessex Typesetters
(Division of The Eastern Press Ltd)
Frome, Somerset

Printed in Hong Kong

British Library Cataloguing in Publication Data
South Asia.—(Sociology of "developing societies").
1. Asia. South Asia—Social conditions
I. Alavi, Hamza   II. Harriss, John
III. Series
954.05'2
ISBN 0–333–27557–8 (hardcover)
ISBN 0–333–27558–6 (paperback)

Contents

III   Ideologies and Realities of Inequality

IV   Regionalism and Ethnicity

V   Classes and Popular Struggles

Series Preface

The question of the so-called "developing societies" lies at the very heart of the political, the economic and the moral crises of the contemporary global society. It is central to the relations of power, diplomacy and war of the world we live in. It is decisive when the material well-being of humanity is concerned; that is, the ways some people make a living and the ways some people hunger. It presents a fundamental dimension of social inequality and of struggles for social justice. During the last generation it has also become a main challenge to scholarship, a field where the perplexity is deeper, the argument sharper and the potential for new illuminations more profound. That challenge reflects the outstanding social relevance of this problem. It reflects, too, an essential ethnocentrism that weighs heavily on the contemporary social sciences. The very terminology which designates "developing" or "underdeveloping" or "emerging" societies is impregnated with teleology which identifies parts of Europe and the USA as "developed". Images of the world at large as a unilinear rise from barbarity to modernity (or vice versa as a descent to hell) have often substituted for the analysis of actuality, as simplistic metaphors often do. To come to grips with a social reality, which is systematically different from that of one's own, and to explain its specific logic and momentum, is a most difficult conceptual and pedagogic task. It is the more so, for the fundamental questions of the "developing societies" are not of difference only but of relationships past and present with the countries of advanced capitalism and industrialization. It is in that light that we encounter as analysts and teachers not only a challenge to "sociology of development", but also a major challenge to radical scholarship itself.

The Sociology of "Developing Societies" series aims to offer a systematically linked set of texts for use as a major teaching aid at university level. It is being produced by a group of teachers and scholars related by common interest, general outlook and commitment sufficient to provide an overall coherence but by no means a single monolithic view. The object is, on the one hand, to bring relevant questions into focus and, on the other hand, to teach through debate. We think that at the current stage "a textbook" would necessarily gloss over the very diversity, contradictions and inadequacies of our thought. On the other hand, collections of articles are often rather accidental in content. The format of a conceptually structured set of readers was chosen, sufficiently open to accommodate variability of views within a coherent system of presentation. They bring together works by sociologists, social anthropologists, historians, political scientists, economists, literary critics and novelists in an intended disregard of the formal disciplinary divisions of the academic enterprise.

Three major alternatives of presentation stand out: first, a comparative discussion of the social structures within the "developing societies", focusing on the generic within them; second, the exploration of the distinct character of the main regions of the "developing societies"; third, consideration of context and content of the theories of social transformation and change. Accordingly, our *Introduction* to the series deals with the general issues of comparative study, other books cover different regions, while a final volume is devoted to an examination of basic paradigms of the theories of social transformation. They therefore represent the three main dimensions of the problem area, leaving it to each teacher and student to choose from them and to compose their own course.

The topic is ideologically charged, relating directly to the outlook and the ideals of everyone. The editors and many of the contributors share a broad sense of common commitment, though there is among them a considerable diversity of political viewpoint and theoretical approach. The common ground may be best indicated as three fundamental negations. First, there is an implacable opposition to every social system of oppression of humans by other humans. That entails also the rejection of scholastic apologia of every such system, be it imperialism, class oppression, elitism, sexism or the like. Second, there is the rejection of "preaching down" each solution from the comfort of air-conditioned offices and campuses, whether in the "West" or in "developing societies" themselves, and of the tacit assumption of our privileged wisdom that has little to learn from the common people in the "developing societies". Third, there is the rejection of the notion of scholastic detachment from social commitments as a pedagogy and as a way of life. True scholarship is not a propaganda exercise even of the most sacred values. Nor is it without social consequences, however conceived. There are students and teachers alike who think that indifference improves vision. We believe the opposite to be true.

TEODOR SHANIN

Acknowledgements

We would like to thank the authors of the papers included in this book for their help and forbearance; and David Arnold, Barbara Harriss, David Washbrook and an anonymous reviewer for criticism and advice.

The editors and publishers wish to thank the following who have kindly given permission for the use of copyright material.

Associated Book Publishers (UK) Ltd for extracts from *Women, Work and Property in North-West India* by Ursula Sharma, Tavistock Publications, 1980.

Roger Ballard for his paper "Effects of Labour Migration from Pakistan".

Cambridge University Press for extracts from "Workers' Politics and the Mill Districts in Bombay between the Wars" by Rajnarayan Chandavarkar, *Modern Asian Studies*, vol. 15, no. 3, 1981.

Frank Cass & Co. Ltd for extracts from "The New Technology, Class Formation and Class Action in the Indian Countryside" by Terry Byres, *Journal of Peasant Studies*, 8, 4, July 1981.

Etnografiska Museet for extracts from "British India or Traditional India?: an anthropological problem" by Chris Fuller, *Ethnos*, 1977, 3–4.

Akmal Hussain for his paper "Pakistan: Land Reforms Reconsidered", December 1982.

Kluwer Academic Publishers for extracts from "Ethnicity and Racialism in Colonial Indian Society" by David Washbrook from *Racism and Colonialism*, ed. R. Ross, Martinus Nijhoff, 1982.

Pacific Affairs for extracts from "Peasant Resistance and Revolt in South India' by Kathleen Gough, *Pacific Affairs*, vol. XLI, no. 4.

The Past and Present Society and the author for extracts from "Communal Riots and Labour: Bengal's Jute Mill-Hands in the 1890s" by Dipesh Chakrabarty, *Past and Present*, no. 91, May, 1981, pp. 140–69.

Sage Publications Ltd for extracts from "Bangladesh and the World Economic System: the Crisis of External Dependence" by Rehman Sobhan, *Development and Change*, vol. 12, 1981.

South Asia Bulletin for extracts from "Ethnic Conflict in Sri Lanka: Perceptions and Solutions" by Newton Gunasinghe, *South Asia Bulletin*, vol. 6, no. 2, Fall 1986.

The University of California Press for extracts from "The Disintegration of the Hali System" in *Patronage and Exploitation* by Jan Breman, 1974; "Changes in Agrarian Economy: Vilyatpur 1848–1968" in *Vilyatpur 1848–1968: Social and Economic Change in a North Indian Village* by Tom Kessinger, 1974; *Business and Politics in India* by Stanley Kochanek, 1974. Copyright © 1974 by The Regents of the University of California.

The University of Chicago Press for extracts from *India's Preferential Policies* by Myron Weiner and Mary Katzenstein, 1981.

Zed Books Ltd for extracts from *Untouchable! Voices of Dalit Liberation* by Barbara R. Joshi, 1986.

Every effort has been made to trace all the copyright-holders, but if any have been inadvertently overlooked the publishers will be pleased to make the necessary arrangement at the first opportunity.

General Introduction

The term "South Asia" has gained currency in fairly recent times to designate the region south of the Himalayan range extending down to the Indian ocean. Geography is not the only unifying factor to denote the region, for it includes countries clustered around British India which were either under British colonial rule or its political influence, which are now independent. They therefore include India, Pakistan, Bangladesh, Sri Lanka and its erstwhile dependency Maldive Islands, Nepal and Bhutan. It is debatable whether Burma, which had close administrative ties with British India, should be so included. Generally it is not. Beyond these borders lie countries like Afghanistan and Iran or Thailand which stood outside the sphere of British colonial rule although the historical and cultural links of these countries with South Asia are close.

The region is unified by a much longer history than British rule alone. Varied influences stretching back over the centuries have woven the intricate tapestry of the region's culture which, perhaps, should not be referred to entirely in the singular, for common threads are overlaid by differentiating local motifs that mark the distinctiveness of its various parts. For the most part, it is the north of the region that has been successfully unified under successive imperial ruling dynasties which have, from time to time, extended their rule southwards. However, Hindu mythology takes in Sri Lanka within its ambit and Buddhist civilization, originating in north-eastern India, has left its mark in Pakistan, in the form of the Gandhara civilisation in the north-west, in Bengal and not least in Sri Lanka where it is the religion of the majority. For over six centuries before the British conquest, Muslim rule was firmly established in northern and central India and was extended southwards. That too has added its colour and texture to the tapestry of South Asian culture and, especially, to its administrative and legal structures on which British colonial rule was later to build.

It is sometimes contended that climatically the region is unified by the seasonal pattern of the monsoons that brings the rain that nourishes South Asian agriculture and times its rhythms. But this does not impose any uniformity, for ecological variations are quite wide, ranging from the barren wastes of Baluchistan and the Sarhad (NWFP), the vast and arid Indus Plain, now enriched by irrigation, to the flood-covered plains of Bengal. Patterns of social organization as well as of agriculture vary greatly between rice-growing regions and wheat-growing areas of the north and the north-west. Problems and conditions of rural development are very different in different parts of the region and over-arching generalizations are often quite misleading.

It is likewise in the case of modern industry which began to develop, but very unevenly, from the latter half of the nineteenth century. The fact that the modern textile industry, which was for long the principal industry in Indian hands, was centred on Bombay and Gujerat may have much to do with the existence of prosperous trading communities in Gujerat ports who had handled the bulk of North Indian exports and imports before the colonial transformation. Their traditional source of livelihood was destroyed by diversion of northern Indian export trade, following the building of railways linking Bombay directly to the interior. These communities responded by moving rapidly into the expanding areas of colonial trade, and later industry. Likewise, Marwari communities (Rajasthanis) who had traditionally acted as middlemen in the overland trade from the north to Gujerat ports, spread all over India and now occupy a dominant position within the Indian capitalist class. Other regions of India were affected by the colonial impact in their rather different ways, and not all of them released entrepreneurial energies on the same scale as the Marwaris and Gujeratis, although the Chettiars of Tamilnadu also produced active entrepreneurs in various fields. In Bengal, administrative employment rather than business seemed to be the most favoured route to upward mobility and there the Jute industry was almost entirely British-owned. In the regions that have come to be Pakistan and Bangladesh, respectively, there was virtually no modern industry before independence. New patterns of industrial development have evolved in those countries since independence.

This volume focuses on what may be the more significant issues relating to India and Pakistan, with some material on Bangladesh and Sri Lanka. For reasons of space, we have not included material on political systems in South Asia nor such matters as the bureaucracy and the military, important though all these questions are. By comparison with most other countries an enormous amount of information is available about India, Pakistan and Bangladesh. The records of the British period are rich; there is an abundance of statistical information (though much of it is probably rather misleading). There has been a great deal of social science research, most of it carried out by South Asian scholars, and a good deal of it published in the pages of the remarkable *Economic and Political Weekly*, published in Bombay. This carries regular weekly reporting on Indian, regional and international affairs, and scholarly articles from the whole field of the social sciences. Other important journals are *Social Scientist*, *Indian Economic and Social History Review*, *Lokayan*, and *Frontier*. Amongst journals published elsewhere in the world are the *Journal of Contemporary Asia*, *Journal of Asian Studies*, *Modern Asian Studies*, and, in view of the frequency with which it publishes work on our region, the *Journal of Peasant Studies*.

Sociological studies of South Asia have generally been dominated by structural functionalism; work on South Asian politics by the liberal pluralist paradigm – and the alternatives have often been framed in terms of a very conventional, stylised form of Marxist analysis. Historical research, too, has been heavily influenced by the "modernization" problematic of functionalist sociology. A need for fresh approaches and for critical examination of basic concepts has come to be recognized, as is shown in some recent reviews of South Asian studies (Harriss; Toye; Washbrook, 1988).

In the selection of contributions for this book we have attempted to present a coherent view of South Asian society, as an historically developing totality of relations, whilst also introducing the wider literature. The first principle of the selection has been firmly to reject the approach, hitherto so powerful, which supposes that there is or was a "traditional" India, which has been or is being changed by forces of "modernization", in conformity with the functional prerequisites of industrialization, urbanization, colonialism and capitalism. We also reject sociological interpretations which rest on "culturalist" premises and maintain that South Asia is somehow "essentially" different from anywhere else because of caste and religion. At the same time, we do not reduce the importance of the ideologies of South Asian people themselves, and recognize that cultural meanings and material conditions combine to determine or constitute any empirical situation. The approach we have taken is an historical one, treating societies in terms of process, assigning causal primacy neither to "economics" nor "politics" nor "ideology", recognizing the organic unity of social structures and processes.

Brief introductions to the various parts of the book are intended to provide an overview of the fields covered.

Part I

The Colonial Transformation

Editors' Introduction

The historiography of modern South Asia is extremely rich and there are many different currents of interpretation running through it. Most writing on the economic and social history of colonialism, however, responds in some way to the propositions of the nationalist historians put forward from the late nineteenth century (Naoroji, 1871; R. C. Dutt, 1956; and see R. Palme Dutt, 1940; and Bipan Chandra, 1966). Their portrayal of India as a backward colonial economy and identification of the cause of the lack of development in India's colonial relationship with Britain has had a profound influence on contemporary theories of underdevelopment, largely because of Paul Baran's *The Political Economy of Growth* (1957). Baran's chapter "On the Roots of Backwardness" takes India as "the outstanding case in point".

Critical elements in the nationalist argument were that there was a continuous "drain" of financial resources from India to Britain; that the British settlements of land revenue impoverished agriculture and created massive rural poverty; that the British first systematically "de-industrialized" India – which in the period before colonial rule had flourishing industries and had had an important place in world trade, as Alavi explains here – and then set up a series of barriers to successful modernization. There is much controversy on all these issues (Charlesworth, 1982; Banerji, 1982; Bagchi, 1983; Stokes, 1973; and Washbrook, 1981).

Much contemporary debate about post-colonial developments, notably in agriculture, turns on assumptions not always explicit, about the manner and extent to which the colonial experience transformed pre-colonial social structures or preserved them. Those who interpret recent developments in Indian agriculture as the beginning of capitalist development, tend to represent pre-existing structures, inherited from colonial rule, as being pre-capitalist in character, e.g. Patnaik (1972). Others, such as Alavi (1982) have argued that structural changes brought about in India during the first hundred years of colonial rule have had the effect of dissolving

1

pre-capitalist structures of social relations of production and establishing the structures of colonial capitalism.

Alavi's argument is briefly summarized in his contribution below, where, additionally, he links the economic drain from India with the underpinning of the Industrial Revolution in Britain. Furthermore, he discounts the prevailing notion that the Indian textile industry was destroyed by the superior competitive power of mechanized production in Britain and shows the development of the British textile industry to have been based on an import substitution strategy, but one that differs in important ways with that recommended in the 1950s by ECLA and undertaken in many Third World countries.

Washbrook, in a recent review of historical writing (1988) has shown that the evidence corresponds quite closely with the arguments of the nationalist/underdevelopment theorists. But as he points out, the underdevelopment view involves the implication that had South Asia's capitalist development not been captured and diverted by Europe, its dynamic "could, would or should have produced industrialisation" – which returns us to a teleological view of the development of capitalism. Second, the underdevelopment view makes it difficult to explain important aspects of South Asia's history in the nineteenth century. In particular, why was there so little political resistance to British rule, and why "after a few early misunderstandings did South Asia's capitalist social classes become the most loyal supporters of the British Raj?" The answer offered is that the magnate groups had probably "never had it so good" in spite of their subordination to the dominance of British capital.

Capitalism in fact flourished in nineteenth-century India. The dynamic of its expansion, however:

> came not from the "dangerous" entrepreneurship of capital but from the pressure of social necessity which forced previously "unproductive" groups and groups productive in now unviable sectors onto the land to work. This pressure, by increasing the competition for land and for subsistence, also increased the dominance of capital and enabled it both to claim a progressively higher share of the social product and to cast off more and more of its responsibilities for the social reproduction of the labour force.

The fact that capitalist development in South Asia depended not on raising productivity through investments in technology and human capital but rather on reducing the share of a more restricted social product accorded to labour, was the result not only of colonialism but also the logic of South Asia's own process of development. It was in the context of this type of capitalist development, the outcome of interactions of colonialism and of "indigenous" processes of change, that class formation and the political developments discussed by Alavi took place.

The two other papers in this part, both emphasize structural changes that occurred during the colonial period. Looking at "Land, Caste and Power" at the local level, Fuller, a social anthropologist, dismisses representation of the late colonial society in India as "traditional" and evaluates important changes that have taken place in the social structure as a consequence of the colonial impact. Kessinger, also a social anthropologist, has produced a fascinating and extremely well-documented study of changes in a Punjab village over a period of 120 years since 1848 when the village came under colonial rule. The extract that we have selected shows changes in the agrarian economy following its incorporation into the global generalised commodity production of the colonial economy. In the light of contemporary "tractor-fetishism", taken to be a symbol of capitalist development, it is well to consider the chain of technological changes and investments in agriculture that occurred during the century which Kessinger has documented.

Colonial rulers and Indian élites were not the only active agents in the making of Indian History. Some contemporary historians seek to write history from the "bottom up", and to describe and explain the struggles of peasants and workers in their own terms, treating these repressed and exploited people as active agents in their own history. As Pandey says "in the case of colonial India the peasants have generally been treated as the beneficiaries (economically) of an increasingly benevolent system or victims of an oppressive one, 'manipulated' (politically) by self-seeking politicians or 'mobilised' by large-hearted, selfless ones. Both viewpoints miss out an essential feature – the whole area of independent thought and conjecture and speculation (as well as action) on the part of the peasant" (Pandey, 1982). He describes the development of agrarian movements and of peasant revolt in Awadh, and shows how peasant mobilization took place well *before* the involvement of urban nationalist politicians – before "Jawaharlal Nehru discovered the Indian peasantry and found the countryside afire with enthusiasm and full of strange excitement". Then the Congress leadership rather quickly turned its back on the peasant movement, for reasons which hinged on "a dim but growing awareness of its own class interests" as the party of the growing urban and rural petty bourgeoisie.

Sarkar, in a synthesis of the recent historiography of India's nationalism (Sarkar, 1983) extends this analysis of Congress politics in a wider context. In the 1930s, Sarkar argues, "The Congress . . . while fighting the Raj was also becoming the Raj, foreshadowing the great but incomplete transformation of 1947 . . . what was involved was the gradual establishment of a kind of hegemony (never absolute or unqualified) of bourgeois and dominant peasant groups over the national movement."

Sarkar's account shows the growing strength of Indian capitalist groups against the background of the complex economic relationships of Britain and India, and suggests that the Congress, while it was never simply the instrument of the bourgeoisie, acted none the less to counter and contain popular struggles. At the same time the attitudes of the Indian bourgeoisie towards the nationalist struggle were inherently ambivalent, the calculation of economic interest sometimes pushing some business groups towards collaboration with the British, and others towards support for the nationalist movement (see Markovits, 1984, for an extended treatment of the relationships of the big bourgeoisie and the Congress). In Sarkar's account of it, the Indian capitalist class can be described adequately neither as a "comprador bourgeoisie" nor as a "national bourgeoisie". It also appears that while it was a strong force by the time of the Second World War, the Indian capitalist class was still not strong enough to make state functionaries unquestionably subservient to its interests. As Anupam Sen says: "This weakness of the bourgeoisie became ever more manifest after independence" (Sen, 1982, 86) – a theme which is continued in Part II of this volume.

Charlesworth (1982) offers an introduction to nineteenth- and early twentieth-century economic history which is a brilliant piece of succinct exposition and the *Cambridge Economic History of India*, vol. II (edited by D. Kumar, 1982) contains a major collection of review articles (reviewed in a special issue of *Modern Asian Studies*, vol. 19, no. 3, 1985). Bagchi's study of private investment (1972) is a work of major importance on Indian industrialization and the same author has reopened debate on de-industrialization in the early nineteenth century (Bagchi, 1976; and see also Vicziany, 1979). Perlin's essay on proto-industrialization (Perlin, 1983), of outstanding importance as a study of India's economic development especially in the eighteenth century, also contains discussion of "de-industrialization". On agrarian history Baker's study of the Tamilnad countryside (Baker, 1984) is path-breaking. Alice Thorner (1982) gives a useful overview of the "mode of production debate"; and Pouchpedass (1980), Charlesworth (1980) and Hardiman (1981) have made important contributions to the study of agrarian politics in the later colonial period.

Formation of the Social Structure of South Asia under the Impact of Colonialism

Hamza Alavi

There is a conventional view of pre-colonial India as a static "traditional society" – rural and agricultural, founded on self-contained corporate village communities bound down by the caste system and confined to subsistence production – on which was superimposed a parasitic state. That society, it was supposed, lacked any endogenous dynamic for development. It followed therefore that it was the shattering impact of colonialism that broke open that closed society and generated new forces of change. Such a view provided the legitimating ideology of colonial rule, of its officials and their masters who thought of British rule as the bearer of a new enlightenment for the natives.

Marx's view of pre-colonial Indian economy and society was somewhat different. His view of the colonial regime was less benign. But as he saw it, while colonialism had brought devastation and much suffering to Indian society, it had also introduced capitalism into India and thereby a new dynamic of social transformation that, ultimately, would be far more significant. His vision of India's ultimate future, as a result, was an optimistic one. "England", he wrote, "has to fulfil a double mission in India: one destructive and the other regenerating – the annihilation of the old Asiatic Society and laying of the material foundations of Western Society in Asia" (Marx, 1960, 77). The colonial impact on the Indian subcontinent would generate new class forces which would turn against colonial rule and liberate India. This dynamic of change would be the result not of paternalism of the colonial regime but of opposition to it by the new endogenous forces.

Indian nationalist opinion likewise shared the view that the old order was static and inimical to progress and had to go. Most of the classical Indian nationalist writing was produced by men who were brought up on an English education, imbued with the conventional wisdom of the nineteenth-century British liberal social philosophy. Their complaints were: first, that there was an unrequited drain of resources from India by virtue of colonial exploitation that was impoverishing India; second, that the colonial regime was doing little to promote indigenous industrial enterprise and, indeed, was doing much to resist its development through discriminatory policies; and, finally, that Victorian Britain was failing to live by its own professed liberal democratic social philosophy by refusing to grant Indians "self-government within the Empire".

Contemporary historical scholarship has refuted the stereotype of "traditional" pre-colonial India, relying on bare subsistence production, isolated from the world and turned in upon itself. Such a view obscures the processes of development that were already in being in pre-colonial India and also the successive stages through which Indian society passed in its encounter with the West, each of which had its own specificity and quite distinct effects on Indian economy and society.

The Age of Trade and Prosperity

Medieval Indian society had already developed manufacturing skills equal to the best that Europe had to offer at the time and it had a flourishing export trade in textiles. It had also achieved a high level of urbanisation. As in feudal Europe, that urban society was parasitic on an economic surplus drawn from the peasantry, in the form of "land revenue". The relationship between the urban and the rural society was asymmetric. The rural economy produced cash crops for sale in urban markets, but only enough to raise money to pay land revenue and no more. It did not raise money to buy urban manufactured goods. The rural economy was itself self-sufficient. Indeed, the village economy was difficult to penetrate from the outside, for village artisans and a variety of "village servants" provided goods and services that were needed by members of the village community and they were in turn maintained by the village community by payment of ritually fixed shares of every peasant's crops that had to be rendered at every harvest. In return the cultivator and his family were entitled to receive from the "village servants" their services or goods on the basis of accepted standards of their needs. The ritual obligation on the cultivators to pay the conventional share of the crop to the village specialists was unaffected by the actual extent of the use that they actually made of such services. Therefore there was little incentive, say, for a peasant to buy shoes from the urban market, foregoing his claim on the village cobbler, for he would not thereby be free from his obligation to pay the cobbler the prescribed share of his crop. The rural economy was therefore resistant to commercial penetration by urban commodity production and its internal self-sufficiency has been very slow to break down. In a sense, therefore, pre-colonial India had two economies, the rural and the urban, relatively insulated from each other, except for the forcible extraction of the agricultural surplus that underpinned the urban economy.

Some scholars have suggested that India was on the threshold of capitalist development on the eve of the colonial conquest (cf. Habib, 1969, and Chandra *et al.*, 1969). This is much too large a question to discuss here. It must be said, however, that if there was potentiality for capitalist growth in pre-colonial India, its scope would initially have been confined to the urban economy and export markets, for the institutional structure that insulated the village economy had not yet begun to break down.

The pre-colonial urban society was a flourishing one. The nobility and state officials presided over it. But being nominees of the Emperor and subject to regular transfer, their presence as individual families in particular towns was temporary. As a class, however, their place in the urban society was a well-established one. This class drew on the wealth that was extracted as land revenue and their disbursements were the source of the wealth that circulated through the urban economy. They and their employees generated a flow of money demand for goods and services which in turn sustained a wide variety of people in profitable employment. To that source of demand must be added the role of foreign trade which was soon to increase by leaps and bounds when the sea route from India to Europe was established.

Urban production itself was in the form of petty commodity production by artisans some of whom employed apprentices and journeymen. It is these classes and the traders, and professionals who were the backbone of the growing towns and cities, since nobles and state officials had no local roots (Naqvi, 1968, 85). The craftsmen were organized in powerful guilds. Evidence points against notions about an obstructing role of caste in development, for the guilds embraced craftsmen of different castes and religions; the Hindu weaver, the *koli* or *kori*, as well as the Muslim weaver, the *julaha*. Guild rather than caste regulated their activities. Apart from craftsmen, nobles and the soldiery, there was a large variety of functionaries in the towns, clerks, accountkeepers, traders and merchants, entertainers and priests who made up a substantial body of urban consumers of manufactured products, sustained by wealth extracted as land revenue from the peasantry.

For several centuries before colonization India was at the centre of a network of world trade, principally as a supplier of cotton and silk textiles to the Middle East, Africa and the Far East. "The cotton plant was first domesticated in India, whose textile trade is so ancient that Indian cotton fabrics have been found in the tombs of the pharaohs" (Twomey, 1983). A mark of that extensive commercial intercourse is to be found in the influence of Indian culture and religions in South-east Asia and the Far East, as well as that of Islam, for Arab seafarers were among principal carriers of Indian trade.

The discovery of the sea route to India by the Europeans at the end of the fifteenth century inaugurated a new era in India's foreign trade and manufacturing, for bulky goods could now be carried to Europe in large quantities and cheaply. As a result, the seventeenth and eighteenth centuries, when the seaborne trade to Europe reached high levels, were periods of great prosperity for India.

It is important to recognize the global character of the colonial enterprise. Indo-European trade was made possible by another colonial link, namely, the Iberian conquest and exploitation of Latin America. Europe did not produce any goods that India needed or wanted at the time which it could therefore offer in exchange for Indian goods. European purchases of Indian goods were paid for in gold and silver bullion and precious stones, extracted by rapacious colonial regimes from Latin America. For India a negative aspect of this form of financing its exports was that its receipts in the form of bullion and precious stones sterilised India's growing wealth, freezing it in jewellery and massive monuments. It contributed nothing to India's productive resources and little to common consumption. It is, nevertheless, noteworthy that in its initial encounter with the West, India played the role of supplier of manufactured commodities in the global trade. That was the reverse of the classical pattern of colonial division of labour, which was to take shape in the second half of the nineteenth century.

European powers vied with each other to capture a share of the Indian textile trade. The rapid expansion of its overseas trade was fully matched by expansion of Indian manufacturing production. Far from being stagnant and inert, the pre-colonial economy was quite responsive to the new demands that were made upon it. Indian techniques of textile production were comparable to the contemporary European technology (Baines, 1966, 115). The East India Company, which had received its charter in the year 1600, had a major vested interest in the preservation and expansion of that trade. It was first and foremost a commercial corporation. It was Anglo-French rivalry to pre-empt Indian trade that set in motion the conquest of India that began in 1757 and led to the subjugation of India as a British colony.

Conquest, Plunder and Disintegration of the Indian Economy

The conquest of India inaugurated the second phase of India's relationship with Europe, the first phase of its colonial relationship with Britain. In that first phase of colonial rule the classical colonial pattern of international division of labour did not take shape. Instead colonial exploitation in that first stage took the form of direct extraction of an economic surplus in the form of land revenue, which was transferred to Britain in the form of unrequited exports. The East India Company took over the privileges of pre-colonial rulers of India in appropriating land revenue. But its accrual to a foreign power was to have devastating effects on Indian society.

Under the regime of the East India Company land revenue was collected with a rapacity and ruthlessness that was unknown under preceding Indian regimes, which were flexible enough to take account of good harvests and bad. Moreover, the magnitude of the revenue burden itself was now increased manifold. "In the last year of administration of the last Indian ruler of Bengal, in 1764–65, the land revenue realised was £817,000. In the first year of the Company's administration in 1765–6, the land revenue realised in Bengal was £1,470,000 ... When Lord Cornwallis fixed the Permanent Settlement in 1793, he fixed it at £3,400,000" (R. Palme Dutt, 1940, 106). In addition vast sums were extorted by officials of the Company who piled up vast private fortunes (Marshall, 1976). The effects of this heavy burden and its rigorous collection were soon manifested in the pauperization of Indian agriculture and loss of food reserves that peasants normally maintained to insure against bad years. Famines therefore became endemic, one of the worst being the great Bengal famine of 1770. The Calcutta Council of the Company, reporting on it to the Court of Directors in London, wrote: "Above one third of the inhabitants have perished in the once plentiful province of Purneah, and in other parts the misery is equal" (R. C. Dutt, 1956, 51–2).

The devastation was not limited to the rural society. There was another, less obvious, aspect of the new dispensation that had far-reaching effects on the Indian urban society. Land revenue, instead of going to an indigenous ruling class, through whom it had fed the urban economy, now accrued to a foreign power, which transferred the bulk of the wealth abroad. The urban society was thus deprived

of the resources that had sustained it. On the other hand, instead of
having to pay for exports of Indian textiles and other goods by
importing bullion and other items into India, as before, the East
India Company now financed its purchases of these goods for export
to Britain and Europe, out of receipts from land revenue. Thus
began the unrequited flow of exports from India that drained the
country of wealth and resources. Not only were the rural economy
and society devastated but also the urban society. Diversion of the
flow of land revenue away from the hands of the indigenous ruling
class took away the foundations on which India's urban society had
rested. There was a dramatic decline in the urban population and
cities were laid waste. For example, Sir Charles Trevelyan reported
that the population of Dacca, the "Manchester of India", declined
from 150,000 to a mere 30,000 (R. Palme Dutt, 1940, 120). Old
cities declined, decayed and many disappeared altogether. New
colonial cities came into existence as the next phase of colonial
development got under way and new centres of the colonial trade
and colonial administration came into existence.

India and the Industrial Revolution in England

The conquest of India began on the eve of the Industrial
Revolution in Britain and it is useful to consider the relationship
between the two. The cotton textile industry was central to the
British Industrial Revolution. The "threshold" of the industrial
revolution in England "was crossed first in cotton manufacture"
(Landes, 1970, 82). British cotton textile manufactures stepped
into the market which Indian textiles had established; an import
substitution strategy of industrialization, similar to the strategy that
was to be advocated in the 1950s for Third World countries, by UN
ECLA under the leadership of Raúl Prebisch. But there was one
essential difference between the two strategies. The eighteenth-
century British "import substitution strategy" of industrialization
was not limited to the production of cotton textiles and light
industries alone. Parallel with it Britain was to develop capital goods
industries also, an integrated pattern of development that contrasts
with the internal disarticulation of peripheral capitalist industrialization whereby there is a one-sided dependence on advanced capitalist
countries for capital goods and access to advanced industrial
technology.

It is almost universally taken for granted that the Indian textile
industry collapsed after the Industrial Revolution in Britain because

machine-produced British textiles were more competitive. The facts show otherwise. Cotton manufacture was established around Manchester by about the middle of the seventeenth century, a time when a flood of Indian imports was coming into Britain. Machine production did not stem this flow. As Baines pointed out, in Britain "Owing to the rudeness of the spinning machinery fine yarn could not be spun and, of course, fine goods could not be woven" (Baines, 1966, 102). Despite attempts to improve spinning technology such as Crompton's mule in the 1780s, British textiles could not match Indian goods either in quality or price. Progressively higher tariffs were imposed on Indian textiles imported into England. Proof that it was not just the fact of machine production that destroyed the pre-eminence of the Indian textile industry may be sought in the fact that in 1813, more than half a century after the Industrial Revolution had got under way, import duty on Indian textiles was increased yet again, to 85 per cent, because they were still coming in very competitively.

Contrary to the conventional wisdom that it was machine production in Britain that killed off the Indian textile industry, we can identify three factors that combined to bring about a steady decline in Indian textile production and exports. All three relate to cutting off sources of demand for them. First of all, in Britain itself, heavy protective duties were imposed to keep the very competitive and high quality Indian textiles out of the British market. The second factor was the closure of European ports during the Napoleonic wars that sealed off the huge European market for Indian textiles. The European market for Indian textiles was of enormous importance to India, and to the East India Company which enjoyed a monopoly of that trade. In 1789, "17/20ths [i.e. 85 per cent] of the whole of the calicoes imported [into Britain, H.A.] were re-exported [to Europe, H.A.] and 12/20ths of the whole of the muslins were re-exported" (Baines, 1966, 330). But there was also a third factor, less visible, namely the effects which the colonial conquest and appropriation of land revenue by the colonial regime had on the internal economy and urban demand in India. With the accrual of land revenue to the East India Company and cessation of the traditional flow of these resources to the local community via the notables, the Indian urban society was devastated and pauperized. Internal demand for Indian textiles also collapsed. It was the simultaneous collapse of demand from all three sources that dealt a heavy blow to the principal Indian industry of the day.

The Indian handloom textile industry was, however, surprisingly resilient. The turning-point in the balance of textile trade did not come until 1830 when India became a net importer of textiles. However, while exports of Indian textiles fell by that time, decline in Indian handicraft textile production itself was a post-1850 phenomenon (Twomey, 1983, 41). Thus Indian handicraft textile production persisted for a whole century after the Industrial Revolution had got under way. The pauperized weavers were to become an important force behind militant anti-colonial movements.

India's "Aid" for the Industrial Revolution

The flow of resources from India to Britain, the "Economic Drain", was India's "aid" for Britain's industrialization. Eric Williams has put forward an argument that profits from the colonial "triangular trade" financed the industrial revolution in Britain. Britain sold textiles in Africa to finance the capture of slaves who in turn were sold at a great profit in the West Indies. This much-enhanced capital was used to buy sugar which was imported into Britain, multiplying the original investment many times. Williams estimated the profits from this trade to amount to £14,000 in 1739, increasing to £303,000 by 1759.

Economic historians have treated Williams's argument with derision, for the scale of that flow of resources was small in comparison with the level of capital formation during the Industrial Revolution. However such an argument takes on a whole new meaning if we take into account the net flow of resources from India to Britain which I have estimated to be of the order of £2 million annually (Alavi, 1982, 63). That may have been an underestimate for other estimates are higher. Mukherjee quotes Martin writing in 1838: "For half a century we have gone on draining from two to three and sometimes four million pounds sterling a year from India" (Mukherjee, 1974, 380). Likewise, Prinsep, writing in 1823, estimated the net flow at between £3 million and £4 million annually between 1813 and 1822 (Prinsep, 1971).

Taking even my own lower estimate of an annual flow of £2 million during the critical period of the Industrial Revolution, we find that such a figure is by no means derisory, compared with estimates of capital formation in England during the relevant period, made by Pollard, Crouzet and Deane, which I have discussed elsewhere (Alavi, 1982). Crouzet's estimates, higher than the others, put gross capital formation in the British economy "in the exceptional boom years of 1790–93" at a total of £9.4 million of which investment in machinery was £2 million, and additional investments in stocks another £2 million (Crouzet, 1972, 33). As against these figures, we put in the balance the annual flow of £2 million (or more) from India, not to speak of large resource flows into Britain from other colonized regions. It is reasonable to conclude that the wealth of Britain, and its industrial might, has been founded on colonialism.

Shaping of a Classical Colonial Economy

A second phase of the colonial transformation of India had begun to take shape by the middle of the nineteenth century. Direct extraction of surplus from the land, by way of land revenue, gradually gave way to new forms of colonial exploitation. First, India became a producer of raw materials required by metropolitan industry and a profitable market for British manufactures trade on the basis of unequal exchange (Emmanuel, 1972). Second, British capital was now being invested in India, most of which went into plantations and extractive industries. In 1911 about 75 per cent of foreign capital in India and Ceylon (Sri Lanka) was in extractive industries of which 60 per cent was in plantations (Alavi, 1964, 118). Indigo production, needed by the British textile industry, was developed earlier by British capital during the first half of the nineteenth century; by 1850 it was among the most important exports from India. The foundations of Indian tea plantations were laid in the second half of the 1850s, worked by "coolies" whose "position was that of virtual serfs for the time of their employment contract" (Gadgil, 1973, 52). 3.7 per cent of British capital was invested in "commercial and industrial undertakings", the jute industry in Bengal being the exclusive preserve of British capital.

The new economic role of India in the global colonial economy entailed commercialization of Indian agriculture, with attendant changes in cropping patterns, encouragement of investment in improved techniques and a shift away from subsistence production. This process and the incorporation of Indian agriculture into a global system of generalized commodity production is described by Kessinger in this volume. Manchester's hunger for cotton was a major driving force in this process of change. The big push came in the 1860s, after the outbreak of the American civil war and the "cotton famine" in Manchester.

Suddenly the colonial government was galvanized into action. It vigorously pursued schemes to facilitate cultivation, transport and export of cotton. In many areas tribal population was turned off its land and peasant cultivators from more densely populated areas were brought in as settlers, to grow cotton. There was an extensive development of canal irrigation, some of it by way of restoration of canals which had fallen into decay and disuse during the preceding century of pauperization of the rural economy under colonial rule. The grandest of such schemes was the irrigation and "colonization" of vast arid tracts of the Punjab so that it was soon to become the richest agricultural region in India. Dormant proposals mooted in the 1840s by British interests to build railways in India were unearthed and set into motion during the period 1868–80, with the benefit of quite exceptionally generous subsidies, so that by 1900 the major part of South Asia's present-day railway system was completed. New colonial cities and towns grew up and prospered at the ports and in the interior.

Colonial priorities had changed. Over the years the relative burden of land revenue began to ease. The rise of cotton prices, after the American Civil War, relieved landowners from accumulated burdens of debt and put into their hand resources which could be applied to improve their land. The pattern of rural development, however, was a contradictory one and it was by no means one that brought wealth and prosperity to the cultivator himself. Parallel with improvements and changes in agriculture there was enhanced exploitation of sharecropping peasants, pauperization of poor peasants and an increase in the number of landless labourers. Official reports throughout the period are a witness to the growing impoverishment of the mass of the peasantry against the background of subordination of Indian agriculture to the needs of the colonial economy. There was a succession of peasant revolts in the nineteenth century. However it was a deliberate policy of the colonial regime to underwrite landlord power, as an essential local component of the structure of its authority. Lord Bentinck put it quite plainly in 1829:

> If, however, security was wanting against popular tumult or revolution I should say that the Permanent Settlement . . . has this great advantage at least of having created a vast body of rich landed proprietors, deeply interested in the continuation of British Dominion and having complete command over the mass of the people. (Keith, 1922, 215)

At the District and Provincial levels structures and relationships were created to institutionalize that partnership. When political reforms and elected forums were established, in response to demands of the nationalist movement, more power in fact accrued to the landlords who dominated the rural electorate. Eventually, when the end of British rule was in sight, the landlords were taken over by the nationalist movements, the Congress and the Muslim League respectively. In the case of the Congress Party in India there was a tension between its urban leadership and its rural power base. In the case ˏof the Muslim League in Pakistan, the landlords became the power in the land.

Emergence of New Urban Classes

Expansion of colonial trade and of the colonial state apparatus brought into being a new pattern of urbanization and Indian urban classes. European traders and bankers presided over the main centres of exports and imports and British officers occupied all key positions at the head of the civil service and the army. However, Indian traders flourished in local produce markets in rural areas and many established themselves as wholesalers, exporters and importers in the cities.

The nodal points for the development of the new urban classes were the three major centres of colonial rule, Calcutta, Bombay and Madras. Bombay was soon to become the pre-eminent centre of colonial commerce, notably in cotton, as well as cotton-textile manufacturing. It became the centre of Indian capitalism. An accident of geography was to leave its mark upon the ethnic composition of the Indian bourgeoisie that established itself in the port towns, the nerve centres of the colonial trade, as well as in major inland centres of trade. The pre-colonial trade of North India used to pass through Rajasthan and the ports of Gujerat, Kathiawar and Cutch. A new railway link between Bombay and Northern India left these regions high and dry and the Gujerati and Rajasthani (Marwari) trading and financial communities – Hindus, Muslims and Parsi – lost their traditional source of livelihood. But on the other hand, at the same time, great opportunities were opening up in the new centres of colonial trade, to which they migrated in large numbers, all over India. Today these communities form the core of the bourgeoisie in India (Pavlov, 1964, and Tripathi, 1984). Gujerati Muslim communities did likewise in Pakistan until the 1970s when they began to give way to a new Punjabi bourgeoisie drawn from army-related families and those with relatives in high places in the bureaucracy.

Bombay was the main base of the new Indian bourgeoisie which soon began to plough its profits from trade into modern cotton textile industry. After a weak start in 1851, the modern Indian textile industry began to get under way in the 1870s. Unlike the jute industry in Bengal which was British-owned, the cotton-textile industry was predominantly in Indian hands. It flourished despite discrimination against it by the colonial regime in a variety of ways. The Indian bourgeoisie therefore was soon to throw its weight behind the nationalist movement which had begun to gain strength by the end of the nineteenth century. Cloth, and the spinning wheel, became principal symbols of the nationalist movement. Later the Indian bourgeoisie extended its range of operations, especially during the Second World War, quite considerably so that by the time of independence in 1947 India had a powerful national bourgeoisie (for excellent complementary accounts see Bagchi, 1972, and Pavlov, 1964). On the other hand the regions that came to comprise Pakistan and Bangladesh had little industry and hardly any bourgeoisie to speak of, although in each of these countries one was fostered by the state (Alavi, 1983, and Kochanek, 1983).

With the development of industry, an urban working class came into existence and made its presence felt on the political as well as the industrial scene. Initially (and in the industrially backward regions that came to constitute Pakistan and Bangladesh) the organized working class was concentrated in transport, in docks and railways; later factory labour became preponderant. Working-class organization was considerably influenced by policies of the colonial state. Labour legislation was a "provincial" subject. In Bengal, where British capital dominated the jute industry, labour laws were far more repressive than in the Bombay Province, with its largely Indian-owned textile industry which competed with British industry. Here labour laws were more paternalistic. Essentially the colonial system of industrial relations allowed for a much greater degree of state intervention – through an elaborate system of laws and rules operated by Labour Departments and Industrial Courts – than is to be found in the Metropolitan societies. Their enforced procedures put a premium on lawyers who were coopted by trade unions as their "leaders". This legacy has continued in the post-colonial states of South Asia. Furthermore, union organization tends to be segmented, with a multiplicity of unions affiliated to rival political parties, which only occasionally form local committees of action during industrial disputes, for united action.

Rapid commercialization of the Indian economy as well as specific needs of a foreign power ruling over India brought about a revolution in the legal and administrative systems. New statute laws were enacted to underpin colonial capitalism and the new legal system needed trained cadres to operate it. Parallel with that there was an elaboration and expansion of the colonial state aparatus and the state became the principal urban employer. A new education policy was set in motion to produce trained Indian cadres who were to occupy middle and lower levels of the state apparatus and mediate between the colonial rulers and the local population. Persian, the pre-colonial official language in Northern India, was replaced by a dual language policy of "Anglo-Vernacular education" (Misra, 1961 and 1977).

A new class of "Western-educated" Indians appeared on the scene, the new professionals and those whom we may label the salariat, namely those who sought formal qualifications required to entitle them to government jobs, at various levels, and who either occupied or aspired to such jobs. This class has played a far more important role in the politics of South Asia, before and after independence, than is generally recognized (but see Basu, 1974, and Alavi, 1987). The state apparatus was the principal avenue for upward mobility and, in the context of colonial rule, the status of the Indian higher civil servants or judges, which did not then extend beyond quite modest middle levels was, nevertheless, generally reckoned to be higher than that of other indigenous classes – the colonial bureaucracy was the new nobility.

The political role of the salariat, however, was quite ambivalent. As individuals it was important for them to demonstrate their loyalty to the colonial regime so that they might be trusted with jobs and secure promotion. As a class, on the other hand, the nationalist movement, with its slogan of "Indianization" of the services, aiming to secure a greater proportion of higher positions in the state apparatus for them, promoted their interests. In the latter part of the nineteenth century it was the professionals and the salariat who initiated and backed the nationalist movement which, after declaring its loyalty to the British crown, would politely petition for a greater measure of "self-government" within the British Empire. Later, when the nationalist movement began to get radicalized and to develop a mass base, these worthies were the "moderate" nationalists. The salariat, as a class, has shown a tendency to split along ethnic lines and to spearhead ethnic, subnational or communal movements (see Part IV of this volume).

The nationalist movement was soon to be backed by the rising Indian bourgeoisie, resentful of discriminatory policies of the colonial regime against them and later by the (mainly) urban masses, activated by the dream of freedom. The Congress Party, leader of Indian nationalism, came to be dominated by the national bour-

geoisie at the centre; some scholars speak of a bourgeois hegemony.
With the emergence of institutions of "representative" government
(limited though their powers were under colonial rule) at local,
Provincial (State) and National levels, in a society in which the
majority of voters are rural, the nationalist leaders made an alliance
with the local level rural power-holders, the landed gentry, and
brought them into the Congress as junior partner. Thus the Congress
came to have a contradictory class base, a contradiction that was to
be reflected in post-independence developments (as Harriss discusses
in his chapter in Part II). In the case of Pakistan, in the absence of
a well-established Muslim bourgeoisie, the political system came to
be dominated by the relatively more advanced Punjabi salariat
through a military–bureaucratic oligarchy, and big landowners,
especially of the Punjab, on the other. Consequently politics of
Pakistan have revolved around the question of "nationalities" – the
claims of underprivileged regional ethnic groups.

During the Second World War Indian capital developed rapidly
in spite of measures (such as Control of Capital Issues Order which
prohibited the formation of corporate enterprises in India without
prior approval of the Government of India) designed to restrict its
growth. After independence, Indian capital made a bid to break
through the colonial pattern of international division of labour that
limited it to the traditional sectors of food and textile industries.
The Mahalanobis Plan Frame (1955) and the Indian Second
Five Year Plan inaugurated the development of heavy industries
producing capital goods, despite much initial resistance from advanced capitalist countries of Europe and North America which
India countered by playing the Soviet card. In the face of Indian
determination to pursue the new economic strategy, the stance of
Western capitalist countries changed from resistance to participation
in new opportunities which this strategy opened up for them. India
has succeeded in diversitying its manufacturing industry so that
now it has a sophisticated modern industrial structure. The share
of the traditional food and textile industries in the output of the
manufacturing sector, which was 67 per cent in 1957 fell to 35
per cent by 1978–9 and, correspondingly, the share of modern
engineering and chemicals industries rose from 14 to 51 per cent
(Balasubramanyam, 1984).

However, India did not thereby manage to break out altogether
from its relationship of dependence on metropolitan capital. In order
to expand engineering and chemicals industries, it needed access to
sophisticated technologies, which in the modern world are produced
and controlled by giant multinational capital. Hence a new kind of

dependence on metropolitan capital emerged through technical collaboration agreements between Indian capital and foreign capital. The measure of the "New Imperialism" was no longer the quantum of foreign investments, in terms of which it has been judged traditionally, but by the degree of control of Indian capital by foreign multinationals by virtue of the technical collaboration agreements (Alavi, 1964, 116ff, and Kidron, 1965). The possibility of India breaking out of the colonial nexus altogether is therefore a moot point. In industrially backward Pakistan (and later Bangladesh) by contrast, the indigenous bourgeoisie was very weak and its economy still remains firmly within the framework of dependency, dominated by foreign multinationals.

Changes in the Agrarian Economy of Vilyatpur 1848–1968[1]

Tom G. Kessinger

Historical accounts of rural India in the British period have generally focused on the significance of land control, and the changes in social and political structure resulting from modifications in the pattern of control during British rule. The emphasis has been fruitful for understanding rural social and political structure and the importance of government policy in shaping it. But the concentration on land tenure and official policy has diverted attention from the history of the use of land and its produce, Indian agriculture generally being treated as a kind of residual category of little significance. Rural people farm only if none of the new occupations are open to them, and agriculture itself simply goes alone, changing slowly if at all.

The form and history of land control was of importance for Vilyatpur. Socially and politically the community was organized around the dominant Sahotas, who owned the village. As part of the proprietary body, individual Sahota property groups (amongst the Sahotas usually equivalent to the *tabbar* – or "family") had influence and esteem in the community based on their share of the land, which allowed them to support some part-time dependents (*sepidars*, tenants, labourers, and the like) through the network of patron–client relationships. But the use of land was of equal importance to the people of Vilyatpur. Agriculture remained the principal economic activity throughout the period 1848–1968. As late as 1958, three men in four were directly engaged in farming as owner cultivators, tenants, and agricultural labourers. Even in 1968, these activities accounted for 64 per cent of the working men in the community. The value placed on agriculture by the owner cultivators, who are also the dominant element in rural society, is an important factor in the history of agricultural development in the Punjab.

Many aspects of agriculture in Vilyatpur show remarkable stability throughout the period 1848–1968. Yet within the stability of the basic occupational structure, cropping, and land ownership, numerous changes in village agriculture have taken place through the interplay

20

of several developments. Improved technology, better marketing facilities, an increase in the total capital devoted to agriculture, an expansion of double-cropping, and an intensification of labour, have brought a gradual increase in village production. A marked change in the organization of agricultural labour also occurred owing to a combination of demographic, technological, and occupational factors. Information on agriculture in the Punjab before the 1880s is scarce because the government – the only source of data on the subject at the provincial level – took time to develop a well-defined interest in cropping, production, and the procedures for collecting detailed and reliable information. The government's only interest in agriculture, beyond its study as part of the revenue surveys and the annual reporting of statistics on cropping before the 1880s, was in the introduction of new cash crops like tea, American cotton, and flax. The most successful project was a tea plantation in the Kangra hills which provided seed and training for British and Indian tea-planters who purchased land in the area. Individual British officers made some scattered efforts to introduce new types of common crops and were also instrumental in the spread of a few improved implements – particularly a more efficient sugar-cane press.

Although information on the period 1860–80 is imperfect, agriculture in the Punjab certainly received a stimulus from the fairly rapid development in railway and road networks and the construction of several large irrigation canals. The development of an adequate transportation system facilitated the marketing of crops, making it possible to export agricultural commodities – particularly wheat, sugar and *ghee* – to other parts of India in the 1860s. The result was an increase in prices for agricultural produce, a welcome development to cultivators in irrigated tracts like Jullundur, where continuous surpluses without a satisfactory outlet had tended to depress prices in the past. The construction of large-scale canal projects since 1859 also contributed to the development of agriculture in the Punjab, increasing the productivity of land already under cultivation and bringing substantial areas under the plough for the first time.

The contention that the development of public works had a substantial impact on agriculture between 1860 and 1885 is supported by the continuing role of railways and canals in the subsequent development of agriculture in the Punjab for which more adequate information is available. The expansion of food grains was about equal to the average rate of population growth in the region, and non-foods increased at a significantly faster pace. In Punjab, as for India in general, expansion in acreage of crops was the most important source of increased output. But in Punjab this was accomplished primarily by a continued development of irrigation in previously uncultivated tracts, rather than by an intensification of present acreage through double-cropping as occurred elsewhere.

Although the total cultivated area continued to expand in "Greater Punjab" the rate of increase slowed noticeably after 1921 when the last of the large canal projects was completed. Thereafter increases in yield per acre became the more important factor for food grains and other crops. Irrigation played the predominant role in increasing production from 1901 to 1911. In the next decade the development and use of new seed varieties took first place. The percentage of the total area under improved varieties in the Punjab and North-west Frontier Provinces was 6 per cent in 1922–3 and reached 33 per cent in 1938–9. Increases in yields were most dramatic for the non-food crops of sugar cane and cotton, but also in a few food crops, particularly wheat.

The isolation of indigenous varieties of high quality and the development of new types suited to the conditions in Punjab villages was the outcome of the research efforts of the Department of Agriculture. The initial step, in 1884, laid the groundwork for scientific classification between 1906 and 1910 of indigenous wheats grown in the Punjab, and the selection of the best varieties from the point of view of yield, durability, and price in the local and export markets. The propagation of pure seed on government farms and its distribution to village cultivators followed soon after. The department made its first recommended wheat variety, Punjab 11, available for distribution in 1913, and by 1920–1 it was sown in more than 600,000 acres. Punjab 11 was slowly displaced by another type introduced in 1919 that was planted over more than 1.3 million acres by 1927–8. Both varieties yielded from 16 to 33 per cent more per acre than the unrefined types used earlier.

The department's success with the acclimatization of American cotton was even more dramatic than in the case of wheat. Experiments started in 1908, and in 1913 the first type was distributed. In contrast to the new wheats, American cotton was valued not so much for its additional yield, as for the premium it fetched in the local and export markets. It was suitable for use in standard textile mills for weaving fine cloth, whereas the short-staple local cottons could only be used for making cheap coarse cloth and guncotton. The American cottons caught on quickly. The other significant development before Independence and Partition in 1947 was the introduction of high-yielding varieties of sugar cane, leading to substantial increases in the output of this valuable crop. Several

types developed in South India were brought to the Punjab in 1918
and their use spread rapidly in the 1920s and 1930s. By 1937–8,
improved varieties yielding 80 per cent more sugar per acre than
the usual Punjab types covered about three-fifths of the acreage
sown to cane.

Although by contemporary standards the spread of the new seeds
may not seem rapid, taking a number of years to cover more than
half of the acreage devoted to a particular crop, it must be
remembered that before 1947 the department depended on word of
mouth communication in rural areas. There was no staff for village
extension work in any district. Given the oft-mentioned conservatism
of village farmers in India, it is surprising that the government's
development efforts met with such success. In fact, local people not
only made use of improved seeds, but worked to propagate and
distribute them as well. Artisans in small towns and cities responded
to the opportunities created by changing agricultural technology.
Some implements introduced by the department that proved particularly popular and effective were quickly copied by blacksmiths and
carpenters – particularly a simple iron plough, the hand-driven
fodder-chopper, and an improved sugar-cane press. Though rough
in finish, the local copies worked well and were considerably cheaper
than imported tools.

Two important features can be traced by the size of operating
units over time. With a declining population for a forty-year period,
the village experienced a stability in the size of farms at the time
when the first improved crop varieties were introduced in the district,
factors which created the potential for significant increases in output
per capita. Although the data is imperfect, information on cropping
patterns and investment in agriculture and indications of an
increased orientation toward the market suggest that this potential
was at least in some measure realized. The nature and extent of
change, however, was conditioned by the land use and management
practices of individual property groups.

Change in the cropping pattern came through the disappearance
of crops that had been cultivated in the nineteenth century rather
than with the introduction of new ones. Between 1885 and 1895 the
crops grown numbered as many as twenty. After 1915 there were
never more than fourteen, if vegetables and fruits are omitted. The
abandonment of the cultivation of several pulses, a food that still
forms an important part of the daily diet of Vilyatpur residents,
accounts for most of this change. Before the turn of the century five
different pulses were raised. After 1905 only *mash* was cultivated,
and that in progressively smaller amounts. *Jowar* and barley, both

important grain crops covering almost 100 acres before 1895, declined since then and vanished finally in the 1940s. The gradual disappearance of these crops, particularly the pulses which still form an important part of villagers' diet, is indicative of a growing orientation toward the market. The available land went for expanded cultivation of wheat, sugar cane, and maize (corn) for consumption and sale, and pulses were purchased in the market.

Increases in total production through the extension of double-cropping and the use of improved varieties were more important in the development of village agriculture than changes in cropping. The number of wells has always been the most important factor determining the productivity of land. There have been two periods of important changes in the second form of investment in irrigation – the apparatus for lifting water. Until 1933–4 all wells were worked with a *charsa* identical to that found in Vilyatpur in 1848. In 1933 Partap Singh, the *surpanch* (headman) of the village, built the first Persian wheel. The general rise of the water table in the area made its use possible. It could be worked with fewer men and animals, and with far greater control of the discharge of water than the *charsa*, which made it desirable even though a number of factors complicated its adoption. It required an initial investment ten times the cost of the *charsa*. The all-iron mechanism had to be purchased outside the village while the wood and leather *charsa* was made by the *sepidar*-carpenter; also the Persian wheel was more expensive to maintain. While I cannot estimate the increment to production from this shift, authorities on Punjab agriculture generally see the existence of the Persian wheel as coinciding with the careful and intensive use of the land. The substantial growth in the intensity of cultivation and increase in double-cropping from 1935 to 1939 probably reflects the impact of this change.

By 1940 all wells in Vilyatpur were fitted with Persian wheels. In 1944 Partap Singh drilled the first deep well, which he operated with a diesel engine. When the first electric line was constructed in 1957, the diesel engine was replaced with an electric motor and two more farmers installed tube wells. Since 1965 ten more tube wells have been bored, bringing the total to thirteen. All other forms of investment in agriculture show two periods of increase. The number of carts and sugar-cane presses increased substantially in the late nineteenth century. The increase was probably an indication of greater marketing of crops in response to the development of roads and railways. Like the growth in outlays for irrigation apparatus, the number of sugar-cane presses and carts has grown since the 1930s. Much new equipment was of an improved type as well –

more efficient presses fitted with a series of iron rollers, and larger carts with inflated rubber tyres instead of wooden wheels. In 1968 there were two tractors and nine power-driven threshers. One tractor belongs to a farmer cultivating more than thirty acres, and the other to a village carpenter who does custom threshing and hauls produce to market on hire.

Labour, the last input of importance for yields and productivity, changed in cost and supply over the past 120 years. Throughout the period most labour was contributed by members of the property groups engaged in farming, while outside labour – hired, or as part of the *sepidar* system – was strictly supplemental except in occasional and extraordinary circumstances. Leaving the question of additions to family labour for the discussion of the family farm, the changes in compensation and organization of non-family labour suggest both an increase in productivity and the growth of the influence of the market in the village economy.

Agricultural labourers formed 10 per cent of the working men in 1848 and grew slowly in numbers and as a proportion of the work force through 1922 when they represented 14 per cent. Throughout the period the *sepidar* system remained intact. Although the compensation for full-time *sepidars* increased from 7 per cent of the annual crop to 10 per cent in 1884, the rates for part-time assistance, the most common type of *sepidar*-agricultural labour, remained unchanged at 2.5 per cent. Since the 1920s, however, the *sepidar* system (for agricultural labour) has slowly disintegrated; the compensation for labour has gradually risen. The practice of a particular *sepidar* working with the same property group for a number of years has been replaced by annual agreements on the amount of work expected and the rate of compensation received: 2.5 per cent for harvesting alone, 5 per cent for weeding, harvesting and threshing, and 10 per cent for full-time assistance in the field and home. By 1947 the last vestiges of the system had disappeared for agricultural labour, the yearly contracts giving way to daily arrangements at cash rates for certain jobs and piece-work rates for others.

The finding that there was no change in agricultural labour's organization and compensation before the 1920s when the district experienced general development and the village population declined, and that rates of payment and employment increased in the period when the supply of labour expanded quite rapidly, contains an apparent contradiction which must be explained. The latter phenomenon is the product of the growth in agricultural investment, the use of improved practices, and the cultivation of improved varieties, all of which effectively absorbed additional labour. As productivity increased, wages rose and changes took place in the organization of labour. The *sepidar* system was replaced first by a series of yearly contracts and then by daily bargaining over the wage to be paid. There was a steady increase in part-time rural employment which supplemented agricultural labour as a source of livelihood for the unskilled labourer. Work in brick kilns, housing construction, whitewashing, painting (as the number of brick houses grew), and, more recently, rural-based industries, have provided supplemental work outside agriculture. The expansion of the canal colonies in the 1920s presented labourers from Vilyatpur and neighbouring villages with an opportunity for seasonal migration during the wheat harvest. In fact, it was the departure of a substantial number of Chamars and village grantees to the canal colonies in the 1920s that irreparably disrupted the traditional *sepidar* system. The web of relationships never recovered from the sudden departure of a large number of its participants.

So much for developments after 1920. But what of the stability in compensation and the *sepidar* system in the earlier period? The first wave of migration to the canal colonies in the 1890s did not have any disruptive effect. Did existing production techniques make labour redundant in Vilyatpur before the developments of the 1920s? If not, why was there no increase in compensation if there was some growth because of better marketing facilities?

Labour in Vilyatpur was not at zero value before the increased investment in agriculture, improved technology, and more complete use of available resources. Rather, village political organization accounts for the absence of change in the organization and compensation for agricultural labour. Before 1848 the Chamars, and all non-Sahotas were dependent on the proprietors for the right to earn a living and reside in the community. No one lived in the village who did not work there. The entire village, including the residential site, belonged to the Sahotas, and no one else had a permanent right to any part of it. The Chamars' time was at the disposal of the Sahotas; they were required to do *begar* (forced labour) for the Jats without payment. Compensation for agricultural labour was regulated by custom and enforced by the Sahotas through their ability to use sanctions which ranged from physical violence to an arbitrary change of wages, and not by any kind of market mechanism.

Numerous indicators point to the increasingly important role of the market as a mechanism for allocating resources in village agriculture since British annexation. In the Sikh period the government tax was paid in cash, and Vilyatpur cultivators were accustomed to marketing wheat and *gur*, although in small quantities.

In spite of the monetization and the practice of selling at least some of the year's surplus production, in 1848 custom and not the market regulated economic life in the village. After annexation, the development first of the roads and railroads and then of the canal colonies brought an increased integration of the village into the economy of the province. The rise in the value of land in Vilyatpur, following the creation of a private marketable right in land, is just one indication of this integration. The development of public works, particularly the canal colonies, created new occupational opportunities in the Punjab, stimulating both short- and long-term migration.

Glossary

Chamar	North Indian caste of leatherworkers, considered "untouchable"
charsa	a simple mechanism for raising water for irrigation; it consists of a large leather bag drawn up by two pairs of bullocks
ghee	clarified butter used as a cooking medium
gur	unrefined sugar, produced in villages
jowar	sorghum
mash	a variety of pulse
sepidar	an artisan, servant or labourer who provides goods and services to a land-owning patron in return for a share of the biannual harvest, as part of an hereditary relationship
surpanch	headman

Note

1. An excerpt from *Vilyatpur 1848–1968: Social and Economic Change in a North Indian Village*, Berkely: University of California Press, 1974.

British India or Traditional India?: Land, Caste and Power[1]

Chris Fuller[2]

"The customary modes of land tenure", writes Stokes (1959, 26), are "the heart of Indian society". It is a characterization which would be endorsed by many Indian historians, but not, I suspect, by many anthropologists whom if forced to identify "the heart of Indian society", would surely point to the caste system. This contrast illustrates an important fact, the division of labour which has grown up between historians and most anthropologists studying Indian society (*cf*. Cohn, 1970).

The Politico-Economic System of Pre-British India

The politico-economic system of pre-British India centred upon control over the land. But it was not control over land *per se* that was crucial. Considered economically, what counted was control over the *produce* of the land. Considered politically, what counted was control over the *people* on the land. The rights to the produce of a particular piece of land were distributed among a number of persons or bodies, from the ruler downwards, and the relations between these persons or bodies constituted a political hierarchy. Force was always a fundamental element in the system and a position in the hierarchy, at least at the supra-local level (by which I mean an area over which power was exercised greater than a village or similar local community), was always in the last resort both established and maintained by force. Conversely, without the ability to claim shares of the produce the instrument of force, men and arms, could not be sustained.

I shall begin by looking at the creation and retention of political rights in the Mughal Empire, and their connection with the agrarian system. Although I take a specific example, the principles underlying it were general in pre-British India. The first crucial fact to be noted is that throughout pre-British India, there was a surplus of land and a shortage of cultivators and labourers. Rulers were therefore reluctant to allow cultivators to leave their land, and conversely the cultivators' ultimate sanction against oppressive rulers was flight to unoccupied land, of which there was plenty. In the same way, cultivators had to ensure an adequate labour supply, and this imposed limits on their effective power over the labourers (Habib, 1963, 115–7, 122; Srinivas, 1975, 66–7, 83). This demographic fact provides the most immediate reason for the emphasis on controlling people, rather than land. The reversal of the demographic ratio in modern times has had a number of serious consequences for relations between dominators and subordinates and it has, where legal restraints have not been effectively imposed, decisively tipped the balance of power in favour of the dominators (Habib, 1963, 117).

Villages in the Mughal Empire could be divided into two basic types: *raiyatwari* and *zamindari* (Habib, 1963, 141; *cf.* Baden-Powell, 1892, I, 144). *Zamindars* formed a rural class standing immediately above the cultivators or peasants (*raiyats*) and their most important right was to a portion of the cultivators' produce. Their right in their estates, which did not invariably coincide with individual villages, however, was not expressed as a right to the land of the estate, but over its occupants and produce. In areas where there were no *zamindars*, villages were of the *raiyatwari* type. Habib (1963, 160) describes the establishment of local *zamindari* rights:

> There is, first, a settlement by members of a caste or clan, perhaps, dominating over peasants settled earlier, or, perhaps, peasants themselves. Then another clan appears, drives them out or establishes its dominion over them; and then still another. At some stage, if not from the beginning, the dominion of the victorious caste crystallizes into *zamindari* right, held by various leading members of it over different portions of the subjugated territory.

Two points are to be noted here. First, that *zamindars* often, if not always, originated as peasants. There was therefore no absolute distinction between them, but rather a continuum of relatively greater or lesser power. Second, what Habib describes is a local "circulation of élites"; in which individual *zamindars* (or their heirs) rose and fell over time, and in which a critical and constant factor was armed supremacy; "armed force appears as the first historical pre-requisite for the establishment, as well as the retention, of *zamindari* right" (Habib, 1963, 163).

Just as there was continuity between *raiyats* and *zamindars*, so there was similar continuity between *zamindars* and those of somewhat greater power, to whom we may refer as chiefs (Habib, 1963, 183).

In the Mughal Empire, *zamindars* had had their power reduced by the state, but the strength of the state was not unfluctuating, either in time or space, and so "the numerous *zamindars*, whom the imperial government had reduced to the status of its servants, could, by casting a glance at these [chiefs'] states, still recall their own past and nurse their political ambitions for the future" (Habib, 1963, 189). These chiefdoms had a degree of political autonomy within the Empire, retained as long as they provided the Emperor with troops and tribute. Their size and the power of their chiefs varied greatly. Some of the most powerful ones eventually became *mansabdars*, the holders of *mansabs*, ranks whose financial rewards and military obligations were fixed by the Emperor (Habib, 1963, 257–9). The Emperor also assigned to *jagirdars* the right to collect the revenue over (at most periods) the large majority of the Empire. The term *jagir* refers to the area thus assigned. Most of the *jagirdars* were *mansabdars*. Royal princes held the highest *mansabs* and the largest *jagirs*, and sometimes they sub-assigned land to their own officials (Habib, 1963, 282–3). The *jagirdars'* principal responsibility was the maintenance of cavalry contingents, the key to Mughal supremacy (Habib, 1963, 317).

The political hierarchy at the supra-local level in the Mughal Empire can be pictured as a gigantic pyramid, the summit occupied by the Emperor and the base by the cultivators. The pyramid had several different levels, each occupied by persons or bodies with some power over those directly below them, but subject to those directly above them. The various levels were occupied by different categories of power-holders – *raiyats*, *zamindars*, chiefs, *mansabdars*, *jagirdars*, the Emperor. The overall structure of the pyramid was maintained by the balance of forces between these different levels, but the balance was often imperfect, and thus there was no sharp division between levels. Power imbalances, whether arising from increase in power at lower or upper levels, gave rise to a circulation of élites within particular regions and also, at its geographical limits, to secession from or incorporation into the Empire. Each person or body claimed rights over a certain territory, ranging from the entire Empire to a *zamindari* estate, and their power persisted for just as long as they could control the occupants and collect a share of the produce from that territory. The number of distinguishable levels may be argued about (*cf.* Fox, 1971, 55; Metcalf, 1969a, 124), but what is important is the Chinese box-like structure of the system, in which there was a fundamental continuity between different levels. To sum up: what we are dealing with when considering the Mughal Empire is a political system in which:

power and authority . . . are distributed among vertically or hierarch-
ically ordered groups . . . Consensus and balance are achieved through
conflict and through the awareness that there are always other groups
ready to step in. [Such a system seems] to be perpetually on the verge
of breaking down. (Cohn, 1962, 313)

I have so far been considering the nature of power at the supra-
local level. Within the village, or on the local estate, the system of
control was not quite the same. Of course, as a cultivator told an
early British settlement officer in northern India, when asked if his
zamindar could evict him, "The man in power can do anything" (qu.
in Neale, 1969, 15). But there was more to it than that. Another
officer, also in northern India at about the same time, wrote that:

the Ryots nonetheless appear to consider that they have some social
tie on a *zamindar* which approximates to a right. If a *zamindar* took
away a Ryot's lands, the Ryot would not dispute his authority to do
so, but he would say that he himself had been deprived of his land by
the *zamindar*'s "violence" or "injustice". (qu. in Siddiqi, 1973, 36)

As Maine (1871, 161) perceptively remarked: "The subordinate
holder who in India states that the superior holder has the power
to do a certain act, but that he ought not to do it, does not make an
admission; he raises a question of the utmost difficulty." In brief, of
course, the answer to Maine's problem is the existence of patron–
client ties and the interpersonal obligations generated by them.
These ties were strongly promoted by the scarcity of cultivators and
labourers (Srinivas, 1975, 83), and Siddiqi (1973, 37) is probably
correct to say that a *raiyat's* "right" against his *zamindar* would only
have been secure while land remained abundant. But such economic
facts fail to explain everything. The caste system was particularly
important here. Not only did the attribution of degradation to the
low castes help to create and maintain a "fixed labour reserve force"
for agricultural tasks and other menial occupations (Habib, 1963,
122), the caste-wise division of labour itself generated cross-caste,
patron–client ties (Srinivas, 1975, 83). Thus within the village, the
caste system both inhibited the development of competition for the
same resources, and promoted, both empirically and ideologically
through the set of values intrinsic to it, ties which were not based
mainly or exclusively on force. I must hasten to add that force was
by no means absent at the local level; it was readily engaged, for
example, against recalcitrant peasants who failed to meet their
revenue demands, and there is little reason to doubt that violence
was not infrequently used against labourers in the village. However,

in the Mughal Empire anyway, it would appear that whereas force was by far the most important factor in the political system at the supra-local level, where it provided the motor for élite circulation, it was tempered at the local level by other relationships and values. That this was so is correlated with the absence of real political competition between different strata within the village.

Let me now turn to the economic dimension, the distribution of produce. "The basis of the whole society [was] the grain heap, in which each constituent rank had its definite interest", wrote Benett, a British settlement officer in eighteenth-century Oudh (qu. in Neale, 1957, 224; 1962, 20–1). The principle was one of distribution; the produce was distributed among both the political superiors of the peasant, up to and including the ruler, and among the peasants' dependents within the village. The distributive system thus operated both above and within the village; above the village, it was the economic dimension of the supra-local political system discussed above. But we should see it as a single system in which every share, including the ruler's, was comparable with that of any village dependent, for the ruler "was one of a large number of people in the rural hierarchy who had rights over the produce of the land, and although he was often the most powerful person, his share did not differ in principle from any one else's share" (Neale, 1957, 29–30).

Anthropologists will recognize that the part of this system operating within the village is what they have studied as the *jajmani* system. Later, I shall consider the implications of studying only a part of the total distributive system. However, as we have seen, in the supra-local portion of the system, rights to a share of the produce were acquired by force, whereas within the village the shares of dependents, such as village servants and artisans, were a customary right deriving principally from carrying out obligations ascribed by caste membership. The village barber, for example, could scarcely ever use force to gain his share of the produce. In pre-British India, however, at least in some areas and at some periods, village dependents' shares of the produce were not guaranteed by "custom" alone, but by the political superiors of the cultivators as well. In the UP, under the Mughals, the state insisted that all details of payments within the village be recorded so that the authorities could check that they had been paid correctly (Habib, 1963, 126–7; Whitcombe, 1972, 42–3). The fact that there was sometimes, if not always, a political guarantee underpinning the *jajmani* system in pre-British India has been noticed, or at least considered, by very few anthropologists, most of whom have tended to analyse the system solely as an

economic aspect of caste alone. (An exception is Gough, 1960, 88–
90; *cf.* also Bose and Jodha, 1965, 123.)

The British Period

British rule in India was extremely expensive, and by far the
largest proportion of the cost was met by revenue from the land. It
is therefore not surprising, as Whitcombe (1972, 120) remarks, that
"official policy and practice as regards the agricultural world of
India should have been dominated throughout by a concern for the
land revenue".

The first task of the new rulers, after each acquisition of territory,
was to collect the land revenue, and to this end it was imperative to
decide who was to be responsible for payment. Early settlement
history was mostly chaotic. "The whole theory of Indian land-
revenue was absolutely strange to the English authorities. They
could not tell who owned the land and who did not" (Baden-Powell,
1892, I, 393). In the UP, for instance, the settlement officers could
find nothing but a "profusion of overlapping claims" (Neale, 1957,
221). Their problem, as we can now see, is that they were trammelled
by a set of fundamental misconceptions. They were seeking the
owners of the land, but there were no owners in the sense in which
they understood the word. Early revenue policy was a bewildering
succession of argument and counter-argument, but the details do
not matter here. What does matter is that the British did eventually
"find" the landowners, "settle with them", and impose the revenue
demand upon them. In addition to the economic considerations of
securing the revenue, there were political ones too. The desire to
create, from those granted ownership rights in a settlement, a stable
land-owning class which would be a reliable political ally of the
British power, was a permanent feature of British policy in India.
It was, though, never thought of as a revolutionary policy (Stokes,
1959, 26); on the contrary, British policy was always designed "to
avoid moves leading to a disruption of the traditional order of local
society" (Whitcombe, 1972, 17). If the British were, in Marx's
phrase, "causing a social revolution in Hindustan" (Marx, 1959,
20), it was not by design.

Why did the British insist on settling with the owners of the land?
Why was the concept of private property so central to their revenue
system? Why could they not collect the revenue as their predecessors
had done, without insisting that any particular person or body had
property rights in the land? The Mughal system had, of course,

collapsed by the time the British arrived. But there was a more general problem, a problem stemming from the particular conceptions of law and property which the British took with them to India, which meant that "the institution of private saleable property rights, through the permanent limitation of the State demand and the relinquishment of a private rent to the proprietor, was a motive common to all types of revenue settlement" (Stokes, 1959).

What is important here is not the introduction of private property rights in land *per se*, but their *universal* introduction as the lynchpin of the revenue system, backed by statute law and, ultimately, by the British power. Crucial to this was the legal rigidity of the British system, in marked contrast to the somewhat arbitrary and elastic revenue demand of pre-British times. The British "revenue-demand shall be assessed according to law . . . with the one idea of making it equal, just, and easily borne: but once fixed, it must be paid in full, *regularly* and to the day" (Baden-Powell, 1892, I, 248; *cf.* Whitcombe, 1972, 14).

The equality, justice and bearableness of the British revenue demand are, to say the least, questionable, but I do not intend to discuss them here. What I do want to consider are the effects on Indian society of the introduction of private property within this rigid legal framework. Let us look first at the distributive system of rights to produce. As we have seen, a series of persons or bodies, both within and above the village, had rights to the produce of the land. Private ownership of land and the British revenue system changed that. Now only one person or body had more or less exclusive rights in the land, subject only to continued payment of the revenue.[3] The claim to a part of the produce by the erstwhile dominators disappeared, while the claims of dependent villagers were no longer guaranteed in any way by the rulers nor, more widely, were they any longer a part of the total distributive system embracing both dominators and dependents. Thus the granting of private property rights in land to those responsible for the revenue destroyed the structure of the distributive system. Where there had previously been a complex hierarchy with many levels, now only its bottom half, the part within the village (the *jajmani* system), remained. The top half vanished and was replaced by a single link between the owner and the government, defined according to principles diverging fundamentally from those of the past.

This leads on directly to a consideration of the effects of British rule on the political system. British rule, in Srinivas's (1975, 53) words, "altered fundamentally the relationship between the rulers and the ruled". The *Pax Britannica* eliminated private control of the means of violence and thus destroyed what had previously been the way to both the establishment and retention of a position in the political hierarchy. The old élite circulation system and the competition for shares of the produce were ended. But the latter had, of course, already ceased, owing to the fixed allocation of rights in land to particular individuals or bodies. Thus the British, at the same time as they destroyed the top half of the distributive system (the economic dimension), also destroyed the top half of the political system. The supra-local political pyramid, with its innumerable levels of power, was flattened and a more uniform landlord class created. In one sense, British political control over their subjects was tighter than any that had previously existed; the district collector was a "more effective instrument of the central authority than any that an Indian ruling power could have devised" (Siddiqi, 1973, 13). But on the other hand, the landlord class was the favoured political ally of the paramount power and the connections between them were no longer through a succession of intermediaries. The reader will see that the British also eliminated the different levels of the political system to which I referred earlier. British rule, just as it finished off the Mughal Empire, also finished off the smaller political domains, leaving only the "little kingdoms" of the new landowners. But the power of the new landowners rested on a basis quite different from that of their predecessors, and their "kingdoms" were not so much political domains as landed estates.

In destroying the old élite circulation system, the British created a new one. But now the dynamic was not provided by force and the competition for shares of the produce; it was principally provided by competition in the market, which had grown up as a result of the allocation of private property in land. Control over shares of the produce was replaced by a new aim, acquisition of actual land in the market.

The effects of British policy on local élites differed from province to province, according to the type of settlement policy adopted and the pre-existing local conditions. In some areas, a new élite tended to rise, while in others the old one succeeded in adapting and maintaining its superiority under changed conditions. What was universal throughout British India, however, was the destruction of the complex hierarchy which had distributed political power at the supra-local level amongst a host of persons and bodies, linked together through the distributive economic system.

There is another, more abstract, aspect to this whole issue which should be mentioned. I began by stating that the politico-economic system in pre-British India centred upon control over the land, and

I distinguished between the economic dimension, control over produce, and the political dimension, control over people. This distinction, though, is primarily one imposed by the analyst, for the supra-local hierarchy was simultaneously economically and politically defined. To control people was at the same time to claim shares of the produce; the one was a means to the other and vice versa. By instituting universal private property in land and destroying the old political system, the British separated politics from economics (Siddiqi, 1973, 36–9; *cf.* Dumont, 1970a, 164–6); political and economic power no longer necessarily went hand in hand.

Traditional India or British India?

A century ago, Maine (1871, 26–7) wrote "It would be absurd to deny that the disintegration of Eastern usage and thought is attributable to British dominion." This judgement, from a contemporary scholar and administrator still regarded as a "founding father" of social anthropology, has a clear implication: that traditional India vanished under the British Raj. I submit that what anthropologists are prone to call "traditional India" is, in fact, British India. Clearly, this allegation needs to be substantiated, and to do so, I shall begin by looking again at the *jajmani* system.

As I have already implied, and as a check of the material will demonstrate, it is no exaggeration to say that very few anthropologists indeed have perceived, or at least explicitly recognized, that the *jajmani* system is only one half of the pre-British distributive system. Mandelbaum (1970, 169), in his massive synthesis of the ethnography, cites Neale, but like nearly all the writers he draws upon, he makes no mention of the fact that the division of grain heap was formerly, directly or indirectly (through the revenue system), a division between political dominators as well as villagers. His failure to remark on this is not at all atypical. Dumont, in his paper on the "Village Community", which so brilliantly undermines the mythical conception of the "independent village", one of the most crucial influences on much anthropological writing about India, does recognize explicitly the fact that cultivators formerly paid over part of their produce to political dominators (Dumont, 1970b, 119, 131). In the light of this, his analysis of the *jajmani* system is all the more surprising. He is right to refer to the system's "orientation towards the whole" and to say that the "distribution on the threshing floor . . . takes place in virtue of the fact that everyone is interdependent" (Dumont, 1970a, 105). He is, however, wrong to claim that this interdependent distribution demonstrates the "encompassed" nature of power, and that this "view of the ordered whole" which the system expresses is "fundamentally religious" (Dumont, 1970a, 107). For, as we have seen, the *total* distributive system linked the entire population from the ruler downwards, and its supra-local part was the economic dimension of what was simultaneously a political hierarchy. Further, the state acted to some extent as a guarantor of the village servants' and artisans' rights to a share of the produce. In no sense can it be claimed that in the Mughal Empire caste or religion provided either the form or the source of these political dominators' rights. And in the Hindu kingdoms, although caste and religion legitimated the politico-economic system, the majority of rights were, as in the Muslim areas, always fundamentally a function of power, often naked military power.

Dumont, although he recognizes the crucial significance of military power (Dumont, 1970a, 158), nonetheless argues – in parallel fashion to his analysis of the *jajmani* system – that the distribution of rights over land to form a political hierarchy was a function of the caste system, which did not relate such rights "exclusively to an individual or a function, but rather to the whole set of functions comprised in the system" (Dumont, 1970a). But the structure of the distributive politico-economic system cannot be derived from the caste system in this way. As we have seen, it must be explained by the competition for control over produce and people. For although it is true that political positions were often legitimised *post facto* in terms of caste or religion, this does not mean that the political hierarchy was derived from the latter. However, an important effect of the British destruction of the supra-local part of the system was to give the village *jajmani* system a degree of autonomy *vis-à-vis* the total politico-economic system which it did not previously have. The British did not create the *jajmani* system – indeed they set in train forces which would eventually undermine it almost completely – but they did bring about a situation in which this local, caste-based economic system could be perceived, by anthropologists and others, as a system in its own right to a degree which would have been impossible before.

In pre-British India, as we have already seen, even the most powerful members of local communities were subject to immediate political domination by more powerful *zamindars*, chiefs, etc. Even those that were not, by some fortunate chance, were permanently under the threat of conquest or subjugation. But under British rule, the subordination or threat of subordination of powerful villagers disappeared. They were now subject, like others, only to the imperial power, which had granted them exclusive proprietary rights in land and regarded them as its main allies.

Within the village, therefore, the effective power of the most powerful villagers increased, and to the extent that it was located in a single caste, because all the most powerful villagers belonged to one caste, the concentration of power in the dominant caste also increased. This does not mean that dominant castes cannot be recognized in pre-British India. They evidently can; for example, the Rajputs or the Jats in northern India. The argument is rather that the *local* power vested in members of these castes, and thus more widely in the castes themselves, increased during early British rule. More recently, it has begun to decline again as the state has been more able to intervene effectively in village affairs (Srinivas, 1966, 151–2). But this is a modern innovation. The "traditional" dominant caste, some of whose members have more or less unchallenged power within their villages, was, I conclude, only widespread during the British period; it did not exist on such a scale before.

The wider conclusion, then, is that the archetypal "traditional" village, with its *jajmani* system and local political structure centred on the dominant caste, is not traditional at all, but was, as Cohn (1970, 45) suggests, mainly a creation of the British Raj. The plausibility of much anthropological writing about Indian society, most of which is concerned with "traditional" village India, is brought into serious question by such a conclusion. The questions relate not only to the social structure of the village, which has been discussed at length, but also to the caste system itself. The issue is raised as to whether the "traditional" caste system is not also a creation of the British.

Very briefly, my argument is that from one standpoint anyway the importance of caste appears to have grown. In the village *jajmani* system, unlike the total pre-British distributive system, the allocation of shares of the produce is primarily a function of caste. Similarly, in the village, political power is distributed along caste lines to a much greater extent than it was in the pre-British political hierarchy. If one focuses attention on what has been taken to be traditional – *jajmani* systems and dominant castes – it is easy to conclude that caste is overwhelmingly significant in the social structure. It can plausibly be argued that caste is the fundamental feature, the heart, of Indian society, for from this point of view, not only does the distribution of economic and political power appear to be a function of caste, the caste system itself also appears to be relatively autonomous. It is not inextricably linked to other social institutions, and in particular not to the system of control over land. In pre-British India, however, the economic and political functions of caste could not be separated from the agrarian system, for the distribution of economic and political power was a function of control over land as much as, if not more than, it was of caste.

Editors' Notes

1. This chapter is an excerpt from a longer essay entitled "British India or Traditional India?: An Anthropological Problem" (*Ethnos*, 1977, 3–4). We believe that the paper's argument about caste and the agrarian system is an important one, though research over the ten years since this paper was written has shown up much more continuity between pre-British and British India. Fuller's more recent position is found in his "Misconceiving the Grain Heap: A Critique of the Concept of the Indian *jajmani* System", in Maurice Bloch and Jonathan Parry, eds, *Money and the Morality of Exchange*, Cambridge University Press, forthcoming.
2. The author would like to thank Professor Kathleen Gough for her detailed criticisms of a draft of this paper, and also Professor Keith Hart for his comments.
3. Those granted ownership rights differed according to the different settlement policies pursued in the various regions. In Bengal, ownership rights were granted to *zamindars*, who controlled much larger estates than the local *zamindars* of the UP, who were the favoured class in that province, except in Oudh, where the more powerful *talukdars* were granted these rights. In most of southern India (Madras, Bombay) settlements were made with individual *raiyats*. For the complete picture, covering all British India, Baden-Powell (1892, I, II, III) remains the authority.

NB In these and subsequent notes throughout the book, where reference is made to a work which appears in the Bibliography at the end of the book, only the author(s)' name and date of publication will be given. Full publication details will be supplied in the note only if the work is not so included.

Part II

The Political Economy of South Asia

Editors' Introduction

Questions about trends of change in agrarian social structures in India and Pakistan are addressed in the next two chapters. Agrarian social structures and trends of change are markedly different in Pakistan, India and Bangladesh. In Pakistan the agrarian economy and society are dominated by very big landowners. Land reforms under General Ayub Khan and again, under Bhutto, were of a token character. Akmal Hussain argues the case for effective land reforms in Pakistan. There have, however, been massive changes in Pakistan agriculture in the past few decades. Tenant family farming with the help of a pair of bullocks has given way to a takeover of the land by landlords of the Indus Plain of Punjab and Sindh for cultivation by tractors, employing a small number of wage labourers. For this they have evicted about a dozen families of share-cropping tenants from the land for each tractor introduced (Alavi, 1973a). The result has been a phenomenal increase in the number of landless labourers who survive by combining casual labour on the farms (especially at harvest time) with work as unskilled labourers on building sites in nearby towns to which they commute by bus. Their fate when the current building boom peters out, as it already seems to be doing, is uncertain. Other regions of Pakistan, such as the Potwar Plateau of the Punjab, are characterized by diminutive and fragmented land-holdings with no irrigation, which cannot yield family subsistence. Their agriculture is in a general state of decay, not least in view of the tendency of able-bodied men of these areas to look elsewhere for their livelihood, either by joining the armed forces or migrating to industrial cities in Pakistan or abroad in search of work. Ballard's chapter discusses the implications of such overseas migration.

In India the issue at the centre of debate is different, namely that of the extent and the manner in which capitalism has transformed Indian agriculture. It might be recalled that before independence the Congress Party was committed to a small peasant strategy of agricultural development which, after independence it proceeded to implement. The main components of that strategy were, first, land

41

reforms, to return the land to the tiller. Second, modern technology was to be made accessible to the small peasants by agricultural extension services and special credit facilities. Third, the peasants were to engage in cooperative endeavour to build the required infrastructure for a more productive agriculture through Community Development Programmes (for a summary of this see Alavi, 1975). Although most studies of land reforms in India were justifiably critical of their shortcomings, it must be said that they have not failed altogether to change the pattern of landholdings in India.

Nevertheless landownership in India remains highly skewed, with much of it in the hands of a relatively small number of rich peasants and capitalist farmers. By the 1960s the small peasant strategy was acknowledged to be a failure, against the background of the crisis of the Second Five Year Plan, and failure to generate a greater amount of marketable agricultural surplus needed to sustain the industrialization process. The Government of India therefore turned instead to a policy of "Betting on the Strong", i.e. the class of capitalist farmers, the strategy that heralded the "Green Revolution".

The influential article by Terry Byres reprinted here represents a widely held view about the direction and extent of development of capitalism in Indian agriculture. He argues that the introduction of "new technology" (improved varieties of seeds, fertilisers, agrochemicals, and machinery) has hastened the process of differentiation of agrarian classes and served to consolidate the rich peasantry as a powerful, dominant class. Yet, according to his analysis, it is far from clear that the process of dispossession of poor peasants and concentration of landholding which has been anticipated with expanded commercialization in agriculture, has been taking place. It appears that the proletarianization of labour is only partial: "[the] most significant contribution [of the "new technology"] has been to throw into increasing wage employment large numbers of poor peasants who continue to own some land". Byres's argument concerning "partial proletarianization" is also borne out by field research on trends in landholding in villages in the semi-arid tropics of India (Cain, 1981), and in a region of South India (Harriss, 1987). Both these authors have found a tendency for landless people and smaller landholders at inheritance to *gain* land over time and for the distribution of landownership to become *more* not less equal.

So it does not appear that the process of dispossession of middle and poor peasants and of the proletarianization of the peasantry has taken place quite as far as it is premised in Byres's analysis or in the comparable work of Utsa Patnaik (1986). They both seem to ignore an alternative form of subsumption of peasant production under capital, without dispossession of the peasant from the land, as analyzed theoretically by Kautsky (1899; forthcoming). In India the Rudolphs show that the class of farmers whom they designate "bullock capitalists" who operate their farm holdings of less than about 15 acres with their own family labour, have actually gained ground as against "tractor capitalists" who own more than 15 acres and operate with wage labour (Rudolph, L. I. and S. H., 1987, ch. 13). The "bullock capitalists" are described as "independent, self-employed agricultural producers" who can be both productive and prosperous, and the Rudolphs argue that it is these cultivators and members of various "backward classes" (an overlapping status category) who are increasingly at the centre of political events rather than "kulaks" or landlords. They suggest, for example, that one cause of the erosion of support for the Congress after 1967 has been its inability to retain the support of the "bullock capitalists".

There is also controversy over the extent of the increase in the proportion of agricultural labourers (see Rudolph, L. I. and S. H., 1984, 314; but also K. Bardhan, 1983). Byres refers to the increasing importance of wage employment, including employment in rural non-agriculture. The question of whether or not such employment is in productive activity, offering higher returns to labour than employment in agriculture is an important one. But there is in any case strong segmentation in rural labour markets, with low-caste labour often excluded from certain types of employment – as Breman (1985) has shown for a dynamic and prosperous region of Gujarat. His is an outstanding study of regional rural development and social change.

It is not part of Byres's purpose to discuss evidence about levels of livelihood amongst the rural masses. But his argument can be linked to the conundrum which is posed by the fact that poverty studies seem to show that the incidence of "poverty" as defined in terms of capacity to purchase a basket of basic commodities, has increased (see the discussion in Pacey and Payne, 1985) while at the same time mortality rates have declined and life expectancy has increased. It does seem that the changes which have been taking place in the countryside may have improved the security of the livelihoods of many people, even if income levels have not been improved, or have not improved by very much. This is what Cain argues (1981), while the fieldwork of Caldwell and his co-workers shows that there are conditions in some parts of India, at least, which encourage reduced fertility (Caldwell *et al.*, 1982). Famines like the Bengal Famine of 1943 analyzed by Sen (1977, 1981) and from a cultural perspective by Greenough (1982) have not occurred since the mid-1960s (though the analytical framework outlined by Sen for assessing vulnerability to famine remains valuable for determining which groups of rural people are most at risk of hunger: see Pacey and Payne, 1985).

In Bangladesh the picture of the agrarian economy is again quite different. Given a proliferation of tiny substandard landholdings, the Bangladesh peasant is given to having recourse to multiple strategies to eke out a living, sometimes leasing out the small patch that he owns, leasing in other land, cultivating his own tiny holding and working as an agricultural or non-agricultural labourer, a patchwork of occupations that defies neat class categorization. Bhaduri, Rahman and Arn have recently shown for a region of Bangladesh how polarizing tendencies are moderated because of the increased availability of other sources of income which makes it possible for small landholders to retain their property so that "there is a marked tendency towards a stabilization of landownership even among the smaller size groups". (Bhaduri *et al.*, 1986 – see also the debate on this paper in *Journal of Peasant Studies*, 14, 4, 1987.) Hartman and Boyce (1983), Van Schendel (1981), Westergaard (1985) and Wood (1981) offer valuable insights on Bangladesh.

Later in Part II Harriss reviews the literature on Indian industrial-ization and the state, and his bibliography lists the more important sources on these themes. The view of the Indian state which is presented is that there is a compromise of power between the bourgeoisie and the dominant rural class (the "bullock capitalists"), inherited (though subsequently modified) from the colonial period. This compromise of power allows some freedom of action on the part of the political élite and the bureaucracy which, with the professionals, constitutes a third propertied class.

This analysis of the state is complemented by a reading of studies of Indian politics. Harriss's remarks about Indira Gandhi's attempts to centralize power, and their effects on the Congress as a political organization are amplified in work by Brass (1982) and by Manor (1983). These authors, and Kothari (1983), give a useful introduction to recent trends in Indian politics, and exemplify contemporary political writing on India. Kohli's recent work (1987), comparing the regimes of West Bengal, Karnataka and Uttar Pradesh illustrates the importance of politics in showing the "small but significant range of redistributive options possible within similar social-structural constraints" (Kohli, 1987, 10).

The outstanding study of the state in Pakistan and Bangladesh remains Alavi's paper on "The State in Post-Colonial Societies"

(1972); and the same author has more recently discussed "Class and State" in a useful volume of essays on the political economy of Pakistan (Gardezi and Rashid, eds, 1983). On Bangladesh, in addition to the work of Sobhan, below, see that of Sobhan and Ahmad (1980).

Amongst the other chapters in this Part, Kochanek's account of the political organization of Indian business is complemented by the same author's comparable work on Pakistan (Kochanek, 1983). There is a short account of Indian labour organizations in Hiro's chapter on trade unions (Hiro, 1976, chapter 10) and a more extended analysis is given by E. A. and U. Ramaswamy (1981). E. A. Ramaswamy has also written an outstanding study of trade union organization in a south Indian city, based on careful field work (Ramaswamy, 1977).

Agrarian Structure, the New Technology and Class Action in India[1]

Terry Byres

Agrarian Structure at Independence and After

In 1947, at the apex of the agrarian structure was a landlord class, not necessarily "owners" in the strict sense, since they might be "occupancy tenants", but with superior property rights in the soil, which allowed them to lease out land and to extract a surplus in the form of rent. Within this class, there were two broad groups, which could be found in all parts of India, but one or other of which predominated in any particular region: a class of large, usually absentee landlords, who tended to hold land in more than one village and were more commonly to be found in *zamindari* and *jagirdari* regions; and one of smaller, normally resident proprietors, who typically held land in one village, and who were most common in *ryotwari* and *mahalwari* areas. It was in the interests of both groups to keep rents as high as possible, and some landlords, in their capacity as money-lenders, drew from the peasant an interest surplus as well as a rental surplus. This appears to have been especially true, in some areas, of the second group, some of whom, or some of whose antecedents, had started as money-lenders, becoming landlords by buying up or foreclosing. We have been reminded by Bhaduri (1973, 122), however, that landlords who act, also, as money-lenders are especially common in West Bengal (a *zamindari* region), for example, but unusual in, say, the Punjab (a *mahalwari* area). Some landlords used hired labour to work the land that was not leased out, drawing the labour from the ranks of poor peasants and landless labourers and paying in money or kind, in a range of unfree and free relationships,[2] which, while they had been changing in the previous century, were still essentially pre-capitalist in nature.

India's agrarian structure had two further, major components (ignoring, for present purposes, traders and the distinct class of money-lenders – i.e. merchants' and usurers' capital – who were crucial elements in the functioning of the mode of production), a peasantry and a class of landless labourers, and a third, a stratum of village artisans and craftsmen, of which we must take cognisance. We may examine each of these in turn.

Among the peasantry some differentiation was fairly evident, varying in degree from region to region, and being most marked where commercialization had penetrated furthest and in *ryotwari* and *mahalwari* areas (that is to say, in the present-day states of Punjab, Haryana, western Uttar Pradesh, Maharashtra, Gujarat, Tamil Nadu). Rich peasants were part-owners and part-tenants, whose land was frequently fragmented, and who obtained significantly lower output per acre than poor peasants. Yet they did accumulate capital, to a certain extent, were market-oriented, and were substantial employers of wage labour, though, as with landlords, the relationship with labour was still of a pre-capitalist kind. Rich peasants were not "masters of the countryside" at Independence – the landlord class was still very much in command, the dominant class *par excellence* – and they were not to be clearly seen in all parts of India. They were far from constituting a class of capitalist farmers. They did, however, have some of the attributes of dominance. The middle peasant stratum was also made up of part-owners and part-tenants, owning a larger proportion of the land they worked than poor peasants and a smaller proportion than rich peasants. They were tenants to a fairly substantial degree, held their land in scattered pieces, were not market-oriented, and employed small amounts of wage labour at peak periods. Poor peasants partly owned and partly rented-in, but were tenants to a greater degree than other peasants. They were particularly likely to be share-croppers (and especially so in eastern India). Among poor peasants, fragmentation was rife; access to credit was via the village money-lender (who might also be the landlord), at usurious interest rates, and the level of indebtedness was high (most of the debt being "deadweight debt"); and market orientation took the form of marketing a "distress surplus" rather than a true commercial surplus. An important characteristic of poor peasants was the degree to which they had to supply their labour to others, in order to survive: in 1950–1, for example, for 15 per cent of rural families with land the major activity was supplying their labour to other cultivators, while for large numbers of the remainder if it was not preponderant it was certainly necessary (50 per cent of agricultural labourer families were, in fact, poor peasant families with land). Such labour might be forced, unpaid labour, extracted by landlords as a condition of tenancy (Thorner and Thorner, 1962, 36–8). Yet, poor peasants, like middle peasants, did employ some wage labour at peak seasons. Throughout

India the highest output per acre was achieved on their dwarf, "uneconomic" holdings.

There had been landless labourers in India since Mughal times, and their numbers certainly increased in the nineteenth and twentieth centuries. In 1950–1 15 per cent of all agricultural families in India were without land. It was a class often in unfree relationship with those who employed labourers, and, therefore, not essentially free in the Marxian double sense (free of the means of production and free to sell its labour power). It might be paid in kind or in money, sometimes a fixed wage and sometimes on a share basis. Debt bondage was common (Thorner and Thorner, 1962, 28–36). Among labourers it is important to distinguish two categories: permanent or attached labourers, or those who are hired for a year or longer; and casual labourers, or those who are hired for a single crop season (such as *rabi* or *kharif*), for a single operation (like ploughing, or transplanting, or weeding, or harvesting), or on a daily basis (Thorner and Thorner, 1962, 22–6). At Independence, there were, of course, virtually no mechanized operations for such labour to work on. Migrant labour was quite common in some areas. Labourers, also, might be employed on a group basis, for a specific operation like harvesting, and might be paid on piece rates (Thorner and Thorner, 1962, 26–7). It is important to remember that the rural proletariat was composed of both totally landless labourers and poor peasants, but that the latter's possession of land effectively prevented a correspondence of interests between the two.

The stratum of village artisans and craftsmen, described in an abundant anthropological literature (which we need not list exhaustively here) included the potter (who might make roof tiles as well as pots), the goldsmith (who might also act as a pawnbroker), the blacksmith (who might make and repair wooden and iron ploughs – to the extent that the latter existed – carts, houses etc.), the carpenter, oil-presser, basket-maker, stone-cutter, etc. They might (or might not) have a hereditary relationship with the village and be paid in kind for performing specific tasks, perhaps earning cash for doing others, and they might own land.[3] This stratum also included, for example, hand-spinners and hand-weavers, as well as other "village functionaries", such as the barber, the washerman etc. (cf., for example, Epstein, 1962, 36–8, 207–10 and Bailey, 1957, 109–17, to choose more or less at random two studies conducted in the 1950s).

Between the early 1950s and the mid-1960s, India's agrarian structure underwent certain changes. Despite a remarkable range of delaying tactics and a host of devices to retain more land than the law allowed, the largest semi-feudal landlords – the *zamindars* and *jagirdars*, the absentee, non-cultivating landlords, who had been the allies of the British in British India and the bulwark of the princes in Princely India – experienced, via land reform, a blow from which they could never quite recover. Their capacity for sustained class-for-itself action was not sufficient to the task, in a struggle against the social forces mobilized in the nationalist movement. From among them a small group emerged which was ripe for transformation into capitalist farmers. The medium to smaller landlords, who were often resident and sometimes cultivating, and more common in *ryotwari* areas, received no such blow. Their survival was assured, but on a rather different basis to their former condition. The attempt to abolish tenancy was unsuccessful and the smaller landlords – as, indeed, were some of the big ones – were able to devise new forms of tenancy ("disguised", often oral tenancies), which successfully evaded the law. Their ability to pursue class-for-itself action was considerable. Another effect of the attempts at tenancy abolition was to encourage non-cultivating smaller and medium landlords to become direct cultivators, which involved an ejection of tenants and their replacement by wage labour. Here was another, larger group within the landlord class which might take to capitalist farming if conditions were appropriate. But these tendencies within the landlord class were nowhere on a scale sufficient to suggest the possibility of widespread "capitalism from above".

There was a quite definite quickening of differentiation among the peasantry over these years. Agriculture grew at around 3 per cent per annum, there was some extension of the irrigated area, some limited development of the forces of production (including, a growth of mechanisation in a certain, few areas), and some rise in commercialization. By far the greatest beneficiaries of these changes, and of land reform, were the rich peasants. Their class-for-itself action became increasingly effective. They were stabilized as independent proprietors, and were on the way to becoming, in many areas of India, the new dominant class in the emerging agrarian structure. Legislation, to the extent that it was successful, extended protection not to all tenants, but to the upper layers of the tenantry. There was an increase in more purely commercial, as opposed to "feudal" tenancy, and in the 1960s a rise in the amount of land rented in by rich peasants, who gained control of a larger proportion of the tenanted area (cf. Bardhan, Kalpana, 1977a, A38). These tendencies have been rather more marked in *ryotwari* and *mahalwari* than in *zamindari* and *jagirdari* areas, especially in those regions which have become centres of tractorization (in particular, in north-west India,

in Punjab, Haryana and western UP). Rich peasants were well on
the way to becoming masters of the Indian countryside, in these
regions in particular, and since these were the location of the largest
concentration of marketed surpluses rich peasants had growing
influence in the polity. They showed themselves to be eminently
capable of exercising political power, not only in the village, but
also at the level of district, state and centre.

Middle peasants must have participated, to a degree, in any
advancement, but poor peasants, landless labourers, and village
artisans and craftsmen gained very little from land reform or from
the other changes that were afoot. In the 1950s there was a mass
eviction of tenants, when fear of future land reform was strong, and
efforts were made to secure as much land for personal cultivation
as possible (cf. Bardhan, Kalpana, 1977a, A38). There was also
some "tenant switching" as tenanted land passed from poor to rich
peasants. But, traditional share-cropping continued to exist on
an extensive scale, while new and insidious forms of "disguised
tenancies" began to emerge. Of landless labourers the Third Plan
document commented: "in some areas their condition may have
actually worsened" (Government of India, Planning Commission,
1961, 375) and the same would be true of village artisans and
craftsmen, with the growing intrusion of factory-made products.
The extent to which poor peasants and artisans joined the ranks of
landless labour is, however, difficult to establish. It does seem likely
that as well as some pauperization (i.e. a fall in living standards)
among landless labourers and artisans, there was also a continuing,
if slow, process of proletarianization (i.e. a complete separation from
the means of production) among poor peasants and artisans.

We wish now to examine the kind of effects the "new technology"
has had upon the agrarian structure whose contours we have
sketched:[4] upon the process of class formation and upon class action.

The "New Technology" and Differentiation of the Peasantry

I have suggested that by the mid-1960s the rich peasant stratum
was already established, in certain areas particularly, as a powerful
class in itself, eminently capable of class-for-itself action. Thereafter,
as the new technology became available, and was, indeed, deliberately steered towards the regions where they were most in ascendancy, and within those regions towards them (a true "betting on
the strong" policy, whose operation they themselves helped to
determine), in the initial stages – i.e. up to the early 1970s – they

effectively appropriated that technology and thereby increased in economic strength. They tended to adopt both the biochemical and mechanical innovations, and their capacity to do this, at first almost exclusively among the peasantry, derived from several of their characteristics. We note that the argument applies, equally, to those landlords who adopted the new technology. Rao observes, *à propos* the supposed scale-neutrality of the biochemical inputs, that they "are not resource-neutral" (Rao, 1975, 44). That is surely so, and, given the likely profitability of the new varieties, the superior resource endowment of rich peasants (and landlords), allied to their considerable class ties, gave them a massive advantage with respect to their ability to apply and to secure a scarce bundle of inputs. Moreover, the profitability (broadly construed) of the mechanical innovations attracted them strongly. First, if we define "resources" to include "knowledge", we may say that rich peasants had far greater access to information about the new inputs and their likely performance: as a result of close ties with the block officials who disseminated information, control of village social clubs which might exclude poor peasants, greater literacy, greater likelihood of ownership of a radio, and deliberate restriction of knowledge (Dasgupta, 1977, 240–2, who cites a study of five UP villages in 1971–2, Hale, 1973). Second, the degree of uncertainty attached to the new varieties is lower for rich peasants (partly because of greater knowledge; partly because of an ability, not possessed by poor peasants, to apply the inputs in the correct proportions; partly because rich peasants, due to storage capacity, can get higher prices), while they are better able to bear risk because of their greater resources (Dasgupta, 1977, 243–4). Third, rich peasants (and landlords) could afford to purchase the new inputs – both biochemical and mechanical – because of greater own resources and because they captured, to a very large degree, the institutional credit (supplied by both cooperatives and commercial banks) that was made available at "reasonable" rates of interest. (See Dasgupta, 1977, 115–9, 123, 244–50, for a survey of some of the evidence. He cites Bapna, 1973; Kahlon and Singh, 1973a and b. See also Farmer (ed.), 1977, 114–5, 121–3, 132, 137–8, 265, 304; Bardhan, Kalpana, 1977a, A38; Rao, 1975, 136–42.) To the extent that rich peasants (and landlords) now used an increasing proportion of own resources for productive investment, rather than, as previously, for money-lending, less credit was available for poor peasants (Dasgupta, 1977, 248). Finally, where the available inputs were scarce (the high-yielding seeds, fertilisers, canal-irrigated water), and supplied through cooperatives or government officials, rich peasants were far better placed to acquire them (Farmer (ed.), 1977, 163, 264–5, 304; Dasgupta, 1977, 79, 88, 121).

That the new technology has hastened the process of differentiation seems beyond doubt. In so doing it has accentuated certain class-in-itself changes. It has served to consolidate the rich peasantry as a powerful, dominant class: the rich peasantry has become stronger economically and has taken on more of the characteristics of a class of capitalist farmers. It seems to be a process of a cumulative kind, though we are not here considering the very real possibility of its being brought to a halt (see, for example, Correspondent, Special, 1975). It is certainly a process which is by no means complete in India's advanced agricultural regions. The middle peasantry may have partaken of this aggrandizement to a certain extent, and a small portion of them may have become rich peasants. There may even have been, in north-west India, some participation by poorer peasants, though on relatively unfavourable terms. That participation, however, may serve to dampen possible antagonism between poor and rich peasants, even where polarization is proceeding. What we must now ask is whether, participation by some "smaller peasants" notwithstanding, the "new technology" has contributed to rural proletarianization, a substantial element in which might be depeasantization. This – and the manner in which it is proceeding, if it is proceeding – has important implications for the kind of rural proletariat that is emerging. Along with other class-in-itself changes it sets up certain predispositions for class consciousness and class action, although, of course, these changes in themselves do not rigidly determine a particular outcome.

The "New Technology" and Rural Proletarianization

I would interpret the available evidence[5] as, indeed, signifying the operation of a process of proletarianization of the peasantry, or depeasantization: one that is complex, but as yet partial in its impact. The new technology has produced conditions in which, by a variety of means, the poor peasantry has lost an increasing share of the *operated* area to rich peasants. Not only that, but the poor peasantry is, in different ways, being transformed more and more into a rural proletariat. Thus, first, "small peasants and tenants have been increasingly pushed out of self-employment into wage labour" (Bardhan, Kalpana, 1977a, A38). The Indian figures on occupational distribution show, between 1961 and 1971, a large rise in the proportion of workers working primarily as agricultural labourers, with the wage-employment proportion of rural workers going up from one fifth to one third (Bardhan, Kalpana, 1977a, A37). In other words, the poor peasant must, increasingly, sell his labour power in order to survive. But he does retain possession of a piece of land. A second form of partial transformation may be seen in the shift from traditional forms of share-cropping to some of the cost-share leasing arrangements that have emerged.

Partial proletarianization has been at work in the Indian country-side: a process not initiated but certainly hastened by the operation of the new technology. That process has added to the already large number of completely landless labourers: some dispossessed tenants, some poor peasants who have sold land, an unknown number of ruined village artisans and craftsmen. It has not done this on a large scale, however. Rather, its most significant contribution has been to throw into increasing wage employment large numbers of poor peasants who continue to own some land, and to bring some share-croppers near to the state of pure wage labour. No doubt it has further manifestations, which we have been unable to identify. Crucial to our understanding of the nature and implications (both immediate and prospective) of this process are the circumstances of employment creation, in both country and town, within which it has proceeded. These circumstances help to explain why it has been a partial process. They also suggest that it is likely to continue to be partial in the immediate future, but in conditions which may worsen for poor peasants and landless labourers.

The "New Technology" and the Emerging Rural Proletariat

We must now consider further the nature of the emerging rural proletariat, or class-in-itself, whose class consciousness and capacity for class-in-itself action are conditioned by the amalgam of foregoing attributes, along with certain others which the new technology appears to have ushered in. Let us see what these other features are. At this point the interaction of class-in-itself and class-for-itself becomes obvious, and the two become difficult to disentangle.

The new labour process, which derives from the application of a combination of the biochemical and mechanical innovations, embodies a change in the structure of the demand for labour. Above, I stressed the distinction between permanent and casual labour. The distinction remains an important one, but the new technology alters the proportions in which the two kinds of labour are used. Some of the work done on mechanization in the Punjab captures the point. Thus, in one study, which attempts a projection to the mid-1980s, an overall decline in the demand for labour is postulated, though one which, through the mechanizing of harvesting and threshing operations, will have a particular impact upon casual labourers (Billings and Singh, 1971). Another study, which examined data for large farms (i.e. above 20 acres in size of operation) throughout the Punjab, revealed that the addition of a tubewell and pump alone induced a shift from permanent to casual labour, while tractorization brought a rise in the demand for permanent labour to replace casual labour (Rudra, 1971) (the latter point, with respect to tractors, borne out by Vashistha, 1975). Thus, one would expect mechanization to have led to a rising proportion of permanent or attached labour among hired labour, and for this proportion to grow as mechanisation spreads.

The change does not stop there, however. The category permanent or attached labourers itself is experiencing significant transformation in its relations with rich peasant employers, in the wake of a qualitatively different labour process. Successful class-for-itself action by rich peasants has brought about class-in-itself changes among the rural proletariat. A new kind of permanent labourer, known locally as the *nauker*, has arisen in Haryana to replace, to an important degree, the traditional labourer; permanent labour contracts have acquired new characteristics: they are now very formal in nature; they are finalized in the presence of three witnesses; and they have built into them a system of advance payment of wages. Each of these serves to consolidate the power of the dominant class over the labourers.

The Rural Proletariat, Class Consciousness, and Class-for-Itself Action

We have delineated some of the structural characteristics of the rural proletariat – the class-in-itself changes – that have accompanied the new technology in the Indian countryside: that have been the product of the qualitatively different labour process in the specific historical circumstances of certain regions of India. We have also, inevitably, touched upon class-for-itself. Some of the changes are obviously general, but, in the nature of the case, much, if not most, of our evidence comes from the wheat-growing belt of north-west India. This is inevitable, inasmuch as if there is anything that one can designate a "green revolution" in India its "heartland" is precisely there (and we do well to recall just how small a part of India that is), and much of the research on the impact of technological innovation in Indian agriculture has, perforce, related to this region. As far as these structural characteristics are concerned, it may well be that in other regions in which technological innovations have been adopted – for example, in rice-growing, and areas with a different set of inherited characteristics, different initial agrarian structures – there are significant variations that we have been unable to identify. It may also be that there are regions whose relations of production are particularly resistant to technological innovations (as suggested, for example, by Bhaduri, 1973). With these provisos – which are considerable – in mind we may turn to some of the possible implications of the observed class-in-itself changes for class consciousness and class-for-itself action. If there are regional differences we will want to consider them.

We start with the concrete circumstances of north-west India. Partial proletarianization, in conjunction with a shift in the structure of the hired labour force away from casual labour and towards permanent or attached labour, longer contracts and the particular nature of those contracts, must certainly mean an inhibiting of class consciousness. They both reflect and lead to such an inhibition. That part of wage labour which comes from households whose main source of income is cultivation, and which constitutes a sizeable proportion of the permanent labour force, is likely to have the most limited proletarian consciousness. Their contradiction with rich peasants is over land. They may even give active support to dominant classes in any struggle over wages and working conditions. At best, they will remain neutral. Those wage labourers from "agricultural labour households with land" (whose major income source is not land) will be similarly, if not so markedly, influenced. The remaining, completely landless, members of the attached labour force are untrammelled by land. They may well have a fairly high degree of class consciousness. They are, however, constrained in any proclivity towards class action by their attachment and the conditions of their attachment. The "permanent labour policy" has certainly contributed to the lack of militancy among permanent labourers that has been observed in north-west India. It has proved, so far, a potent class weapon in the hands of the dominant classes. It is one they have evolved in order to cope with the conditions which the new labour process has created, in particular the "worrisome improvement in the bargaining position of labourers" (Bhalla, 1976, A28).

Among casual labourers, too, partial proletarianization exercises an influence, which may be reinforced where the casual labour force includes migrant labour from depressed areas. On the other hand,

while casual labourers are as likely to come from households whose
main source of income is cultivation, they are distinguished from
permanent labourers in not coming from holdings above 2.5 acres.
It has been observed that "casual labour . . . appears to be much
more militant than the permanent agricultural labourers" (Bhalla,
1976, A29). This is probably a reflection of the tighter constraints
imposed by the "permanent labour policy", plus the presence of
members of middle (and even rich) peasant households. Yet, one
should not exaggerate the militancy of casual labour. It may have
an increasing class consciousness, but:

> this has not led to collective bargaining . . . Individually, the casual
> agricultural labourer can, and does, say on occasions to one of the
> cultivators who regularly hires him: "I will not work today" . . .
> Collectively, in action – far removed still from collective wage
> bargaining – labourers in a village may arrive at some sort of consensus
> that for the coming harvest each should stick to a demand for Rsy per
> day instead of the lesser sum of Rsx, which was paid last year. But
> this is a consensus which is implemented by individuals (Bhalla, 1976,
> A28).

The Rich Peasantry: Class-in-Itself and Class-for-Itself

We have already pointed to the major characteristics of the rich
peasantry, although, again, much of our evidence relates to north-
west India. Among rich peasants, clearly, class consolidation has
proceeded apace and has been hastened by the availability of the
new technology. They are, more and more, a class of capitalist
farmers. Class-for-itself action has been pursued with relentless skill
with respect to both subordinate rural classes and to the urban
bourgeoisie (and urban proletariat). We have seen some of the
implications of this for class formation in the countryside, and how
it is by no means uniform in its effects. It carries significant
implications, too, for urban class formation, which we may at least
mention. Elsewhere, I have argued that the rich peasantry has
exercised its class power, with great success, to avoid taxation, to
maintain high agricultural prices and inter-sectoral terms of trade
favourable to themselves, to subvert attempts to nationalize the
grain trade, to prevent further land reform (Byres, 1974; 1979).
There can be no doubt that the new technology, by increasing their
economic strength has added considerably to their capacity to pursue
their class interests in this fashion. I have also argued that this is a

significant factor in the failure of industry to grow. That this impedes the growth of the urban proletariat and reflects the essential weakness of the Indian urban bourgeoisie is obvious enough. We cannot pursue that issue here.[6]

Rich peasants are now organized very effectively as a class: aggressively, cleverly, and extensively constituted as a class-for-itself, capable of pursuing its interests with skill, ruthlessness, and success. Between 13 and 15 May, 1973, a Farmers' Convention met in Delhi, with representatives from all the states of India, and an attendance of 3000 on the first day (Correspondent, Special, 1973). In the printed welcome address the following words appeared:

> the sleeping rural giant has awakened from his age-old slumber. The days of government proposing and farmers disposing as obedient children have gone. He [the farmer] is no more a docile, dumb and obedient child to accept whatever the government says . . . Government can plan and propose . . . but they themselves cannot perform (*loc. cit.*).

The awakened rural giant is the rich peasant. The gathering in question was scheduled to discuss:

> recent developments in agricultural research and their operational aspects for higher farm production; problems of small and marginal farmers and of farmers in tribal and dry areas; rural unemployment and means of gainful employment; social justice and farm productivity; and problems relating to agricultural input supplies, pricing and taxation etc. (*loc. cit.*).

That was the public face. There were, indeed, one or two brief speeches by invited agricultural scientists on recent research, but the seminar, in fact, was devoted almost exclusively to:

> issues directly and immediately affecting farmers, such as procurement prices and the foodgrain takeover, shortages of and irregularities in input supplies, land ceiling and agricultural taxation (*loc. cit.*).

The Agricultural Prices Commission was subjected to indignant criticism . . . and so on. So much for the public face. These are the concerns of rich peasants. One can be sure that there were no poor peasant delegates.

Our observer at the Convention comments:

> The Indian big farmer is certainly not a parallel of the Russian *kulak*. Other differences apart, the relationship of this class with the ruling

party and the government in the two situations make them qualitatively the opposite of each other. The Bolsheviks coerced and crushed the *kulaks*, whereas the Indian establishment has always nursed and pampered them (*loc. cit.*).

Let us pursue the analogy a little further. During the debate which raged in the Soviet Union between 1926 and 1929 (the last debate to rage in the Soviet Union), Trotsky declared, in one of his memorable phrases, that "the *kulak* . . . is knocking at the door of politics' (*Times Literary Supplement*, 1969). In India, the *kulak* (if we may use that word) has marched boldly through the door of politics and is very much a force to be reckoned with in the Indian polity. Indian state power has been exercised on his behalf. One cannot understand the nature of the Indian state – its class basis – unless one recognizes this. It may be too much to say that the rich peasantry has captured state power in India. But it most certainly exerts an immense influence upon the Indian state – an influence that the new technology has magnified.

Editors' Notes

1. First published in Journal of Peasant Studies, 8(4) July 1981.
2. These relationships are discussed by Breman in his chapter on "The Disintegration of the *Hali* System" in Part III.
3. For a discussion of the hereditary relationships between specialist artisans and craftsmen, and landowners, in the context of the so-called "*jajmani* system" see the chapter by Fuller in Part I.
4. The term "new technology" refers to the biochemical inputs of the "green revolution" – new higher-yielding varieties of the major cereals, fertilizers and agro-chemicals.
5. Byres refers in particular to work by Bardhan, Kalpana, 1977a; Bhalla, S., 1977a and 1977b; and by Rao, 1975.
6. The issue is pursued by Harriss in his chapter in Part II.

Pakistan: Land Reforms Reconsidered[1]

Akmal Hussain

Introduction

Before the introduction of the high yielding varieties of food-grains in the late 1960s the argument for land reform was a simple one. It was observed that small farms had a higher yield per acre than large farms,[2] so it was argued that a redistribution of owned land in favour of the smaller farmers would improve average yields in agriculture. Hence land reforms were considered advisable both on grounds that they would reduce the degree of inequality of rural incomes, as well as on grounds of efficiency. The efficiency argument for land reforms in Pakistan gathered momentum in the 1950s when agricultural stagnation began to constitute a fetter to the growth of industry.[3] Agriculture provided not only food-grains for the rising urban population but also provided most of the foreign exchange with which industrial machinery and raw materials were imported.[4] Accordingly slow agricultural growth generated both a crisis in the balance of payments as well as food shortages in the urban sector.[5] In such a situation even the technocrats who were merely interested in the growth of GNP joined the cry of the social reformers for a land reform. It began to be seen as a necessary instrument for accelerating agricultural growth and thereby releasing the constraint on industrial growth.

When the Green Revolution technology became available in the late 1960s, the ruling classes could breathe a sigh of relief. The new technology made it possible substantially to accelerate agricultural growth through an "élite farmer strategy" which concentrated the new inputs on large farms. Now the crucial determinant in yield differences became not the labour input per acre in which small farms had been at an advantage, but the application of the seed–water–fertilizer package to which the large farmers with their greater financial power had superior access. Thus the technocrats felt that the Green Revolution had made it possible to accelerate agricultural growth without having to bring about any real change in the rural power structure.

Today after more than a decade and a half of the "élite farmer strategy", the imperative of land reform is re-emerging, albeit in a more complex form than in the pre-Green-Revolution period. As the large farms approach the maximum yield per acre with the available technology, further growth in agricultural output increasingly depends on raising the yield per acre of smaller farms. The small-farm sector whose yield potential remains to be fully utilized, constitutes a substantial part of the agrarian economy. According to the Pakistan Census of Agriculture 1972, farms of less than 25 acres constitute 88 per cent of the total number of farms, and 57 per cent of total farm area. From the viewpoint of raising the yield per acre of small farms (i.e. farms with less than 25 acres) the critical consideration is that 54 per cent of the total farm area in the small-farm sector is tenant-operated. Since tenants lose half of any increase in output to the landlord, they lack the incentive to invest in technology which would raise yields. Because of their weak financial and social position they also lack the ability to make such investment. Their ability to invest is further eroded by a whole nexus of social and economic dependence on the landlord which deprives the tenant of much of his investable surplus. Thus the objective of raising yields in the small-farm sector is inseparable from removing the institutional constraints to growth arising out of the fact of tenancy. A land reform programme that gives land to the tiller is therefore an essential first step in providing the small farmer with both the incentive and the ability to raise his yields. However the imperative for land reform today arises not only from the need to accelerate agricultural growth, but also from the need to prevent the developing social crisis associated with the impact of the Green Revolution on Pakistan's rural society. We shall argue in this paper that in a situation where the distribution of landownership was highly unequal the adoption of the Green Revolution technology set in motion powerful economic forces which, while rapidly enriching the large farmers, also induced a sharp increase in rural poverty, unemployment and the pressure on big urban centres. We shall discuss the following four contradictions generated by the growth process in Pakistan's agriculture during the Green Revolution period:

1. the rapid mechanization of large farms in an economy characterized by a "labour surplus";
2. the polarization in the size distribution of farms accompanied by a growing landlessness of the poor peasantry. The polarization consisted of an increase in the percentage shares of large and small farms at the expense of medium-sized farms (8–25 acres);
3. the growth of capitalist farming together with a growing social and

economic dependence of the poor peasantry on large landowners;
4. an absolute deterioration in the economic condition of the poor
  peasants alongside the growing affluence of the large farmers.

The Attempts at Land Reform and their Failure

Before embarking on an analysis of the four contradictions
specified above, and their link with an unequal distribution of
landownership, let us briefly examine the impact of the land reforms
of 1959 and 1972.

The Land Reforms of 1959   The 1959 land reforms fixed the ceiling
on the private ownership of land at 500 acres irrigated and 1000
acres unirrigated. The fundamental feature which rendered this
reform incapable of significantly reducing the power of the big
landlords was that the ceiling on ownership was fixed in terms of
individual rather than family holdings. This enabled most of the big
landlords to circumvent the ceiling by transferring their excess land
to various real and fictitious family members. Moreover a number
of additional provisions in the 1959 land reform allowed landlords
to retain land far in excess of the ceiling even on an individual basis.
For example, an individual could keep land in excess of the ceiling
so long as his holding was an equivalent of 36,000 Produce Index
Units (PIUs). A PIU was estimated as a measure of the gross value
of output per acre of land by type of soil and was therefore seen as
a measure of land productivity. The lacuna in this provision was
that the PIUs were based on pre-Partition revenue settlements.
Since the gross value of output was dependent on the quality of
land and prices, values of PIUs fixed before 1947 would grossly
underestimate land productivity in 1959. M. H. Khan (1981)
estimates that even if the PIU values published in 1959 were taken
as a correct representative of land productivity, the allowance of
36,000 PIUs for an individual holding would leave a substantially
larger area than that specified in the ceiling. Another provision
which enabled landlords to retain land above the ceiling was that
an additional area was allowed for orchards.

Given the fact that in the 1959 land reforms the ceiling was fixed
in terms of individual rather than family holdings, and given the
existence of additional lacunae in the provision, most big landlords
were able to circumvent the ceiling and retain their land without
declaring any land in excess of the ceiling. Those who actually
declared excess land were super-large landlords who even after

making use of exemptions still could not conceal their entire holding. Thus the average owned area per declarant landlord in Pakistan was as much as 7208 acres and in the Punjab province was 11,810 acres. It is interesting that even out of the land declared in excess of the ceiling only 35 per cent (1.9 million acres) could be resumed by the government. After the government had resumed whatever excess land it could, the average owned holding retained by the declarant landlords was as much as 4033 acres in Pakistan and in the Punjab province 7489 acres.[6] Thus the land reforms of 1959 failed to affect the economic power of the landed élite in Pakistan. The final gesture of benevolence by the government towards the landlords is provided by the fact that of the land actually resumed under the 1959 land reforms, as much as 57 per cent was uncultivated land. Most of this area needed considerable land improvement before it could be cultivated. Yet the government paid Rs39.2m to the former owners as "compensation" for surrendering land which was producing nothing (Khan, 1981, chap. 5).

The Land Reforms of 1972   The 1972 land reforms shared with the 1959 land reforms the essential feature of specifying the ceiling in terms of individual rather than family holdings. However the ceiling in the 1972 land reforms was lower, being 150 acres for irrigated and 300 acres for unirrigated. The 1972 land reforms allowed an area equivalent to 12,000 PIUs (with a bonus of 2000 PIUs to owners of tractors or tubewells) which made possible a *de facto* ceiling on an individual ownership far above the ceiling. The reason for this discrepancy between the *de jure* and *de facto* ceiling was that the revenue settlements of the 1940s still formed the basis of estimating the PIUs. The considerable improvement in yields, cropping patterns, and cropping intensities since the 1940s meant that the use of obsolete PIUs in 1972 considerably understated land productivity. M. H. Khan has estimated that due to the understatement of land productivity through the PIUs provision, the actual ceiling in the 1972 land reforms was 466 acres in the Punjab and 560 acres in Sind for a tractor/tubewell owners. If an owner also took advantage of the provision for intra-family transfers the ceiling came to 932 acres irrigated in the Punjab and 1120 acres in Sind (Khan, 1981).

Of the land that was declared above the ceiling by landlords after they had made use of the provisions for circumventing the ceiling, only 42 per cent was resumed in the Punjab and 59 per cent in Sind. The area actually resumed by the government under the 1972 land reforms was only about 0.6 million acres, which was even less than the area (1.9 million acres) resumed under the 1959 land reforms. The resumed area in 1972 constituted only 0.01 per cent of the total farm area in the country. Moreover in the Punjab 59 per cent of the area resumed by the government, was uncultivated. Consequently the land reforms of 1972, like the land reforms of 1959, failed to affect the power of the big landlords significantly.

Agrarian Structure and the Impact of the New Technology

The discussion in the preceding section has suggested that both the land reforms of 1959 and 1972 failed to change the highly unequal distribution of landownership in Pakistan. We find that as much as 30 per cent of total farm area in Pakistan is owned by large landowners (i.e. owning 150 acres or more). These landowners constitute only 0.5 per cent of the total number of landowners in the country.[7] The overall picture of Pakistan's agrarian structure has been that these large landowners have rented out most of their land to small- and medium-sized tenants.[8] In such a situation when the HYV technology became available in the late 1960s the large landowners found it profitable to resume some of the land they had rented out to cultivate themselves on large farms, using hired labour and capital investment (Hussain, 1982). It is this process of the development of capitalist farming which has generated new and potentially explosive contradictions in Pakistan's rural society. Let us examine each of these contradictions.

Farm Mechanization and the Problem of Employment

During the period when the HYV technology was being adopted in Pakistan there was also a rapid introduction of tractors. The number of tractors increased from only 2000 in 1959 to 18,909 in 1968. The rapid increase in tractors continued and by 1975 there were 35,714 tractors in Pakistan. Between 1976 and 1981 an additional 75,859 tractors were imported into the country.[9]

What was significant about the increase in the number of tractors was not only the rate of growth but also the fact that most of the tractors were in the large-size range. According to the report of the Farm Mechanization Committee, 84 per cent of the tractors were over 35 horse power, while only 1 per cent were in the small-size range of less than 26 horse power.[10] The question that arises is why predominantly large-sized tractors were introduced in a rural sector where 88 per cent of the farms are below 25 acres in size.[11] This is integrally linked with the question of why tractorization occurred at all in what is commonly regarded as a "labour surplus" economy. Both these questions can be understood in terms of the fundamental features of Pakistan's agrarian economy arising out of the highly unequal distribution of landownership. These features are:

1. The distribution of land *ownership* in Pakistan is much more unequal than the distribution of *operational* holdings. Our estimates based on the 1972 Census of Agriculture show that as much as 30 per cent of total farm area in Pakistan was owned by landowners in the size class 150 acres or more; by contrast the percentage of farm area *operated* by farmers in this size class was only 9.2 per cent. The observed divergence in the degree of concentration of farm area between owned and operated holdings suggests that many of the larger landowners must be renting out some or all of their owned area to smaller farmers. This proposition is supported by the data which show that compared with any other category in Pakistan and Punjab respectively[12] the large landowners (those with 150 acres or more) were the biggest renters out of land, even in 1972.

2. The larger landowners attracted by the high profitability of owner cultivation following the availability of HYV technology, tended to resume their formerly rented-out land to cultivate themselves on large farms with tractors. Evidence for the resumption of land during 1960 and 1978 for owner cultivation on large tractor farms is provided by our field-survey data. We found that farms in the size classes 50 to 150 acres, and 150 acres or more, have experienced a substantial increase in their area over the period.

In the case of farms in the size class 150 acres and above, the increase in farm area over the period 1960 to 1978 constituted half their total farm area in 1978. In terms of the source of increase, 65 per cent of the increase in farm area of large farms came through resumption of formerly rented-out land. Thus resumption of formerly rented-out land was by far the biggest source of increase in farm area of large farms. There is evidence that the resumption of rented out land for owners to cultivate themselves on large farms was associated with the purchase of tractors by those farmers. My field-survey data shows that whereas in 1960 almost 60 per cent of the farmers in the large-size class (150 acres or more) were without tractors; by 1978 *all* of them had at least one, and 41 per cent had three or more tractors.[13] Evidence at the all-Pakistan level is provided by the Report of the Farm Mechanization Committee. It shows that within the farm area operated by tractor owners, the percentage area operated by large farmers was as high as 87 per cent.

It appears from the foregoing discussion of the available evidence that an important reason why large-sized tractors began to be introduced during the 1960s was that large landowners responding to the new profit opportunities began to resume rented-out land for cultivation on large farms. Given the difficulty of (a) mobilizing a large number of labourers during the peak seasons in an imperfect labour market, and (b) the problem of supervising the labourers to ensure satisfactory performance, the large farmers found it convenient to mechanize even though there may have been no labour shortage in an absolute sense.

Polarization in Rural Class Structure and the Increase in Landlessness

An examination of census data for the period 1960–72 shows that in the Punjab province (where the new technology had its greatest impact) a polarization occurred in the size distribution of farms, i.e. the percentage shares of both large- and small-sized farms increased while that of lower-medium-sized farms (7.5–25 acres) decreased. This polarization was essentially the result of large landowners resuming for their own cultivation some of the land which they had formerly rented out to tenants.[14]

The dynamic process underlying the polarization phenomenon consisted of the following elements:

1. Large landowners resumed for their own cultivation land which they had rented out to both small- and lower-medium-sized (7.5–25 acres) tenant-farmers. However the resumption hit lower-medium-sized farms to a much greater extent than it did small farms because of the considerably greater degree of tenancy of the lower-medium-sized farms.
2. As lower-medium-sized tenant-farmers lost some but not all of their land following resumption, many of them shifted into the category of small farms over the inter-censal period.

The evidence shows that the phenomenon of polarization in the size-class of farms was accompanied by growing landlessness amongst the poor peasantry. Our estimates based on population census data show that during the period 1961–73, 794,042 peasants entered the category of wage labourers, i.e. 43 per cent of the total agricultural labourers in Pakistan in 1973 had entered this category as the result of the proletarianization of the poor peasantry.

Our discussion in this section has suggested that given the unequal distribution of landownership in Pakistan, when the new technology became available, it induced a process of land resumption by big landlords: this resulted in a polarization in the size distribution of farms on the one hand and an increased landlessness of the poor peasantry on the other.

The Growth of Capitalist Farming along with a Growing Dependence of the Poor Peasantry

The growth of capitalist farming was accelerated considerably in the late 1960s as large landowners began to resume their rented-out land to operate their own farms with hired labour and capital investment. However the particular form of the development of capitalism in Pakistan's agriculture was such that instead of being accompanied by a growing independence of the poor peasantry (as in Europe), in Pakistan capitalism in agriculture was accompanied by an increased social and economic dependence of the poor peasantry on the landowners. The reason for this was that capitalist farming in Pakistan developed in a situation where the power of the landlords was still intact. Consequently the emerging market was mediated by the social and political power of the landlords. The local institutions for the distribution of agricultural inputs and credit and for the sale of output are heavily influenced by the big landlords. The result is that the poor peasant in order to acquire the inputs, credit and facilities for transporting his produce to the market has to depend on help from the landlord. In many cases the poor peasant who lacks collateral cannot get credit from the official agencies at all, and has to depend on the landlord for loans. In addition to this he often has to purchase the tubewell water from the landlord and use the landlord's transport to take produce for sale to the market. Thus as the inputs for agricultural production become monetized and in so far as the access to the market is via the landlord the poor peasant's dependence has intensified with the development of capitalism in agriculture.

The Deteriorating Economic Condition of the Poor Peasantry

With the development of capitalist farming, the poor peasant is subject to a triple squeeze on his real income. This squeeze has the following elements.

(1) *Money costs have increased*

(a) Inputs which were formerly non-monetized (e.g. seed, animal manure) or inputs which he formerly did not use at all (such as tractor ploughings, tubewell water, pesticides) he now has to purchase with money. In this context it might be asked why the poor peasant now has to buy fertilizer and hire tractors. The answer lies in the inability of the poor peasant (whether owner or tenant) to maintain as many farm animals as before. The reasons for this are: (i) Pastures devoted to fodder have been reduced on poor peasant farms as farm size declined following loss of some of his rented in land due to resumption by landlords; and (ii) The poor peasant's access over the fodder and pasture lands of the landlords was reduced as the latter mechanized and began to grow cash crops over much of the area formerly devoted to pastures or fodder.

Thus mechanization and the development of capitalist farming on large farms has adversely affected the poor peasant's ability to keep animals thereby making him more vulnerable to market pressures.

(b) The second factor in the rise in money costs is the shift from share-cropping to money rents which are rising sharply. The money rent is often fixed by the landlord on the basis not of the actual yield of the tenant-operated farm, but of its *potential* yield if it were being cultivated at peak efficiency.

(2) *Slow growth in yield/acre*

While there has been an increase in cash rents payable by the poor peasant and thus in his rental burden, his yield per acre has not increased proportionately because the poor peasant does not have the financial and political power to acquire all the required inputs (seed, fertilizer, supplementary tubewell water and pesticides nor does the poor peasant have control over their timing.

(3) *Selling grain cheap and buying dear*

The third pressure on the real income of the poor peasant is that in a situation of rising cash requirements and indebtedness, he is forced to sell a part of his subsistence output at harvest time. These harvest sales are at low prices. However at the end of the year he has to buy grain in the market at high prices. Thus selling grain cheap, and buying dear is another squeeze on the poor peasants' real income which is discussed in this section and which is reflected in the changes in the quality and quantity of their diet since 1965. The class of poor peasants (with farms of less than 25 acres) contains a substantial number of farmers who have suffered an absolute decline in the quantity of food, and an even larger number of farmers who have suffered a decline in the quality of their diet (Hussain, 1980).

Conclusion

In this paper we have argued that in Pakistan, given the highly unequal distribution of landownership, the introduction of the new technology in agriculture has unleashed powerful contradictions which are not only likely to become constraints on continued agricultural growth, but are also generating acute social tensions: the nature of the economic process, in the absence of an effective land reform, is such that it is enriching the rural élite at the expense of the rapid deterioration in the economic and social conditions of the majority of the rural population.

Each of the contradictions specified above stems from the fact that the new technology became available in a situation where economic and social power was concentrated in the hands of the big landlords. Agricultural growth during the 1960s and 1970s was predicated on the rapid increase in yields of the relatively larger farms. Continued growth in the next two decades will have to be derived from increasing yields per acre of the small farmers. An essential precondition for this is the institutional and economic change which will give the small farmer better access over the new inputs, and greater control over his production process and investable surplus. In this sense, an effective land reform is now not only an imperative of a more equitable economic growth, but of growth itself.

Notes

1. Originally delivered as a paper at the Group 83 Seminar at Hotel Intercontinental, Lahore, December, 1982, under the title "Contradictions of Land Reforms in Pakistan".
2. There was a lively debate on the factors underlying the inverse relationship between farm size and productivity. One of the more elegant explanations for this phenomenon was offered by A. K. Sen who suggested that with traditional technology, small family farms

could produce a higher yield per acre than large farms, through a higher labour input per acre. This could happen because small farms using family labour applied labour input beyond the point where the marginal product equalled the wage rate, while large farms using hired labour could not afford to do so.

3. Annual growth rate of large-scale manufacturing during the period 1950–5 was 23.6 per cent, while that of agriculture during the same period was only 1.3 per cent. During the period 1955–60, annual growth rate in large-scale manufacturing declined to 9.3 per cent, while that of agriculture was only 1.4 per cent. See S. R. Lewis Jr., 1969, p. 3, Table 1.

4. Cotton and jute constituted 85 per cent of total commodity exports up to the mid-1950s. See S. R. Lewis Jr., 1969, p. 7, Table 5.

5. Import of food-grains and flour as a percentage of total commodity imports increased from 0.5 per cent in 1951/2 to 14.6 per cent in 1959/60. See A. Hussain, 1980, p. 16, Table 3.

6. Land Reforms in West Pakistan, vol. III, Appendix 18, Government of Pakistan, 1967.

7. These figures are estimated on the basis of combining Land Reforms Commission data and the Agriculture Census data. The 1972 Agriculture Census data alone gives an incorrect figure of land owned by the large landowners because its sampling procedure is such that absentee land is systematically excluded. For details of my estimating procedure see A. Hussain, 1980, pp. 219–21, Appendix 2.

8. As late as 1972, 46 per cent of the total farm area in Pakistan was tenant operated, and of this tenanted area, 50 per cent had been rented out by large landowners (owning 150 acres and above). My estimates show that as much as 75 per cent of area owned by large landowners in 1972 was rented out to smaller tenants. See A. Hussain, 1980, chap. 3.

9. Pakistan Economic Survey, 1980–1, Government of Pakistan, Finance Division, Economic Advisor's Wing, Islamabad.

10. Report of the Farm Mechanization Committee. Ministry of Agriculture and Works. Government of Pakistan, March 1970, p. 60.

11. Pakistan Census of Agriculture: All Pakistan Report, Agriculture Census Organization, Ministry of Food and Agriculture, Table 1.

12. See A. Hussain, 1980, p. 194, Table 5(a), and p. 198, Table 6a.

13. A. Hussain, 1980, chap. 5, Appendix.

14. This picture emerges when the 1960 Census data is adjusted for biases inherent in its methodology in order to make it comparable with the 1972 Census methodology (A. Hussain, 1980, chap. 3).

Indian Industrialization and the State

John Harriss[1]

Introduction: State Intervention and Industrial Development in India

State intervention has affected industrial development in India by the following broad means. The state has sought to regulate industrial development both through measures of control, such as the allocation of certain sectors of production to public sector enterprises or to "small-scale industry", and by requiring the licensing of capacity in large-scale enterprises; and through offering incentives to particular developments by making available funds from state financial institutions. It has affected industrial development (crucially, according to some economists) through its own investments (a good many economists concur in the view that a major reason for the general sluggishness in the growth of industrial production after the mid-1960s was the decline in public investment) and through the means whereby it has raised resources. It has affected industrial development through its handling of foreign capital, through its exchange and tariff policies – and in many of its actions it has been profoundly influenced by the requirements of international financial institutions (perhaps increasingly so – witness the IMF agreement of 1981). It has also had a most significant effect on industrial development through its interventions in labour relations. In all these major areas of intervention it is generally agreed that the mid-1960s – the period of what was called at the time "the crisis of Indian planning" – marks a watershed. It cannot really be disputed that the rate of growth of industrial production was higher and more sustained in the period before the mid-1960s than after, and that attempts to plan the Indian economy were diluted very much just after that time – though the way in which these tendencies are to be related together is, of course, very controversial.

"Before the Crisis": The State and Industry 1947 to circa 1966

The Congress regime which took over state power in 1947 had a

complex and contradictory character. The Freedom Struggle had
brought to positions of leadership men drawn mainly from the
intelligentsia and professional groups, but whose political philos-
ophies ranged from the strongly conservative over to commitments
to the establishment of socialism in India. The Gandhian philosophy
which influenced all of them was itself susceptible to both conservative and radical interpretation. The ideological influences upon the
regime thus pulled in different directions. There was, in addition,
an important contradiction between the aims and objectives of a
major fraction of the leadership, committed to socialist objectives –
and this fraction became dominant for a time in the 1950s and early
1960s – and the base of the Congress movement. This was not really
a *mass* base, so much as a dependence upon locally dominant rural
élites. Even before Independence the radical section of the leadership
had discussed the need for agrarian reforms – reforms, in fact, which
conflicted with the personal interests of precisely the people on
whom the Congress Movement essentially depended for its support,
and this contradiction became very much more clearly apparent
after 1947. Throughout the 1950s the Congress leadership pressed
the need for reform of the agrarian structure and for the development
of cooperative and collective forms of production. But all attempts
to implement these policy aims foundered on the rocks of the interests
of the dominant people in the countryside, who came to acquire
even more clout through their control of state legislatures – especially
after the establishment of linguistic states in the mid-1950s. There
was indeed a quite fundamental ambiguity – reflected in the major
policy pronouncements of the 1950s, such as the commitment to the
socialist pattern ratified in the *Lok Sabha* in 1954, or in the Industrial
Policy Resolution of 1956 – in the stated objectives of the Congress
regime of bringing about a socialist transformation of Indian society,
and the means by which it proposed to achieve the objective, through
a politics of consensus and compromise. Hanson (1966) and Weiner
(1962) both report speeches of Nehru's made close together, in the
Lok Sabha and to gatherings of business people, the first of which
seemed to promise almost immediate nationalization of the most
important business interests, and the second of which offered solid
reassurances to big business. Such flat contradictions are indicative
of the inherent weakness and ambiguity of "the Indian road to
socialism".

In the first three or four years after Independence rather *ad
hoc* economic policies were pursued though these were generally
favourable to private enterprise. The removal of wartime controls
on essential commodities led to great price rises but also to booming

profits, whilst at the same time corporate and personal taxation was reduced in favour of increased indirect taxation – especially sales tax. But in the early 1950s, after the death of Patel, and as Nehru acquired for a time almost undisputed authority, a new approach to social and economic change began to take shape and was put forward in the final version of the First Five Year Plan (which was published as late as December 1952, reflecting the fact that this "plan" was a *post hoc* rationalization of a modest bundle of pro-grammes). The Plan statement outlined an attack on the position of private enterprise, as the planners announced their intention of increasing supervision and control over the private sector under the framework of the Industries (Development and Regulation) Act of 1951. This provided that no new industrial units or substantial expansions to existing plants could be made without a licence from the central government, and it empowered the government to investigate the operations of any industry to make regulations concerning the quality and price of production. Further, the displace-ment of the private sector as the pre-eminent agency of industrial development was emphasized.

These thrusts were confirmed in the Industrial Policy Resolution of 1956, which asserted that the state was to "assume a predominant and direct responsibility for setting up new industrial undertakings" and classified industries into three categories depending on the state's role in the development of each of them. At the same time the Resolution reassured the private sector that it was to have "the opportunity to develop and expand". The terms of this Resolution thus further expose the ambiguity and the vagueness of the commit-ment of the Congress government to "socialism" and they reflect the contradictions inherent in an attempt to implement radical social change by gradualist methods in a polity in which power lay with groups which stood to lose most from "socialism" – the rural rich and private industrial entrepreneurs (who often displayed a capacity for meeting plan targets which greatly exceeded that of public sector enterprise – Hanson (1966) discusses instances of this at length).

In fact the 1950s and the early 1960s saw rates of industrial growth (about 7 per cent per annum) which were absolutely, and not just relatively, quite high, and the composition of industrial output became very much more diversified than it had been in the colonial period. India built up a solid industrial infrastructure at this time:

> the industrialisation which India has achieved is unique in some respects. First, she has been able to diversify the structure of her

manufacturing sector relatively quickly. Second, she is one of the few developing countries which possesses a sophisticated modern industrial structure despite the low level of her per capita income. While, in 1957, the traditional food and textile industries accounted for 67 per cent of total manufacturing output, their share had declined to 35 per cent by 1978–79; that of modern chemicals and engineering industries increased from 14 to 51 per cent over the same period. These changes in the composition of manufacturing output are also reflected in the pattern of import substitution the country has achieved . . . while the First Five Year Plan years were marked by a high degree of import substitution in consumer goods industries, the Second Five Year Plan years were marked by a high degree of import substitution in capital goods and intermediate goods industries . . . *It should be noted, however, that the industrial structure has changed very little since the mid-sixties* (emphasis mine – J.H.). (Balasubramanyam, 1984, 112)

The creation of an industrial infrastructure was the achievement, above all, of the Second Five Year Plan, which (unlike the First Plan) was the result of protracted debate and calculation, and attempted to bring about a fundamental break from the colonial pattern of international industrial division of labour by developing capital goods industries. It was not a simple "import substitution strategy" such as that advocated by the UN Commission for Latin America, the logic of which was to develop light consumer goods industries. The Second Five Year Plan strategy, formulated in the Plan Frame devised by P. C. Mahalanobis, was carried through under Nehru's leadership against a great deal of opposition internally and externally. The Plan as it was actually implemented, however, was a watered-down version in which a smaller proportion of total resources than the Plan Frame had proposed was allocated to the capital goods industries. The strategy was attacked by some economists at the time on the grounds that a country with India's endowments should aim at labour-intensive investments and so give priority to agriculture and small-scale industry. Much the same criticism has been advanced more recently by Mellor (1976) in the context of advocacy of a "food-and-employment"-led strategy of growth, and it appears too in Lipton's attack on the "urban bias" in Indian planning (Lipton, 1977). There are substantial theoretical arguments on both sides. But we should not neglect the context of competition of capitals. As Patnaik has argued: "the economic regime erected in the fifties sought to promote a relatively autonomous and rapid capitalist development in the country by expanding the economic space available for Indian capital . . . it is this precisely which drew the ire of metropolitan capital, notably of the United

States" (Patnaik, 1986, 1015). As we go on to explain, there have been serious problems with India's strategy of industrialization, which seem to lend weight to criticisms of the "Mahalanobis model". But it is important to note the context of the Second Five Year Plan, as Patnaik has done, and the extent of its achievement.

There is a good deal of consensus amongst economists that the high growth rates of the 1950s and early 1960s were based on the greatly increased volume of public development expenditure which, together with import restrictions, provided a wide market for producers in the private sector; while the growth of capacities through public investment, especially in the basic and intermediate goods sectors, made a real expansion in the economy possible (this is the formulation of Patnaik and Rao, 1977; but see also Bagchi, 1975; ISI, 1975; Mitra, 1977; Patnaik, 1979). In this period the government spearheaded investment in crucial and high-risk sectors "while making finance available to the private sector to take advantage of opportunities as a consequence of its own investment and its protectionist policy" (Patnaik, 1979, 6). And because the logic of this framework rested in practice on the notion of a mixed economy with incentives to private investment, public investment could not be financed by a heavy reliance on taxation of property incomes. The resources for public sector investment came from deficit financing, indirect taxation and foreign aid. Foreign aid and deficit financing – narrowly defined as borrowing from the RBI only – together account for 43 per cent and 42 per cent respectively of the total public sector plan outlays in the Second and Third Plans; the additional tax revenue mobilized in both these plans came largely from indirect taxes, the share of which in the total tax revenue increased from 61.9 per cent in 1955–6 to 70.7 per cent in 1965–6.

Patnaik argues that

> Since the impact of indirect taxes and deficit financing tends largely to be a regressive one, markets for mass consumption goods did not increase to any substantial extent in the course of the industrialisation process itself. And this tended to reinforce the reliance upon protection and public investment as stimuli for industrialisation, giving it a "top-heavy" character. (Patnaik, 1979, 6)

In spite of the introduction of legislation as early as 1951 giving the government quite extensive powers to control industrial growth, it has been established that not only did the government fail to check the development of monopolistic tendencies in the economy, but also that the licensing regulations actually accentuated them.

At the end of the Third Plan [1966] the private sector's contribution to the output of the organised industry was still approximately 80 per cent of the total. Data prepared in the late 1960s indicated that the licensing system not only had failed to prevent the growth of capacity in less essential industries, but actually had worked to provide a disproportionate share of new licenced capacity to the few firms belonging to the larger business houses. Over the years, the share of total approved investment allocated to the four largest business houses – the Birlas, Tatas, J.K. and Shri Ram – actually increased. (Frankel, 1978, 334–5)

In sum, there is little reason for doubting that the period of planning, from 1951 to 1966, was a period in which the industrial interests of big business generally prospered, in spite of the hostility of the dominant political culture to them (as Kochanek, 1974, has explained).

The Crisis of Planning in the mid-1960s

Why was it, then, that this quite long period of high industrial growth rates came to an end in the 1960s? Patnaik, Bagchi and others refer to several important features of the industrial development of India in the 1950s and the early 1960s:

(i) growth was accompanied by a considerable increase in the country's indebtedness (aid flow increased from 5.9 per cent of national investment in 1950/51 – 1955/56 to 17.2 per cent in 1960/61 – 1965/70);

(ii) alongside external financial assistance, technological dependence increased, and with it the role of MNCs. (The significance of foreign capital in explaining India's pattern of industrial development is a matter of controversy. Data are not readily available, but it is argued that what there are show that though "the amount of private foreign investment in India is not insignificant, it is not large enough to dominate and influence the course of the economy" (Balasubramanyam, 1984, 147). The quantum of private foreign investment is less important than the influence of technological dependence. This is not reduced by the "technical collaboration agreements" which the Government of India has preferred to the establishment of foreign-owned subsidiaries.);

(iii) the industrialization drive had a negligible impact on the

employment situation or the sectoral distribution of the workforce (for the entire period 1951–69 the annual compound growth rate of factory employment was 2.9 per cent, or only just about enough to absorb the natural growth of the employed labour force);
(iv) industrial growth was accompanied by stagnation in real wages, and the share of wages in industrial output declined.

It is argued that these features reflect the structural constraints which finally brought the period of high growth to an end. They reflect the inability of the government to raise resources domestically at the expense of property incomes, and by the mid-1960s the state was unable to sustain increased public development expenditure because of resource constraints. Toye (1981) has shown that the deceleration of industrial growth from that time was not a general phenomenon but one concentrated in the capital goods industries and to a lesser extent in intermediate goods. The abandonment of the policy of state-promoted capital accumulation which character-ized the Second and Third Five Year Plans caused the slowdown in industrialization. A number of economists argue that the effective shift in policy was most crucially the result of the inability of the government to raise resources domestically at the expense of property incomes, in a context in which the Congress party had an increased need for legitimacy. By the middle 1960s the state was unable to sustain increased development expenditure because of a fiscal crisis, arising from increased non-developmental expenditure commitments combined with inability to raise more resources domestically, and consequent heavy dependence upon regressive indirect taxation, on deficit financing and on foreign aid.

Industrial development in the early period after Independence was also "top-heavy", being "based mainly on capital goods and a few luxury consumer goods, all of which are highly technology-intensive and all of which at the prevailing level of imported technology are incapable of generating substantial employment for any given level of investment" (Patnaik, 1979, 12; and see also, for example, Sau, 1972, 1977). This pattern of industrialization reinforced itself because, along with regressive taxation, it meant that new incomes were concentrated in upper groups, leading to stagnation in the sales of traditional consumer goods and limited demand for consumer durables (C. P. Chandrasekhar's work shows that the textile industry exemplifies this "dualistic" pattern of industrial development very well; Chandrasekhar, 1978).

To these critical features of the economy we must add the further constraint of the instability and restricted growth of agricultural output. Again, most commentators, representing a diversity of theoretical and ideological backgrounds, concur in assigning a fundamental role to the failure of the Congress regime to effect a reform of the agrarian structure on India. Hanson (1966), for example, drew attention to the role which was assigned to increased agricultural output in the financing of the Second Five-Year Plan, and showed how it was expected that agricultural output could be increased without the allocation of any additional resources to the agricultural sector. He refers then to the failures of attempts to increase production primarily through reliance on institutional reform and innovation – a theme taken up more extensively by Frankel (1978, but see also Patnaik, 1972; Raj, 1976; Mitra, 1977). The aim of bringing about a transformation of the agricultural economy from below, by building up popular pressure for reform, was fundamentally in conflict with the conciliatory style of the Congress and its claims to represent the interests of all groups including the propertied classes.

The constraints to which we have alluded showed themselves in severe resource limitations even before the middle 1960s. These, in turn, were expressed in "the crisis of planning" and the interruptions that came about in the sequence of Five Year Plans (though in emphasizing the importance of resource constraints we should not neglect serious weaknesses in the planning process itself and in the implementation of the plans). And they were shown up in increasing reliance on foreign aid – Hanson (1966) comments that, in the end, the Second Five Year Plan was bailed out by American Aid. A retreat from socialist objectives had in fact already begun before Nehru's death in 1964, and it was quietly completed during Shastri's brief tenure of office. As the growth of the economy slowed down, so the ability of the Congress at the Centre and in the States to satisfy the demands of different groups that it sought to accommodate, declined. Frankel notes that by the early 1960s:

> growing demands on static resources led to bitter internal disputes inside the Congress Party. Factional alliances frequently broke down . . . [and] social goals of reducing disparities and economic aims of rapid industrialisation were both being sacrificed while the achievement of political consensus began to be imperilled by economic failures and visible signs of growing corruption. The very fact that Congress promises of rapid economic growth and reduction of disparities failed to materialise was successfully used by all opposition groups, radical and conservative, regional or communal, to denigrate the policies for democratic socialist reform embodied in the Five Year Plans. (Frankel, 1978, 203)

These trends were shown up in the indications of declining support for the Congress in the 1962 General Elections and in the electoral gains of the Jan Sangh and Swatantra, and also of the Communist Party in West Bengal, Kerala and Andhra. The China War of late 1962 then dealt a serious blow to the socialists within the Congress because it inflicted so much damage to Nehru's personal prestige and led to the ousting of Krishna Menon and K. D. Malaviya who were Nehru's mainstays in the cabinet on social and economic planning.

The crisis of the Third Plan in the early 1960s, with stagnation in agriculture, shortages of power and essential raw materials, increasing prices, and – crucially – yawning budgetary deficits, led to increasing pressures for reductions in plan outlays and for greater reliance on the private sector. By-election reverses in 1963 further showed how the opposition could harness discontent and continued the undermining of Nehru's own prestige. A series of ideological and policy battles ensued as Nehru sought to reaffirm the commitment of the Congress to democratic transformation, and to reconstitute the party as an instrument of popular involvement (this partly through the so-called "Kamaraj Plan"). But with Nehru's death, the change in the means and objectives of public policy which was being actively pursued by Congress conservatives such as Morarji Desai even in the later part of Nehru's lifetime, was soon completed. Shastri lacked an independent power base and he did not pursue Nehru's attempts to reform the party organization; and, giving in to both domestic critics and to criticisms by international aid-giving agencies "of overly ambitious industrial plans in the public sector and inefficient methods of development both in agriculture and in industry that ignored incentives to private (domestic and foreign) investment" (Frankel, 1978, 246), he allowed a complete reorientation of the approach to the economy. The Planning Commission was effectively displaced as a policy-making body; it was at this time that "the new agricultural strategy" was adopted; at this time too, there was a shift from controls to incentives as major instruments of development planning, and an enlarged role for private domestic and foreign investment was encouraged. Shortly after Shastri's death, and before Mrs Gandhi had fully taken control of the reins of government, the power of international capital and the direct influence of the US government was shown in the 1966 devaluation, which was strongly opposed within India.

In sum, it appears that the very important shift in policy and direction which came about in the later 1960s was due to serious weaknesses in the attempt to bring about planned social and economic change in India. These, in turn, resulted from basic structural constraints within the political economy of the country and from the ambiguities of the gradualist approach of accommodative politics, but they provided the basis for opposition which was mobilized around a variety of issues and ideologies. The adjustments which resulted did not, however, tackle the fundamental constraints to which we have referred and it may be argued that they have actually exacerbated them.

After "the Crisis": Industrial Development after 1966

Since the mid-1960s the performance of the Indian economy as a whole has been unsatisfactory, as growth has been slower and subject to sharp fluctuations from year to year. Agriculture has made the main contribution to growth, but the overall growth rate of agriculture has not accelerated and the impact of "the new strategy" has been restricted to a few crops and regions. Meanwhile, compared with a 7 per cent growth rate in industrial production between 1951 and 1965, the period 1965–70 witnessed a mere 3.3 per cent growth rate and that between 1970 and 1982 4.3 per cent per annum – just above the average for twenty-three low income countries listed in the World Bank's *World Development Report* for 1984 (see Ahluwalia, 1985).

There was no real upswing after the return of Indira Gandhi to power in January 1980. The industrial growth rate in 1979–80 declined by 1.4 per cent, and though it increased again in 1980–1 – to 4 per cent – there were negative rates of growth still in some basic industries (see Kurien, 1982; and the *Economic and Political Weekly* (*EPW*) Editorial of 29 May 1982 which suggested that the industrial growth rate of 8.5 per cent recorded for calendar 1981 had already petered out and that "There is growing evidence that wide range of industries are coming up against a situation of insufficient demand" . . . *plus ca change!*). More recently, after the supposed "liberalisation" of the economy which followed Rajiv Gandhi's succession to the office of his murdered mother in 1984, it has been claimed that the Indian economy "is now on a new growth path" (*Economic Survey 1986–87*, Government of India). The *Economic Survey* points out that the average annual rate of growth in the 1980s has been 5 per cent, "much higher" than the historial trend of growth. Estimates of the rate of growth in the 1980s are influenced, however, by the fact that the base year, 1979–80, saw a decline in real GDP of 4.7 per cent. The growth rate in key production sectors –

agriculture, mining, manufacturing and electricity generation – taken together, has not reached 5 per cent in a single year, except in the recovery year of 1980–1:

> On the whole, then, agriculture and industrial production [has kept] ahead of population growth by the most modest of margins. By contrast, the contribution of banking and insurance to gross domestic product expanded by 11.5 per cent in 1985–6 and by 11.3 per cent and 9.1 per cent in the two preceding years. Even more impressive has been the performance of public administration and defence which witnessed growth rates of 12.5, 13.4 and 12.4 per cent, respectively, in the same three years. (*EPW*, Editorial, 28 February 1987)

What Shetty (1978) refers to as "structural retrogression" in this period is shown by the facts (amongst others) that services have grown faster than commodity-producing sectors; that the growth of basic and capital goods industries has been slower than the meagre average growth in industrial output; and that production of mass consumption goods has lagged behind that of élite-oriented consumer goods (again, Chandrasekhar's analysis of the textile industry provides an excellent illustration with its picture of a steadily developing dualistic structure – see below). At the same time there is evidence of a great deal of underutilised capacity, there has been virtually no growth in organized sector employment and the real wages of industrial labour have declined. None of these features of the economy has changed in the 1980s.

S. L. Shetty's is one of the more comprehensive reviews of economic development as a whole from the mid-1960s (Shetty, 1978). His basic argument is that "The primary cause of the structural retrogression of the Indian economy is the decline of planning" (1978, 185) – referring to the twin phenomena of the reduction of rigorous industrial controls which he shows to have given rise to distortions in production and investment patterns in the private sector, and of serious financial mismanagement which is shown both in the frittering away of a significant proportion of public sector outlays in non-development expenditure, and in the distorted system of resource mobilization. Shetty shows first that savings and investment efforts have been curtailed since the mid-1960s, especially in the public sector, and points out how this is reflected in much lower rates of capital formation. He comments:

> the major source of strength of the economy during the eleven year period from 1955–56 to 1966–67 was the average growth of over 12 per cent per annum in fixed assets formation. By the same logic, the

major factor responsible for the ills of the national economy during the subsequent decade is the failure to achieve a commensurate increase in fixed assets formation. The actual increase over this decade worked out to a little over 2.0 per cent per annum . . . (Shetty, 1978, 216)

He goes on to argue that there has been misallocation of resources in the public sector, as Central budget data show that development expenditure has made up a decreasing share of all expenditure. Contrary to a widely held view, this is not attributable to rising defence expenditure but to a disproportionate growth of non-developmental expenditure, including subsidies – especially those for export promotion, which have been shown to have been singularly inefficient, and for the public procurement and distribution of food-grains – and transfers to state governments for purposes other than development and capital formation:

> Such transfers from the Central Budget to third parties (i.e. both subsidies and transfers to state governments) had formed an average of about 24–5 per cent during the first three plan periods but they rose to 33.2 per cent for the Annual Plans period and further to 37.5 per cent for the Fourth Plan. Though their share came down to around 33–5 per cent thereafter, they nevertheless remained far higher than the 24–5 per cent of the first fifteen years". (Shetty, 1978, 222)

Transfers to state governments include allocations for famine relief assistance, of which the Sixth Finance Commission "implicitly brought out that the relief expenditure encouraged by the centre was largely determined by political patronage extended to a few states" (Shetty, 1978, 223). Further, certain states in particular have persistently resorted to overdrafts with the RBI – beginning principally in the drought years of 1965–6 and 1966–7 – which have had to be cleared in a routine way every year by a grant of *ad hoc* and special assistance from the central government. Meanwhile – and partly accounting for the persistent needs of some states for this special assistance – state agencies like the state Electricity Boards and Irrigation Departments have made huge losses for want of prompt recovery of dues, especially from rich farmers. Shetty builds up a picture of enormous wastage of financial resources, whilst showing at the same time that the system of resources mobilization has been distorted because of (i) the government's refusal to touch the richer segments of the farm community who have mainly benefited from the new agricultural strategy; (ii) reductions in the marginal tax rates on personal incomes and wealth in the non-farm sector; (iii) its continued reliance on indirect taxes which are regressive; and (iv) its resort to a disproportionate amount of deficit spending (then see Shetty's summary, 1978, p. 228).

At the same time the declining trend of investment in the public sector has had important repercussions on the level of capital formation in the private sector, where – in the words of one Economic Survey – "investment activity . . . has been in recent years generally subdued". The cut-backs in public sector investment in the 1960s had immediate effects on a range of basic and capital goods industries, many of which have continued to experience demand constraints, so that they have shown scant increases in output and high levels of underutilization of capacity. But the preponderant part of the investable funds deployed by the private manufacturing sector throughout the period since the mid-1960s has been provided by public financial institutions (mainly as loans). Promoters' contributions have been allowed to be kept at unusually low levels. Shetty believes that the large amounts granted have been out of all proportion with their impact on industrial investment and output growth in real terms, and especially on employment. He suggests that the easy availability of investable funds at relatively low cost, and the low personal stakes of promoters, has induced higher capital intensity as well as siphoning-off of funds and general lack of cost consciousness. Here Shetty's argument and that of Ahluwalia are comparable. Ahluwalia (1985), however, emphasizes that the setting up of a high cost industrial structure was the result of an environment which discouraged competition.

Alongside these developments there has been a general relaxation of industrial controls (the passing of the Monopolies and Restrictive Trade Practices Act in 1969 is considered to have been largely a matter of "show" for the provisions of the Act were almost immediately undermined: for more recent comment on industrial controls see *EPW* editorials of 8 May 1982 and 30 May 1987). The results have included the build-up of underutilized capacity in some industries while in some others there are capacity constraints; and there has been a shift of investment in favour of commodities which supply the luxury end of the market. (More so after the "liberalizing" budget of 1985). There has been, in short, an increasing tendency towards industrial dualism, such as Chandrasekhar described in the case of the textile industry: in which a small number of firms have been able to modernize their plants and to cater for the higher-income market, which has required high levels of investment, some foreign collaboration, and sophisticated marketing. "These firms constitute an oligopolistic group in the market for sophisticated fabrics, while the majority of firms compete with each other and with the decentralised sector in the production of a large number of less sophisticated and cheaper varieties of fabrics" (Chandrasekhar, 1978). The former group has generally shown high levels of profitability, while the latter has included large numbers of "sick" units. Chandrasekhar shows that there exists a "structural break" in the industry. Within this pattern of industrial development – not only in the textile industry – foreign companies have tended to increase their share of sales and to obtain relatively higher levels of profit, while the top twenty business groups have increased their assets at a much faster rate than the private corporate sector as a whole and have generally maintained higher rates of profit.

Shetty's analysis of public policy and its impact shows that the same basic constraints that we found to be crucial in the period up to the mid-1960s – the inability of the state to raise sufficient resources domestically through direct taxation of property incomes; the failure of agrarian reform; and serious market constraints which have been exacerbated still further by regressive taxation and associated with top-heavy industrialization – have persisted in the later period and have even been intensified by the relaxation of attempts to control and to plan the economy. The principal beneficiaries of this relaxation appear to have been the top business groups and the rich farmers who have benefited from the "new strategy" whilst paying very little indeed to the state through taxation.

Shetty's explanation for the "structural retrogression" that he observes is that it has come about because of "the decline of planning", but this is an intermediate level of explanation of course, and it leads us to ask the further question of *why* planning should have declined. We ourselves suggested earlier that the decline of planning came about in the 1960s precisely because of resource constraints and failures in the implementation of planning which resulted, amongst other factors, from the power of the rural rich to resist taxation and to turn measures of agrarian reform to their own advantage, and from the power, especially of big business, similarly to "turn" industrial controls and to resist taxation. Fundamentally, the failure of planning came about because of the dependence of the Congress government, for its control of the state, upon the classes which would have had to have sacrificed most for planning to have been successful. The failures of planning became self-reinforcing because, as we saw, as plan targets were not fulfilled discontents increased and were given political expression in the rise of opposition parties.

Comparable arguments have been advanced by Mitra (1977), by Patnaik (1972, 1979) and Patnaik and Rao (1977), and by Bagchi (1975) (see also Rubin, 1985, on the extent of consensus over explanations for industrial stagnation). Mitra's view is that the decline in the rate of industrial growth since 1965–6 is causally related to a continuous movement of the terms of trade against industry and in favour of agriculture. The simplest form of the argument is that this has squeezed profit margins in industry (where real wages have fallen only marginally), and that the profits squeeze has resulted in lower investment in the private sector (where investment is governed by profitability considerations). Further, since surplus-producing agriculturalists are taxed relatively lightly, a shift in income distribution in their favour adversely affects public revenue and hence public investment. Patnaik (1979) shows that the evidence on company profits means that "the simple *modus operandi* of the terms of trade explanation does not hold much water", but he goes on to save the argument as a whole. Bagchi's explanation emphasizes that a higher level of growth was not attained because: "First, absence of suitable innovations in industry and of suitable organisational changes and change in agrarian relations (which) kept the growth of productivity low – and have borne down heavily on the profitability of new investment and its stability . . . Secondly, new incomes became concentrated among upper-income groups and led to stagnation in the sales of traditional consumer goods. Thirdly, the State – because of its dependence on the richer sections of the population who were unwilling even to make the adjustment necessary for creating an efficient fiscal apparatus – was unable to sustain the programme of increasing public development expenditure" (Bagchi, 1975, 159).

State Power and the Determinants of Industrial Development

Mitra and Patnaik argue explicitly that the trends which they observe in the economy as a whole have come about as a result of the basis of state power on a coalition between the bourgeoisie and large landowners – or, in Mitra's words, "a duopolistic arrangement between the rural oligarchy and the industrial bourgeoisie". This conclusion is based partly on observation of the determinants and the effects of policy referred to above, but also on ideas about the political process. Mitra suggests that the rural rich play a crucial role in state power because they control the majority of votes. They are especially strong in state legislatures, while the big bourgeoisie enjoys greater power and influence at the centre. This formulation, expressed by other writers more graphically as "the strangulating embrace" of rural oligarchy and industrial bourgeoisie (Djurfeldt and Lindberg's evocative phrase, 1975), is close to that of the Communist Party of India (Marxist) (CPI(M)), with which both Mitra and Patnaik are associated. The CPI(M) line is that "The present Indian state is the organ of the class rule of the bourgeoisie and the landlord, led by the big bourgeoisie who are increasingly collaborating with foreign finance capital in pursuit of the capitalist path of development". This differs really only in emphasis from the CPI formulation.

Mitra's argument is too heavily dependent upon his discussion of trends in the terms of trade, for Tyagi's analysis (1979) of the way in which the price series used by Mitra (and others) have been computed is a convincing argument to the effect that very little indeed can be concluded with confidence from these data. Nonetheless, even if we accept Tyagi's own conclusion that the available data suggest that in the recent period the terms of trade have remained more or less constant, the data and the argument offered by Shetty – who does not even refer to the terms of trade issue – still provide strong support for the conception of state power in Mitra's and Patnaik's analyses. Certainly there seems to be little room for dispute (*pace* Lipton) that the rural rich – the rich peasant/landowners – have succeeded in resisting taxation by the state and that they have quite effectively mulcted public resources through their non-payment of electricity and irrigation dues and through their exploitation of institutional finance. We believe that this argument holds even though there remain questions concerning the profitability of agriculture in some regions of the country (such as West Bengal) where the relationship between product prices and the prices of essential inputs – principally fertilizers – appears to be unfavourable to investment in production. At the same time Shetty's data on private-sector industry suggest that, in spite of the general sluggishness of the industrial economy since about 1966, the big business houses have done relatively well. In general, the conception of state power presented by Mitra and Patnaik appears to be strongly substantiable.

Thus far we have presented what is almost the conventional wisdom of the mainstream left in India, though this interpretation seems to lurk in Frankel's pages too, and might even be deduced from Hanson's classic study of the planning period. Frankel's work (1978) has the merit, however, of describing political trends and developments in detail. Her theme is that the disjuncture between the socialist rhetoric of the first fifteen years of independence and the practicalities of the mode of accommodative politics (like Harry Blair, 1980, she suggests that the pluralist model of the Congress system of one party dominance was quite a good portrayal of the reality of the period) came to create a situation in the later 1960s in which, though a liberal capitalist orientation in public policy had taken the ascendancy in central government, there was no longer any possibility of a political consensus around such an orientation. Thereafter, she portrays the government of Mrs Gandhi as having been trapped by conflicting forces, including pulls to right and left around which were mobilized various communalist and regionalist sentiments. An important aspect of the political situation which is alluded to in Shetty's economic analysis is the considerable increase in tensions between the centre and the states in the later 1960s and the 1970s, which probably lies behind the drain of resources – to some states more than to others – mainly for non-development purposes, which Shetty describes. The states – or some of the states – have become much more powerful in relation to the centre than before, in the days of Congress dominance, *because of* (rather than "in spite of") Indira Gandhi's attempt to centralize power by dismantling the party machines at State level. Finally, Frankel portrays an administration which, to maintain political support, has always had to make gestures towards a "socialist" programme, but which has lacked the organizational means to implement them, because of depending – still – on social groups which are fundamentally opposed to "socialist" reform. The results have been a series of half-baked politics which in general have contributed to the stagnation of the economy and have created inertia in government. Political commentators found this inertia increasingly pronounced in Indira Gandhi's administration between 1980 and 1984 which was often preoccupied with the maintenance of power over state governments (e.g. the affairs of Andhra, Maharashtra, Kerala and Haryana in that period). And there is little doubt of the increasing extent of graft and corruption (for a detailed study of which, in relation to the irrigation bureaucracy, see Wade, 1982).

Theories about India's Political Economy, and the Explanation of Recent Developments

The principal alternative to the view of Indian political economy presented here is found in the work described as "the new political economy", within the neoclassical paradigm, which "has been based on empirical studies of government intervention in trade and industry and the varied effects that such policy actions in India have had" (Toye, 1988). Empirical studies by Bhagwati and his collaborators sought to show how exchange controls leading to the overvaluation of the rupee, and bureaucratically discretionary methods of restricting imports and sanctioning investments in industry, led to economic distortions and inefficiency. The "origin of the new political economy was in the implications that were drawn out of their economic analysis of the consequences of bureaucratic controls" (Toye, 1988). Essentially what is argued is that India is a "rent-seeking society" – or, more accurately, that India is a society with a rent-seeking government:

> the misguided adoption of certain economic policies, especially import quotas, itself creates a society with certain economic irrationalities such as permanently under-utilised industrial capacity, a corrupt administration and a political structure dominated by interests fed financially by windfall gains (from bureaucratic rents, based on the system of controls). This latter feature is important because, almost by definition, it rules out the possibility of achieving the reforms which the neo-classicals are seeking, at any rate in a democratic polity like India. (Toye, 1988)

Recognizing the insights in this argument, whilst also being aware of its limitations in terms of the specification of political dynamics, Bardhan (1984) has brought this explanation together with the conception of the Indian state as "a duopolistic arrangement between the rural oligarchy and the industrial bourgeoisie" (Mitra's formulation; Mitra, 1977) which informs the account of India's political economy offered above. Bardhan's argument is that the trends of Indian economic development can be explained as the outcomes of conflicts and compromises between three dominant propertied classes: the industrial capitalist class, the class of "rich farmers" and a class of public sector professionals. An important expression of conflict between the urban industrial and professional classes, and the dominant rurals, is observed in the struggles over farm prices and input costs which have become a recurrent feature of Indian politics (most recently in Gujarat and UP; see *EPW* 28 March 1987). There is a complex net of transfers and payments between "sectors" which no one has adequately sorted out quantitatively. But what does seem to stand out is that compromises are being made all the time between the interests of different groups of rural people and those of the industrial bourgeoisie and the working class; and that while the government at the centre may favour industrial interests, state governments have used their resources to

maintain political support, which has often meant making concessions to rural interests at the expense of those of industrialists (such,
perhaps, as is implied in Devi Lal's pledge to cancel outstanding
farm loans in the state elections in Haryana in June 1987). At
the same time, for Bardhan, public-sector professionals constitute
another distinct set of proprietorial interests – in conflict over
bureaucratic rent creation and distribution with industrial capitalists
and to a lesser extent with farmers. So he presents:

> a picture of the Indian government as managing class conflicts by
> expanding subsidies on food, agricultural inputs, and public-sector
> produced inputs with little regard for their impact on raising pro-
> ductivity. This expansion is seen as driven by the rising stakes in
> electoral competitions and the rise of gangs led by a large number of
> MLAs and MPs, political middlemen who over the years have
> specialised in the profession of brokerage services . . . (Toye's sum-
> mary, 1988)

The actual trends in public finance in India have seen the
expansion of public expenditure associated with increased reliance
on deficit financing, on indirect taxation, and latterly on commercial
borrowing, and they have involved a divorce between development
goals and actual resource allocation, increased decentralization of
public expenditure decisions and a preference for consumption
over investment spending. These trends are the outcome of the
government's quest for legitimacy and the compromises that have
been made between conflicting interests of the three dominant
properties classes. The Indian political system (the Congress "dominant party system") worked effectively to accommodate different
interests up to the 1970s. The event of the Emergency between 1975
and 1977 shows the breakdown of that system (see Blair, 1980), as
a result of the kind of fiscal crisis depicted by Shetty and the inability
of the system to supply sufficient resources to meet divergent
demands, as well as Indira Gandhi's attempt to centralize power
by destroying the local organization of the Congress. The period of
Janata rule saw first, relief of the pressures of managing legitimacy,
and then their renewal in a context in which "bullock capitalists"
(rich peasants/landowners) were more strongly represented at the
centre than before. They were relieved again by Indira Gandhi's
triumphant return to power in January 1980, and yet again by the
support generated by Rajiv after her assassination in 1984. But the
dominant trends of the 1980s have seen the government at the centre
increasingly embattled in the face of violent separatist and regionalist

movements, especially in Punjab, Assam and elsewhere in the north-east, and by its "isolation" as never before, as the non-Hindi speaking states have come under the control of non-Congress governments. There is, in Bardhan's terms, a crisis of political legitimation which has called forth increased expenditure on defence and internal security, so exacerbating yet further India's basic fiscal problems.

In the light of this view of India's political economy the economic liberalization proposed in the 1985 Budget can be seen as an attempt by the Central government in a phase in which it was relatively strong in relation to society – given the strength of electoral support for Rajiv – "to reshape the relation of the Indian state to economic interests" and "to reassert the autonomy of high politics" (Rubin, 1985). That Budget reduced income, corporate and wealth taxes, cut import duties on capital goods, provided tax breaks to exporters and largely eliminated licensing restrictions on investments in twenty-five industries. It really did reflect, therefore, "an attempt to change at least some of the conditions that the theoretical debate has pointed to as causes of slow industrialisation" (Rubin, 1985, 948) – inefficiencies resulting from the industrial policy regime, and the problems of inadequate demand. Prabhat Patnaik, from the left, concurs to an extent with this view when he argues that the declaration of a "new economic policy" was more the result of a strong build-up of internal pressures than a response to external forces – these pressures being the outcome of the crisis that had developed in the earlier regime "consisting in the fact that the ability of the regime to generate substantial industrial expansion got progressively impaired over time" (Patnaik, 1986, 1015). Patnaik's argument is that industrial stagnation has substantially been the result of the stagnation in public investment (cf. Toye, 1981, cited above) and that this, in turn, has been the result of the "fiscal crisis" depicted earlier. Internal pressures for liberalization have come, he thinks, from big business because it has found growth of investment opportunities constricted relative to the growth of its command over capital. It has to do deals with metropolitan capital in order to enter the international arena in any significant way. But metropolitan capitalists insist on the opening up of domestic markets. It is for this reason, as well as because of interests in expanding into hitherto closed domestic channels for investment, that big business has given cautious and qualified support to the liberalization urged by the World Bank from the early 1980s.

But though there were, and remain, powerful groups with interests in effective liberalization, it has become clear that others are threatened, by the possible removal of the system of controls from which they have benefited because of being able to manipulate it, by direct competition from imports, or by indirect competition mediated by shifts in demand away from old goods to new ones. And events have shown that the regime is unable to resist the political pressures which have created and perpetuated India's basic fiscal problems. So there has been fudge, and the underlying tendencies – towards increasing public expenditure, increasing imbalance in taxation, and increasing resort to commercial borrowing – have been intensified in practice. The move to "liberalize" the economy was perhaps even half-hearted in intention. Rubin argued of the Indira period that:

> in the area of industrial policy the autonomy of the state in Bardhan's sense (the ability of the class of state officials to define a distinct set of interests), together with the power of other dominant classes, limits the autonomy of the state in the Marxist sense. Private deals negotiated among politicians, bureaucrats and industrialists . . . render difficult the pursuit of policy in the interest of "capital as a whole" or, for India, the dominant coalition as a whole . . . (Rubin, 1985, 947.)

In this context the attempt under Rajiv "to reassert the autonomy of high politics" was very short-lived, as Rubin surmised it might be. Both the "new economic policy" promised in 1985 and the rapid retreat from it in practice, should be seen as outcomes of the compromised nature of class power and the weakness of the state as an organization. India does not present an instance of "the developmental state in retreat" in the 1980s. It remains, as it has been, a weak but plastic state, though also one with a sufficiently developed industrial base of its own in capital and intermediate goods to be able to resist external pressures in favour of liberalization. It seems that here a real attempt to liberalize the economy probably would require the establishment of a much more authoritarian regime, able to ride over the powerful interests represented in the dominant coalition.

Note

1. I am grateful to Hamza Alavi for comments on the earlier version of this chapter.

Business and Politics in India[1]

Stanley Kochanek

Despite the socialist rhetoric of Indian politics and heavy investment in the public sector, the private sector – which includes agriculture, trade, small-scale industry and handicrafts, as well as modern, large-scale industry – still holds a predominant position in the Indian economy. Prior to the first Five Year Plan, the private sector generated 92 per cent of India's gross national product. It continued to generate over 90 per cent during the 1950s and slightly over 85 per cent in the 1960s. By contrast, the private sector in Japan provides less than 80 per cent of the gross national product and even in the USA it accounts for under 75 per cent.

The public sector in India is concentrated primarily in the capital goods sector of the economy. Public sector units account for one-seventh of the total output of capital goods and have played a significant role in helping to restructure the character of Indian industrial production. In the 1950s, two-thirds of Indian production was confined to consumer goods, and capital goods and intermediate goods accounted for only one-sixth each. By the 1960s, however, the proportion of the three sectors was about equal. In some subsectors of the economy, the public sector dominates completely. For example, Hindustan Machine Tools Ltd accounted for half the output of machine tools in India; Hindustan Steel Ltd produced 60 per cent of all finished steel; and Heavy Engineering Corporation (Ranchi) and Heavy Electricals (India) Ltd (Bhopal) were the sole producers of some types of heavy machinery. At the same time, however, although the public sector dominates the commanding heights of the economy, the total gross sales of public sector manufacturing, excluding Indian Oil Corporation, amounts to little more than 10 per cent of the industrial sector.[2]

Private sector business in India is therefore still important. It is not only responsible for the bulk of the total output in the industrial sector but also plays a dominant role in internal trade and commerce. The elements which make up the private sector, however, are extremely heterogeneous and consist of traders, small-scale manufacturers, and large-scale indigenous and foreign manufacturers organized into conglomerates called business houses and modern corporate units. It is this very size and diversity of the business community that has made it so difficult to mobilize into organized cohesive groups and which has inhibited the development of a united business class.

In terms of numbers and diversity, the largest sector of the business community consists of 6.7 million persons employed in wholesale and retail trade. Assuming an average family of five, the total strength of the trading community in 1961 would be over 33 million out of a population of 437 million. Moreover, transport, communications, and commerce contributed 14.9 per cent to the national product of India in 1967–8.[3]

The middle-class trader in India feels threatened and insecure. He feels he is being systematically destroyed by the actions of government and big business. Government has been slowly eroding traditional trading functions by channelling more and more trade through the government-owned State Trading Corporation. At the same time, private business has steadily encroached on the traditional livelihood of traders by opening retail outlets and channelling all their products through their own marketing organizations. Feeling insecure and threatened, large sectors of the trading community have become closely identified with the revivalist politics of parties like the *Jana Sangh*.

Despite their numbers, the vast majority of small businessmen and traders in India remain an unorganized reflection of the fragmentation of the larger society, each basing his behaviour on family, caste, and community norms rather than on any large appreciation of class identification or interest. Because most small businessmen are still not conscious of the potential benefits of collective action, they have proved difficult to organize; their demands on the political system tend to be sporadic and anomic in origin and uncertain in impact.[4] It has, thus, generally been the representatives of the unorganized or intermittently organized traders and small business sector who have resorted to demonstrations, strikes, and violence. Such groups as have agitated for specific demands from time to time have been bus-fleet owners, restaurant owners, cycle-shop owners, grain traders, vegetable sellers, and sweets sellers. It is also this vast army of traders, shopkeepers, and middlemen belonging to the noncorporate, largely unorganized sector of Indian business that has generated the greatest amount of public resentment because of highly questionable practices, including food adulteration, creation of artificial shortages, price gouging, black marketeering, and petty bribing. Such offences, more visible than abstruse white-collar crimes, go far toward creating anti-business sentiments, even among those with no particular commitment to the socialist pattern or to another more radical pattern of society.

Although smaller in size than the group of small businessmen and traders, manufacturing contributed 13 per cent to the national product of India in 1967–8.[5] Within the manufacturing sector, large-scale industry contributed 8 per cent to the national product, and the small-scale sector contributed 5 per cent.[6] The small-scale sector in India has grown very rapidly in recent years, as a result of strong encouragement from government. As late as 1961, there were only 36,000 small-scale industrial units registered with the various directors of industries in the states, but by 31 March 1971 there were 281,781 units registered.[7] It is estimated that small-scale industrial units covered under the programmes of the Small Industries Development Organization had a fixed investment in 1970 of Rs 4750m and an output of Rs 40,500m, and that they employed 3.3 million workers. Half the manufacturing product and 92 per cent of all registered factories in India – that is, one-half the value added in the industrial sector – was produced by the small-scale sector.

The small-scale sector is primarily concentrated in the consumer goods sector of the economy and accounts for 77 per cent of the value added in that sector. The small-scale sector produces such things as buckets, trunks, nails, hand tools, plastic goods, electric fans, sewing machines, bicycle parts, pharmaceuticals, and a wide variety of other consumer products. The predominant field, however, was textiles, and in 1967 the small-scale sector produced 43.7 per cent of all cloth manufactured in India as opposed to only 56.3 per cent for the large-scale, organized mill sector. The government of India has specifically reserved 128 items of manufacture for the small-scale sector. At present, thirty-three items are exclusively produced by the small-scale sector, and the bulk of production of another fifty-four items is contributed by the small-scale sector.

The small-scale industries sector of the Indian economy faces a host of problems which are quite different from those of the large-scale sector. Although small-scale industries have proved difficult to organize and somewhat ambivalent toward joining business associations, they are now represented through their own apex organization: the Federation of Associations of Small Industries of India (FASII). The federation maintains close liaison with a whole host of government bodies especially created to assist in the development and finance of small-scale industry.

The organized large-scale sector of Indian industry has grown proportionately even faster than the small-scale sector, as a result of government planning, tariff protection, national development policies, and its own initiative. Unlike the small-scale sector, which is scattered throughout the country, big business is highly concentrated. It is centred in the older industrial regions of India, is drawn from a small group of traditional trading castes, and is responsible for a substantial share of the total industrial production. The gross output of organized industry in 1968–9 was Rs 54,210m based on Rs 45,000m gross investment.

Despite the government's commitment to reduce disparities in levels of development between various regions, the fastest growing areas tended to be the old port cities of Madras, Calcutta, and Bombay. From 1953 to 1961, 40 per cent of all industrial licenses were granted for units in these areas. Of the three areas, the Greater Bombay area grew the fastest and was to have a significant impact on the post-independence development of business associations in India.[8]

During the decade of growth, many of the old business houses were able to expand, diversify, and develop into major forces in the Indian economy. Because of its historical development, Indian capital had been highly concentrated, even at the time of independence. In 1951–2, the total share capital of all non-government-owned companies was estimated at Rs 13,960 million. "In that year the four largest business groups – Tatas (a Parsee firm), Birlas and Dalmia-Jain (Marwari groups), and Martin Burn (a Bengali–English group) – had full control by sole ownership or majority stock holding of approximately 15 per cent of the total share capital of both non-government public and private limited companies." If their minority holdings were added, their proportionate share of the total was 19 per cent. The top thirteen business houses had complete or partial control of 28 per cent of the total share capital.

The effect of a decade of rapid growth was to increase the absolute number of large business houses and to change their relative ranking. A government study in 1965 revealed that the modern industrial sector of business in India was dominated by seventy-five British and Indian conglomerates or business houses which controlled almost half of the non-governmental, non-banking assets of the country. The top thirty-seven business houses were predominantly drawn from the traditional trading communities. Despite their later start, the Marwari houses ranked first, with Rs 7.5 billion in assets, followed by the Parsis with 4.7 billion, and the Gujaratis with 3.8 billion.

Foreign controlled assets in India represented a relatively small but important part of the total. In 1961, foreign capital controlled more than two-fifths of the total assets in the organized large-scale private sector.[9] The bulk of this investment was new investment which had flowed in after independence. Foreign investment in 1961 was heavily concentrated in a small number of industries. Some of these had been the long-standing original preserve of foreign capital, and others had grown up since independence. Three areas – tea, petroleum, and manufacturing – together accounted for three-quarters of the total foreign investment in India. Half of the investment in manufacturing was concentrated in a relatively small group of industries – chemicals and drugs, cigarettes and tobacco, jute textiles, and light electrical goods. Generally speaking, older forms of investment, like tea and jute manufacturing, grew slowly or declined in relative importance after independence, because most fresh foreign capital was directed into petroleum and into newer, technologically complex and patented manufacturing industries.

Originally foreign capital in India meant British capital. At the time of independence, three-quarters of foreign investment in India was British. Although British capital continues to play an active role in India, its power and influence have been diluted. The substantial influx of foreign capital in the past twenty years has resulted in a greater diversity of the national origins of capital. Indian affiliates have been developed by American, German, French, Swiss, Japanese, and Italian corporations. These affiliates were usually established in collaboration with the larger Indian business firms, thereby augmenting the trend toward closer liaison between foreign and indigenous capital.[10] Thus, despite the original hostility of the government of India and the ambivalence of foreign investors, foreign investment in India has increased in size, diversity, sophistication, and national origins.

Unlike the activities of the traders and small-scale businessmen, the activities of the organized corporate sector of the business community are neither sporadic nor anomic. Demands are articulated through two types of permanent structures. The first is the business house itself, functioning through its "industrial embassy" in Delhi. The embassy is capable of continuous and calculated self-representation based on family and kinship structures. It also employs the highly personal system of liaison and lobbying developed after independence as an attempt to influence the political élite largely for individual benefit, although some collective benefits might incidentally accrue. The second type of representational structure includes a series of specialized structures for interest articulation: chambers of commerce, trade and industry associations, employers' associations, and peak associations. Together these associational groups constitute the oldest, most bureaucratized and politically autonomous structures for interest articulation in India. They function through a highly regularized and formalized pattern of access and are designed primarily to achieve collective rather than individual benefit. And – because of their growing organizational capacity – they have become one of the few kinds of groups in the society capable of sustained rather than intermittent action. Because the leadership of the specialized business organizations is provided by the leadership of the top seventy-five houses, the two structures are linked and capable of more or less coordinated action.

The advent of planning and the introduction of a pervasive system of government controls made business heavily dependent on government initiatives. Business houses immediately organized themselves for the purpose of securing maximum benefit from the system of licensing and controls under which they were expected to function. In the early years of planning, individual businessmen had been principally concerned with the expansion and growth of their own business empires and made limited use of associations. Individual growth and protection of individual interests were of such primary importance that each business leader used the influence acquired through individual contributions to Congress party leaders, patronage, and hospitality to obtain benefits for his own house.

As business grew it became more complex, and with complexity came the need to consider the organizational dimension of business. Indian business had moved relatively quickly from the traditional manufacture of textiles to more complex types of industry requiring greater organizational skills and expertise. In addition, as enterprises began to grow larger and more complex, traditional family patterns of control and organization no longer sufficed. The Sarabhai organization, for example, was made up in its early years of a series of informal personal relationships between the managing agents and other managers within the organization. This series of relationships was complicated by close family ties between the managing agents and other members of the company. Although no organization chart with formal lines of communication existed, there was a recognized and accepted order of seniority among managers and direct contact between managing agents and managers at all levels. "The pattern was not dissimilar to that of the management of family business in other countries than India, but in India, more than in the West, it was supported by the traditional joint family system . . ." The eldest male was the head of the firm. All other members looked to the head of the family for decisions and accepted his authority, whereas "authority and responsibility among the other members of the family are diffused, informal, and personal". In hiring, also, the needs of the family prevailed. The tendency was to find jobs for people, not people for jobs.

As Indian business grew, it became more efficiently organized; it began to emphasize professional and managerial skills in recruitment; and the slow process of dissociation of management and ownership was begun. The older generation of industrial giants began to die out and a new generation of owner-managers began to emerge, not just as sons and heirs of the old boss but as competent managers in their own right. More self-confident, more highly educated, politically and socially more aware than their elders, the members of the younger generation were all also more alert to the importance of organization.

Interest in organization extended beyond concern with the internal organization of the individual business firm to the value of links to others in the same industry and the business community at large. Businessmen were faced by a common set of problems emerging from business interactions with government. And so they became more concerned with the substance of government policy which impinged upon business activity collectively, rather than being preoccupied solely with gaining individual distributive benefits for their firms. In addition, they became concerned with the problem of building a better image for business. Their conviction of the worth of the business contribution for the society left them no longer content with merely affecting the detailed implementation of public policy. Businessmen, they felt, must be concerned with influencing the actual formation of public policy in the open and direct manner employed by any legitimate interest group.

In many ways, the character of business associations in India began to change under the impact of changes in the Indian political system after independence. The emergence of Congress party dominance, the centralization of decision-making in the hands of the cabinet and bureaucracy, and the development of a government policy emphasizing planning, rapid industrialization, a mixed economy, protectionism, regulation, and control and restrictions in regional disparities – these factors forced business to develop institutional patterns of access and professional staffs to handle the complexity and all-embracing nature of government action. Big business in India felt compelled to pour large amounts of resources into business associations so that they could work at both the personal and institutional level. Individual problems could be taken up personally with ministers and the higher echelons of the bureaucracy. But business still needed a way to formulate collective views and reactions to government policy as a means of setting limits on Nehru's socialism, of securing greater government protection and support, and of handling more generalized problems of policy or administrative action.

Small and medium-sized businesses also became more organizationally conscious. Big business had always enjoyed relatively easy access to government on an individual basis, but small and medium business had to approach government through organizational channels or not at all. Government in fact encouraged them in their efforts, for it was becoming clear that unless business approached government jointly through organized channels, the channels of access would become flooded by a multitude of individual petitions. As a result of this complex of recent developments, business associations in India have grown phenomenally in size, variety, resources, organization, and even in unity as business has become more organizationally conscious.

Notes

1. First published as chapter 5 of Kochanek (1974).
2. By the late 1970s the public sector accounted for about 14.4 per cent of total GDP originating in manufacturing (Balasubramanyam, 1984, 115).
3. In 1979–80 they contributed 19.3 per cent of national product.
4. Whilst substantially confirming this account of the political action of small businessmen and traders, B. Harriss also shows how powerful they can be because of being able to manipulate state interventions (Harriss, 1984).
5. In 1979–80 they contributed 16.2 per cent of national product.
6. In the late 1970s small scale industry contributed between 16 and 21 per cent of total manufacturing output (Balasubramanyam, 1984, 118).
7. The number had grown to 1,275,000 by 1984–5. Their output was worth Rs 505,200 million and they employed 9 million workers.
8. More recently, in the 1970s and 1980s there has been more industrial growth in other cities, such as around Delhi, Hyderabad and Bangalore.
9. In 1973 foreign capital controlled only 22 per cent of the total value of assets of joint stock companies in the private sector (Balasubramanyam, 1984, 147).
10. Latterly joint ventures, collaborative agreements of the kind described have become even more important, in the wake of the attempted

"economic liberalization" of 1985 (on which see J. Harriss, in the previous chapter).

Glossary

1 crore = 10,000,000.

Bangladesh and the World Economic System: the Crisis of External Dependence[1]

Rehman Sobhan

Introduction: The Nature of Dependence

On the face of it Bangladesh would appear to represent a relatively low level of interaction with the world economic system. If this process of integration is measured in terms of the contribution of external trade to GDP or to the control of foreign investment over the domestic economy, Bangladesh comes fairly low down in any league table of external penetration into various developing economies. It is the central theme of this paper, however, that within the prevailing structural constraints of Bangladesh society, the process of development has itself contributed to the growth of external linkages, dependency and domination of the domestic polity. These external linkages have in turn become critical to the emergence and development of an indigenous bourgeoisie, whose entire fortunes are intimately tied up with access to external resources in the name of development.

This particular pattern of dependent development has contributed to the increase in poverty, along with concentrations in the ownership of wealth and inequality in the distribution of income without leading to a significant expansion of the reproductive forces within the economy. This growing immiserization of the masses in juxtaposition to the parasitic and unproductive character of the dependent bourgeoisie has accentuated the need for external resource flows both to sustain subsistence consumption and to feed the growing appetites of the aspirant bourgeoisie. The incapacity of the system to involve the masses in the development process and their consequent marginalization from the productive process is likely to threaten the stability of the domestic social order and, by extension, will affect Bangladesh's linkages with the world economic system.

The Crisis of the Old Order Bangladesh's dependence on aid is not a new phenomenon and, in fact, has progressively increased over the years. Its dependence is tied into the compulsions of demography, geography, history and politics. Bangladesh inherited a situation

100

where the size of its domestic population and its rate of increase was juxtaposed against acute scarcity of cultivable land and natural resources.

This unfavourable environmental situation could have been compensated by a systematic attempt to optimize available resource use. More productive use of available external assistance could have enabled Bangladesh to move to a higher threshold of productive activity from which it could cope with the mounting pressure of population. At a time when other countries were moving towards independence, however, Bangladesh's emergence in 1947 as part of the independent nation state of Pakistan was characterized by a form of internal colonialism practised by the Pakistani-based ruling élite (Nations, 1975). Monopoly of state power to the exclusion of Bangladesh was used initially to divert Bangladesh's export surplus to finance the industrialization of West Pakistan. By the 1960s, when this surplus had been exhausted, the rising volume of aid designed to cover Pakistan's external resource deficit was channelled towards financing West Pakistan's development. As a consequence of this incapacity to utilize Bangladesh's own resources and subsequently to derive an equitable share of external aid, Bangladesh faced economic stagnation which helped to accentuate its inherited environmental and structural problems which had constrained its development capacities.

At liberation in December 1971, Bangladesh inherited an economy where external dependency on food had increased, its external resource gap had widened, the number and proportion of landless peasants had increased. Along with the incidence of rural poverty, its exports were stagnating and indeed facing a decline in the world market, and its rate of domestic resource generation was contracting. Its limited capacity for self-reliant growth had thus been substantially eroded. The traumatic legacy of the liberation war with its massive visitation of death, dislocation of millions of people, damage to the infrastructure of the economy and, last but not least, the major social dislocations caused by the withdrawal of the Pakistani bourgeoisie, posed a crisis of survival for the infant nation state.

This crisis, inherited as a legacy of nature, demography, history and politics, could have been confronted by a major effort in social engineering to mobilize the collective energy of the masses to share austerity and to rebuild the war-shattered economy on a drastically restructured social base. But the political leadership of the day, constrained by its political support base, was hesitant to embark on such heroic feats of social reconstruction for fear of aggravating the dislocations inherited from the war (Sobhan and Ahmad, 1980).

The logical consequence of this incapacity to use the dynamic of the liberation war to transform the social order was to condemn Bangladesh to a pattern of dependent development. Foreign aid became the initial source for rehabilitating the 10 million refugees displaced by the war and for reconstructing the war-damaged infrastructure of the economy. This external dependence became cumulative as the food gap, the foreign exchange gap, the savings gap, and the revenue gap, all came to be covered by foreign aid. The incapacity to generate domestic resources owed in part to narrow margins of surplus left within the domestic economy, but it also reflected the political constraints in extracting resources from those segments of the élite groups which monopolized these resources. To the extent that parts of the aid channelled into the economy were used materially to benefit these same classes and enhance their power within the polity, the scope for generating internal resources deteriorated rather than increased over the years.

The Institutionalization of External Dependence The violent change of regime in 1975 was designed to legitimize the power of those classes which sought to institutionalize their monopoly over domestic and external resources (Lifschultz, 1979). The contradictions which characterized the post-liberation regime were subsumed in the united pursuit of bourgeois accumulation and integration of the economy into the world economic system. State power was directed towards channelling a rising pool of external resources towards building-up an indigenous capitalist and rural bourgeoisie. Conversely, there were few compulsions to improve the utilization of installed capacity and to generate domestic revenues from increased output generated by increased availability of external assistance.

The consequence of this growing tendency towards a dependent development strategy was the proliferation of aid-dependent projects and of people seeking to enhance their fortunes from them. Starting from grandiose capital-investment projects at the top, to small infrastructure development projects at the village level, these came to be tied to the specific interests of particular élite groups and their need to appropriate more resources to enhance their power base. As a consequence, it was rare for any autonomous development initiative to emerge which was not underwritten by state patronage from above and by external resources mediated through the local administration and local power-brokers who provide the base of the ruling party. This strategy seems destined to perpetuate a nation of consumers, and a system which disproportionally rewards those with access to power at the expense of those who actually work. The system therefore carries certain built-in disincentives to sustained productive effort, internal resource mobilization, and reduction of external dependence.

The low exposure to foreign penetration of the Bangladesh economy may have owed to the historical legacy of Pakistani rule, but it was compounded by Bangladesh's low exploitability. The country has few natural resources which are internationally marketable. Jute is the only resource with a significant external market where Bangladesh enjoys any sort of international comparative advantage. As a consequence, Bangladesh's external trade is heavily dominated by exports of jute and jute goods which account for around 80 per cent of commodity exports. In turn Bangladesh accounts for around 75 per cent of world exports of raw jute and 50 per cent of exports of jute goods (World Bank, 1973).

Apart from its jute, foreign capital has found little occasion to rush to Bangladesh. It had involved itself in tea plantations in the north-eastern region of the country from the period of British colonial rule. The British originally had also dominated the export trade of jute. But they gradually gave ground to local traders, initially from India, then from Pakistan and finally from Bangladesh itself, so that today the trade in Bangladesh is largely in indigenous hands, both in the public and private sector. A large part of the international market for jute and jute goods, however, even now continues to be controlled by intermediaries operating from London and New York who cream-off part of the surplus. As a result, the jute economy in Bangladesh remains highly sensitive to the level of activity in the world economy, which contributes to considerable instability in the earnings of jute growers and the jute industry.

Besides renewable resources such as jute and tea, Bangladesh's sole non-renewable resource is natural gas, where it has an estimated reserve of 9 trillion cubic feet. Current levels of exploitation are low, its use being limited to feeding an indigenous fertilizer industry, power generation, and domestic consumption in a few urban areas. Its extraction and marketing are currently within the state sector. External involvement has been marginal though attempts are now underway to involve transnational corporations (TNCs) in the liquefaction of natural gas for export.

Apart from exploitation of natural resources, TNCs have been only marginally involved in import-substituting industrialization and industries with foreign equity still do not account for more than 1 per cent of fixed assets in the manufacturing sector, so that the TNC presence, whether in resource exploitation, import substitution, or export of labour-intensive products, is negligible. To this extent, the various cycles of dependence identified by various writers on the world system are not fully relevant to the Bangladesh experience.

Dominant Class Forces in Bangladesh

The absence of foreign control in the classical sense over the domestic economy has meant that the dominant social formations within Bangladesh are largely indigenous. In the initial period after liberation the state sector, dominated by petty bourgeois elements which had led the nationalist struggle, became the dominant decision-maker. This became an important factor in abridging the scope of penetration into Bangladesh by external capital. With 85 per cent of fixed assets in the manufacturing sector, along with the bulk of banking and insurance, foreign trade, communications, and power all under state ownership, decision-making and investment priorities, on the face of it, were largely indigenously determined.

This tendency experienced some erosion as a consequence of a change of regime in 1975 following the assassination of the then-President Shaikh Mujibur Rahman. Power then moved from the regime which had led the liberation struggle into the hands of a more affluent segment of the bourgeoisie deriving its power from the military coup, which put a regime favourably disposed towards the West in control. The new regime sought to promote the development of a local capitalist class and to open up the economy to private foreign investment. Though some enlargement of the private sector has occurred in recent years, there has as yet been no quantitatively significant erosion of the dominance of public enterprise over the non-traditional sector of in the indigenously controlled character of the domestic economy.

But this recent strategy of promoting, under state patronage, some segments of the local bourgeoisie to constitute a private capitalist sector has had important consequences for opening up the economy to external penetration. The historical legacy of external political domination up to 1971 over the areas that now constitute Bangladesh, meant that the indigenous bourgeoisie remained an underdeveloped social entity (Sobhan, 1980). The growth of a domestic bourgeoisie from the outset of liberation thus came to be tied up with access to external resources. For the aspirant private bourgeoisie who enjoyed limited control over productive assets, it meant that their only vehicle for linkage with the world system was through the role of an intermediary.

The volume and distribution of earnings from performing the role of intermediary depend critically on the volume of external assistance coming into Bangladesh and on access to state patronage. The higher the inflow of external assistance, the more profits accrue to this class. External resource inflows directly and indirectly further the growth and prosperity of this class of intermediaries. Directly, the intermediaries function as commission agents for foreign suppliers, tendering for development projects and supplies of a wide range of intermediate and finished goods such as raw cotton, fertilizer and cement. Indirectly, this class derives profits from the distribution of goods imported by the state trading corporation or finished goods manufactured in public enterprises through the processing of imported intermediates. The volume of external resources available to the economy was and remains a critical determinant of the fortunes of this class.

To the extent that Bangladesh came to be dependent on foreign aid to fund 60 per cent of its investments, 85 per cent of its development budget, and 63 per cent of its commodity imports,[2] the level of external resource inflows was critically dependent on the volume of aid available to the economy. This aspirant bourgeoisie has thus come to acquire a material stake in an aid-dependent regime. Any trend towards abridging external dependence, at least in the short run, is likely to be directly inimical to the interests of these commission agents of foreign suppliers. To the extent that the growth of self-reliance remains contingent on expansion in import-substituting domestic production of goods and services, the bourgeoisie could be compensated through control of domestically traded goods produced in the state sector or even directly produced by the private sector. Insofar as the level of domestic output is itself contingent on aided imports, however, even this class of distributors of manufactures remains critically dependent on maintaining the levels of aid-financed imports.

In the case of the private sector, liquid resources generated from agency commissions provide the basis for diversification into capitalist production, but few of this class are inclined to reinvest their trading capital directly in industry. As a result, under state patronage extended to the local bourgeoisie through loan and equity financing from state-owned financial institutions, the state itself has become the main source of capitalist growth in Bangladesh. The capacity of these state institutions to promote expansions of the capitalist sector is itself contingent on foreign loans to the state financing institutions, largely extended through multinational financial institutions such as the World Bank and Asian Development Bank. Thus, capitalist development in Bangladesh has become a direct function of aid availability intermediated by the state.

The Role and Interests of the State Bourgeoisie

The dependence on aid flows is not restricted to the growth aspirations of a domestic capitalist class. A growing state bourgeoisie, including members of the permanent bureaucracy and the executives of the state enterprises, has also become heavily dependent on inflows of external assistance to further its sectional interests. Part of this compulsion originates in the power and patronage which derives from initiating and executing large aid-financed development projects. Both in terms of intra-bureaucratic power and within the polity, control over such projects becomes a major resource for those contending for state power. Patronage derived from such projects extends over employment as well as the dispensation of favours to suppliers of goods and services and to construction contractors. Vast fortunes can accrue to both these categories of beneficiaries as a consequence of expenditure decisions within the state sector. Some of these benefits may even return to the decision-makers, who thus acquire a material stake in aid-financed projects.

The built-in drive to seek more and more foreign aid is thus a common feature of the development process in Bangladesh. Many state functionaries, however, seek more aid to serve as a cushion for their own managerial inadequacies. Thus, for example, the incapacity to ensure capacity utilization of mechanized irrigation facilities provided by the state to farmers, generates pressure for more aid-financed import of irrigation equipment rather than for fuller utilization of installed capacity. Thus, new aid becomes the main source for expanding acreage under irrigation or even for maintaining current levels of irrigation. Aid in these situations becomes the soft option designed to mitigate the consequences of deteriorating operating performance within the economy. Given the contingent benefits which accrue to particular classes from aid, we can get some insight into the low and deteriorating performance of some state-run enterprises.

The aid compulsion of the private and state bourgeoisie is reflected in the character and aspirations of the political leadership. The dominant political party currently administering the polity in Bangladesh is itself an expression of the interests and ambitions of the aspirant local bourgeoisie. This element seeks to control the state machine in order both to dispense patronage as a basis for expanding its power over the polity, and to seek material benefit from the dispensation of this patronage. This entente between the party and state machine, however, tends to be strained by intra-class conflicts over control of the patronage derived from access to foreign aid. Indeed, where the ruling party expresses its class character through the aspirations of the private sector, some element of contradiction arises with the state bourgeoisie over control of foreign aid and attitudes towards it.

The Character of the Comprador Bourgeoisie

The critical role of foreign aid in the development of the bourgeoisie is reinforced by the essentially parasitic and unproductive character of this class. The private sector has shown little capacity to generate surpluses to finance capital formation. The low level of private savings, manifested directly in direct equity investments and in contributions to direct taxation, is a measure of the unproductive character of this class (Government of Bangladesh, 1980). A low savings capacity is compounded by high levels of conspicuous consumption based largely on consumption standards and on goods imported from abroad. The appetite of this class even absorbs the savings of overseas migrants, who provide a growing and variable source of foreign exchange remittance to Bangladesh (Mahmood, 1980). To the extent that state controls over investment limit the extent of import-substituting investment derived from imported consumption standards, both imports and overseas travel to spend their earnings have become an outlet to the comprador bourgeoisie for the incomes derived from acting as intermediaries to foreign suppliers. What investment is made by this class is in part channelled abroad, both for profits and as an insurance against domestic upheaval. At home a high rate of investments in luxury housing is encouraged by state-financing institutions and generates *rentier* income from foreigners who come to live in Bangladesh as another by-product of the aid regime. Along with urban landlordism, preferred domestic investments of their equity by the bourgeoisie are directed to trade and speculation.

The pattern of the urban economy is paralleled in the rural areas where rich farmers use their access to state power to monopolize imported fertilizer, irrigation facilities, pesticides and aid-financed credit programmes (Devylder and Asplund, 1979). To this end, the growing affluence of a section of the rural bourgeoisie has emerged as another by-product of the aid regime.

The Extent and Nature of Aid Dependence

It would be misleading, however, to see aid serving solely as a prop of the bourgeoisie in Bangladesh. Within the present social framework, aid has now become central to the expectations and conditions of life of a much wider segment of the urban and even rural populations of Bangladesh. Some of the main social classes who are directly or indirectly dependent on aid for their subsistence consumption and livelihood are drawn from the following social groups: rural poor, urban population of six major cities, government employees, workers in public enterprises and in large-scale manufacturing enterprises, school teachers in state educational institutions, college and university students resident in hostels, the armed forces and other instruments of state power. The nature of this dependency may be reviewed in relation to the rural and urban segments of the population.

The Rural Poor   The dependence of the rural poor is part of a built-in structural crisis within Bangladesh society. At present, 50 per cent of all rural households are classified as functionally landless, whilst another 25 per cent find it difficult to ensure subsistence from their cultivable land and have to seek supplementary sources of income.[3] This indicates that some three-quarters of rural households in Bangladesh are now dependent in all or part on the market economy, as opposed to subsistence cultivation, for their basic staple diet. This large category of the rural population is now directly touched by the world economic system to the extent that the market regime for food-grains in Bangladesh over the years has become critically dependent on imports. Today some 12–15 per cent of food-grains consumed in Bangladesh are imported, but at least 50 per cent of domestic output is not marketed. Of the grain entering the market, imports account for 30–50 per cent, depending on the size of the domestic crop and the marketable surplus derived from this. The availability of grain imports has a crucial importance for the volume of marketed grain and consequently the market price of grain. Both factors are critical to the level of consumption of the rural poor, for whom scarcity of grain on the market, operating through the price mechanism, may make all the difference between starvation and subsistence. This was made apparent in 1974 when the delay, for political reasons, by the US government in sanctions US PL 480 food aid, precipitated a severe famine in Bangladesh where some 30,000 perished (Sobhan, 1979).

Food-grain aid has acquired a further dimension in the lives of the rural poor. It is now being used to underwrite the Rural Public Works Programme and the Food for Work Programme which are becoming increasingly important as a source of livelihood for a growing segment of the rural poor. To the extent that aided imports of fertilizer and irrigation equipment determine the spread of higher yielding variety (HYV) cultivation, this is again affecting the lives of share-croppers and wage labourers who benefit from the employment-enhancing features of the new technology.

The Aid-supported Rationing Programme Apart from the rural areas, food aid is directly instrumental in providing basic staples to the entire population of six major urban centres in Bangladesh. These areas are covered by what is known as "statutory rationing": a basic supply of rice, wheat, sugar, edible oils and kerosene is guaranteed to all households through the issue of ration cards. Ration shops sell a fixed quantity of these basic items at a controlled price. This ration is extended to cover all government employees wherever they are posted in Bangladesh, workers in state enterprises and large industrial units, students resident in college and university hostels, government school teachers, and all personnel of the armed forces and other related law and order agencies. An estimated 4.5 million people are covered by this ration programme (Zahir and Kamal, n.d.). A large and at times overwhelming part of the ration programme is sustained by food imports, mostly procured under various aid programmes. These people identified above are a priority group for determining access to food aid, which includes both food-grain and edible oil, and are particularly vulnerable to any major change in the level of external assistance, though less so than the rural poor since any cut in aid flows is usually passed on to the latter as long as government policy gives priority to meeting obligations to the statutory rationing areas and special groups identified above. The political assumption underlying this policy is that these groups are politically the most volatile.

Dependence in the Manufacturing Sector The mechanism of aid dependence, however, is not restricted to direct consumption of food items. Many items of daily consumption produced by the domestic manufacturing sector have come to depend on aid-financed imports. The level of output of the textile industry depends on aid-financed imports of raw cotton. The textile industry not only provides a basic need for the whole industry, but is a source of livelihood for 160,000 industrial workers and another 300,000 artisan households who depend on supplies of yarn made available by the state-owned textile industry to feed their handlooms. Cuts in the supply of raw cotton thus have wide ramifications in the price of cloth and in the income of those involved in its manufacture.

In other import-dependent sectors of industry such as steel which produces corrugated iron sheets, a basic item in rural housing, the engineering industry which contributes to rural development and public transport, and the chemical industry which produces soap and refined petroleum products, commodity aid is crucial to ensure capacity utilization. If one allows for the crucial role of spare parts and supplies of other intermediates, then in most sectors access to foreign exchange for imports is a critical variable in determining levels of domestic output. Because of foreign exchange constraints scarcities in domestic output cannot readily be compensated by imports. Thus, a reduced level of imports of intermediates as a result of aid cuts can have far-reaching repercussions on domestic price levels and levels of consumption of basic necessities.

The Parameters of Aid Dependence

From a review of the basic indices of dependence it becomes apparent that employment for the rural poor, domestic revenues, development expenditure, fixed investment, imports, the balance-of-payments deficit and levels of output in specific sectors of the economy, are all directly or indirectly dependent on levels of external resource flows. If to this we add the role of aid in specific sectors to finance expansion of capacity and enhancement of services, aid would appear even more critical to the performance of the economy.

Clearly any sudden suspension of aid or even an appreciable decline in its availability would have far-reaching consequences for the economy, society and polity of Bangladesh: We have seen that significant segments of the urban and rural populations now depend on aid for their employment, income and consumption. Virtually every area of government activity in relation to revenue generation, development, external trade and provision of goods and services, is now contingent on aid availability. Bangladesh, in consequence, is as integrated into the world economic system as any classically dependent Latin American or African country. The policies of aid donors in the developed world, specific not only to aid but to decisions affecting the production and the pricing of commodities imported into Bangladesh, e.g. food-grains, cotton, soya beans, petroleum products, fertilizer and steel, are of growing consequence to a rising proportion of Bangladesh's population. This factor gives policy-makers abroad an unusual measure of leverage over countries such as Bangladesh, and drastically abridges Bangladesh's autonomy of action in matters of domestic policy, investment priorities, choice of technology, and programming of its development expenditures. In each area its decisions have to be tailored to the ideological predilections of donors, the types of aid provided, and the terms on which it is made available.

Bangladesh and the World Economic System

Bangladesh therefore appears to need the world system for its survival within its current social system. On the other hand, the only concern in the world system relating to Bangladesh arises from the potential for endemic and proliferating social chaos growing out of the unresolved contradictions and problems within this country, and the possible incapacity of the existing political structure to mediate the crisis within the framework of the prevailing system. Fear that the crisis within the existing social order may not contain the repercussions of this upheaval of humanity within its national boundaries has given Bangladesh a place in the concerns of the aid donors. In this situation the leverage of a regime whose survival, both as a regime and as a class, is dependent on external donors, is nominal and must remain subservient to those who keep it alive. This uneasy entente, however, is likely to prove increasingly unviable as the donor countries' own internal crises make them less capable and less inclined to undertake the apparently unrewarding task of keeping the social order in Bangladesh afloat. In these circumstances the incapacity of the dominant groups in Bangladesh to sustain a productive and stable social order is likely to make it another crisis state during the remaining years of this century.

Notes

1. First published in *Development and Change*, vol. 12 (London: Sage, 1981).
2. Computed by author from data available in *Bangladesh Current Economic Position and Short-Term Outlook* (World Bank, March, 1980).
3. Data derived from *Summary Report of the 1978 Land Occupancy Survey of Bangladesh* (Bangladesh Institute of Statistics, Dacca, December 1978).

Effects of Labour Migration from Pakistan[1]

Roger Ballard

Emigration is nothing new in the history of the subcontinent. It has been going on for centuries. But in recent years the migratory outflow has grown so large that its consequences are now of great structural significance. Thanks to the growing ease and efficiency of communications, migrants can now keep in much closer touch with those whom they left behind. Many send a substantial proportion of their overseas earnings straight back home, where their remittances are having an ever-increasing impact on the local social, economic and political order. Nowhere has this been more salient than in Pakistan. By the early 1980s over 2 million men – nearly 10 per cent of the country's adult male labour force – were working overseas; and their remittances, in both cash and kind, amounted to at least $4 billion annually – well over half the country's total foreign exchange inflow. Manpower had become by far the largest of Pakistan's exports, and remittances its most important source of external revenue.

Yet what have been the consequences of Pakistan's growing dependence on remittance income? How, and to whose benefit, has this huge new inflow of resources been deployed? Has economic development been enhanced or hindered? And given that the employment prospects of overseas migrants are extremely insecure, especially in the Middle East, just how sound are the economic and social structures that have emerged in the wake of their departure?

These questions can be explored at a number of levels. First, from the perspective of the migrant and his family; second, in terms of the effects of the huge inflow of remittances on the local economy in migrants' villages of origin; and third, with respect to their impact on the national economy as a whole. Processes at each of these levels are closely interrelated, for although it is individual migrants who have sought employment overseas, and who make investment decisions on their return, it is the national economy which enjoys the benefits of the foreign exchange content of their remittances, and which sets the parameters within which individual returnees have to operate. Finally the whole process must also be located within the global economy; for it is in that context, far beyond the control of anyone in Pakistan, that the demand for labour, rates of pay, and the security of employment for migrant workers is determined.

Patterns of Demand for Overseas Labour

Mass migration from Pakistan has arisen primarily as a result of labour shortages in Britain and the Middle East. Like many other highly industrialized countries, Britain became acutely short of labour during the 1960s, and so a new industrial sub-proletariat was recruited from overseas. Although the jobs available were those which indigenous workers found unattractive, they offered Pakistani villagers access to unparalleled prosperity. Those that could made the trip to Britain, and although the combined impact of recession and rising levels of white hostility are now causing Britain's 300,000 Pakistanis many problems, they have at least acquired the security of permanent rights of residence in a developed economy.

The 2 million or so Pakistanis living and working in the Middle East have been a good deal less fortunate. Although they originally set off in pursuit of the high wages and apparently limitless opportunities which seemed to be available when the oil boom began in the early 1970s, economic prospects in the Gulf today are very different. Most of the huge construction projects in which they found employment have now been completed; competition for the remaining jobs has increased sharply, as migrants have flooded in from all over South East as well as Southern Asia; and as both oil prices and production levels have plummeted, most Middle Eastern states have brutally pruned their development plans. The bonanza is over. Wage rates, especially for the unskilled, have fallen sharply, and migrants are returning home in large numbers. Unlike those who went to Britain, very few migrants to the Middle East have been able to acquire local citizenship, and with it rights of permanent residence.

The Migrants' Own Perspective

Nevertheless the prospect of working overseas at wage levels which, in local terms, were quite unbelievably high, seemed to offer Pakistani peasants a wonderful chance of achieving social and economic mobility. In seeking to make the most of this opportunity, few, if any, expected to stay permanently overseas. Their aim, instead, was to save most of their wages, not so much to supplement their families' everyday incomes, but to accumulate enough capital to enable them to transform the basic conditions of their existence – by building a new house, buying more land or starting a business. Working overseas also gave them access to much-sought-after consumer goods, from watches and radios to refrigerators, televisions and VCRs. By the late 1970s "Dubai-fever" was sweeping through many parts of Pakistan.

But overseas migrants were not recruited equally from all sections of the population. Relatively few were of urban origins, or had professional and technical qualifications. To be sure the departure of many of its small but expensively trained stock of doctors, engineers and accountants was a loss which Pakistan could ill afford – especially since it was the most competent who were the most likely to leave – but in the overall scheme of things migrants of this kind have been very much in the minority. The great majority were neither of urban origins, nor were they professionals, technicians or even craftsmen. Instead they were typically the sons of small peasant farmers, well over half of whom were recruited from a broad swathe of villages stretching across north-eastern Punjab and the North-west Frontier Province. This area, which is dependent on rain-fed (*barani*) rather than irrigated agriculture, has always been relatively densely populated, and young men have long sought employment elsewhere to supplement their families' incomes. It was, for example, one of the principal recruiting grounds for the Army during the British Raj, and remains so to this day for the Pakistani Army.

As a result of mass migration, very large sums of money are now being injected into the economy of this relatively restricted area. But with just what consequences? At least in principle the arrival of large amounts of capital in these otherwise under-resourced villages might have been expected to lead to rapid economic growth. But in northern Pakistan, as indeed in so many other parts of the Third World from which heavy emigration has taken place, this has not occurred. It is worth exploring why.

Migration to Britain

Let us take the case of migration to Britain first. The great majority of British Pakistanis originate in and around Mirpur District, which lies right against the Indian border in the southern tip of Azad Kashmir. Migration from this area has a long history.

It began with Mirpuris taking jobs as stokers on board British steamers sailing out of Bombay at the turn of the century; and it was ex-seamen who were drafted to work in munitions factories in Birmingham and Bradford during the Second World War who pioneered the Pakistani settlement in Britain. When the post-war industrial boom took off, they were well-placed to write and tell their kinsmen about the new opportunities. A process of chain migration soon ensued, as a result of which over half the population from many parts of Mirpur District now live in Britain.

The most notable consequence of this mass exodus has been a transformation in local housing conditions. Prior to migration, most villagers lived in small *kaccha* (adobe) dwellings. Today virtually all houses, even in the most remote settlements, are built of brick and reinforced concrete; most are much larger than before, and many are elaborately and expensively decorated. But their size may be deceptive. Very often they are only partially inhabited, usually by those few – often elderly – members of the family who have not yet moved overseas; many houses are locked up, and only reopened during their owners' increasingly rare visits to their homes.

The other most obvious change is the development of bazaars. Even the most remote villages now contain rows of shop units, but these too tend to share the half-abandoned look of so many absent migrants' houses. Many stand unlet, and even where they are in business, activity is desultory. Yet competition is intense, so only the very largest and most well-established businesses are at all profitable: travel agents do best of all. But this is not for lack of money. Bank branches can be found everywhere, even in the most remote settlements, and all have large sums on deposit: in the village in which I conducted intensive fieldwork, whose resident population was around 3000, they amounted to more than Rs 50 million. But transactions are few, and loans non-existent: cashing villagers' British pensions is now one of the banks' most active forms of business.

What, then, has become of the very large sums of money that Mirpuri migrants have sent back from Britain, and why has its arrival not had a more positive economic effect? Although agriculture was and remains the District's only indigenous source of wealth, it has attracted very little investment. On the contrary, the land has been neglected: an ever-increasing area is now left fallow, and even that which is still under the plough is much less intensively cultivated than it once was. Mirpur is no longer self-sufficient in food grain. Instead, wheat and a wide range of other foods and consumer products are imported from elsewhere – though thanks to the continuing inflow of remittances, villagers have plenty of money to pay for it. In the short term, at least, the onset of dependency does not matter.

Yet why should agriculture be neglected? Although the land is by no means infertile, it makes little sense, from the villagers' perspective, to put much effort into its cultivation. Not only has peasant farming long been regarded as an unprestigious activity, but such judgements are now strongly reinforced by its lack of profitability. Given low grain-prices, the inflation of local wage-rates caused by the arrival of remittances, and the paucity of local infrastructural resources – for despite the high levels of private wealth the District still lacks decent roads, irrigation facilities, or an effective agricultural extension service – agricultural activity has virtually ceased to be economically worthwhile; most forms of agricultural investment now offer insignificant, and possibly even negative, returns. When I asked returning migrants why they did not invest their money more positively – whether in agriculture, business or manufacturing – rather than leaving it in the bank, all gave the same answer. The prospects of making a profitable investment were, in their view, and indeed in their experience, minimal. Despite its richness in capital, Mirpur has become economically stagnant.

But it was not always so. In the early 1970s, when the inflow of remittances was at its peak, the local economy seemed to be in much better shape. Houses were being built everywhere. Not only was there a huge demand for construction materials – bricks, cement and steel reinforcement rods – but also for trucks and camels to transport these materials to the migrants' often remote settlements, as well as for building workers to construct the new houses. Thanks to the inflow of wealth from overseas local wage-rates rose rapidly, so much so that large numbers of migrants from elsewhere in Pakistan were attracted into the District. With so much commercial activity all the bazaars expanded very rapidly, and well-placed businessmen made a lot of money.

Since then much has changed. Once most families had rebuilt their houses construction activity declined; and with the reunion of families in Britain – which became increasingly commonplace from the mid-1970s onwards – as well as the onset of severe economic recession at the end of the decade, the volume of remittances to Mirpur has also declined sharply. Since the boom of the 1970s was construction- and remittance-led, it soon collapsed as these fell back: the little dynamism which is still present in the local economy depends almost totally on what remains of the remittance inflow. Nevertheless expectations are still high, especially amongst young people. Since local prospects are so limited, they now, even more than ever before, equate success with securing the magic visa which will permit them, too, to settle overseas.

Migration to the Middle East

Since the late 1960s entry to Britain has effectively been closed to everyone but those whose close kin had already settled there. Instead the most frequent migratory target, not just in Mirpur, but right across the *barani* region of Northern Pakistan, has been the Middle East. Although the intensity of migration to the Middle East has nowhere been quite so great as that to Britain from Mirpur, its impact has been far more extensive; but it seems to have been very similar in character. Just as in Mirpur in the early 1970s, a huge building boom is now in progress, and the bazaars – and indeed the whole service sector – are expanding very rapidly throughout the *barani* areas. This bustle of activity certainly gives an appearance of progress, but a comparison with Mirpur must give cause for alarm. For just as in Mirpur there has been next to no investment in agriculture, or indeed in any other kind of productive activity, and in comparison with Mirpuris experience in Britain, the window of opportunity in the Middle East is proving to be much narrower.

Migrants to the Middle East are now returning to Pakistan in very large numbers, and they are well aware that they have little chance of finding further employment overseas. But they are also facing many difficulties at home. Having built themselves a new house, most hoped to use their accumulated savings to start a business. But there is now so much competition in the market-place that it is becoming ever more difficult to do so successfully. And once the volume of remittances starts to fall, and the market to stagnate as it has in Mirpur, the squeeze will become tighter still. For a short while returning migrants can cushion themselves against adversity by spending their accumulated savings – and as long as they are able to do so the additional money supply will help to keep the local economy afloat. But that cannot last for long, since their savings are not limitless.

A new source of income will soon have to be found, and as the returning migrants themselves are only too well aware, the range of choices with which they are now faced is unenviable. They could, of course, try to return to the Middle East, though if so they know it would only be for very much reduced wages; or they could look for work in Pakistan's already overcrowded cities, in which wages are certainly no higher; or they could return to subsistence farming on their long-neglected land. To look to the only resource which they themselves control might seem to be the best option in principle, especially since the potential productivity of their land is very great. But if they were to make such a choice, they would have little alternative, at least at the outset, but to fall back on traditional labour-intensive methods, even though they now live in expensive *pakka* houses, and are proud owners of such consumer durables as refrigerators and VCRs.

If this does happen – and they may well find that they have no alternative – their income will fall sharply, so much so that they will be unlikely even to be able properly to maintain their houses, let alone their televisions. So despite all their exertions overseas, the hoped-for transformation in their conditions of existence has remained elusive.

Explanations?

But just why has the arrival of remittances done little more than to precipitate a superficial boom in the service sector, while leaving the productive base largely unchanged? Why has so little that is positive been achieved? One possible explanation is to blame those who are returning. Government officials in Islamabad, for example, generally take the view that because migrants were predominantly of peasant origins their "backwardness" and "illiteracy" has prevented them from deploying their wealth more positively. "Spoiled" by their access to consumer goods, they argue, returning migrants are either too lazy to be bothered to work, or too commercially incompetent to be able to invest their savings more effectively.

However plausible such self-serving arguments may seem to members of the cocooned and privileged élite, they soon collapse in the face of rural experience. As far as most returnees are concerned, their central problem is to identify *any* investment strategy which offers some security and as well as reasonable prospects of profitability. And it is certainly quite wrong to argue that Pakistani peasants lack entrepreneurial skills: in Britain many have become very successful small-scale businessmen. Interestingly enough, in recent years a number of Mirpuris with experience of small-scale manufacturing in Britain have sought to replicate their success back home. But with the exception of those who have moved into property speculation and other forms of financial manipulation, no one has achieved very much. But the reasons which they give for their lack of success are most instructive. Virtually without exception, they argue that the business climate in Pakistan is far more hostile than that in Britain, despite all the problems of racism and recession which led them to consider shifting to Pakistan in the first place.

What all this suggests is that the problem is not so much individual as structural. What must also be considered is the role which remittances have come to play in the structure of the economy as a whole, as well as who controls that structure, how, and to what ends.

A National Perspective

Rich though it is in natural resources, Pakistan is currently facing an acute economic crisis. Although the population is growing rapidly, agricultural and industrial production is almost static; moreover infrastructural investment – on roads, canals, education, health-care and so forth – remains minimal, especially in rural areas. But the cities are rather better provided. Not only are infrastructural facilities concentrated there, but they have a superficial air of prosperity, since imported consumer goods of all kinds are also freely available – at a price. Beguiled by all this, many young men are drifting to the towns, however difficult they may find it to earn a living.

In addition to this rural–urban divide, Pakistan is also a highly inegalitarian society in terms of class. But in this case privilege comes not so much from the ownership of industrial capital, not even of extensive tracts of land, but through control of the state. The élite, composed mainly of senior bureaucrats and military officers, is small, but its members live extremely comfortably, mainly as a result of bending the economy to their own interests.

In managing the economy the élite has not only sought to protect its economic interests, but also to sustain its political dominance. So although much lip-service has been paid to rural development, the interests of the rural population have counted for little in the calculus of power – for it is *urban* revolt which has brought down each of Pakistan's increasingly authoritarian regimes. With this in mind it is easy to see why infrastructural resources have been concentrated in urban areas, and why grain prices have been held as low as possible. However much damage such policies may have done to the rural economy, they do at least provide some insurance against challenges to the established order. Given this structure, it is scarcely surprising that returning migrants should have found agricultural investment unrewarding.

Nevertheless their remittances now play a crucial role in the operation of the Pakistani economy as a whole. Since Partition Pakistan has for the most part pursued an extremely liberal trade policy, particularly with respect to consumer goods: imports have been rising almost exponentially for many years. While such imports are disproportionately consumed by the élite, they also have to be paid for, and in foreign exchange. Where, then, has the money come from? In the early years it was raised primarily from the sale of Bengali jute, later from the inflow of remittances from Britain, and more recently still from the Middle East. And unless that inflow is sustained, most of Pakistan's current veneer of urban prosperity – which is once again confined primarily to the survice sector – will evaporate.

The instability of this whole structure is only too obvious, especially since, contrary to the hopeful expectations of the recent Five Year Plan, it is quite unrealistic to expect an endless future growth in remittances. They have already begun to decline, and despite frantic efforts to promote further manpower export, an even sharper decline is clearly in the pipeline. Nor is there any plausible alternative source of external finance. Thus the evaporation of opportunities in the Middle East seems likely to precipitate as severe an economic crisis nationally as the one which already looms more locally.

Nevertheless this structure has not been without its beneficiaries, for although established policies may be about to leave most sections of the population high and dry, the élite has done much better. Not only have the rich been enabled to sustain their position of affluence: they have enriched themselves still further.

The windfall inflow of remittances has served many purposes. Most straightforwardly it has made it possible to continue running a liberal imports policy, which has allowed the élite to surround themselves with expensive imported consumer durables. And by deliberately overvaluing the Pakistani rupee, a hidden tax was effectively placed on migrant remittances, cheapening the cost of imports, while devaluing the rupee value of the remittances themselves. Finally the inflow of remittances has also enabled the very rich to export a large part of their capital. Although accurate figures are quite impossible to find, it is common knowledge that many of Pakistan's much famed "twenty-two families" have by now shipped the bulk of their wealth overseas, and that many senior members of the military and bureaucratic élite – when they are not members of those self-same families – have done just the same. So should the current edifice collapse, those who have been running it for the last few years will only need to find their way to the nearest Jumbo jet to begin a prosperous life elsewhere. The fruits of the labours of millions of Pakistanis overseas will largely have been transferred into other, more prosperous hands.

Conclusion

Need it necessarily have been thus? Quite clearly not. Those parts of rural Pakistan from which heavy overseas migration has taken place are now effectively capital rich. Had those resources been deployed locally, rather than deposited in the banks (from which, once again, the élite are the principal as well as the most delinquent borrowers) it would have been possible to begin to liberate the productive capacity of the local environment; if agricultural prices had been set higher, cultivation would have been more profitable, and much more actively pursued; and if the import of consumer goods had been prevented (as in India, for example) indigenous manufacturing would have expanded instead of collapsing. But such changes in policy could only occur in the wake of a political upheaval which removed the beneficiaries of the current order from power; ironically enough, the illusion of prosperity generated by the inflow of remittances has so far largely contained all such pressures for change.

But as remittances decline and the underlying contradictions are more nakedly exposed, those pressures will surely increase. But by then the window of opportunity will have closed, for it is most unlikely that the huge demand for unskilled labour which emerged in Britain and the Gulf over the past two decades will ever be repeated. If so Pakistan will have little alternative but to look inwards towards the potentialities of its own, still largely undeveloped, resources. But in that process televisions, VCRs and long-since exported capital assets will be of little utility.

So although migrants may have worked for long hours in appalling conditions overseas to send billions of dollars back to Pakistan, it may well be that there will soon be little to show for their efforts. But if they themselves are to be blamed for this sorry state of affairs, it is not because they lacked individual initiative; rather it is because they failed to realize just how easily an inegalitarian social order can vitiate individual enterprise.

122   Roger Ballard

Note

1. This chapter is based on research conducted in Pakistan between 1984 and 1986, and which was supported by a grant from the Economic and Social Research Council. A Report on the project, entitled "The Context and Consequences of Emigration from Northern Pakistan" has been lodged in the British Library.

Part III

Ideologies and Realities of Inequality

Editors' Introduction

Much sociological writing on South Asia has been preoccupied with ideological dimensions of inequality because of starting from the view that "society is in good part constituted by the ideas and relations of caste" (Hawthorn, 1982, 204). Here in Part III ideological aspects of South Asian society are considered, but without leaving behind a concern with power and the social relations of production. An important part of the purpose of the papers by Harriss and Omvedt is to critique the large body of work on the sociology of South Asia which is premised on the proposition that the ideology of caste structures society. At the same time both these authors are opposed to the kind of reductionist thinking which holds that caste is quite unimportant beside class relations. Harriss provides a guide to important work on the sociology of caste and from the tradition of studies of rural society based on ethnographic fieldwork at the village level. Caste, it is argued by some scholars, is important amongst Muslims as well as amongst Hindus and this may well be so in the case of Muslims of Northern India (see Ahmed [ed.] 1973).

Colonialism fostered the tendency for what Sarkar refers to as "the expression of socio-economic tensions through a kind of false consciousness of caste solidarity" (Sarkar, 1983, 55). For example:

during the colonial period ... the landless labourers' capacity to bargain with landowners was greatly weakened. The scarcity of opportunities overall locked a great many into the occupation of last resort: landless labour. Unable to stand up to the village landowner, the landless labourer had little of the stamina needed for wider political activity. The landowner in most regions could in any case insulate his labourers from the political worker from outside: the insulation took the form of economic sanctions for labourers and physical ones for political organisers. With the labourer's increasing dependence went an increasing sense of insecurity [see Breman's paper in Part III]; and he would seek relief from it by staying well within the familiar, unthreatening shell of his kinsmen and neighbours within the caste group. The larger society locked him into landless labour; he locked himself into his caste group. (Saberwal, 1979, 260–1)

Amongst economically rising groups, too, caste as an identity became more significant, for example, as people sought to establish wider-ranging alliances. S. A. Barnett (1975, 1977) gives an account of a striking example, in which an upper non-Brahmin landowning caste decided in the late 1920s, through a caste assembly, to allow marriages across village clusters and to endorse inter-district marriage. The effect, as he explains, was to bring about a fundamental shift in the basis of caste ideology, which may be understood as a transition to "ethnic-like regional caste blocs" (S. A. Barnett, 1977, 402; though see Shah, 1982, for criticism of Barnett's approach to change in caste ideology). The actions of the colonial administration and its endeavours to classify the population in terms of caste, added to these tendencies (see Sarkar, 1983, 54–9, for a brief review of the literature).

The relations of caste and of other dimensions of inequality in South Asia are brought out strongly in labour studies, especially those concerned with the structure of labour markets and access to different types of work. Breman's (1985) work on rural labour in Gujerat complements his studies of urban workers (in the chapter in Part V of this book). Holmström (1984) synthesizes a large literature and also gives a detailed analysis of the labour market in Bombay, while Harriss (1986) offers a similar analysis for the South Indian city of Coimbatore. In part what is shown in these studies is how the operation of a "principle of particularism" in entry to different types of work, in the context of an abundant supply of labour, continually creates conditions in which caste identities have a peculiar salience.

An aspect of inequality which is not considered in very much detail in the articles here concerns local power structures and political organization. There is a rich literature focused on the organization of factions both in local and supra-local politics. Seminal work was done by Bailey (1963) and by Nicholas (1968), and subjected to a major critique by Alavi (1973b).

The final chapter in Part III, by Ursula Sharma, introduces another major sphere of power relations in Indian society, that of gender. Discussing the conclusions of her field research in north-west India, Sharma treats the ideological and material aspects of male/female relations. She argues that "If there is any explanatory 'key' to women's position in both Punjab and Himachal (Pradesh) it is more likely to be women's dependence on men than their submission to men." One result of the subordination of women by men, in the view of a number of authors, is the unusually high ratio of men to women that obtains in India, especially in North India, reflecting high female mortality rates particularly in early childhood and in the reproductive years. The explanation of these facts is one critical issue in the understanding of gender relations in South Asia. Valuable studies are those by P. Bardhan (1974). Dyson and Moore (1983) and Miller (1981), which, with other work, are reviewed critically by B. Harriss and Watson (1987). A sensitive study of gender relations affecting Muslim women in north India is by Jeffrey (1979); women's roles in production are the subject of work by Agarwal (1984; 1986), and Mies (1981); women's politics are the subject of studies by Omvedt (1978; 1980). The women of Pakistan are the subject of a book edited by Mumtaz and Shaheed (1987).

The Formation of Indian Society: Ideology and Power

John Harriss[1]

A great deal of social analysis of India starts from the view that the ideology of caste and the way in which the caste system works in practice are of fundamental importance, that "Indian society is in good part constituted by the ideas and relations of caste" (Hawthorn, 1982, 204). In the 1950s and 1960s the main focus of research was on village studies (see Marriott (ed.) 1955; Bailey, 1957; Beteille, 1963, and Mayer, 1960, for outstanding examples). These studies, which mainly treated the village as an elementary unit of real significance in Indian society, were concerned with explaining the sources and nature of social order and emphasized the importance of caste relationships as the base of it. It is remarkable that in the majority of village monographs rather little space was devoted to analysis of agriculture, of land-holding or of economic relationships in general (for comment on this see Fuller, in Part I of this volume, and Beteille, 1974; and for an outstanding study published more recently which does concern these issues, Gough, 1981). Most were concerned to some extent, however, with the impact of contemporary economic and political changes on the caste order, and saw the village as being "encapsulated" by the state and expanding markets (classically in Bailey, 1957). The institutions and practices of caste were seen as undergoing change, while remaining of fundamental importance.

At much the same time an alternative approach to the study of Indian society was expounded by Dumont and Pocock (1957). Critical of the empiricism of the conventional village studies, critical too of the notion that the village constitutes an elementary unit of Indian society, these authors proposed that the proper way to study Indian society is through ideology:

> Methodologically, the initial postulate is that ideology is central with respect to the social reality as a whole (man acts consciously and we have direct access to the conscious aspect of his action) [though] it is not the whole of social reality, and the final goal of the study is the difficult task of placing the ideological aspects in positive relation to what may be called the non-ideological aspects. (Dumont, 1980, 344)

Following these premises Dumont was concerned to elucidate the intellectual principles of caste ideology, relying as much on Hindu texts as anthropological observation. The argument is that if we accept Mauss's precept that "A sociological explanation is finished when one has seen what it is that people believe and think, and who are the people who believe and think that" (Dumont and Pocock, 1957, 13) then we are led first to understand the centrality of caste ideology in Indian society and then to perceive that Indian society is organized on quite different principles from those of the West: "On the whole, the essential form of the system is of a hierarchical polarity. One might say that India has institutionalised inequality just as much as we are trying to do the same with equality" (Dumont and Pocock, 1957, 18).

So whether in the vein of the structural functionalism of most village studies, or in that of interpretive sociology, sociologists have emphasized caste. Political scientists, too, have found caste of fundamental significance. Studies like those of Harrison (1960), Kothari (1970a; 1970b) or of the Rudolphs (1967) show the apparent importance of caste identities and organization in political processes. Contemporary newspaper accounts of elections continue regularly to emphasize the idea that outcomes often depend crucially on the way particular castes vote (see Omvedt's critical remarks on these analyses, in the next chapter).

Set against the prevailing judgements of social scientists that caste, however it is understood, is of central importance, are the arguments of some scholars and political activists, that the concern with caste, which perhaps stems from an orientalist curiosity, has completely obscured the significance of key aspects of the economy – such as the distribution of land-holding in rural society – and of class relations (see Fuller's view of this in Part I, and Omvedt's in the next chapter; and for a pointed critique of Dumont's sociology in particular, Mencher, 1974). One of the outstanding sociologists of India, Beteille, argued as much when he suggested that "We have made some progress in developing a sociology of ideas for India. There should be some place by the side of this for a sociology of interests." (Beteille, 1974, 1955.)

Some other social scientists and historians have argued, however, that colonial understandings of caste, and the way these were projected back onto Indian society, have set up a misleading conception of the ideological premises of the society. They suggest that other values and institutions than those encompassed by the conventional understandings of caste may have been more important historically, including "little kingdoms" and the institutions of kingship more generally. Fuller touches on these ideas in his chapter in Part I, but they have not yet been well incorporated into analysis of contemporary India (though see Washbrook 1988, and Stein, 1983).

The chapters in this section are concerned with the ideas inherent in caste and with caste relations and treat them as being of vital interest whilst all are also critical of the view that they "constitute" Indian society as substantially as has been held in the literature to which we have referred. The following short account of a fairly orthodox view of the sociology of caste may be of help to readers.

Caste ideas and relations (defined by Omvedt in her paper here) are grounded in religious beliefs, amplified in what may be called the *"varna* model", a kind of all-India reference model which explains the principles on which actual relationships between caste communities (*jati*) in local caste systems depend. The *varnas* are four different categories or orders of people, believed to have been derived originally from different parts of the body of a primal being. According to the *Purusa Sukta* hymn of the *Rg Veda*, the four *varnas* emerge from the body of Purusa: those of the *brahmin* (priest); *kshatriya* (kings/warriors); *vaishya* (husbandmen); and *shudra* (labourers, tillers of the land). These four orders of society all have important roles in relation to each other and to society as a whole. The *brahmin*, as the one of purest moral substance, acts as a vital intermediary between the rest of society and God. The purity of the *brahmin* depends in part on his avoidance of actions which would be defiling. The shedding of blood is defiling, yet it may be necessary for the defence of society. This task is undertaken by the *kshatriya*. Similarly the task of reproducing the material requirements of society is undertaken by the *vaishya*, while the most polluting actions, including physical labour and the removal of "biological matter" like excrement, or the cleansing of spilled blood (especially menstrual blood) are undertaken by the *shudra*. The material needs of society are supplied by the labour of the *shudra* and the management of the *vaishya*, under the control of the *kshatriya*, who redistributes the social product for the maintenance of all. All four orders of society are necessary to each other, but their different roles involve different levels of pollution (or differences in moral quality), so that there is a clear moral hierarchy. It is important to note that the different roles have both material and religious aspects. Thus the *shudras'* role includes not only the function of supplying physical labour, but also a religious one, when through their actions such as scavenging or the washing of cloth soiled with menstrual blood, they absorb potential impurity from others. It has been suggested that they may be seen as "contra-priests" to the *brahmins* because of the religious services they perform for society, though they are of an opposite kind from those performed by *brahmins* (see Gould, 1967). Although the social hierarchy is defined by differences in purity, it clearly depends upon the possible exercise of power: the power to devolve impurity downwards. As Omvedt puts it, it is "impossible to speak of a 'caste system' and a 'class structure' as separate concrete phenomena, the two were in fact interwoven".

The relationships thus defined schematically in the *varna* model may be observed in practice in the relationships between local caste communities, at the level of a village or a small group of villages, in what has been called the *jajmani* system (see the classic works on this by Wiser, 1936; Beidelman, 1959; and recent contributions by Commander, 1983, and Good, 1982). This system centres on those who are in the structural position of the *kshatriya* in the *varna* model, the members of the locally dominant caste – the caste community which, through its control over the land, also exercises control over labour (see Srinivas, 1959; and Beck, 1972, 15–16; and Fuller, in Part I of this volume). In return for labour services and for religious services supplied by *brahmin* priests and by other specialists whose activities have a religious as well as a purely economic content, the land-controlling members of the dominant caste supply traditionally defined shares in the product of the land (see Breman, in the next chapter but one: "In south Gujarat it was the Anavil *brahmins* who, as dominant landholders, regulated the distribution of agricultural produce").

Epstein (1967) has shown how this system of economic and moral transactions may operate in practice as a system of patronage which supplies minimum guarantees of the "right to subsistence" to all the members of a village (see also Fuller, in Part I of this volume, and Harriss, 1982, 235–44). Thus, following the general propositions advanced by Scott concerning the "moral economy of the peasantry" and the significance of patronage in legitimating the social order (Scott, 1976), it can be argued that caste relationships in the *jajmani* system are held to be legitimate because they supply "the right to subsistence", and in spite of the fact that they are predicated upon real material inequality. As Fuller observes: "within the village, the caste system promoted both empirically and ideologically through the set of values intrinsic to it, ties which were not based merely or exclusively on force". The first study by Breman analyzes the breakdown of such a system of relationships, under the impact of commercialization, without, however, there being any immediate challenge to the power of the land-controllers following the disintegration of patronage: "the agricultural labourers cannot escape the control of the dominant landowners. Attachment as farm servants symbolises the dependent condition in which more or less the great majority of Dublas lives. They still depend on the landlords for their livelihood." The significance of the acute weakness of labour in the South Asian context for capitalist development is discussed by Washbrook (1988).

For orthodox Hindus the doctrine of *karma* entails the belief that the individual goes through a cycle of birth and rebirth, occupying different positions in the hierarchy of creation in different existences according to action in past lives – essentially the extent to which the individual acted in conformity with the *dharma* associated with his/her station. The concept of *dharma* is one which it is difficult to translate, though it conveys the sense of "duty" (the obligations associated with particular social positions). According to Hindu belief action in conformity with *dharma* carries the individual towards *moksha*: "*Moksha* is the realisation of the purpose of each individual. On the attainment of perfection the historical existence terminates" (Radhakrishnan, 1927, 46). Following from these essential ideas, all individuals may be seen as being born endowed with a particular physical and moral substance or "quality" which reflects their past actions. This "substance" may be affected by relationships with others imbued with a different quality, and interactions are therefore carefully regulated. Reproduction vitally affects substance and there is thus a rule of endogamy, restricting marriage to the confines of a group of people considered to be of closely similar "quality". It is this rule which, in principle, defines the effective caste communities (those groups often called *jati* in the literature).

But substance is affected by a wide range of possible action and contacts between people. Close physical contacts with others may pollute individual substance, and there are therefore restrictions on them, and on the extent to which commensality between people is possible. These restrictions are roughly scaled according to the distance which is thought to obtain between groups of people in terms of their substance (or relative purity/impurity). Thus people who believe themselves to be of comparable substance may share food or water, but people who think of themselves as having a high moral standing may refuse to take certain items of food or drinking water from others whom they think of as having a lower, more polluted substance. Broadly, those actions, too, which involve close contact with "gross biological matter" (especially blood, excrement and hair, pieces of skin and nails – that can be detached from the body) are believed to be polluting, and those who believe themselves to be of a high moral standing must seek to avoid such contacts.

The principal features of caste relations follow from these ideas. As Dumont and Pocock (1957) argued, caste relations are defined by separation, hierarchy and an hereditary division of labour. Separation between groups and their hierarchical organization follow from beliefs about the inherent differences of moral substance between individuals and groups, and the division of labour is related to these differences, too, because different activities involve varying degrees of contact with biological matter, which, in turn, affect moral substance. Dumont and Pocock argue that at a more abstract level caste relations are structured by a conceptual opposition – pure/impure.

But the question of the relationships between caste ideology and what Dumont refers to as "the non-ideological aspects" of social reality is clearly a vital one. We have argued that the *varna* model shows how caste relations also depend on the exercise of power. Fuller in his chapter in Part I of this volume takes this argument much further. His case is that "the structure of the distributive politico-economic system" of pre-colonial India cannot be derived from the caste system in the way that Dumont suggests: "it must be explained by the competition for control over produce and people. For although it is true that political positions were often legitimized *post facto* in terms of caste or religion, this does not mean that the political hierarchy was derived from the latter". Fuller shows that there was in pre-British India a distributive system that operated both above and within the village. But the supra-local part of this system was destroyed by the British when they destroyed the top half of the political system. Anthropological observers, unaware of this, have generally failed to recognise that the local *jajmani* system is only one half of the pre-British distributive system and, in fact, that their "traditional India" of the village with its *jajmani* system and local political structure centred on the dominant caste "is not traditional at all, but . . . mainly a creation of the British Raj". It has been a crucial misperception for:

> if one focuses attention on what has been taken to be traditional . . . it is easy to conclude that caste is overwhelmingly significant in the social structure . . . [and it] . . . appears to be relatively autonomous. It is not inextricably linked to other social institutions, and in particular not to the system of control over land. In pre-British India, however, the economic and political functions of caste could not be separated from the agrarian system, for the distribution of economic and political power was a function of control over land as much as, if not more than, it was of caste.

Dumont's argument that caste ideology "encompasses" power, will not do.

The religious beliefs and ideas associated with caste certainly represent a powerful screen of material exploitation, as Mencher (1974) has argued. The *jajmani* system, where it is social practice (as it is still in some south Indian villages; Harriss, 1982, ch. 6), constitutes a system of patronage which may legitimate the social order and its inherent inequalities. Beyond this, caste ideas offer a well-defined religious explanation for different social positions. In so far as people really believe these ideas then it might be argued that power is not being exercised and that people regard their different positions as natural. The view that caste ideas constitute an hegemonic ideology gains support from the observation that caste relations are reproduced amongst those at the very bottom of the social order – amongst those considered "untouchable". Moffatt (1979) has shown how untouchable communities, too, are organized on the same principles of separation as the society as a whole. But as Lukes (1974) has pointed out, we cannot, finally, accept that power is *not* being exercised in caste relations because there are too many instances, recorded over a long historical period, of individuals and groups having sought to change their positions within the system. Power, clearly, is exercised in caste relations when it is known that subordinates within the system do seek to act in ways which are held by those who are higher up in the hierarchy to be counter to their interests. It has to be recognized that caste ideas and values do not now, and have not historically, occupied the entire ideological space of Hindu society. There is a long tradition of religious movements opposed to orthodox Hinduism and the caste practices associated with it (on Veerasaivism – one of these movements – see Ramanujam, 1973). Bhakti cults constitute a devotional form of religion, opposed in important respects to orthodox Hinduism, as in the way they are anti-hierarchical and emphasize the individual rather than the group (see Holmström, 1972). In the present inconsistencies in the behaviour of high-caste people, like those described by Harriss (1982, ch. 6) when some low-caste people are treated by members of high castes with deference and respect (on account of their wealth or political influence), reinforce an awareness of alternative values and modes of action (and see Omvedt, too, on anti-caste struggles of the colonial period). Concepts of inequality and other values which are absent from caste thinking, are not excluded from Hindu thought and belief.

In sum, power clearly should not be treated as secondary and "encompassed" by ideology in the way that Dumont suggests.

Equally, though caste can be seen as a screen of exploitation, it should not be treated as a mere ephiphenomenon of fundamental class relations. As Omvedt says: "the idea that . . . 'caste is only a form, the reality is class struggle' does not explain why the form of caste has become so important, what its material base is, and how the revolutionary movement should deal with this". She offers her answers to those questions in her chapter here. The view which is reflected – though not uniformly – in all the chapters vigorously rejects the idea that caste effectively "constitutes", or defines the "structure" of Indian society. Caste is treated as a very important aspect of social relations, closely tied up with power and the control of economic resources, and subject to historical change (see Fuller in Part I). We substantially support Eric Wolf's position when he argues that:

> Caste categories involve notions of corporate membership, common descent and endogamy . . . I conclude that the caste phenomenon is tied up intimately with power and control of economic resources but that the corporate nature of descent-based groups must be taken into account in trying to understand the workings of the Indian system of classes. (Wolf, 1982, 398)

Note

1. I am grateful to Hamza Alavi, Chris Fuller, Barbara Harriss and Mark Holmström for comments on a draft of this chapter.

Class, Caste and Land in India:
An Introductory Essay[1]

Gail Omvedt

"Farmers' agitations" and "atrocities on *Harijans*" – these seem to be vying for space on the front pages of India's daily newspapers. On the one hand, in the name of "peasants unite!" rural militants have been blocking roads, burning railway stations and going on marches hundreds of miles long. On the other hand, caste, the age-old source of rural disunity, has been apparently coming to the fore in brutal attacks on low-caste labourers in Belcchi, Bajitpur, Pipra and in the massive programs in Marathwada, the campaign against giving land to the landless at Kanjhawala, and the month-long battle of *dalits* and caste Hindus in Gujarat.[2] And such agitations and attacks are occurring not only in the more feudal, backward and impoverished areas of the countryside such as Bihar but even more in the "modern" and capitalistically developed regions like Gujarat, Punjab and Maharashtra.

One thing seems clear and that is that though caste is a crucial factor in these struggles, the current events are a disproof of Western-derived academic theories of politics which have emphasized the integrative and even "democratic" role of caste.[3] Such theories, with their functionalist and idealist biases, have seen peasants as passive, villagers as torn only by factional conflicts among the rural élite, and untouchables and other low-caste labourers as too helpless and dependent to revolt. The farmers' agitations and the organizations behind them – however much they may be in the interest of and led by the rich farmers – have shown peasants ready to surpass local factionalism to go into battle. And in the case of the attacks on *dalits*, Marxist analyses have clearly shown the class factors lying behind these, the struggle between share-croppers and landlords or labourers and *kulaks* and – a qualitatively new factor – the increasing readiness of the most suppressed and proletarianized sections of Indian society to rise up and fight for their rights even in the face of the most brutal repression.

Similarly, the old models of caste-based "vote banks" and politics as a game of the village "dominant caste" are clearly incapable of explaining the varying political alignments of the last decade – the

134

swings from Indira Gandhi to Janata and back again – or the underlying factors which are influencing voting.[4] The new forms of political parties, in particular the Congress (I) and the BJP,[5] their tendencies/efforts to become cadre parties while building up a single "supreme leader" in their efforts to make ideological appeals to all sections of the population, reveal the inadequacy of the old model of the Congress and its opposition parties. These old models were themselves based on a particular image of the Indian village (in which class factors were much less significant than caste-based alignments and in which political, social and economic life was solidly controlled by a "dominant caste élite") which itself is no longer true: the village is now revealed to be increasingly torn by a complex of class and caste contradictions which are bursting out everywhere on the national political arena.

So those who claimed that "class" and "class struggle" have no place in the unique society of India have been silenced by the emergent historical reality. However, the traditional Marxist analyses are also showing themselves as inadequate. The view that though there are class differences among the peasantry (rich, poor, landless, etc.) these are non-antagonistic and the main contradiction is between "peasants" as a group and landlords has left the major communist parties tailing after the rural rich rather than building an independent political movement based on the rural toilers.[6] And the idea that in regard to atrocities "caste is only a form, the reality is class struggle" does not explain *why* the form of caste has become so important, *what* its material base is, and how the revolutionary movement should deal with this. Similarly it has to be admitted that though there is a heroic tradition in India of both anti-caste and left-led peasant and agricultural labourer struggles, these have largely also failed to deal with the present crisis – or rather, shown their limitations.

What is the connection between "class" and "caste" in rural India today, and what is its role in relation to both the old and developing forms of agrarian relations of production?

Theoretical Background

An analysis should begin with some basic definitions. First, what is *caste*? Though there is often violent disagreement among scholars, Marxist and otherwise, about the origins of caste, its relation to the rest of the social structure and in particular to the economy, there is a surprising amount of agreement about what caste actually *is*.

Caste is a system in which a person's membership in the society is mediated through his/her birth in a particular group which is assigned a particular status within a broad social hierarchy of such groups; this group has a particular "accepted" occupation or range of occupations and only within it can a person marry and carry on close social relations such as interdining. This group is *a corporate group* that has certain defined rules of behaviour for its members and exercises some degree of authority over them, including the right to expel those who defy its authority. A person is born into such a group, is a lifelong member (unless expelled) and is not able legitimately to join any other group.

The most basic groups or units of the system are not actually the *jatis* or "castes" but rather the subcastes. These are the actual functioning units of the system which regulate marriage, and are known to their members by special names (e.g. Agamudaiyan Mudaliars, Somvanshi Mahars). Their membership has been estimated at a median of between 5000 and 15,000 each (Marriott and Inden, 1974, 985). In turn, these groups are known to the broader society largely by the name of their *jati* (e.g. in the cases cited as Vellalas or Mahars). During the medieval period, when the caste system was maintained by the state, the *jatis* themselves had a concrete social existence as the basic unit of the social division of labour (and the *jati* name most commonly was an "occupational" name, meaning "peasant", "barber", "potter" or the like), but today the *jatis* exist only as clusters of subcastes. In turn these *jatis* claimed and still claim a certain broader status as Brahmans, Kshatriya, Vaishya or Shudra within the all-India hierarchical *varna* system.[7]

In pre-capitalist Indian society, unpaid surplus labour was pumped out of direct producers via a system that was itself defined and organized in terms of caste. While the subcastes were a basic unit of the kinship system, the *jati* itself was a class phenomenon and was a basic unit of the division of labour; with this, caste structured the very nature and existence of the exploiting and exploited sections. The result was that it was impossible to speak of a "caste system" and a "class structure" as separate *concrete* phenomenon; the two in fact were interwoven.

Caste-Feudal-Society

By the time of the British conquest the Indian social formation was primarily feudal in character,[8] characterized by the fact that the most important means of production, the land, was essentially controlled by exploiting classes at the village level. Periodically the ruling states (both the Mughals and Hindu states) laid claim to "ownership" of the land but in practice were not able to enforce this; while on the other hand the main producing classes (peasants, artisans and labourers) had certain types of rights to the land and to the means of production. They were primarily subordinate tenants dependent on the village feudals for their access to the land and the performance of their functions.

But the nature of these village classes and the very structuring of the relations of production they dominated were defined in terms of the caste system. To understand how this worked, we shall begin with two points about the traditional system. First, André Beteille has pointed out that along with the thousands of castes, there were also in fact indigenous "class" – type classifications that divided the rural population of India into four or five main socio-economic groups according to their position in the system of production. In Bengal these are *zamindars*, *jotedars* (most often big *ryots* or big tenants), *bargadars* (share-croppers) and *khetmajdur*; along with these of course were merchants and artisans (Beteille, 1974, 126). Almost identical classes can be identified in nearly every region of India. In all these classifications, it can be seen that there is not only a division between the exploiting classes (village landlords, merchants, priests and state officials) and others; there are also divisions among the village toilers between peasant cultivators, with peasants usually divided into two sections – artisans, and labourers – and the latter divisions coincide with *jati* divisions. A second point stressed by many scholars is that access to produce within the village was almost never on the basis of market exchange. Rather it was through caste (*jati*), the services performed by the different castes and a right to a share of the produce traditionally claimed on the basis of such services. This is often described in terms of a division of the grain heap at harvest time: members of the different castes or subcastes (from barbers to carpenters to untouchable field labourers to priests) who had performed their traditional duties throughout the year at that time claimed as their right a prescribed proportion of the grain. Besides this, they also had various other kinds of socio-economic rights, from prescribed places and tasks at village festivals to certain shares of food at specific times to (occasionally) allotment of land for self-cultivation. Of course this system did not work "automatically". In fact the allotment of the shares of grain or of other goods (along with the major share of village land, was under control of the dominant subcaste or lineage at the village level; it was these in fact who were the village feudal rulers and they are sometimes referred to as the "managerial caste" or "dominant caste".

Pavlov's analysis (1978) helps to show one important way in which this structuring differed from European feudalism. This was not simply in terms of the existence of "birth-ascribed" class membership nor in terms of the fact that religious and cultural factors shaped the economic structure – all feudal societies are "ascriptive" in some sense and in all religious and political factors directly enter into production relations. The difference was in the relationships *among* toilers. In Europe, though membership in the exploited peasantry was defined by birth, there were no such birth-limits to performance of specialist functions. A peasant might do his own carpentering or other work, or there might be specialist carpenters, but even if there were, a boy from a peasant family faced no absolute barriers to entering such occupations. In various ways guilds might regulate entry into skilled crafts, but this was not part of the basic social rules. Similarly an impoverished family that lost its land might be forced to mainly work as wage-labourers (and there were in fact wage-paid field labourers in medieval Europe), but again it was only economic obstacles which placed people in such positions or prevented them from moving out of them, and not social ones which assigned them to groups who were held to be by birth and nature fit only for tasks as labourers.

In contrast, Indian caste feudalism split the exploited classes into several permanent major sections. Pavlov decides to reserve the term "peasant" for "only the tillers of the soil among the upper castes who held the land as *rayats*" and he notes that this section constituted only a minority of the population in contrast to the European notion of the peasant as a land-tilling majority.

Below these cultivating *rayats* were inferior tenants and share-croppers of lower castes or subcastes. And along with them was another numerous section in rural society, the artisans (*kamins, balutedars*). They included a wide range of castes from relatively high-status goldsmiths down to leather-workers, rope-makers and others often classed as untouchables; but they were always socially and economically subordinated not only to the landlords but to most of the cultivating peasants as well. A very important fact stressed by Pavlov is that production of the means of production for agriculture (carts, rope, leather, iron) was carried out through the *jajmani/balutedari* system in which the craftsman was not paid in exchange for each item he produced but was considered as a village servant entitled on an ongoing, hereditary basis to rewards that included the allotment of grain at harvest time, a whole bundle of social and economic perquisites and occasionally the allotment of land for self-cultivation. In contrast to this, production of consumption goods such as cloth, jewellery etc. was nearly always carried on for exchange though again by members of specific castes (Pavlov, 1978, 51–7).

The lowest of the castes within this system were usually considered untouchable on the grounds that they performed polluting occupations, and were forced to live in separate settlements outside the village boundaries. Significantly, almost everywhere there were one or two large untouchable castes who not only did specific craft duties but were also bound to the performance of general menial labour that included acting as general plough servants and field slaves for landlord families, carrying and fetching services for the village headman and higher state officials, woodcutting and other general casual labour for the village.

Would village servants and labourers be called "peasants" in any sense? In fact their position was an ambivalent one. On the one hand they were agricultural producers in the sense that they performed functions that were crucial for agricultural production. But they had no recognized right to the land itself, and they were never considered to be "peasants" or "tillers of the soil." In contrast to European labourers and artisans, their economic position did not result from impoverishment or choice of a specialization, but was rather an ascriptive one within a system that maintained a permanent class of field labourers as well as village – resident artisans.

Thus besides the exploiting classes of merchants, Brahman administrators and landlords, there were three major sections among the exploited producers in Indian feudal society; the *kisans* or peasants; the *kamins* or artisans; and the untouchable labourers. The *kisans* were almost always drawn from the main "peasant" or landtilling caste of the region, and in fact their *jati* name was also frequently the word for "peasant" in a local language. They were Kunbis, Jats, Kurmis, Reddis, Vokkaligas, Kammas, Vanniyas, etc. and they were always classed as *shudras* in *varna* terms. Similar in status and almost in the same category were castes whose "traditional" function was that of sheep-herding, cow-herding or vegetable gardening (Malis, Yadavas, Ahirs, Dhangars etc.) but who often became cultivators and sometimes constituted the dominant caste in villages where they were a majority. It is important to note that while the *kisans* were mainly an exploited section of toilers, the village feudal classes (from *patils* to *zamindars*, *deshmukhs* and others) could be drawn from their ranks, and in this sense they had an access to economic and social mobility that other sections lacked.

Below these, the artisans were always drawn from specific castes known by the name of their function to the wider community; they were also classed as *shudra* in *varna* terms. Finally there were the labourers, who were untouchables or *ati-shudra* in *varna* terms and were the most exploited (though not the only exploited) section at the base of the system. Next to the major *kisan* caste, these were often numerically the biggest caste in the village and today also they represent castes that are quite big in the Indian context – Chamars, Chuhras, Mahars and Mangs, Malas and Madigas, Holeyas, Puleyas, Paraiyans and Pallans.

Should these three sections be called different "classes" or different sections of a single exploited class? What is important is that in the Indian caste-feudal mode of production, the economy was structured and the surplus "pumped out" in such a way that it maintained in existence such highly subdivided and unequally exploited sections of toilers. For anti-feudal struggles the conclusion is important: while it would be correct to say that in India as elsewhere "agrarian revolution" (the revolutionary transformation of relations of production on the land) was central to the anti-feudal struggle, this could not be attained simply through the abolition of landlordism. Rather it required a thorough attack on the caste system itself and a transformation of relations of production within the village and among the toiling masses in a way that would assure that artisans or village servants and labourers as well as the *kisans* could gain basic rights to the land itself and to its produce.

Colonial Rule and Anti-Feudal Struggles

Indian feudalism was not, of course, revolutionized by an indigenous development of capitalism. Rather it was transformed by the imposition of British colonial rule, which subordinated the entire Indian social formation to the needs of the development of capitalism in Britain. The concrete form in which colonial rule both sowed the seeds of capitalist development and maintained semi-feudal structures in existence in India provided the conditions under which anti-feudal as well as anti-imperialist movements developed in India. An important aspect of this was the transformation/maintenance of the caste system and its relation to the rest of the society.

First, the British abolished the pre-existing purely caste-defined access to land and other goods and imposed legal relationships of land ownership and tenancy backed up by courts operating on a definition of legal private property.[9] Along with this, new factories, mines and plantations as well as the new schools and bureaucracy recruited their workers, students and employees on a basis of formal equality in which caste membership did not in and of itself bar any section from entry. The state ceased to be a protector of the traditional caste hierarchy enveloped in the feudal relations of land control, and instead began to emerge as a colonial-bourgeois state. To this extent, new classes began to come into existence and important democratic and capitalist transformations began in India.

But these transformations were not equivalent to the abolition of caste or feudalism, and they could not automatically lead to such abolition. First, the very subordination of the Indian economy to imperialism meant that the openings in the new factories, mines and schools were limited because the growth of Indian industry was limited and because the British needed only a small section of "clerks" to man their bureaucracy. In spite of formal openness, the pre-existing power, wealth and social traditions of the upper castes gave them an overwhelming advantage in filling the higher positions opening up. The majority of the population remained dependent on agriculture. And here the British alliance, for political reasons, with the land-controlling village feudals and higher landlords and with the merchants ensured that their power was maintained at the local level. This was both an "economic" power (in fact they had control of the majority of the land) and a "political" power, for the limitations of the colonial administration meant that in most cases the village landlords with their gangs and their unquestioned social privileges normally exercised coercive and "judicial" powers as well.[10] Further, within the village much production continued to be organized via the *jajmani* system which did not really wither away until after independence, and this in turn meant a continued subordination of artisans and the untouchable labourers whose traditional caste duties became a major part of the unpaid labour (*vethbegar*) extracted by landlords.

Under British rule there was a broad correlation between caste and class which duplicated the main classes of the pre-colonial caste-feudal period. Nevertheless it was only a correlation, and not an identity, and in every caste there could be found some individuals who could get education, a little bit of land, some access to new opportunities. The fact that artisans and even untouchables had formal rights to land ownership, to education and to new occupations was connected with the emergence of "caste" and "class" as separate structures, separate but highly interconnected, and this was the material base on which the very complex anti-feudal struggles of the colonial period emerged.

These anti-feudal struggles included the *kisan* movements, the non-Brahman anti-caste movements, and the *dalit* and agricultural labourer movements. Of these, the *kisan* movements have been the most thoroughly studied; they centred on demands for abolition of *zamindari* and so primarily involved the interests of middle and rich peasants who had traditionally recognized claims to the land as tenants or as cultivators. But they also included a large number of related issues – demands for restoration of certain lands grabbed by the *zamindars*, opposition to forms of forced labour collectively termed as *vethbegar*, opposition to moneylending, demand for cheap access to water resources, etc. – and they frequently involved poor and low caste peasants. Further, both the climactic struggles of the *kisan* movement – the Tebhaga movement in Bengal and the Telengana revolt – transcended the limitations of the earlier *kisan* movement and involved large sections of the rural poor.[11]

Anti-caste movements, in particular the broad non-Brahman movements of South India, were also generally anti-feudal. Just as the *kisan* movement could generate a "united front" allying both peasants and labourers against the landlords, so the more radical non-Brahman movement could emerge as an alliance of *shudras* and *atishudras* against the high castes. For the large section of peasant and artisan masses, their oppression was in terms of caste as well as class, and as some educated sections began to develop within each *jati* these took leadership both in more conservative forms of organizations (caste associations which essentially accepted the caste hierarchy but sought to use caste identity to compete for a higher position within it) as well as in more radical challenges to the system itself. Toilers as well as many educated sections began to reject their hitherto accepted position as *shudras* within an established *varna* hierarchy and to see themselves as non-Brahmans or non-Aryans or *bahujan samaj* fighting an exploiting Aryan élite or *shetji–bhatji* class which had organized the caste system as a means of subjugating and dividing them.[12] The Satyashodhak Samaj in Maharashtra and the Self-Respect movement in Tamilnadu[13] at times took the place of the *kisan sabhas* in these areas and engaged in sometimes direct attacks on moneylenders or landlords as well as in a fierce challenge to the ritual status of the élite. In north India anti-caste organizations generally took a more conservative form in which the middle castes mainly claimed *kshatriya* status. In Bihar the middle peasant *kisans* organized through the Triveni Sangh as well as in the Kisan Sabha, while in north-west India the Arya Samaj and Kisan Sabhas became interwoven expressions of the (mainly Jat) *kisans* against their (mainly Rajput) feudal exploiters.

At the same time the untouchable labourers, inspired by such struggles but only partially included in them, began to organize separately. Movements based on their notion of themselves is the original "sons of the soil" (Adi-Andhras, Adi-Hindus, Ad-Dharm, etc.) began to emerge in the 1920s, and a new term expressing a totality of socio-economic exploitation, *dalit*, began to be used from about 1930 in Maharashtra and north India. Struggles began to take place not only in the towns to claim education, legal rights or use of tanks, and temples (the Mahad *satyagraha*, the Vaikom *satyagraha*), but also in the villages to claim land (either forest land or cultivable waste), higher wages and the ending of *vethbegar*. The late 1930s, the same period in which the All-India *Kisan Sabha* emerged as a united organization under left leadership, saw the emergence of separate *dalit*-based agricultural labourer organizations in Bihar (led by Jagjivan Ram)[14] and Andhra (led by Ranga and the Communists). In the same period Ambedkar founded the Independent Labour Party to link *dalit*, peasants and workers' struggles. Finally, people in the tribal areas, now subordinated to new consolidated feudal exploitation, also began to organize in a new fashion that stressed their identity as adivasis.

The Telengana revolt (1946–50) was in many ways a climax of all these movements. While both the *Kisan Sabha* and agricultural labour organization had been strong in the Andhra region, in Telengana itself the mass organization which was a base for the revolt was the Andhra Mahasabha – which combined social reform, anti-caste and nationalist features. It had earlier taken up anti-untouchability and anti-*vethbegar* as well as cultural campaigns; and to these a new Communist leadership linked militancy and anti-landlord struggles. Thus *dalits*, artisans and the landless as well as substantial village landholders were involved in the revolt, and when the revolutionaries took up both abolition of *zamindari* and distribution of "excess land" to the landless – the first time this really was brought forward as an issue in the struggle – in practice they were meeting the needs for land of the low castes as well as the cultivating *kisans*.

But in spite of these achievements and in spite of the long history of sustained struggles, by and large they remained under rich-peasant and middle-class hegemony. In the end it was Gandhi and the Congress, rather than the socialists and Communists, who maintained leadership in the anti-imperialist as well as over the anti-feudal struggles.

This Gandhian leadership succeeded quite brilliantly in forging a policy for a bourgeois form of anti-feudal and national struggle that did bring together under Congress leadership all aspects of the anti-feudal movements but only in a distorted, conservative and fragmentizing manner. One aspect of Gandhi's genius was in fact that he could give an all-round programme that promised something for every section of society. In the case of the *kisan* movement, the Congress supported or even organized struggles where they had no choice or where they could be controlled, and always with certain conservative policies: to accept the principle of compensation and the ultimate right of landlords, to avoid "violence", etc. (Desai, 1978). At the same time it sought to avoid connecting the *kisan* movement with that of the issues of labourers. In turn the Congress very cautiously encouraged a limited form of organizing agricultural labourers but only (under Jagjivan Ram) where this was useful as a counter to a left-led *Kisan Sabha*. But for the *dalits* as such, Gandhi's main emphasis was to avoid their economic issues entirely; to avoid also any militant action against caste oppression as such; and in fact to avoid organizing them altogether except as *"Harijans"* who were objects of paternalistic sympathy and "uplift" from caste Hindus who were consciously given control of the organizations such as the *Harijan Sevak Sangh*. The brilliance of Gandhi's "constructive programme", (from the viewpoint of the bourgeoisie) was that it provided something for the *dalits* and those who were motivated by their plight, but only in a way that increased their subordination to the rural élite and diverted them from radical struggles. In other words, the Congress policy almost consciously fostered disunity among the various sections of the toiling masses while at the same time preaching a harmony with the exploited; while the left led many militant struggles and sought to intensify contradictions in the countryside according to their understanding but failed to build up a militant unity of all sections of the oppressed.[15]

Thus the promise inherent in the mighty Telengana revolt, in the all-round participation of Communists in anti-landlord and anti-untouchability struggles among agricultural labourers and peasants in such areas as Andhra and Kerala, or in the attempt of Ambedkar in the late 1930s to formulate a programme to unite workers, peasants and *dalits* remained unfulfilled. Congress hegemony was maintained; the *kisan* movement ended up serving the needs of the rich peasants; the non-Brahman movements fell under middle-class leadership and the *dalit* and anti-caste movements in general failed to become a thorough *dalit* liberation movement. When independence was won in 1947 it was under the domination of the bourgeoisie and in the form of a bourgeois state.

Caste and Class in Post-Colonial India

A close look at the notorious "atrocities against *Harijans*" that seem to be going on everywhere today will reveal the significant changes that have occurred in Indian agriculture since Independence. The cases of Kilvenmani, Belchi, Bajitpur, Pipra may appear to be feudal in the violent, *goonda* nature of the onslaught, but the very ferocity of the attacks shows the growing rural tensions and the degree to which *dalit* labourers are beginning to challenge the village power-holders. In the case of Kanjhawala, Marathwada, and now Gujarat, a new phenomenon is evident: along with riots and pogroms, are sustained organized campaigns, demonstrations, mass-oriented slogans designed to win over the caste Hindu toilers against the *dalits*. And everywhere a simple question reveals a crucial difference from the feudal, pre-Independence period: who is attacking the dalits? Now it is no longer Brahmans, Rajputs, Deshmukhs, Vellalas or high-caste landlords, but most often the middle castes, the new rich farmers, those who were once middle peasants and tenants fighting against landlords and who now still call themselves *bahujan samaj*, *kisan* and *shetkari*. Those who were once allies of *dalits* in the anti-feudal struggle now appear to be the main enemy.

These attacks themselves show the coming of capitalist relations in agriculture. They indicate that the main lines of conflict are no longer between middle- and low-caste peasants on one side and high-caste landlords on the other, but are now between the rich farmers and the agricultural labourers/poor peasants. And they show that the caste structure of rural India has changed in this new emerging class struggle; caste is one of the strongest weapons which the rich are using to divide and attack the rural poor.

In very general terms, ignoring regional variations for a moment, we can define the new shape of agrarian classes and their caste composition (see Omvedt, 1980, for empirical data). First about 15 per cent of all rural families can be classed as rich farmer families, including capitalist farmers, capitalist landlords, a minority of feudal landlords existing in more backward areas, and families who also include merchants and rural employees. In caste terms this section includes both the traditional feudal classes (Brahmans, Rajputs, Vellalas, etc.) as well as the middle *kisan* castes. But it is the *kisan* castes who are now dominant among them (there are only a few, a minute proportion, a family from artisan caste or *dalit* background in this class) especially in the more capitalist, regions, where Patidars, Marathas, Jats, Vokkaligas, Lingayats, Kammas, Reddis, etc. seem almost equivalent to the new *kulak* farmers.

These rich farmers have an ambivalent, almost dual political character. On the one hand the proportion of ex-tenants and peasants among them, the fact that they have a heritage of struggle against landlords and the upper castes, allows them to take on a surface appearance of being "peasants" (*kisans, shetkari, bahujan samaj*) and leaders, not simply oppressors, of the rural masses. Their role in the new capitalist institutions of dominance (*gram panchayats* cooperatives etc.), the fact that they are now largely educated, their ability to exercise a sophisticated, coopting form of rural power in which some patronage is dispensed and some members of low castes are given a place, is part of this. But on the other hand, their own background as village power-holders and their readiness to take on even the most brutal feudal traits of the classes they once fought against means that they are also ready to exercise their power in the most corrupt, violent and gangster forms. Similarly, their relative caste homogeneity in many regions means they are often able to put on an appearance of being less "casteist", but this is the section that most strongly uses caste associations and caste appeals to rally people behind them, that relies on kinship and caste ties for "influence" in education, employment and other concessions, and gives the strongest support to all the religious and cultural institutions that uphold casteism. Their specific class interests lead them into a dual political battle, facing the urban industrial bourgeoisie on the one hand in claiming more credit and higher prices (though here their contradiction is non-antagonistic) and facing the rural semi-proletariat on the other. Generally they attempt to use a rhetoric of "peasant unity" to win over middle peasants and sometimes poor peasants to their side, but with this also they use caste ties and appeals to win over the poor peasants and agricultural labourers of their own caste in dividing and concentrating their attack on *dalit* labourers.

Middle peasants, about 25 per cent of all rural families, are again primarily of *kisan* caste background but include a small but significant proportion of artisan castes and other allied castes and even some *dalits*. Though they are continually threatened with problems of unemployment, price-rise, and with the corruption and bossism of the rich farmers, their own aspirations as petty-property holders and their caste ties with the rich farmers at present mainly lead them to tail after this class.

Finally, the poor peasants and agricultural labourers, the proletarianized rural majority, perhaps 60 per cent of rural households, are the most divided in Caste terms. They include not only *dalits* and *adivasis*, but Muslims and other minorities, and members of all the former Hindu *shudra* castes, both artisans and the traditional *kisan* castes. In capitalist areas (such as western Maharashtra) one can find that not only are the "dominant" caste like Marathas fully differentiated in class terms, but in each village practically every clan of this caste may be equally differentiated, including both rich farmers, middle peasants and landless agricultural labourers.

Among the rural poor toilers, the continued existence of caste divisions and the continued, if varying forms of the special oppression of *dalit* labourers means that a struggle against social cultural oppression and an anti-caste struggle is a crucial part of their general battle for liberation. But this is no longer a simple anti-feudal struggle as before. For one thing the main enemies now are the rich farmers, including capitalist farmers, and the bourgeois state as such, for another, the *dalits* can no longer find their allies as the ex-*shudra* peasantry fighting against the "twice-born". Now the question has become one of uniting the *dalits* – and breaking the false, cross-class "caste unity" of the middle castes in order to bring the middle-caste toilers into alliance with *dalits*; it is now a question of a *dalit* liberation movement along with the formation of a broader militant class unity among the rural poor under the slogan of "*dalit–shramik* unity". So far, however, this has barely begun.

Editors' Notes

1. The major formulations of this chapter were initially developed in an article co-authored with Bharat Patankai, "The *dalit* Liberation Movement in the Colonial Period" and revised and elaborated in the course of our mutual discussions. The chapter first appeared in a more extended form in Omvedt, G. (ed.) *Land, Caste and Politics in Indian States* (Delhi: University of Delhi, Department of Political Science, 1982; Authors Guild Publications, Delhi 110035).

2. The references here are, first, to the so-called "Farmers' Movements" which have sprung up in several regions of India since the mid-1970s and have articulated demands over farm prices, inputs costs, electricity tariffs and the repayment of debts to public credit institutions (on which see the commentary by Harriss in his chapter in Part II); and, second, to notorious incidents of inter-caste violence, in Bihar, in Marathwada, in Maharashtra in 1978 (see the references in the chapter by Engineer in Part IV), and in Gujarat (on which see the short discussion by Joshi in her chapter in Part IV).

3. Important exemplars of the "Western-derived academic theories" referred to are: Barrington Moore, Jr, 1966, *Social Origins of Dictatorships and Democracy* (Boston: Beacon Press); and Rudolph, L. and S. H., 1967.

4. An influential statement of what Omvedt refers to as "the old models" was in the work of F. G. Bailey. See his "Politics and Society in Contemporary Orissa", in C. H. Philips (ed.), *Politics and Society in India* (London: Allen & Unwin, 1963).
5. The Bharatiya Janata party, on which see note 5 to the chapter by Engineer in Part IV.
6. The chapter by Gough in Part V shows up the ambiguities in the agrarian programmes of the Indian communist parties to which Omvedt refers here.
7. See the explanation of the *varna* system given by Harriss in the preceding chapter.
8. Omvedt claims that "there is broad agreement amongst Marxist scholars" on this characterization of the Indian social formation of the eighteenth century, but there remains a good deal of controversy on the point. See H. Mukhia, 1981, "Was there Feudalism in Indian History?", *Journal of Peasant Studies*, 8, 3, 273–310.
9. Scholars now argue that the institution of private property was not unknown in pre-colonial India. See, for example, C. J. Baker, 1984.
10. An excellent account of the relations between the British administration and village notables is in Washbrook's chapter on "The Governance of Madras" in his *The Emergence of Provincial Politics: the Madras Presidency 1870–1920* (Cambridge: Cambridge University Press, 1976).
11. The contemporary historiography of the *kisan* struggles of the later colonial period is synthesized by S. Sarkar, 1983. Hamza Alavi's "Peasants and Revolution", *Socialist Register, 1965*, offers one analytical account of the Tebhaga and Telengana struggles. See also D. N. Dhanagare, *Peasant Movements in India 1920–1950* (Delhi: Oxford University Press, 1983) especially chapters VII and VIII.
12. On the non-Brahmin Movement in Western India see Gail Omvedt, *Cultural Revolt in a Colonial Society: The non-Brahman Movement in Western India 1870–1930* (Pune: Scientific Socialist Education Trust, 1976); and in Southern India: M. R. Barnett (1977).
13. See Editors' Notes to the chapter by Washbrook in Part IV.
14. Jagjivan Ram was to become one of the most powerful politicians in India in the 1960s and 1970s. He held a number of senior cabinet posts.
15. See S. Sarkar, *Modern India* for an extended analysis on these lines.

The Disintegration of the *Hali* System[1]

Jan Breman

In the earliest reports of British administrators, during the first decades of the nineteenth century, there was mention of a system of attachment – *hali-pratha* – which later became known as a form of bondage.

Hali was the term applied to a farm servant who, with his family, was in the permanent employ of a landlord, a *dhaniamo*. The service was not contracted for a definite period; as a rule it continued indefinitely. It usually began when an agricultural labourer wished to marry and found a master who would pay for the marriage. The debt thus incurred attached the servant to the master for life. It increased in the course of the years, so that repayment was practically impossible. The service relationship ended only when the *hali* was taken over by another master. Although in such a case the original master received compensation, the transfer was not a business transaction; in several reports it was stated emphatically that *halis* were never sold.

Not only was entering into bondage the beginning of a lifelong service relationship, but the unfree elements in it were reinforced by some hereditary features. It is true that the debt incurred by the *hali* during his lifetime could not be passed on to the next generation, but the master had a claim to the son of his servant, as it was thanks to the master's beneficence that the boy had grown up, living on the *dhamiamo*'s food. When the son married, usually at the age of 16, it was therefore natural that he should enter the employ of his father's master. Only when the master did not need another servant was the boy free to look for another master. These hereditary features were so essential to the relationship that, according to some reports, only those agricultural labourers who had been attached to the same family from father to son were called *halis*.

As elsewhere in India, the servants came from castes of tribal origin. Most of the *halis* in the plain of south Gujarat were Dublas but not all Dublas were permanently attached to a master. Lack of data makes it impossible to determine proportions; we can only say with certainty that bondage was the prevailing service relationship. There was, however, no clear-cut difference between bound and free agricultural labourers. The *chuta halis* (literally: free *halis*) belonged to the latter category. They, too, were indebted to a landowner, though not as deeply as the *bhandela halis*, the bonded servants. Unlike the latter, they did not work for the same farmer all the year round, but only when he needed them, and at other times they had to provide for themselves. The difference is not always very clear, but what it amounts to is that the *chuta halis* were less bound and, on the other hand, had less security.

The servants were invariably in the employ of members of prominent castes. In the northern part of the plain, *halis* worked for Kanbi landowners, but it was pre-eminently the Anavil Brahmans who employed *halis*. They were the dominant caste in south Gujarat and, as such, the owners of the best and largest plots of land. The *hali* system, in other words, is especially identified with these two agrarian castes. *Hali* means literally, "he who handles the plough (*hal*)". It is not an arbitrary designation, but indicates an activity which members of high castes in many regions of India try to avoid because of its impure character. The *hali* bound not only himself, but also his wife and children. The farm servant worked chiefly on the land, but he was also the personal servant of the landlord – an odd-job man who attended him, ran errands for him, in short, assisted his master in everying and did what could reasonably be expected from him. Neither the work nor the working-hours of the *hali* were clearly defined. At all times of the day, and if necessary of the night, he was at his master's beck and call, always ready to carry out orders.

His wife, the *harekwali*, served as maid in the house of the master, usually only in the mornings. Her tasks ranged from grinding grain, fetching water, sweeping the floor, washing up after meals, and cleaning the stable to emptying the chamber pot on the dunghill. She did the rough household work which elsewhere was done by members of the impure castes. Moreover, she helped out on the land in the busy season.

The servant's daughter assisted her mother in the household of the master. His son – as *govalio* (cowherd) – tended the cattle and did various light jobs. In this period the master could test him to see whether he qualified both on ability and in personal behaviour for later employment as a servant.

Attachment for an indeterminate period, severance of the relationship only in exceptional cases and often its prolongation into following generations, work obligations for the servant's whole family, and finally the non-specific and exchangeable nature of the service were the chief elements of servitude in the past.

The counterservice expected from the master could be summarized in the obligation to provide for his servants. As one of the first reports on the *hali* system commented, "rearing and feeding in years of scarcity and the charges of settling them in marriage (about 30 rupees) are all borne by the master." On the days that the *hali* worked, he was entitled to an allowance of grain – the *bhata* – which varied according to the size of his family. Instead of this grain he sometimes received a piece of land to till with his master's land; he was allowed to keep the produce for himself. In addition, he was given a slight breakfast in the master's house, and in the busy season also a midday meal on the land.

The master allotted him a site where he could build his hut, and supplied the materials for it. Each year the *hali* received some clothing: a headcloth, a jacket, a loincloth, a scarf for the winter, and a pair of shoes. His wife was entitled to a *sari* and some brass ornaments every year, and a meal daily after work. Further, the *hali* was allowed to gather firewood on the master's land. When the day's labour was over he received some tobacco and sometimes some toddy (fermented coconut milk). When he was ill, the master provided medicines, and if he lived to old age, the master gave him food every day when he could no longer work. As is evidenced by the extent of the benefits enjoyed by the *hali*, he received total care, that is to say, he depended for his every need on what the master put into his hands.

The Anavil landlords seem to have had the *halis* completely in their power. The members of the tribal and landless Dubla caste had no choice but to put themselves in the keeping of a master. This explains at the same time why the relationship began and continued with the approval of the servant. The tie attaching him to the master became increasingly close, and only on the master's initiative could it be severed. It is true that in the course of time the amount of support to which the *hali* was entitled had become standardized, but if necessary he had to accept less. The exceedingly unequal division of mutual rights and obligations was due to the difference in position between *dhaniamo* and *hali*. In theory, the right of the servant was the obligation of the master, but the former was not guaranteed in any way. The great economic, political, and social power of the Anavil made it possible for him to dictate, and in any case interpret, the service conditions one-sidedly. His obligations were rather in the nature of favours to be granted as he thought fit. The paternalistic attitude of the master could barely conceal the elements of enforcement that were inherent in the relationship. The servant was at his master's beck and call. Together with his family he had to comply with the latter's every wish, which might include sexual intercourse with the *hali*'s wife.

On the other hand, the element of patronage prevented any pronounced tyranny and complete exploitation, which would have detracted from the esteem in which the Anavil was held. Then, too, he had to rely on the support of his following. The patron's position stood or fell by his willingness to provide for and aid a group of followers, to let them participate in his goods, his power, and his esteem. The master must carry out a minimum of the obligations he owed to his servant. In the end, it was on the latter's labour that the success of the crop depended. In the traditional agrarian system, patronage not only served as a corrective of the lopsided distribution of scarce goods in traditional village India, but also accentuated inequality in all spheres of life. The presence and the symbols of subordination of the clients enabled the patron to demonstrate his superiority. As the economic and ritual distance between them widened, the relationship came to contain an element of exploitation, which in the case of the low-classed agricultural labourers was mitigated only by the mutual intimacy and sympathy inherent in the personal, usually hereditary tie with the landlord's family.

In south Gujarat it was the Anavil Brahmans who, as the dominant landowners, regulated the distribution of agrarian produce. It would be wrong to conclude that instead of production based on profit for a few, fulfilment of the material needs of all was aimed at. The Anavils were not altruistic to that extent. A more plausible explanation is rather that, for the landlords, maximization of income took second place to maximization of prestige and power, which in the nineteenth century amounted to behaviour as a patron in the village. This objective required a minimal fulfilment of the need of clients for aid and protection. At that time, the Dubla *halis* were objects in the endeavour of the members of the dominant caste to acquire more power and esteem, not subjects in a surplus-oriented market economy.

On the basis of all these considerations it can be concluded that servitude in south Gujarat during the nineteenth century was essentially a form of unfree labour that was complicated and mitigated by a relationship of patronage.

Depatronization

The disintegration of the *hali* system marked the disappearance of patronage. The possibility of selling an increasing proportion of the agrarian output on the market led to commercialization of the relationships between landlords and agricultural labourers. The allowance paid to Dublas, which in the subsistence economy had been based on various "obligations" towards the landlord, increasingly took on the character of a wage payment in exchange for a labour performance in the market economy, and it was paid in money. The amount was no longer related to the minimally defined needs of the agricultural labourers, but was based on the supply of labour and on the control exerted over them by the landlords.

The patron–client relationship has not disappeared in all respects, but the locus of patronage has shifted to a supralocal level and is framed in a more limited context, being chiefly economic or political in nature. I have related "depatronization" to an enlargement of scale which put an end to the closed nature of the traditional social and economic order, but both the course of this process and its results were determined to a large extent by the reactions of the parties involved towards these outside influences.

The Landlords There is no doubt that the landlords desired and promoted the disruption of the *hali* system. The change in the scale of preferences of the members of the dominant caste – high investments in education and in a consumption pattern adopted from the urban culture – was to the detriment of their subordinates. The changeover to market production made possible alternative ways of spending the crop profits and diminished the superiors' social responsibility towards their servants. Many Anavils seized the opportunity of cultivating fruit trees so as to free themselves from agricultural labour. Even without employing farm servants they can now lead a landlord's life as behoves a member of the dominant caste.

Their integration in the urban environment has given importance to other standards of values than the traditional ones, especially as to education, income, and a profession outside agriculture. The village community is now only in part the framework in which the position of the Anavils is determined. The dependence of members of other castes is no longer an aim in itself, but has become a means to enhance the masters' own prosperity and to finance preparation of their children for non-agrarian professions. Ostentatious leisure is now possible without a landlord's life, and the desire for conspicuous consumption is satisfied by the display of riches. Even where the landlords are still actively concerned in agriculture, the grip of the members of the dominant caste on the Dublas has become more depersonalized, being dictated by income maximization. The agricultural labourers' right to work is no longer recognized, their social security no longer guaranteed. In the endeavour of the members of the dominant castes to attain more esteem and influence within and outside the village, the Dublas have been changed from subjects into objects.

The Agricultural Labourers   Descriptions of the disappearance of the *hali* system often create the impression that it was the agricultural labourers who initiated it – that when alternative employment arose, increasing numbers of them severed the relationship of servitude. My data confirm this assumption only to a limited extent. The need of the local landlords determines whether any Dublas succeed in finding work outside the village, and if so, what proportion of them. Once a migration tradition has arisen, this changes. Contact with alternative sources of income in the cities then takes place through the Dublas' own mediators, the *mukadams*, and is no longer controlled by the Anavils. Even then, escape is often only temporary, because of the unskilled, low-paid, and unstable character of urban employment that is available to Dublas. The termination of the traditional service relationship may also be connected with the Dublas in another way. It might be argued that the rapid growth of their number makes it impossible for the landlords to provide for them all. This fact undoubtedly reinforced the effect of "depatronization," but it did not cause it. The agricultural economy of south Gujarat could have been much more labour-intensive if the crop system had been different. The abundant supply of labour, in other words, is not traceable simply to the rapid demographic growth of the population of agricultural labourers, but is also connected with the preference of the dominant landowners for pursuing a kind of agriculture that is not highly intensive.

Although indeed aspirations have been aroused among the Dublas that are incompatible with the bondage inherent in attachment, with dependence, and with subordination in general, it seems that the members of that caste were above all subjected to the process of depatronization. In more than one respect they were the losing party.

The Present Situation

What relations between landlords and agricultural labourers have replaced the *hali* system? – this was the question that I posed at the beginning of my field work. The labour system in a market economy is primarily determined by labour supply and demand. Whereas in some regions the demand has remained about equal, and in other parts of south Gujarat has considerably shrunk, the caste from which the labourers were traditionally recruited has grown rapidly. Opportunities for employment outside agriculture have not kept pace with these developments. The kind of work available to Dublas in the urban centres reduces them to a life of pauperism, and their condition is not much better than that of the rural Dublas, whose labour conditions are imposed by the landlords. The living standard of the agricultural labourers, low to begin with, deteriorated further when allowances in kind were replaced by money wages. Most of them are continually indebted, and this is the main reason why, in budget calculations of households of agricultural labourers, expenditure always turns out to exceed income. The debt binds the Dublas and provides the landlords with a means of pressure. In the long term it is cheaper and safer for the landlords to give a limited loan to a farm servant than to hire day-labourers. Moreover, they select the most industrious and obedient labourers for farm service.

The mutual rights and obligations have always been one-sidedly weighted. Disguised exploitation could be perceived in the *hali* system. On the other hand, patronage-like elements still occur in the present relations between landlords and agricultural labourers. I know of a number of Anavils who still feel obliged to aid and protect their subordinates, and these servants, in their turn, sometimes speak of their masters in terms of affection and devotion. As for the landlords' endeavour to acquire political support within the village for the purpose of obtaining advantages outside, it might be described as patronage for new ends.

To the conclusion that exploitation was inherent in the *hali* system, and that patronage may occur in a situation of exploitation, should be added the comment that the difference between past and present is more than one of degree.

It would, therefore, be incorrect to interpret as a form of patronage the network of obligations with which the Anavils have surrounded themselves. Although the landlords wish to preserve their traditional rights, they are not prepared to accept the attendant responsibility for the well-being of the Dublas who depend on them. On the contrary, they try to limit their obligations to the utmost, that is to say, to specify them and reduce them to a minimum. In other words, the Anavils do not behave as patrons, but still expect a maximal benefit of varied counterservices. Their demands increase as the dependence of their subordinates grows. All agricultural labourers among the Dublas depend on them, but dependence is particularly inescapable for farm servants. They are bound to about the same extent as the *halis* were, but they do not receive the aid and protection that their predecessors enjoyed. The farm servants in their turn therefore try to confine themselves as much as possible to a fixed amount of work, to render their obligation specific instead of diffuse. Whenever possible, they sabotage any claims by the master that exceed that amount. Both parties have exorbitant expectations towards each other, but they try to get away with fulfilling partial roles as employer and employee, respectively. In the end the Anavils, by virtue of their dominance, succeed better at this than do the Dublas. The risk of subsistence has been shifted onto the agricultural labourers. The widening social gap is even harder for the Dublas to accept than is the growing economc disparity. The Anavil who used to work alongside his subordinate now keeps aloof from agricultural labour. By freeing himself as much as possible from his undignified work the landlord has at the same time made the landless labourers more conscious of their humble position.

The Dublas are increasingly aware of the fact that their subjection is one of the main causes of their low social status. Economic disadvantages aside, weakness and dependence are looked upon as dishonourable and deplorable. Their resistance takes various forms. They no longer submit to beatings, nor do they tolerate landlords maintaining sexual relations with Dubla women. In the tense situation that now exists, incidents of this nature occasionally lead to sudden and violent explosions.

To sum up, however, the agricultural labourers cannot escape the control of the dominant landowners. Attachment as farm servants symbolizes the dependent condition in which more or less the great majority of Dublas lives. They still depend on the landlords for their livelihood. Those who have escaped and have found work outside the village and agriculture are highly esteemed by their fellow caste members but are looked upon with great irritation by the local power élite. When the members of the dominant caste oriented themselves towards the urban environment while maintaining their interests in the village community, their indifference to the fate of the Dublas became even more evident. Dependence in an economic sense is used by the landlords to further political ends as well. This explains why the Anavils, though not very numerous, have largely been able to maintain their supremacy in the rural area of south Gujarat. They mobilize the support of the members of the lower castes to legitimize their dominance, and thus to perpetuate it in the new political structure.

The process of "depatronization" has left the agricultural labourers in a condition of isolation. The landlords are averse to being reminded of their former obligation to look after the interests of their subordinates, and sometimes flatly refuse to intercede for them with a third party. Nor are there any indications that the Dublas are trying to join forces with other weak categories, for instance the small farmers. The basis for such a collaboration is lacking.

The Dublas have not succeeded in turning their numerical strength into political power. Nor has mobilization of their dissatisfaction by political parties yet been attempted. Especially in the Surat district, communist leaders have tried in recent years to win agricultural labourers over to their party, but in the state of Gujarat this party is too weak to have any influence. The votes of the Dublas in the villages are controlled by the landlords or by social workers. The emancipation movement that is operating in south Sujarat has founded a society to promote the welfare of Dublas (*Halpati seva sangh*), with a leadership consisting mainly of social workers and landlords who are affiliated to the Congress Party. At a conference that I attended, for instance, the Dublas were exhorted by the guest of honour, Morarji Desai, to break their bonds of dependence and not to submit to the bad treatment that falls to their lot, but at the same time they were urged to be patient. To control the increasing protest and rebelliousness seems to be the main function of this organization, but stabilization of the existing relationships amounts, for the Dublas, to stagnation, if not to deterioration of their condition.

The landless labourers have no access to the centres of power, and the isolation in which they find themselves is part of their economic and social pauperism. If we take their rapidly growing numbers into account as well, a prognosis cannot be other than pessimistic. It seems unlikely that the Dublas will soon know better times. Legislation which will guarantee a higher wage for the agricultural labourers is inadequate, as are other measures aimed at bettering their lot. Government intervention to this effect may aid in improving their material circumstances, but it must include economic and social reforms that will reinforce the position of the Dublas in the labour market. Industrialization progresses too slowly in India to provide a solution. The ratios between urban and rural population and between agrarian and industrial employment in south Gujarat have not appreciably changed in recent decades. This means that Dublas increasingly compete for the available labour places in agriculture – to the greater comfort and gain of the landlords.

Wider employment in agriculture appears to be a more realistic possibility. The much-discussed "green revolution", a programme of measures in the field of agricultural economy and technology, which has recently led to a spectacular rise of agrarian production in several regions, could enhance, and sometimes has enhanced, the labour-intensity per land unit. This does not, however, necessarily imply a rise in the real income of the agricultural labourer. There are, on the contrary, many indications that, because of the green revolution, the economic and social gap between landowners and landless labourers in the rural areas has widened further. Improvement of the condition of the Dublas can be expected only if there is a fundamental change of the relationships of power and property, but the possibility of this is remote. The administrative decentralization that has been introduced, as well as the consequent tendency of the local government bureaucracy to become politicized, have, on the whole, had advantageous consequences for the dominant landowners.

Among the Dublas, there is increasingly a collective awareness of their condition of subjection, a feeling of being wronged, and the beginning of an attempt at collective opposition against their exploiters. But it must be added immediately that the conditions that are prerequisite to implementing their protest organizationally in an effective and lasting way are lacking. Their rebelliousness is of short duration and is often directed against individual landlords. Like their companions in misery elsewhere, the Dubla agricultural labourers have become sunk in apathy and suspicion. Their lives offer them no prospects of improvement and they show themselves indifferent to what the future may bring. It can never be better than it is today – and that is not good enough.

Notes

1. First published in 1974 in *Patronage and Exploitation* (University of California Press).
2. Cf. also the statement of Vyas in a report on the conditions of agricultural labourers in four villages of west India: "In most of the regions there are no organisations of agricultural labourers which can represent them adequately before the employers and secure for them higher wages and better conditions of work. The attitude of the State in this field is reflected more in pious hopes than in any active steps. The way the provisions of the Minimum Wages Act for Agricultural Labourers are flouted in almost all areas is a significant indicator. Because of all these factors it is quite possible that though the demand for agricultural labour may show an increase in relation to supply, the wage rates may remain

depressed, as has been happening for the last decade or so. In such circumstances, even if there are no large-scale disturbances, a situation of accentuated tension may arise in many areas." (See also the discussion by Byres in Part II of this book.)

Women, Work and Property in North-West India[1]

Ursula Sharma

Women in Himachal and Punjab certainly see themselves as divided by enormous differences. From my own point of view it felt very different to be living among Himachali women after six months spent in Punjab. Punjabi women "come across" as more open and assertive in their personal manners than Himachali women, yet they also appear more housebound and more restricted in their movements and public activities. The contrast between the restrained public demeanour of Punjabi women and their spontaneity in the private company of other women is striking. Himachali women seemed to me more reserved at all times though less obliged to refer their behaviour and movements to men (if only because so many of their menfolk were absent from the village for so much of the time).

Yet I concluded that whilst these differences were experienced as very important, when it came to analysis they were less significant than they seemed. The similarities in the underlying structure of the female situation turned out to be much greater than I had expected. In reality the chances for economic independence and the control over their own activities which this might bring are as limited for Himachali women as for Punjabi women, even though the former are more actively involved in agricultural production. I found, for instance, that it was not automatically the case that women who perform such agricultural work have any greater say in agricultural decision-making than women who perform little agricultural work or none at all. Or if they do have greater say, it is as likely to be due to the negative fact of their husbands' absence as migrant labourers as to the positive fact of their own productive activity. In other areas of social life, women's capacity to influence decisions and exert control was just as likely to depend on factors unrelated to the kind or amount of productive work which they do. One particular sphere which I examined in some detail was that of matchmaking; here the power which women wielded and their importance in determining household policy depended on factors quite other than their capacity to work or generate income. Their control in this field had much more to do with their structural position as links between households in a system which favours

160

marriage outside the circle of immediate kin and neighbours but within the caste group. If some women (e.g. low-caste women and some of the poorer high-caste women in Himachal Pradesh) seem to have greater freedom to leave their husbands or to make second marriages with men of their own choice, this is not primarily because they are economically more independent of men than are other women. It is probably more closely related to factors such as the organization of property, and patterns of marriage payment, especially the distribution of the *kanya dan*[2] type of marriage with its associated ideology. In theory we might certainly expect to find that women who work for wages (and even women who work as family labourers) have a greater say in household matters than women who perform domestic work only, and this is an assumption that has often been made both by anthropologists and others. But the female labourer usually earns wages which are too small and sporadic to lend her any special leverage in household politics, and the work of female family labourers does not give women any particular control over the products of their labour.

There are variations in the internal structure of the household and its political machinery which are related to the kind of work which its members do and especially to the sexual division of labour. But these are not as conspicuous as the broad similarities in role patterns and the organization of authority. A wife is a wife, in whatever kind of work she spends her time, and a daughter-in-law a daughter-in-law. The subordination of female to male and junior to senior pervades family life in both areas and in all classes, whatever modifications we find in particular groups. I have not dealt with women's participation in collective political processes in the village, largely because it was difficult to make any worthwhile observations in the short time available in each area. But here also, what I was able to observe confirms the impression that there was much overall likeness between the two areas, at the village level at least. In both places, women's participation in community affairs is severely limited by general standards of female behaviour in public which stress women's invisibility and passivity and which circumscribe their movements, especially their contacts with men. Their political effectiveness, whatever their role in production, depends on their domestic power and their contacts with other women; the direct routes to political influence are blocked and for the most part they have to exploit the opportunities offered by their situation within the household.

This review shows that considered as a determinant of women's social power, their participation in agricultural work is only one variable among many. It cannot (on its own) explain differences in marriage practices, dowry payments, and divorce arrangements, as has often been assumed by anthropologists and others.

There is a fund of common norms and images which all the women I studied recognized as bearing on their lives, a warp of common values regarding women's special role which underlies all the differences due to class and regional culture. There are general similarities in the rules which govern women's public mobility, the organization of marriage, kinship terminology and the domestic role system. The dominant images of female behaviour which are carried in popular culture – the dutiful wife, the revered and indulgent mother, the modest and submissive bride – remain as strong and attractive as ever and are now disseminated by a variety of powerful media (the press, cinema, popular religious literature, and mythology). It is possible that further ironing out of regional differences will occur.

So do we simply have a case of "Ideology Rules OK"? Perhaps the traditional functionalist approaches are valid after all? After all, why trouble to scrutinize the precise tasks which women perform or the exact degree of their control over production processes if we can explain everything that is important about female roles by appealing to the force of ideals of proper female conduct (which do not vary much for women of different groups)?

I hope it will be clear that I do not think that this is the way out. If there is any explanatory "key" to women's position in both Punjab and Himachal it is more likely to be women's dependence upon men than their submission to men. Women depend on men because men may own land and hold tenancies and women (on the whole) cannot. The etiquette of public invisibility, the avoidance of male affines, the subordination of women within the household, the tendency to educate women to lower standards than men – all these practices elaborate secondary sources of dependence upon men (moral, practical, and ritual) which feed and reinforce their primary economic dependence. Variations in the pressure and force of these practices can now be seen as responses to differences in the economic sources of women's dependence upon men rather than as "just" regional and cultural differences. The ideology of dependence is required by the material structure of production.

But this does not tell us why the economic dependence of women is required in the first place. This is a much harder question to answer. The most important factors here are the allocation of property (especially land) and the allocation of the right to work, i.e. to command wages.

Women and Property

The main kind of property which it is relevant to consider is land, or rights in land. These rights are transmitted through a thoroughly male inheritance system. Familial values are not merely congruent with this male property sytem, they are actually geared to maintaining its maleness. Sons must be produced at all costs. In spite of a general rise in age at marriage in the past fifty years, marriage still takes place at a relatively early age in rural families (few of the women in the sample households were married at more than 20 years old). Couples therefore have many years in which to try to produce a male heir. Those who do not produce sons at first will go to great lengths, both magical and medical, to ensure that sons are conceived. As is well known, sons are given a religious and cultural value that is not given to daughters; the birth of a son is marked with much more elaborate ceremony than that of a daughter, and women who cannot produce sons are regarded with pity. Any woman of child-bearing age who has not already borne sons will constantly be reminded by others that she has not yet done her duty by her husband and his family and this pressure is kept up until she either produces a male heir or resigns herself to failure. A man who fails to produce sons by his first wife may by custom marry again. Even the Hindu Code Bill, which prohibits polygamy among Hindus, has not been effective in this respect, so forceful is the imperative for male heirs. Adoption (usually of a brother's son) is another solution. Lastly, in the past, female infanticide was not unknown among the propertied class in Punjab and some other parts of north-west India, and even now it is likely that male children are given preferential treatment when resources like food or medical treatment are limited (the demographic imbalance of the sexes in most states in India can scarcely be explained otherwise).[3]

In short, while female children remain (legally) the residual heirs of male property, as far as it is within their power, people see to it that there are male heirs to inherit.

Another point is that I do not think that it is useful to regard dowry as it is practised in North-west India as a form of inheritance, although this might be a useful way of analysing dowry in other societies. Or, if we do wish to consider dowry as a form of inheritance, then we might just as well regard it as inheritance on the part of the son-in-law as on the part of the daughter. Dowry gifts go *with* the daughter *to* the son-in-law (or his parents) rather than to the daughter herself. Also dowries in north-west India consist of particular types of property, and the chief difference between the kinds of property transferred at marriage and those transferred to sons at a man's death is that the former does not usually include wealth-generating forms of property. As far as I know, land is never gifted as dowry.

If we want to understand the system of property and inheritance which obtains in northern India today it is necessary to look at practice rather than at legal codes alone. The statutes which allow for equal participation in inheritance on the part of daughters are not a dead letter by any means, but they are appealed to in certain circumstances – in cases of disputes among siblings or where land ceiling legislation makes it expedient for large estates to be broken up "on paper" among male and female heirs. Ordinarily daughters waive the rights which the law gives them and would be considered selfish sisters if they did not do so.

In addition to inheritance practices we need to look at the pattern of effective control, since it is clear that many women who do inherit land or who have land registered in their names have only minimal control over the land they officially own. This happens because norms governing women's movements in public inhibit them from taking an active part in the management and administration of estates and in all the legal business attendant upon landholding. Usually a man – the husband or the brother in most cases – will act on the woman's behalf.

So what we actually find is a system of inheritance only slightly modified by modern legislation, in which daughters are certainly preferred to a man's more distant collateral heirs, but in which they do not actually inherit very often. Everything in the system of property which I have described tends to establish the primary control of income-generating property in the hands of men. Women may have a good deal to say in the way in which land is administered and farmed and they may also have effective control of other forms of property (domestic goods, furniture, clothing, and jewellery), especially as they reach positions of seniority in the household. But they have little direct control over wealth-generating forms of property.

Even those forms of property which do not of themselves generate new wealth (household equipment, agricultural implements) are passed on from father to son, with daughters entering only in the absence of sons. For many men, this is the only kind of property which they are likely to inherit since their fathers have no land to leave them. But even among labourers, once the tiniest plot of land is acquired, the property rules which I have just outlined assert themselves.

All this means that *pace* the Indian legislators who have attempted to shift things in favour of female inheritance, the system is still firmly male. Now it is possible to see such practices as purdah, avoidance of male affines, women's public invisibility, etc., not so much as antidotes to misalliance (though they certainly do perform this function) as a system of practices which reinforce the male control of productive resources. Specifically they protect this system against modern attempts to modify it through legislation in favour of women. The ideology of the good sister ensures that women do not claim land which their brothers might inherit, and the ideology of the deferential and dependent wife ensures that a woman will find it difficult to control land registered in her name independently of the assistance of her husband or some other male relative. The norms governing female roles by no means exclude women from an active role in agricultural and other productive work but they limit the ways in which women can actually use whatever economic power they may derive from their role in production, whether collectively (in the community) or as individuals (in the household).

These ideological constraints sustain the "maleness" of the property system in a very direct way. We are not strictly obliged to appeal to the need for women to marry status equals in a class society in order to explain purdah and associated practices, when a more direct connection between property and gender roles can be traced. However, this does not mean that these less direct paths of causation are irrelevant for all purposes. Had I been writing about the class structure of north Indian villages rather than focusing upon gender roles, I would have had to make the connection between property and purdah via the problem of status group endogamy and the dominant classes' need to prevent dispersal of the productive resources they control. Those writers who have seen purdah in relation to social differentiation are not incorrect in their views, only in their tendency to stress the dimension of "status" or "prestige". The surveillance of women and the restriction of their movements and autonomy, especially as they affect the possibility of women marrying outside their own group has an important function in relation to the organization of property if we consider that even if daughters rarely gain direct control of their fathers' estates, a son-in-law may well gain access to the household's productive resources in the absence of sons.

The subordination of women within the household also plays an important role in respect of class, which is not diminished by the fact that some assertive and strong-minded women exercise far more control within the household than the ideologies of the submissive daughter-in-law and the deferential wife allow to be recognized. In rural households at all socio-economic levels it is quite usual to find a number of different class interests represented through the diverse activities and sources of livelihood of their members. The solid structure of the household authority system, with its emphasis on the subordination of women and junior members' interests, may well explain why divergent interests do not tear such households apart.

Purdah, then, has a double ideological function. It favours the consolidation of property-owning groups (and the emulation of these groups' values and culture by others). It also favours the concentration of the direct control of property in the hands of the male members of the group.

Capitalism, the Cash Economy, and Women

In capitalist economics, some workers have a status which is superior to others in relation to the right to work. Some, for instance, enjoy greater security of tenure, even in periods of unemployment, and if they do lose their jobs they are offered more substantial redundancy payments or better retraining opportunities. The right to work is explicitly denied to some (children) but there may be other groups for whom it is very limited or offered only conditionally. These may include blacks, immigrants, the elderly or disabled, and (the largest group) women. These groups often constitute a reserve of labour which can be drawn into production during times of boom or emergency (wartime) and excluded or relegated to marginal positions in the economy of times of recession. The historically prior domestic orientation of women made it easier to exclude them or offer them only marginal and insecure forms of employment. Indeed the domestic orientation of women has been accentuated since the industrial revolution with the development of the full-time "housewife" role and the ideology of home-based consumerism. Should we expect the progress of capitalist production in India to have very different results so far as women are concerned?

On the whole there seems reason to suppose that it will not. Existing modes of agrarian production and property already emphasize women's role as dependents of men. In some senses, peasant and labouring women were already a kind of rural reserve force, being drawn into or excluded from agricultural production as the need arose – honour (women are disgraced if they work in the fields) or necessity (women have to work in the fields because no one can afford to hire other labour) being appealed to, as the case might be.

On the whole the male head of the household retains some control over the labour of its female members. A girl can only train for paid work if her father wishes it and is prepared to pay for her education, and it will be difficult for a wife to work after her marriage without the goodwill of her husband and his parents. Women who do take paid employment cannot always find suitable work in the same place as their husbands, and Indian courts are now being asked to determine whether a wife has an independent right to decide where she should work, and, if necessary, maintain a separate establishment from that of her husband – independent, that is, of her husband's consent. On the whole there has been a tendency to deny that right as an automatic entitlement.

Male control of female labour power continues, although this control must be attenuated when the women work for others. Therefore if women are entering the industrial and bureaucratic work force, it is not on the same terms as men and it is under conditions which encourage their continued subordination to men in the household. So things seem set fair for a reproduction of the western pattern of female dependence upon male wages, albeit for somewhat different historical reasons.

However, this is only a very general truth and it is important not to lose sight of the different ways in which these broad trends affect particular areas. Obviously there are considerable differences in the ways in which capitalist production and the cash economy have affected the two areas studied here.

Punjab is relatively urbanized and industrialized compared with Himachal Pradesh. There is a good deal of industry in its cities (light engineering, textiles) and considerable scope for employment in the public services (irrigation, schools, etc.). Many men can get paid work near to their own villages, even within commuting distance, and can retain an active interest in their land. But at the moment there are few opportunities for urban employment for women in Punjab, nor even of rural employment; farming among the larger landowners becomes organized on a capitalist basis, women continue to constitute a fund of seasonal labour, becoming ever more marginal as agricultural work becomes more mechanized. It is not so much that capitalist development has taken away women's traditional work and given it to men – women in Punjab never did have much chance to earn an independent income. It is rather that capitalist agriculture and industry have offered women nothing very specific as yet and so they remain as dependent on men as they ever were.

Himachal Pradesh differs in two important respects from Punjab. First, men have to travel much further to find waged work and communications are poorer, so they really have to choose between being full-time wage earners or full-time peasant farmers or tenants. There is no way in which they can participate in wage labour whilst retaining an active involvement in the day-to-day demands of a farm. Even more agricultural work devolves upon women (as family labourers) in addition to the extra domestic work which they must undertake when men are not at home to help in fetching water, going to the *bazar* etc.

Second, land in the foothills is not productive enough to make it worthwhile investing large sums of cash earned in employment in its improved exploitation. Some workers do invest in buying more land, but this extra land must be farmed by traditional methods. Again, it is the migrant's wife who will do the extra work, with perhaps very occasional hired help, unless land is rented out to share-croppers. The peasant households whose men go to the cities to work can only achieve the standard of living they enjoy (which is not always very high) because they depend on the double sources of agricultural production and waged work. The land is an important source of security against old age or unemployment and will not lightly be abandoned, but there is increasing specialization within the household. Working on the land becomes the concern of the women, and earning wages becomes the business of men. This specialization in agriculture does not bring women any particular rewards however, other than more work, and it certainly does not bring them an income of their own or any other kind of wealth which they could use on their own account. It does mean that their daily lives are relatively unsupervised by men and they have somewhat more freedom of movement than most Punjabi women, but these are not necessarily seen as valuable assets. As one migrant's wife complained, "It is all very well for people like my husband. We women stay at home and do back-breaking work even if we are feeling ill or if we are pregnant. There is no sick leave for us. But we do not have any money of our own and when the men come home we have to cast our eyes down and bow our heads [i.e. act submissively] before them."

In neither area does the development of a cash economy and capitalist production mitigate the dependence of women on men. If anything it increases it by adding to their old dependence on men as property holders a new dependence on men as wage-earners. In spite of this, women in Punjab probably feel that they have had a better deal than Himachali women since these developments have at least brought many of them increased leisure and comfort. The main thing which they have brought for Himachali women is an increased work load.

Editors' Notes

1. This article is abstracted from the conclusion of a book with the same title, published by Tavistock in 1980 which is based on very detailed ethnographic studies. Here Ursula Sharma summarizes conclusions which are richly supported in her book, and which relate to *rural* women in north-west India. Sharma has subsequently conducted research amongst urban women in the same region: *Women's Work, Class and the Urban Household: A Study of Shimla, North India* (London: Tavistock, 1986).
2. *kanya dān*: the gift of a virgin daughter in marriage; according to Sanskritic tradition, the noblest form of marriage. In this kind of marriage a dowry is customary but no payment is received from the groom's family.
3. On the demographic imbalance see Bardhan, P., 1984 "On Life and Death Questions: Poverty and Child Mortality in Rural India", in *Land Labor and Rural Poverty: Essays in Development Economies* (New York: Columbia University Press); Harriss and Watson, 1987; and Miller, 1981.

Part IV

Regionalism and Ethnicity

Editors' Introduction

Much of "the news" about South Asia which appears in the international press concerns conflicts based on regionalism and ethnicity, such as the continuing conflict in Punjab (discussed here by Alavi. See also Akbar, 1985; and Tully and Jacob, 1985); struggles in Assam and elsewhere in north-east India; incidents of communal violence between Hindus and Muslims, such as occurred in Meerut in May 1987 (see Engineer, 1987); or between different groups amongst Muslims (such as in Karachi in December 1986), or Hindus (as in Gujarat in 1981; see Joshi here).

Amongst the social changes of the colonial period in South Asia some of the more important were those which gave new salience to caste and to religious affiliation as identities. Hindu and Muslim "communalism" was fostered by colonialism. Sarkar notes that "Instances of local conflicts between Hindus and Muslims may certainly be found occasionally in past centuries . . . But communal riots do seem to have been significantly rare down to the 1880s" (Sarkar, 1983, 59). Communalism largely sprang from élite conflicts over jobs and political favours (see Sarkar, 1983, 76–82 and Alavi's contribution in this section) but "the tragic fact has to be admitted that communalism also acquired a mass dimension from an early date" (Sarkar, 1983, 59) – for reasons like those explained by Chakrabarty here, and which clearly have their echoes in present day communal violence as discussed here by Engineer (and in a book; Engineer (ed.) 1984). There is, however, a broad consensus amongst scholars that communal conflict is grounded in competition of material interests. Such competition is examined in some detail by Weiner (1978) who in that work looks particularly at movements directed against immigrants from other parts of India into particular regions such as Assam and Hyderabad. Brass (1974) offers an excellent study of language, religion and politics in Northern India. Such élite competition has also manifested itself in regional movements, such as movements for linguistic provinces in India. These are examined by Bondurant (1958), Srivastava (1970), Bose

171

(1967) and others, while Gankovsky (n.d.) provides an excellent survey of ethnic groups in Pakistan.

As Washbrook notes in the next chapter, in both the colonial and post-colonial periods "A crucial feature of the constitutional or legitimate political process is the way that 'particularist' interests mobilize themselves to compete for rewards and favours from the institutions of the state . . . [in these circumstances] A strong incentive exists to maximize the public support on which pressure groups and local interests can call and the symbols of ethnicity are especially advantageous agencies of popular mobilization and group solidarity." He goes on to note that "The way that republican India structures her system of government guarantees a continuing undertow of ethnic politics" – for reasons which are explored in the chapters here by Weiner and Katzenstein, Joshi, and by Alavi. The book by Weiner and Katzenstein, from which we have taken the extract published here, gives an account of the working of the quota system in India and the communal politics that revolve around them. At a wholly different level, Barbara Joshi's contribution brings to our attention the special position of *dalits*, India's "untouchables", whose problems are not simply those of competition for jobs and favours of the state but which demand fundamental transformation in Indian society and its values and ideologies before the *dalits* can hope to secure emancipation. Finally, Alavi in looking at the politics of ethnicity in India and Pakistan singles out those whom he calls the "salariat", as the class that plays a central role in them. In looking at India and Pakistan in comparative perspective, he is struck by the fact that the politics of ethnicity take different forms in the two cases, taking the form of localized communalism in India and that of subnationalism in Pakistan – although he is careful to point out that local communalism is not absent in Pakistan and, in the case of India, the case of the Punjab appears on the surface at least to be one of subnationalism. He offers explanations why there should be such a contrast between the two countries. Furthermore, Alavi does not take the view that over the decades, ethnic categories have become set and crystallized, because of colonial policies referred to above, for example. On the contrary, he finds that ethnic definitions are contingent on kaleidoscopic political changes currently in motion so that changes in political circumstances precipitate ethnic redefinitions or, indeed, as the Sindhi case shows, alternative definitions are contested vigorously to decide who should be included and who should be excluded when defining the boundaries of the ethnic group.

In view of the frequency with which journalists in India and outside discuss the possibility of the break-up of India in the face of ethnic and regionalist forces, Washbrook's judgement that "The politics of ethnicity have been remarkably ineffective in directing the course of modern Indian history" might be found surprising. His discussion of the way in which the processes of class formation from the late colonial period set up "strong imperatives against weakening the forces of territorial integration" is correspondingly important. At the same time it should be recognized that the politics of the Congress Party, particularly after Indira Gandhi's attempts to centralize power in the 1970s, have given rise to particular tensions between the centre and the states (which, indeed, seemed to immobilize Indira Gandhi's last government between 1980 and 1984). As Manor says:

> During the early 1970s, by abandoning the principle of representation within the party, by clumsily over-centralising power within the organisation . . . she severely damaged the party's ability to arrange workable bargains among varied interests and between levels in the political system . . . She clearly misunderstood a central element in the logic of power relations in India under the East India Company, the Crown and Nehru's Congress – that the influence of those at the apex of the political system penetrates downward most effectively through bargaining and compromise rather than coercion. (Manor, 1983, 90)

It is in the context of a political system weakened in this way that the forces of fragmentation seem to have grown stronger in the recent past.

The last chapter in this section concerns ethnic relations in Sri Lanka, and also introduces a different perspective from that presented by Alavi, in emphasizing the social consequences of perceptions. Newton Gunasinghe gives a succinct account of the bases of ethnic conflict in Sri Lanka in his remarks on the Sinhalese world-view, the actions of the Sinhala-dominated state, and on the responses of Sri Lankan Tamils (expanded upon by a number of authors. See Jayawardena (1984) for a brief historical account of Sinhalese communalism; Roberts (1979) for an important collection on collective identities in modern Sri Lanka; Ponnambalam (1983) for an account of the Tamil struggle; and de Silva (1982) for a short, judicious view). Gunasinghe's analysis of different perceptions and their dynamic relations, as well as his outline of possible lines of action, remains apposite even after the events in Jaffna of 1987, when the Indian army entered into action against Tamil separatist guerilla fighters.

Ethnicity in Contemporary Indian Politics[1]

David Washbrook

Why was India not fully "Balkanised" after 1947 into a series of autarchic, ethnically based nation-states, or deeply federated according to such principles, or even given a constitution which closely reflected the "plural" status of her society? With the exception of Pakistan, a case unique both in its significance to the Raj and in the underlying strength of its symbolism, none of these developments took place. India emerged from the British Empire as a secular nation-state based upon territorial principles and with a centrally biased constitution. While, indeed, the forces of vernacular ethnicity have helped to reshape her system of regional government, that system is quintessentially subordinate to the power of the centre. The politics of ethnicity have been remarkably ineffective in directing the course of modern Indian history. It is, however, this very ineffectiveness which gives rise to a second problem. Why do these politics still persist at all? If the logic of political development since independence has been towards secularism and territorial integration, why do movements reflecting particularist ethnic sentiments continue to operate and to vociferate apparently hopeless demands?

Some light can be thrown on the first problem by looking at the inconsistencies and inherent contradictions of ethnic movements as primary principles of mobilisation. In the first place, if ever one wanted a case from which to challenge Ernest Gellner's belief in the necessary association of language with ethnicity, it would be this one (Gellner, 1964). In India, religion and caste, as much as language, provided the symbols of ethnicity. Clearly, this created major practical difficulties, for every individual was potentially open to mobilization along several different lines of affiliation simultaneously, was implicitly the member of several different ethnic communities at once (Barnett, 1977). A close examination of the politics of ethnicity shows rapid and kaleidoscopic changes in "identity" as first one set of symbols became critical and contentious and then another. In these circumstances, it was very difficult for ethnic movements to provide themselves with a stable, long-term following. The unique success of Islam perhaps derives from the degree to which lines of linguistic, religious and life-style differentiation converged upon it, although even here its political appeal varied greatly over relatively short stretches of time (Robinson, 1974). A second problem was posed by the lack of correspondence between ethnicity and discrete territory. The strongest political sanction available to ethnic movements, that of "withdrawal" into their own state, was available only to very few. Indeed, it was less seen to be available than forced on the Pakistan movement which, while it always proclaimed territorial ambitions, originally designed them in a way which made nonsense of the ethnic principle and which served more the purposes of gaining special privileges in a still-united pan-Indian state. The logic of territory has perhaps had most to do with the greater spread of the politics of vernacular ethnicity since independence for it offers a stronger bargaining counter against the centre.

Yet the ineffectiveness of ethnic movements may lie in causes deeper than these. The politics of race and ethnicity, in effect, were but part of, and were set in the context of, a much greater whole. In examining this whole, it is possible to see a range of distinct disadvantages in or limitations to the politics of ethnicity in comparison with other available models of mobilisation. The most obvious of these limitations lay in doing battle with the Raj. The pluralist theory of society was a valuable aid to the maintenance of imperial rule, and while Indian political activity which was informed by it could bring a range of benefits within the colonial system, it was in a very weak position to break that system. Indian nationalism always contained, and its leadership always tried to preserve, a strong emphasis on territorial and secular principles of social identity and political loyalty. From the 1930s, when the final struggle with the Raj was joined in earnest and began to take precedence (and itself to determine) the more restricted competition of domestic politics, the nationalist leadership moved to the centre of the political stage. Their principles bound the colonized society together in ways which were crucially necessary and they both organized and negotiated India's final independence. On the other side too, the Raj was given reason to question a total devotion to pluralistic premises. These were most useful in the situation of a distant enervate authority ruling over a stagnant society for they broke up and neutralized the bases of opposition. But for a state forced into an active role in a more dynamic society, they could carry awkward implications and, particularly, raise contradictions with the class and bureaucratic requirements of rule. In north India, for example, the British had partially rested their regime on the greater territorial landlords whose authority was coming to be undermined by the growth of class tensions. These tensions were especially open to ethnic expression and forms of political mobilization for the Islamic or Islamized culture of the landed magnates distinguished them visibly from their more demotic and folk Hindu tenantry. The preservation of landlord authority now started to conflict with the premises of Hindu–Muslim divide and rule. In the 1920s and 1930s, the British tried to develop a more secular, class-based system of government through the Legislative Council while, perversely, it was the forces of nationalism which mingled ethnic with class protest (Robinson, 1974). At a much less significant level, pluralist principles of representation and the needs of "good government" came into conflict in south India. By the mid-1920s, the British discovered that were the non-Brahmin Justice Party[2] allowed to "communalise" appointments, as had first been intended, they would have had to face the new, deepening and more expert tasks of administration, which were being imposed upon them, with a civil service consisting increasingly of semi-literates and ministerial placement (Baker, 1976). Few of the communalist promises of the Justice Party government were, or were allowed to be, fulfilled. As India's national class and state structures evolved towards independence, the principles of ethnic affiliation within them came into increasing conflict with alternative principles of state-craft and nation-building.

Indeed, that this was an unlikely conclusion can be seen by probing further into some of these contradictions. As noted by Dumont, the modern ideology of ethnicity is predicated on the value of equality. This is expressed not only in appeals for a social equality between ethnicities but also in the corollary to the proposition that the individual's social identity is founded in his ethnicity, which is that all members of the same ethnic group share a common identity and therefore are equal. The egalitarian implications of modern ethnic ideology make it a very radical social philosophy. It was no coincidence or mere opportunism, for example, that E. V. Ramaswami Naicker should have taken his non-Brahmin "self-respect" movement[3] to Moscow and towards communism. Fully extrapolated, the logic of the modern ideology of ethnicity leads to social revolution – albeit one rather more in keeping with Hitler's than Lenin's vision. This logic inextricably entwined the history of ethnicity with that of class and, in the world of Indian political praxis, it was always going to be extremely difficult to generate the former's revolutionary potential out of the latter's context. On the one hand, appeals to social equality met resistance from the more traditionalistic conceptions of, particularly, caste ethnicity, which were located in the kin- and craft-based organization of the continu-ing, if distressed, *"petit"* economy. On the other, and even more significantly, they met resistance from the inegalitarian logic which arises out of the "free" capitalist system and legitimates the social differentiation of class. The development of Indian class relations under colonialism was very complex and we cannot discuss it at length here. But it would be possible to argue that an important theme was the emergence of a dominant class alliance under bourgeois direction (see Patnaik, 1972). While this alliance was born of growing conflict with other groups, it was not yet under severe stress. Indeed, it was being consolidated as the imperial–national contradiction within the bourgeoisie was progressively resolved, or at least moved to a different plane. In short, the class history of the period made it "unripe" for revolution and extinguished the possibilities of radical change from the ethnic as much as the class perspective. Ethnic movements and associations remained critically reliant on the patronage and support of members of the dominant class alliance, whose self-preservation instincts ensured that their programmes were moderated. It was again not opportunism but an acknowledgement of harsh realities that led E. V. Ramaswami Naicker back from Moscow to the Bobbili palace and an electoral pact in 1937 with the conservative Justice Party. Except by attaching himself to the bandwagon of one or other of the dominant class parties, there was no way that his movement could hold any political importance.

The processes of class formation in the late-colonial period, however, can be seen to have done more than limit the radical component in ethnic ideology. They also circumscribed the extent to which its more malleable liberal components could be built into the institutions of the "new" society. At least at the heights of the state and economy, the Raj had imposed systems which operated on unitary territorial principles. These set the framework within which the struggle for independence took place. They also set the framework of institutions within which Indian class relations evolved. As, with the expansion and devolution of government and the beginnings of industrialization, these *"haute"* systems became more penetrative, so they increasingly helped to determine the distribution of wealth and power in society. Membership of the "All-India" Congress party came to be necessary for effective participation in the state; influence over national policies of protection, subsidy and labour repression, important for success in the market-place. There were strong imperatives towards territorial integration at work on the dominant class sections of the emergent national society (if not on all sections, as "integrationist" modernization-theories assume). Contrariwise, of course, there were also strong imperatives against weakening the forces of territorial integration. What could ethnic principles of political federation or even autonomy offer to the dominant bourgeoisie to compare with the security of a central umbrella of coercive force, the rewards of a large protected market and the weight lent to international bargaining strength by size? Ethnic movements, resting on liberal social principles and appealing to a bourgeois following, were obliged to subordinate their aspirations (however tacitly) to the premise of continuing territorial unity or risk compromising their leading members' class interests. The logic of this subordination can be seen in two enduring features of Indian political behaviour. First, there seems a strong propensity for the leaders of ethnic movements to sell out their principles as soon as they break into the corridors of power and for movements to moderate their own demands as they get nearer to the apparatus of power. The strength of the Tamil separatist demand, for example, appears to move in an inverse direction to the success of Dravidian parties in constitutional politics (Barnett, M., 1977). And second, there seems a strong propensity for ethnicity to reach its most extreme manifestation in racialist social theories only among those groups who have no future in the dominant class structure. If ideologies which focus closely on the significance of subnational ethnicity make territorial integration difficult, those which hypothesize racialism make it impossible. In these, there is no basis for transregional relationships to develop by means other than political domination, which the historical processes through which the Indian nation was built rule out. It is very striking that the Bengali *bhadralogh*'s[4] lurch towards racialism had its counterpart in their progressive alienation from the Gandhian Congress and the mainstream of the national movement (Gordon, 1974; Gallagher, 1973). And that this too had its counterpart in their declining position in the Bengali class structure. The forces of national and class history ran against the prestige and privilege of high-caste landed gentries. Their racialism may have represented a legitimate protest against the times, but it was the protest of dead men passing into political insignificance.

But if integrationist themes dominate the development of modern Indian society, why do fissiparous ethnic themes continue to persist and, more than this, strongly to influence the forms in which political competition takes place? At the subordinate levels of the political system, the symbols of regional, religious and caste ethnicity play an important role even though, when transposed to the national arena, their meaning is wont to become obscure. Part of the answer may perhaps lie in the extent to which, for all its utilitarian value, a national identity based largely on the claims of territory is aesthetically unsatisfying. It can give the relations of society no legitimacy in a theory of organic unity. Attendant upon the process of nation-formation have been recurring attempts to give the Indian identity a firmer cultural base, most obviously through association with the symbols of the Hindi language and Hindu religion. But the historical parochialism of these symbols makes them problematic agents of unification. The more vigorously they are manipulated, the more vehement become the reactions to them and the stronger the juxtaposition of subnational ethnicities. In Tamil India, for example, the Hindi language seems to be seen more as the symbol of northern domination than as that of national unity. The secular logic that brought India to independence left an important vacuum which is filled by a continuing dialogue between her many cultural traditions.

Another part of the answer, however, may lie in the concept of state corporatism which is as relevant to the republican as to the colonial context. A crucial feature of the constitutional or legitimate political process is the way that "particularist" interests mobilize themselves to compete for rewards and favours from the institutions of the state. These interests are manifested in many forms – as pressure groups cohering around specific issues and as geographically defined local constituencies. The role of the state in this process is to be seen in the extent to which its own design elicits such particularistic responses. The executive agencies of government enjoy a wide measure of discretion in the allocation of patronage. They do not treat individuals as anonymous atoms, each of whose claim on the state is inherently equal and to be adjudicated against standards of merit and efficiency. Rather, they distribute quotas, grants, protection in the market-place, etc., to individuals as members of prior social categories with differential rights and privileges. These categories form obvious nodal points around which pressure groups can gather. Similarly, local government systems tend to operate by allocating block grants, licensing powers, etc., to lower-level, geographically defined "self-governing" institutions which administer their immediate distribution. What this means, however, is that these lower geographic units are placed in competition with one another for resources from the state and impelled towards a local particularist identification of their interests. Of course, neither pressure group nor locality particularism need engage ethnic affiliations, but a number of factors make this a likely outcome. The state frequently designs social categories/pressure groups around ethnic criteria. The geographic divisions separating competing localities often overlie lines of potential ethnic differentiation (reflected in old dominant caste territories, sectarian religious centres, areas of linguistic peculiarity, etc.). Moreover, the tendency is encouraged by a further aspect of the political process. Pressure groups and local administrative institutions gain much of their weight from their role in vote-gathering and vote-banking. If "government" flows down the political system from above, democratic power flows up it from electoral constituencies beneath. But how is this power to be organized, consolidated and projected? A strong incentive exists to maximize the public support on which pressure groups and local interests can call and the symbols of ethnicity are especially advantageous agencies of popular mobilization and group solidarity. They obscure points of possible class conflict and, as "social mobilization" theorists have seen, possess multivocal properties and sentimental attachments which are capable of drawing support from the widely spread corners of an otherwise much differentiated society. The way that republican India structures her systems of government guarantees a continuing undertow of ethnic politics (see Kothari, 1970b).

But recognition of this political logic creates a further problem. Why should a state whose historical struggle to freedom and dominant institutions so heavily emphasize the virtues of national integration and territorial identity function in a manner which seems to promote disintegration and subnational ethnic identity? The colonial rationale for a pluralist sociology ended in 1947. What now informs the republic's adoption of these same assumptions? The answer perhaps might be seen in the difficulties and dangers to the existing territorial state and the class interests which it enshrines of attempting to realize the ideal of national integration and, reciprocally, in the practical advantages which accrue to the regime from the maintenance of internally competing ethnicities and particularisms. The lack of uncontentious points of cultural reference cuts the republic off from the easiest means of developing, or imposing, a meaningful and uniform national identity. It also shifts the focus of any desirable identity onto strictly secular criteria. It may be, indeed logically it ought to be, that a secular territorial national identity is capable of arising, or at least generalizing itself, only on the social facts of effective national integration and secularization. But if this is so, then there lies the Indian rub. It is hard to see how, in the context of the international and social contradictions of capital, India ever is to produce these transforming social facts. Integration and secularization are parts of the ideal-typical programme of modernization. They require the equality (or at least potential equality) of individuals, an open-market society, the protection of secular freedoms, etc. Unless these requirements are met, the individual's life-chances will continue to be bound up with a host of particularistic institutions (of family, ascriptive corporation, parochial organization, etc.) which protect and determine his welfare, career opportunities, etc. Yet the costs in social overhead capital necessary to bring these facts into existence are enormous. They require a huge expansion in the institutions of the state, to equalize life-chances by providing equality of access to education, welfare, etc., and a "perfection" of the communications, specialization and articulation of the market-place. They demand a modernizing transformation of the economy. No such transformation has attended India's history since independence nor, given her reliance on capitalist processes and specific situation in the world of capital, can it reasonably be expected in the foreseeable future (even if it were accepted that the dynamic of capitalist development made the notional properties of the "modern" society fully realizable, which is highly arguable). In effect, the condition and situation of Indian society turn the generalization of the secular territorial national identity into an improbable dream.

In the light of this improbability, those who remain committed to the values implicit in the dream may better protect their position by seeking to subordinate and neutralize the forces of ethnicity than by trying forthrightly to oppose and destroy them. What the territorial principles of the republican regime are most vulnerable to are general critiques from the premises of cultural nationalism and territorially coherent pressures for withdrawal. The structure of the state can be seen, paradoxically, to inhibit both of those developments precisely by granting a limited recognition and legitimacy to ethnic principles of affiliation. First, by offering special and particular grants of patronage and protection, the national centre encourages ethnicities to compete against one another rather than itself. It provides the favours which ethnic pressure groups pursue and stands as a potential friend to them all. But to get these necessarily scarce favours, these groups must mobilize against their rivals. The tactic prevents the groups from merging their particularistic interests into general principles of criticism. Its efficacy is well seen in the history of southern India, which witnessed two major vernacular mobilizations among the Tamils and Telugus at almost the same time. Yet the conflicts between the two, for appropriate territory and patronage from the centre, far outweighed any tendency for them to move together. Second, by recognizing and supporting widely various criteria of ethnic identity (caste, locality, religion and language), the centre ensures that may different foci of loyalty converge on the same social field and makes difficult the construction of large-scale territorial solidarities. Through policies which promote internal divisiveness, the territorial secular state can keep itself out of and above the fray of ethnic politics. Indeed, it can do more and stand as the independent arbiter between the claims of rival ethnicities whose members perceive themselves to have more to fear from one another than from it.

The logic of class relations also can be seen to promote this partial and contradictory solution. First, it is arguable that the personal material interest of members of the dominant class alliance, which holds the national regime, inhibits them from pursuing the realization of the secular national ideal. At present, they enjoy the benefits (of access to monopolies, subsidies, governing institutions, etc.) which flow from possession of the state apparatus. Were society to be effectively secularized and modernized, switched to a value-base in individualism and equality, one consequence would be a great increase in competition in the market-place and political arena. But this in turn would place an increasing strain on their personal positions of dominance. It is very noticeable that a utilitarian willingness to take advantage of the national government has never implied a reciprocal willingness to accept the secular ideals on which it formally stands. But second, and more importantly, the imperatives of general dominant class interest also sustain subnational ethnicity. As the British discovered in the last decades of their regime, sociological pluralism can be as useful in dissipating and controlling class as nationalist threats. On the one hand, it breaks up lines of potential cohesion and divides subordinate classes against them-selves. On the other, it organizes society into cross-class categories which give subgroups with interests or position in the dominant class alliance leadership roles and authority over their weaker brethren (see Mencher, 1978). The radical component in the ideology of ethnicity is thus moderated. In the Indian context, the class functions played by the relations of ethnicity may be especially significant to the development of capitalism. If one accepts the argument that the progress of capitalism in Third World societies faces peculiar and severe problems, is unlikely in the short term to produce a general increase in material benefits to offset the effects of its social disruption and is likely to involve an exceptional degree of coercion and brutality, then the political means of coping with class resistance lie at the centre of the process and prospects of capital itself. The propagation of subnational ethnicities is, for India, one of the most advantageous means.

For this very reason, however, it may also provide an advantageous point of attack on that capitalism. The interpretation offered in the last few paragraphs leans heavily on Marxist functionalist formulations. These, seeing the role played by its divisiveness in maintaining the class and state structures, are inclined to write off ethnic consciousness as lacking in political potential. But this may reflect an analytical confusion: that because ethnicity may be used as a control mechanism by the dominant institutions, it has its origins in and is simply imposed by those institutions. On our wider arguments, this does not follow. We have tried to show that the tendency towards ethnic politics also arose from certain features of the social structure and, further, that it could express demands for radical change. Traditional ethnicity might emerge as a protest and reaction against pressures on the corporate organization of the relations of production. The egalitarian component in Modern ethnic ideology might draw in revolutionary aspirations. A history of class conflict and change lies behind that of ethnic politicization. Indeed, it is only by virtue of the fact ethnic movements and organizations contain radical "material" and are related to class issues that they can be, or need to be, used as instruments of control at all. But such instruments are two-edged weapons and, should they be turned back on their current masters, the political implications could be immense. Cultural nationalist campaigns, for example, could weaken the centre of the territorial state and greatly limit its coercive umbrella which, at present, represses the possibilities of radical movements taking place in any one region. Equally, a greater emphasis on the egalitarian ideals implicit in modern ethnicity would open out vast contradictions in the structure of the state. The extent to which the state recognizes ethnic appeals allows them to be brought inside its own regulating systems. Once there, however, the demand for effective equality would confront the class partialities of the regime. The demand could not be met from the class premises of the state, whose legitimating ideology would then stand clearly contradicted by its reality. Given the importance and yet ambiguity of ethnicity to the maintenance of the dominant class alliance and its state, its evocation as part of a radical programme seems one of the most promising of all revolutionary tactics.

Whether or not the tactic comes to be used, of course, is another matter. The Indian Left, whether from doctrinal purism or post-colonial nationalist atavism, has shown a great disdain for the politics of ethnicity and a great reverence for the territorial principle.

By most standards, its history over the past thirty years also has been one of dismal failure. In contrast, the star of political parties such as the DMK(s)[5] offering an American-style populism tied to ethnic symbolism, has been in the ascendant. But however the future develops, it is hard not to feel that changing configurations around the nexus between class and ethnicity will play a very large part in it.

Editors' Notes

1. This chapter originally appeared in "Ethnicity and Racialism in Colonial Indian Society" in R. Ross (ed.) *Racism and Colonialism* (The Hague: Martinus Nijhoff, 1982).
2. The Justice Party was formed in the Madras Presidency in 1917 in order to secure the uplift of non-Brahmins and to oppose the nationalist movement, which would, in its view, replace the neutral administration of the British with a Brahmin oligarchy. The Justice Party held power in Madras until 1934, when it was routed by Congress.
3. E. V. Ramaswami Naicker was a major non-Brahmin political leader in the Madras Presidency who founded a "self-respect movement", aimed at purging South India of Brahmin tyranny and the religion by which the Dravidian people of the region were held in submission.
4. The term *bhadralogh/bhadralokh* refers to the educated gentry of Bengal.
5. The DMK (*Dravida Munnetra Kazhagam*, or "Dravidian Progressive Federation") is an important political party in the south Indian state of Tamil Nadu. It was founded by C. N. Annadurai, a journalist and film writer, in 1949, as a breakaway faction of the DK (*Dravida Kazhagam*, or "Dravidian Federation"). The DK had been formed by E. V. Ramaswami Naicker by reorganizing his "self-respect movement" (see note 3), in order to pursue the objective of creating a separate Dravidian state. The DMK retained the "rationalist", anti-Brahmin, anti-Hindi character of the DK and remained formally committed to secession until 1963. Unlike the DK, however, the DMK combined electoral activity with agitational politics, and the party became increasingly oriented to pragmatic economic issues. Though the separatist objective of the DK came to be dropped by the DMK, it has appealed powerfully to Tamil nationalist sentiments and it has always demanded greater state autonomy. Its platform has emphasized the ideals of a classless and casteless society, and its economic programme has been characterized by radical populism. The party succeeded in extending its support in successive elections, appealing to a wide range of social groups – partly by effective use of popular media, especially the cinema. It succeeded finally in "going over the heads" of the local Congress political bosses to take power in Tamil Nadu in 1967. It remained in office until the declaration of President's Rule in the state early in 1976, during the

Emergency, and then lost the post-Emergency election of 1977 to the
ADMK (Anna DMK) which was formed by a split in the DMK in 1972.
The split came about largely because of personal rivalry between the
DMK leader M. Karunanidhi and 'a famous film star and politician,
M. G. Ramachandran ("MGR").The ADMK platform and methods
are not substantially different from those of the DMK. "MGR" was the
Chief Minister of Tamil Nadu from 1977, until his death in December
1987, and pursued an increasingly authoritarian style of populist
government.

Communal Riots and Labour: Bengal's Jute-mill-hands in the 1890s[1]

Dipesh Chakrabarty

The Early 1890s: A Communal Culture Emerges

Calcutta and its suburbs appear to have enjoyed a fairly peaceful history of communal relations over large parts of the nineteenth century. But from the early 1890s onwards a communal culture grew in the northern parts of Calcutta and its northern suburbs, areas which had concentrations of immigrant merchants and labourers. The first recorded Muslim riot broke out at Shyambazar in north Calcutta in 1891. The issue was the demolition of a building alleged to be a mosque. Immediately after the Shyambazar riot several incidents of conflict between Hindus and Muslims took place in the area loosely described as Chitpur, especially at Machuabazar which had a large settlement of immigrant Muslims. A significant rumbling of communal demands was also heard in the years 1894–5 in the jute mills. Sections of the mill workers became extremely assertive about observing their religious festivals, including those of Id, Bakr-Id, Muharram and Rath Jatra.[2] Disturbances occurred over demands for paid leave during these festivals.

The most interesting point about these demands is of course their novelty – "Last year [1894] and in the former years they were never demanded." This new accent on religious and community festivals revealed to the authorities "quite a new attitude on the part of the mill coolies". The demands also reveal a new community consciousness on the part of the workers. The Muslim worker was emphasizing the Muslim part of his identity; the Hindu, the Hindu part of his. In 1894–5 this did not yet lead to communal (that is, Hindu–Muslim) conflicts, but the 1896 Bakr-Id riots in the jute mills over the issue of the sacrifice of cows by Muslims, were indeed communal. Such community consciousness on the part of the mill worker, especially the immigrant, was only to grow over time both in its depth and spread.

What is the import of this sudden emphasis placed by mill-hands on communal issues such as cow-killing? The very fact that cow-killing became such an important issue in the 1894–6 riots strongly suggests the up-country social origins of the rioters. For cow-killing riots had never been seen in Bengal to any significant extent, whereas they raged in districts of Bihar and UP such as Ballia, Benares, Azamgarh, Gorakhpur, Arrah, Saran, Gaya and Patna throughout the years 1888–93, that is, the period just preceding the troubled years at the Calcutta jute mills. The districts affected were also typically the supply area for immigrant labourers in Bengal's jute mills and other industries. "Cow-killing" thus seems to have been an "imported" issue. (Some observations of contemporary officials confirm this.)

By 1894–7 there was a sizeable component of up-country mill-hands, a number of whom were, in addition, entirely new to industrial work. It was natural that their past attitudes, memories and prejudices would also form "fresh recruits", as it were, in the formation of a social outlook of this group of people. A telling piece of evidence is the argument which one worker gave as his reason for insisting on killing a cow on Bakr-Id, claiming that "he had every year sacrificed a cow *in his own country*, and it was hard that he should now be prohibited from doing so, merely because he had changed his residence". There was thus an "immigrant mind" at work.

Community Consciousness and the Labour-market

What was happening, however, was not just a mere transfer of past attitudes into a new situation of industrial work. Life in industry had elements which helped such attitudes to persist and grow. To explain that phenomenon, we now turn to a discussion of the jute mill labour-market. In the absence of any significant growth of other industries in the narrow industrial belt around Calcutta, especially in the absence of any significant engineering industry,[3] the jute mills were the most important employer of industrial labour in a market where supply of labour always outstripped demand. In 1911, for example, jute mills employed more than 73 per cent of the factory labour force in the industrial areas of Hooghly, Howrah, 24-Parganas and Calcutta.

Work in the jute mills required a low degree of skill and little rigorous training. Workers therefore were highly replaceable, and since the mills had a pull on the entire labour-market of Bihar, UP and Orissa, the industry could easily afford to change the social composition of its work-force whenever this was to its advantage.[4] Stability of labour was not in itself a crucial concern to the industry as, over the long run, labour supply was abundant, though there were some periods of temporary scarcity.

What concerned the industry most, then, was a steady supply and control of labour. Also, being a labour-intensive industry where labour alone accounted for more than 50 per cent of the "cost of conversion", the jute industry had to find a relatively less expensive means of recruiting and controlling its labour force. The industry's answer to its problem of supply and control was the *sardari* system.

Sardari, or "jobbery" as it was called in English, is probably an example of a pre-colonial, pre-capitalist institution being made an essential feature of the process of industrialization in a colony.[5] Simply put, the *sardar* was both a recruiter and supervisor of labour. He was of the same social origin as the ordinary worker. He had the power also to effect dismissal. He indulged in all kinds of financial extortions, which included taking a *dastoory* (commission) from each of his recruits. In the jute mills he was also the workers' money-lender and landlord, and his major economic instrument of control was debt-bondage.

The *sardar*'s mode of operation had some crucial pre-capitalist elements. For one thing, he always recruited on the basis of the often overlapping networks of community, village and kin, making such links extremely valuable to the worker. The basis of the *sardar*'s social control of the work-force lay in manoeuvring these relationships, and the ideologies and social norms associated with them. *Sardars* would thus have dominated the caste *panchayats* of up-country Hindu workers which were already in existence in 1890 and which the contemporary Factory Commission reported on. Muslim *ulama* (priests), whose influence over up-country Muslim workers was so visible during the riot at Rishra in 1896, must have had the *sardars* as their patrons and cohorts. For the *ulama* were attached to mosques, and mosques in working-class localities situated in jute-mill districts are still named after important *sardars*.

Thus the *sardari* mode of recruitment and control went hand in hand with the retention of community consciousness and other forms of pre-capitalist ideology in the working-class milieu. In the mid-1890s, as demand for jobs grew, the *sardar*'s powers increased, and with that the worker's community consciousness became more manifest.

The 1890s were a period of over-supply in the jute-mill labour-market, when immigration from UP into Bengal reached its peak. The operations of *sardars* could only have added to the actual physical competition in the labour-market, as *sardari* corruption (that is, the taking of bribes for every recruit) usually led to a high turnover in the mills. The growing crisis of the jute mill labour force in the mid-1890s shows through some of the events of the time. In October 1893 at a Howrah jute mill, "old and new workmen" fought with each other. "The former struck work as their pay had been reduced". There were strikes, and managers were attacked in a few mills. Workers were essentially fighting wage cuts. The scramble for jobs (especially when the mills were expanding in the mid-1890s) and the consequent weakening of the workers' bargaining power is reflected in the wage data. The index of the average real wage (taking the average for 1890–4 as the base) for the jute-mill workers fell first from 108 in 1895 to 105 in 1896, and then to 91 in 1897.

In such a scramble for work, the *sardar* in his capacity of recruiter would undoubtedly have been crucial to the worker's life. Communal connections through which the *sardar* found his recruits, and therefore community consciousness (which *sardari* control fostered anyway), would have become extremely important to the worker, especially to the migrant in search of work. Such community consciousness was indeed revealed in the demand for holidays in 1894–5. In fact the new accent on cow-killing in 1896 shows a recent tightening of communal bonds, for the price of a cow was such that it could not be bought without raising subscriptions from the community.

Community consciousness was then, in a sense, the migrant workers' substitute for closed-shop trade-unionism. Yet surely it was much more than just that. In a life characterized by the preponderance of men, unstable marriages, precarious living conditions, and desperate gambling in years of rising prices, socialization usually took place according to communal lines. Hindus and Muslims often lived in separate *bustis* (slum dwellings). The caste *panchayats* of the Hindu migrants, or the Muslim *ulama* acting as communal figure-heads for the Jolaha weavers from UP, would all serve the same function: to fulfil the immigrant's need to hold on to certain constants in a hostile and changing environment. Community consciousness thus also gave to these socially marginal people psychological comfort and security.

This is what made Muslim workers receptive to the politics they received at the hands of the city's Muslim leaders who controlled the Muslim (especially Urdu) press, and from the itinerant "*maulavis* and *oolamas*" who naturally spoke a religious language. This is not to suggest that the Hindu migrant was any less (or more) communal. It was just that for the Hindus, as the following discussion will show, such organized leadership was not available.

Workers and Communal Leadership

The character of the social leadership that these community-conscious working men often sought in this period is remarkably brought out in a letter written by the *imam* of Rishra, Nazir Mian, to Haji (*Hadji*) Nur Muhammad Zakaria, an important Muslim trader living in north Calcutta, asking for help during the Bakr-Id riot of 1896:

> It is informed that in village Rishra, police station Serampore, district Hooghly, the Hindus are going to create a row during the *Bakr-Id* [cow] sacrifice; they say they do not sacrifice here, if you do so, we [Hindus] will create row. Therefore, I request that you all assist us. We are poor people and work in mills. You better give this information to Muhammadans in the Friday prayers that it is religious act and everybody should assist as possible

The letter is significant. Part of it merely shows the poor man's sense of his position ("We are poor people and work in mills"), but the invocation of a "religious act" and the whole purpose of writing the letter clearly bring out my point about the growth of community consciousness.

The latter further suggests a situation. We have here at the end of the nineteenth century a group of up-country workers, acutely conscious of their being Muslims, approaching a wealthy Muslim of the city for his support of their communal demands. The *haji* must have appeared in their eyes as a community leader.

Evidence is lacking on the question of how, or what sort of, connections were formed between the *haji* and the Muslim mill-hands. But we may use the Talla riot in Calcutta of 1897 and the events connected with it to prove indirectly a basic point: a person like Haji Zakaria was accepted by the poor Muslims in and around the city as their protector and guide. It is to men of this sort that they repeatedly turned for leadership in trying to solve their problems.

The Talla riot was the first-ever large-scale riot to break out in Calcutta. It started on 29 June over the issue of the eviction by court order of a Muslim mason named Himmat Khan from a piece of land at Talla in north Calcutta. Maharaja Jotindra Mohan Tagore held a life interest in the plot of land. Himmat Khan, faced with the court order, declared his hut to be "a *Musjid* of long standing". The "mosque" was subsequently demolished by the police, and this sparked off the riot.

Throughout the history of the riot Haji Zakaria and other leading Muslims of Calcutta figure as the people involved in the events leading up to the outbreak of the riot, as in those which finally culminated in its quelling.

It is true that the physical involvement of Muslim mill-hands in the Talla riots remained mostly marginal, being confined mainly to the few mills that were situated either within or very close to the city, including those at Sealdah, Garden Reach and Baranagar. But certain events which occurred some days after the riots had subsided in the city served to bring out the importance and esteem in which the *haji* was held by some sections of the Muslim mill-hands. It seems that they would not come and help the Talla rioters without the *haji* asking them to do so. That was the extent of the hold that Haji Zakaria had on their minds.

Zakaria, His Audience, and Community Consciousness

Haji Zakaria was an important member of the Kutchi Memon community living in the Chitpur quarters of the city. What might otherwise have only been conjectured from the letter of Nazir Mian, the *imam* of Rishra, can now be seen as reality. In 1897 we have a wealthy Muslim trader who is at the same time a "religious" man (as evidenced by his founding a mosque) and who enjoys a great deal of social importance, commanding a following from among the more indigent Muslims in the city. The *haji*'s followers were a motley crowd, men of different labouring occupations. In the absence of court documents it is indeed difficult to depict the people who constituted the "crowd" in the Talla riot. Besides, motives for joining the riot varied widely. But looking through some newspaper reports on rioting at Talla near the site of the mosque, we do indeed catch glimpses of the mob, and can identify some faces in an otherwise anonymous crowd. The identifiable are no doubt very few in number, but they may be indicative of the social composition of the men who fought for saving the demolished mosque.

It was the poor up-country Muslims of the city who made up the Talla rioters and accepted the social leadership of Haji Zakaria – the mason, the thatcher, the bricklayer, the coolie, the jetty worker and the labourer from a jute press in north Calcutta. These and many other up-country Muslims working in mills north of the city shared certain communal bonds and were, in other words, community conscious. This is reflected in their acceptance of the leadership of Haji Zakaria and in the fact that on the first night of

the Talla riot Muslims came over from different places such as
Chitpur, Kashipur, Baranagar and Nikaripara to fight the police,
and that mill-hands at Garden Reach felt restive on the same night.

Haji Zakaria was also one of the earliest and most confirmed pan-
Islamists in Calcutta.[6] Even in these lean years of pan-Islamism in
the city, Haji Zakaria remained a consistent follower of the creed.
People who stood by him in this were also the men who had signed
his religious *fatwa* during the Talla riot,[7] the men who were described
officially as enjoying the confidence of the rioters. Of course they
were not anti-British as such, and showed "every disposition to
please the authorities". But in their pan-Islamism, they did form a
"party" which was described as having been:

> active in holding up the Sultan as the head of Islam, in representing
> him as being unjustly harassed by Great Britain and the European
> powers and in magnifying his might as manifested by victories over
> the Greeks.

If the men who gave social leadership to the Talla rioters were pan-
Islamist, it is interesting to observe that pan-Islamism also formed
an important part of the feelings that circulated during the riot. The
Talla incident, wrote a correspondent to the *Amrita Bazar Patrika*,
"has its origin in a current of feeling which was inspired by the
manner in which the news of the victory of the Sultan over the
Greeks were so freely circulated among the Mahomedan population
in the country". "The educated Mahomedans were the agents in
circulating the news", so much so that the Talla rioters often thought
that they were fighting "the cause of the Sultan and the [Afghan]
Amir".

Rumours current during the Talla riots also point to the pan-
Islamist content of the riot. The *Amrita Bazar Patrika*, in an editorial
after the Talla events, wrote of the "very many" stories circulating
on the subject of the rioters.

It was not only the distant reality of the Sultan that came to be
looked upon with pan-Islamist eyes by the poor Muslim; the ideology
of pan-Islamism seems to have gone deeper. Even things nearer to
the daily lives of the city poor often received a pan-Islamist
interpretation. The mid-1890s were problem years as much for the
city poor as they were for the jute-mill workers. There had been,
first of all, a very sharp drop in real wages. The city had suffered a
bad attack of cholera that began in March 1897. Besides, at the end
of 1896 fear of plague had gripped the city. This fear and resentment
of attempts by the government to effect "plague regulations", were

assuming by early 1897 almost all-India proportions.

Early in the year, Calcutta was "restive with rumours about plague regulations", and the "wildest possible notions" were being "freely supported". The Muslims especially disliked the restrictions the government had put on *haj* pilgrimage; in April 1897 the pilgrimage had been temporarily stopped by the government under the Epidemic Diseases Act and this was interpreted by the Muslim labourers as an action which ran counter to pan-Islamism.

On top of everything there was surely the urge of an immigrant community to settle down. For, behind every protest against the demolition of "illegal" *musjids*, there must have been an objective demand for land and settled habitation. And if some of these alleged mosques were performing the roles of real ones, then their demolition would only upset the life of a settled community.

Thus, fear of plague, resentment of plague regulations, a drop in wage rates, the predicament of a migrant labouring population, the Sultan, the British raj – all these issues were becoming one. This in the end lent the Talla riot an anti-British character that worried the authorities. The poor migrant Muslims of the city and the mills had indeed received and accepted the politics of the pan-Islamist Muslim élites in the city.

The Communal Question and Problems of Social Leadership in the 1890s

Why were the immigrant Muslim traders of the Chitpur area so interested in linking up with the Muslim poor? Muslim charity or factional politics may have been important factors in these developments, but a police document of 1910 suggests an interesting alternative explanation. Such explanation can again only be speculative in the absence of hard data.

The document in question relates to anti-cow-killing agitation in Chitpur in 1910. The agitation was led by the immigrant Marwari traders from Rajasthan, Hindu or Jain by religion, who were to dominate much of Calcutta's business history in the twentieth century. The document shows that by 1910 Marwaris were pushing into the residential areas of Muslim traders and labourers, and were prepared to use communalism to displace them. The Marwaris, who were deeply entrenched in the trade of rice and jute, the two principal twentieth-century crops in Bengal, brought with them new chains of retail and wholesale trade connections. Their entry into the Chitpur area, the central business district of the city, may have been of importance to their interests.

Marwari incursions into the Muslim residential areas of Chitpur and Burrabazar did not start in 1910. Indirect evidence points to an earlier beginning. The formation of a Marwari-inspired Cow Protection Society in Burrabazar in 1894, or Marwari gambling that was particularly rife in 1896 in Chitpur, suggest a growing Marwari presence in these areas in the 1890s. If this is true, the it would partly explain why in this decade the poor migrant Muslims were often fighting the demolition of "alleged mosques". Their settlements were under pressure from developments in the local land-market. The residential areas of the old Muslim traders were being invaded by the Marwaris. They may have faced business competition, too, from the Marwaris. The Zakarias and Ariffs were probably on the defensive and therefore keen to link up with the poorer migrant Muslims so as to be able to use their own "communalism" against that of the Marwaris. In this, a pan-Islamist ideology could be a very good bond to cement the Muslim rich and poor. The leadership of the up-country mill-hand, by contrast, went by default. His communalism may have received occasional support from Hindus important in the locality. But the chain of patronage would hardly go beyond the locality.

The Bengali *bhadralok* ("respectable person" of the middle class) in the nineteenth century, with his "education, clean clothes, and hands unsoiled with manual labour", perhaps felt distant from the world of men who worked in the mills. In the 1890s, with a large number of immigrant mill-hands, the gulf between the *bhadralok* and working men was only to grow wider. The Bengali *bhadralok* were not sufficiently equipped culturally to communicate with such groups. Their premier political organization, the Indian Association, reacted to the Talla riot by petitioning the viceroy to "open a volunteer corps and train the Bengalis in the use of arms . . . [which] would . . . help them to resist the rowdy rioters".

It was in this context of a social and cultural hiatus between the *bhadrolok* and the migrant workers that the community consciousness of Hindu mill workers found foster-parents in the idiosyncratic communalism of an Annapurna Devi or a Hindu mill babu, while Muslim migrants found similar support in the broader community politics of someone like Haji Zakaria. Bengal did not provide them with any alternative social leadership.

Some of the beginnings of twentieth-century mass-communal politics in Calcutta may be discerned in this story. The cultural gap between the mill worker and the Bengali intelligentsia remained.[8] The Marwaris and the Hindu Mahasabha party were to become in time the chief patrons of Hindu communalism in the city. The tradition of Haji Zakaria or Golam Ariff found twentieth-century successors in men like H. S. Suhrawardy or Y. C. Ariff (a descendant of Golam Ariff) who organized "black" Muslim trade unions in the jute mills and the Calcutta docks in the 1920s and 1930s. The crucial continuity was of course in the labour-market, where the migrants were to grow in number, and the *sardari* system much stronger. The labour-market thus continued to churn out human material that communalist-minded politicians in the city were only too happy to use. The Calcutta riots of 1918 and 1926, and to some extent the Great Calcutta Killings of 1946, bear gruesome testimony to this.

Notes

1. This is an abridged and revised version of a paper originally prepared at the Centre for Studies in Social Sciences, Calcutta, and published in *Past and Present*, no. 91. Thanks are due to several friends and colleagues for comments on drafts, especially to Partha Chatterjee, A. K. Bagchi, R. Das Gupta, Majid Siddiqi, Diana Tonsich, Stephen Henningham and Roger Stuart. I am also grateful to E. P. Thompson for detailed, helpful criticism. My greatest debt, however, is to Barun De. All errors are mine.

2. The Id festival occurs at the end of Ramadan, the ninth month of the Muslim year during which strict fasting is observed during daylight hours. The Bakr-Id festival commemorates the Patriarch Abraham's sacrifice of his son Isaac. The Muharram festival celebrates the end of the period of fasting and public mourning observed during the first month of the Muslim year in commemoration of the deaths of Hassan and Hussain. Rath Jatra is the chariot festival of the Hindus.

3. The slow growth of the engineering industry is traced in A. K. Bagchi, *Private Investment in India, 1900–1939* (Cambridge, 1972) 302–3.

4. Thus it is interesting to observe that the replacement of Bengalis by up-country workers in the mills in the mid-1890s took place at a time when mill work was becoming more onerous and Bengali workers had started complaining. Electric lighting was introduced to the mills in 1895. The "working day was increased to 15 hours, Saturdays included, which involved an additional amount of clearing and repairing work on Sundays", but not everywhere with a corresponding increase in wages.

5. Professor Ashin Das Gupta has encountered jobbery in his research on pre-British Surat (personal communication to the author). For an instance of jobbery in Bengal, in the pre-factory days of the early nineteenth century, see D. Chakrabarty and R. Das Gupta, "Functions of the Nineteenth-Century Banian: A Document", *Economic and Political Weekly*, ix, no. 35 (August 1974) M73–5. For a discussion of jobbery

as a ubiquitous form of labour recruitment and control in Indian
industrialization, see *Report of the Royal Commission on Labour in India*, 11
vols. (London, 1931).

6. In the late nineteenth century the examples of German and Italian
unification suggested the potency of movements for unity of divided
territories. This idea formed the basis of pan-Islamic euphoria which
swept many parts of the Muslim world in the last quarter of the century.
See M. Hasan, 1986, "Pan-Islamism versus Indian Nationalism?",
Economic and Political Weekly, XXI, 24, 14 June.

7. A religious decree.

8. This is not to belittle the heroic efforts of leftists and communists in
Bengal to bridge the gulf, but their organizational basis, down to the
1950s, remained somewhat limited to a minority of mills having a mainly
Bengali work-force. See Indrajit Gupta, *Capital and Labour in the Jute
Industry* (Delhi, 1953) 42.

India's Preferential Policies[1]

Myron Weiner and Mary F. Katzenstein

India has two types of preferential policies. One provides special benefits and exclusive preferences to members of scheduled castes and scheduled tribes; these policies are analogous, though not identical, to affirmative action programmes for minorities in the USA. These communities are given preferences in admission to schools and colleges (and special stipends), and in recruitment and promotion in government employment. They are also given reserved seats in state legislative assemblies and in parliament. Some of these preferences (not including reserved seats in legislative bodies) have also been extended by many state governments to a list of disadvantaged "backward" classes.

Another set of policies provide preferences to *local* ethnic groups in competition for higher-salaried jobs with migrants from outside the state. There are domicile rules for employment by government, and the private sector is also "encouraged" – the pressures are often acute – to hire locally. In addition, preferences are also provided to local people for admission into educational institutions, especially into engineering and medical colleges. To the extent that the local ethnic group is disadvantaged in relation to outsiders, it is argued, they too deserve preferences. Both sets of policies share common assumptions about the responsibility of the state for the achievement of ethnic equality. They differ in that the first set of policies is intended to provide preferences to minorities, while the second provides preferences to a majority which considers itself educationally and occupationally subordinate to a minority.

Of the many consequences of these policies for India, there are four that emerge as particularly important. The first is that preferential policies in India are primarily directed at expanding educational and employment opportunities for the middle classes within each ethnic group that considers itself "backward". Members of these middle classes have been the primary beneficiaries of preferential policies, although we suggest that there is at least some evidence that the position of these groups might have improved even in the absence of such preferences.

Second, the extension of preferences to local ethnic majorities has meant that an ever-increasing proportion of the middle classes in almost all ethnic groups is assured of a "share" (though often an unequal share) in education and employment.

Third, various ethnic groups, therefore, politically fight for a share of that labour market. The major political struggles are often over who should get reservations, how the boundaries of the ethnic groups should be defined, and how large their share should be. There are also political struggles over whether there should be reservations in both education and employment, in private as well as in public employment, and in promotions as well as in hiring. The preferential policies themselves have thus stimulated various ethnic groups to assert their "rights" to reservations.

Finally, we emphasize that the response to demands for preferential treatment and the incorporation of preferences within governmental policy must be understood in terms of political logic: we thus attempt to identify how those who make policy perceive the costs and benefits of preferential treatment. We look not only at the social and economic linkages between policy-makers and ethnic claimants, but also, even more important in our view, at the political gains and losses which policy-makers must attempt to calibrate as they react to demands for preferences.

The Demand for Restructuring the Ethnic Division of Labour

In those regions and urban areas of India in which migrant minorities were educationally and occupationally more advanced than the local population, the expansion of local secondary schools and colleges subsequently created an aspiring middle class that was dissatisfied with the existing ethnic division of labour. As the local community, or at least the educated portions within it, felt blocked by migrants and descendants of migrants, they sought state intervention to provide job reservations for the local population.

The demand was not simply for equality of income – there was no demand, for example, for more equitable income-tax policies – but rather for equality of employment *in the modern sector of the economy*. Newly educated natives, seeking jobs in the modern sector, viewed the successful migrants from other cultural–linguistic regions as barriers to their own social and occupational mobility. The demand for ethnic equality was not a demand for state-subsidized assistance to compete in the labour market, or for the elimination of discrimination in employment, but for a set of policies that would restrict or even exclude migrants and their descendants in order to improve the position of local ethnic groups. In other words, the demand was that the state intervene *to restructure the ethnic division of labour.*

One argument for intervention is that the existing division of labour is the result of a historical set of policies adopted by the British rulers. The British had made it possible for the more educated (from the more economically developed regions) to take control of the administration and to occupy positions in the emerging modern sector of the economy. The state should intervene to remedy what the state had itself created. To permit equal competition for positions would not reverse this historic division of labour since the two groups, the natives and the migrants, continue to be unequal in education and skills. Only a system of preferences in employment, it is argued, can change the existing division of labour.

A second argument is that local people have a right to employment in the modern sector created within their territory. They are entitled to whatever benefits modernization and industrialization bring to their region since the region provides the resources which make development possible Hence, it is only right and proper that for example, the tea plantations in Assam be managed by Assamese, and that industrial houses in Bombay be staffed by Maharashtrians.

A third argument is that social justice requires that all ethnic groups share equally in the benefits of modernization. According to this argument, all ethnic groups – and by ethnic is meant linguistic, tribal, religious, and caste groups – ought to have the same internal division of labour that exists in the society as a whole. Thus, according to this argument, each ethnic group ought to have its share of positions in the modern sector of the economy – in administration, in the professions, in the factories, and so on. If, to place a numerical value on the principle, 10 per cent of the jobs are in the modern sector, then 10 per cent of each ethnic group ought to be employed in this sector.

Such numerical quotas were initially established for the employment of scheduled castes and scheduled tribes in the state and central administrative services. Members of scheduled castes and tribes have reservations for seats in the state legislative assemblies and in the national parliament, admissions into colleges and technical institutes, and jobs in the central and state administrative services. These reservations or quotas are in proportion to the population of the scheduled castes and tribes within each state; in a state where 10 per cent of the population belongs to scheduled castes and another 5 per cent to scheduled tribes, 10 and 5 per cent respectively of political offices, college admissions, and civil service appointments are reserved for these communities.

A number of state governments also provide preferences for a category known as "other backward classes". A Backward Classes Commission established by the central government in 1953 presented a list of 2399 groups entitled by its criterion to government benefits, totalling 116 million members, or about 32 per cent of the total population of India. Nationally, the scheduled castes, scheduled tribes, and other backward classes together total 54 per cent of the population.

The demand by other local groups for reservations was thus a logical extension of the system of reservations for the scheduled castes, tribes, and OBCs – with one significant difference. While reservations for scheduled castes, tribes, and OBCs were intended to benefit disadvantaged minorities (though collectively they may form a majority), the demand by local people for preferences against migrant communities was a demand on behalf of a disadvantaged majority. Moreover, while the case for preferences for the scheduled castes and tribes in part rested on the argument that they suffered from social disability as a consequence of their place in the Indian social order and the discriminations which they experienced, the case for preferences for the local population did not rest upon the notion of discrimination, but rather on the argument that for one reason or another they had been left behind. The principle was thus argued and accepted that disadvantaged groups – that is, those that have a disproportionately small share of jobs in the modern sector – irrespective of the cause and irrespective of their size, are entitled to preferences.

The demand for preferences for the local population comes primarily from those who do not receive them as members of scheduled castes, tribes, or other backward classes. This explains in part why the political movements for local preferences have their social base among caste Hindus and particularly among the more "advanced" higher castes within the local community (approximately 34 per cent of the Indian population). In every state these are the groups that would otherwise receive no preferences and hence no protection in the competition for admission into colleges and universities and in employment. For example in the city of Bombay, the Shiv Sena, a local political party, demanded that special job rights be given to the local Marathi-speaking population (42 per cent of the city) in preference to middle-class migrants from south India (see the discussion by Engineer in the next chapter). Underlying the various arguments for preferential treatment on the basis of ethnicity is the assumption that the position of an individual in India's hierarchical society is largely shaped by the position or rank of the ethnic group to which he belongs. Hence, any effort to improve one's position rests upon changing that of the group as a whole. This is a different argument from one which says that one's position is affected by the prejudice of society. Although many Indians recognize that there is prejudice, especially against scheduled castes, the argument for preferences rests more broadly on the notion that individual success requires an improvement in a group's standing.

The Debate on the Use of Ethnic Criteria

Some Indians have argued against the use of any ethnic categories in employment on the grounds that within each of these ethnic groups there is a wide range of educational achievement and that preferences simply give jobs to those most qualified to compete while doing nothing for those who are the least qualified. Some critics have also argued that it is unfair to treat locally born descendants of migrants as "outsiders" simply because they belong to another ethnic group, and that it is also unfair to give preferences to a local person (or to a member of a scheduled caste) from a well-to-do family while those who are excluded from the preferred groups may come from a less-advantaged background. Finally, some have argued that industry and government need the most qualified individuals without regard to ethnicity or place of birth, especially for managerial personnel and for the more technically sophisticated jobs.

The objection to preferences by ethnic criteria thus has two possible grounds: rights and justice, and efficiency. In this debate both the state governments and the central government have rejected the rights argument, concluding that the disadvantaged ethnic groups have legitimate claim for preferences, but accepted the efficiency argument. Thus, the laws and administrative regulations were written in such a way as to minimize the impact of preferences on employment where a high level of skill is required or where efficiency seems essential for the work of others. The central government, for example, declared that local people would be given preference in employment in centrally run public sector firms, but that technical jobs and senior administrative positions – an arbitrary salary level was defined – would be recruited nationally on merit alone. Similarly, private employers were informed that they might make a similar distinction; national recruitment (hence merit) for some categories of jobs, local recruitment (hence ascription and ethnicity) for others. However, state governments were generally reluctant to accept what they viewed as a dangerous loophole, so they have preferred to hire local people for all categories of employment.

It would be a mistake to assume, however, that preferential policies in India are based upon a clear set of logical, consistent principles which make it possible to determine who should and who should not be given preferences, what kind of preferences, and for how long. Preferential policies have been adopted in India, as elsewhere, because of political pressures. There is in fact a political logic to preferential policies which accounts for the many inconsistencies and ambiguities in the policies themselves.

Critics of reservations have argued that the policy itself intensifies ethnic identifications, since politicians seek support by promising benefits to their caste, tribal, or linguistic constituents. And as politicians make these demands, and win support from ethnic groups, a struggle for benefits takes place which leads to a clash between backward and forward castes, Christian and non-Christian tribals, scheduled castes and caste Hindus, sons of the soil and migrants.[2] Competition that might otherwise have taken place among individuals for education and employment now takes place among groups for political control as each group seeks to carve out a benefit for its exclusive use.

Moreover, the critics continue, once a caste, tribe or local group is given preferences, it will fight to retain reservations even if it is no longer backward in education and employment. In the name of seeking equality, reservations thus perpetuate caste and undermine efforts to create a casteless society.

Leftist critics further argue that policies which provide benefits along ethnic lines serve to encourage individuals to give primacy to their ethnic rather than their class interests. Class differences within ethnic groups are muted, and the opportunities for creating class-based political organizations that cut across ethnic lines are thus made more difficult. In Assam leftists have argued (not without some evidence) that attacks against Bengalis are in part attempts to undermine the leftist parties.

More conservative critics have argued that reservations are detrimental to the functioning of the administrative system since jobs are given to those less qualified. Administrators, judges, engineers, doctors, and others appointed to government through reservations on the basis of ethnicity (either explicitly or indirectly through domicile requirements) may not be unqualified, but they are less qualified than those who would have been appointed had recruitment been through open competition without reservations.

But whatever the economic and social costs of preferential policies for those who are excluded, the political costs of dismantling preferential policies are very high for both state and central governments. Once policy-makers have redefined the disadvantaged to encompass the majority, the decision becomes virtually irreversible. Which majority is likely to give up benefits when it has the political clout to keep them? Why should the central government intervene in a state government policy that has widespread local popularity and thereby risk a politically costly clash between central and state authority? And what leverage do the excluded minorities have? They may seek loopholes in the laws, turn to the courts or to the central government, or appeal to the government of the states from which they come, but they do not have the political power to pressure the state governments to reverse the preferential policies.

At present, however, it seems politically more likely that preferences will be extended than that they will be curtailed. So long as the educational system continues to expand the middle class more rapidly than the economy can provide it with employment, the middle class within each state and within each ethnic group will fight to carve out a protected niche in the labour market; a labour-surplus middle class will want protection extended from the public to the private sector, from the state-run to the central-government-run public sector, from already-included categories of employment to those that have thus far been excluded. Only if India's economy expands rapidly enough to meet the employment needs of the middle class does it seem likely that the demand for preferential policies will abate.

Once preferential policies for the local population were in place, the state governments themselves became interested parties in their maintenance. The main reason, of course, is that the state governments became dominated by the very ethnic groups that demanded the policies, a process accelerated by the policies themselves. The result is that the state governments – the bureaucracies as well as elected officials – have become advocates of the policies and wish to see them extended; from public employment to private employment; from the lower to the higher categories of employment; and from employment and education to housing and other public benefits. For this reason it seems unlikely that the tendency to extend preferential policies can be brought to an end by the political process within a state. They can be arrested only through intervention by the courts or by the central government, if at all.

Editors' Notes

1. From the book of the same title, published in 1981 by the Chicago University Press.
2. See Joshi's discussion of recent caste conflict in Gujarat in the next chapter but one.

Bombay–Bhiwandi Riots in National Political Perspective[1]

Asghar Ali Engineer

The Bombay–Bhiwandi riots[2] which shook the country for nearly ten days should not be treated merely as a local phenomenon, although local factors were not without significance. Many journalists and some others have propounded various theories, many of them quite shaky or based on doubtful evidence. The most talked-about theory was the one about smugglers and builders having financed the riots. While it is undoubtedly true that anti-social elements have played a definite role in these riots it would be erroneous to ascribe the principal organizing role to them. A probe by this writer does not indicate any systematic involvement of builders or smugglers-turned-builders.

These riots, like other major riots, must be viewed against the background of political developments in the country. The politicians are the principal, and the anti-social elements at their beck and call, the subsidiary agents in promoting and inciting communal violence. Those who hold smugglers and builders to be the principal agents minimize the role of politics and politicians.

It would be useful to refer to the political situation in the country in order to understand the background to the ever-increasing communal violence. The makers of the Indian Constitution adopted secularism as the sheet-anchor of state policy and this suited the emerging bourgeoisie very well. However, putting secularism into practice and achieving national integration are not easy given uneven capitalist development and the stresses and strains produced by it.

With capitalist development a host of forces are released sharpening conflict among regions, castes and communities. The Telengana, Assam and Punjab agitations on the one hand, and the increased manifestation of caste and communal violence on the other, are the result of this process of uneven capitalist development. The role of anti-social elements in caste, communal and regional violence should be treated, by serious social scientists, as contingent upon the political consequences of the socio-economic developments taking place within the capitalist framework. The fast-emerging caste, communal and regional conflict, also manifesting itself in the form

205

of greater emphasis on ethnic identities, has created a severe political crisis for the ruling classes. In view of this crisis, the bourgeoisie finds it difficult to fulfil its commitment to secularism, although it continues to pay lip-service to it.

The ruling classes have, of late, sought to adopt the strategy of encouraging and making unabashed alliances with the rank communalists among the Hindus, Sikhs and Muslims. It is no secret now that Indira Gandhi very subtly encouraged the emergence of the Vishwa Hindu Parishad and its blatant Hindu communalist posture. Her role in the emergence of Bhindranwale as a militant political force is too widely talked about to be repeated here.[3]

Shift in Alliances

In this connection one has to take note of an important development which has taken place over the years and which has brought about a shift in the alliances among the ruling classes. The caste composition of the ruling classes is fast changing. When the country achieved freedom, the Brahmans and a few other top castes, comparatively few in number, were dominant. The middle and other backward castes did not play any crucial role. The ruling Congress, in order to widen its support base, wooed religious minorities, especially the Muslims, often exposing itself to the charge of appeasing them.

The middle and backward Hindu castes, so long as their political profile was low either did not resent the wooing of minorities by the ruling Congress or even approved of it.

The latter part of the 1960s was a period of deep economic as well as political crisis. Indira Gandhi split the Congress by widening her support base among the Muslims and the lower Hindu castes. By now the middle and backward castes had begun to assert themselves politically. The socio-economic transformation taking place both in rural and urban areas increased their aspirations and adult franchise helped them to bargain effectively for a share in economic and political power. Thus the middle and lower castes are acquiring greater political and economic clout. The political parties are now trying to widen their support base with the help of these castes. Yadavas, Jats, Bhoomihars, Ahirs, Marathas, Reddys, Patels and several other similar castes are becoming politically and economically predominant.

Among Muslims too a similar process is underway. Hitherto lower Muslim *biradaris* like Qureshis (those who deal in goats, buffaloes, etc), Ansaris (weavers, loom-owners, etc.) and similar other artisan *biradaris* are acquiring greater economic clout and consequently their political aspirations also soar high. The minorities as a rule tend to emphasize their religious identities which pays rich political dividend in view of their emotional appeal. The lower Muslim *biradaries* are mainly concentrated in middle-sized towns like Bhiwandi, Malegaon, Moradabad, Meerut, etc. These also happen to be the areas where the Hindu middle castes are prospering. The situation of confrontation develops between the Muslims and these Hindu middle castes and the Hindu middle castes are thus fast becoming communalized.

In view of these developments it now suited Gandhi and her party to try to win allies among these middle castes. Being more numerous, these castes could ensure greater mobilization of votes. The Muslims, on the other hand, for a variety of reasons, including greater political consciousness and consequent assertiveness, were not in a mood to go the whole hog with the ruling Congress. In view of all this there was a perceptible shift in Indira Gandhi's electoral strategy. She was inclined to give greater weight to Hindu upper-caste and middle-caste votes and minimize the significance of minority votes. She was even reported to have said in one of her speeches after the Bhiwandi–Bombay riots that the majority community also had feelings which must be respected. Such a statement by her in the late 1960s would have been unthinkable. The army action in Punjab was also partly inspired by this changed electoral strategy. The Hindus of the North welcomed the army action, thus enhancing her electoral appeal. She intended to cut into the BJP votes. She had done so effectively in the Jammu region with subtle RSS support and intended to repeat the performance in UP and Bihar.[5]

Shiv Sena's Role

The Bhiwandi–Bombay riots also must be seen against the same background. The Marathas in Maharashtra are an important support base for the ruling Congress. The Marathas, now a powerful ruling caste, have assumed an arrogant caste and communal posture. It was the Marathas who played the principal role in organizing the Marathwada riots on the question of renaming Marathwada University.[6] The Maratha Mahasangh had played a very active role in promoting the Pune–Solapur riots in 1982. The leader of the Mahasangh had made virulent anti-Muslim speeches in the Pune–Solapur region before and during the riots.

It would not be wrong to maintain that the Bombay–Bhiwandi riots were incited mainly by Shiv Sena[7] and were mainly between Maharashtrian Hindus and the Muslims. The role of other Hindus was either passive or neutral, with some exceptions, of course. The ruling Congress and the state government led by Vasant Dada Patil chose to remain silent spectators in view of the mounting offensive by Shiv Sena, precisely because they could not afford to alienate the Maratha sentiment roused by the communal fury. Indira Gandhi too remained silent on the issue refusing to blame anyone (restoration of peace is more important than blaming anyone, she maintained in a press conference she addressed at the Raj Bhavan after touring the riot-affected areas of Bhiwandi and Bombay) as she too did not want to alienate the powerful sentiments of her political allies. If she really meant to check violence she could have asked the Chief Minister to swoop down on the culprits. Firm action did check communal violence when it erupted again in the Kherwadi area of Bandra East on 19 June. The arrest of forty Shiv Sena Shakha Pramukhs brought the situation under control. A second serious outbreak of communal violence would have meant total loss of credibility for the government making its position utterly ridiculous and hence its decision to put down the violence firmly.

The foregoing discussion mainly focuses upon the national political scene and the changing alliances of the ruling party to suit its election strategy. The Indian bourgeoisie, despite its commitment to secularism, which is essential requirement of economic integration of the country as a whole, is resorting to casteist and communal politics in order to resolve the emerging political crisis. The caste and communal violence, occuring on an ever-increasing scale in the country must be primarily viewed against this background.

However, the discussion should not make us oblivious of the local factors responsible for building up communal tension and finally causing the conflagration.[8] In dealing with these factors the role of migrant-labour population cannot be ignored. Bhiwandi is a fast-developing powerloom centre. The majority of the looms are owned by Uttar Pradesh (UP) Muslims and the workers are also Muslims from UP. The Muslim population of Bhiwandi has been expanding due to migration from UP. Some of these migrants, hard working and enterprising, soon succeed in raising their economic status and come to own a couple of powerlooms thus acquiring economic prosperity.

Some important consequences follow from the dynamics of this socio-economic situation. The propaganda by the Hindu communalists that the Muslims do not practise family planning and breed much faster acquires credibility among general Hindus. In fact the immediate provocation for these riots was the speech delivered by the Shiv Sena Chief Bal Thackeray on 22 April, wherein he described Muslims as a growing cancer in India which required an operation. It is being said by the communalists that the Muslim population in India is around 170 million (according to the 1971 Census it was a little over 60 million only) and even many Hindu advocates of the Bhiwandi court dismiss the Census figure and tend to believe the higher figure. Ironically, even Muslim communalists keep complaining against alleged deliberate suppression of Muslim population by the Census authorities.

Migrant Muslims from UP belong to lower *biradaris* and are religiously conservative. They spend more on religious rituals and other related activities than on acquiring economic clout. They are, therefore perceived to be religiously aggressive and fundamentalist, thus reinforcing another stereotype about Muslims. In view of all this the lower-middle-class Hindus easily swallow the Hindu communal propaganda that the Muslims, if not checked in time, would succeed in carving out another Pakistan. In this connection it is interesting to note that the rioting in Bhiwandi began after the flag war on the eve of the Muslim religious festival, Shab Barat, in which a few Muslim youngsters were involved. The flag war was projected as religious aggressiveness on the part of the Muslims. It is also interesting to note that the youth involved in the flag war were mostly lumpen elements, connected with no organization or political party. The elderly Muslims, connected with different organizations and political parties, had exercised due caution and had resolved to check all the facts about Bal Thackeray's reported speech.

In understanding the genesis of a communal riot, apart from the political factors at the national level discussed above, it is also necessary to understand the sociology of religion in a developing industrial middle-sized town with its potential for attracting migrant labour, the different classes to which it gives rise and the varying perceptions among these classes of their counterparts in the rival community. The communalists, pushing under the carpet all these facts, indulge in sweeping generalizations about the whole community.

Religion not Causative Factor

Religion, it must be stressed, is not the causative factor but an instrumental factor. However, in common perception, on both the sides of the communal divide, it is taken to be a causative factor. It is necessary to combat this erroneous perception, if one intends to strike seriously at the root of the problem. It is necessary to throw some light on this in the context of the present riots also. In order to make religion appear as a causative factor, the Shiv Sena Shakha offices had put up boards saying "*Koran chodo* or *Hindustan chodo*" ("leave either the Koran or India"). This clearly implies that as long as the Muslims follow the Koran, they cannot become part of the national mainstream and the conflict with Hindus would remain. Thus religion becomes the main causative factor in the conflict between Hindus and Muslims.

The falsity of this approach becomes apparent is we examine the Hindu–Sikh conflict in Punjab. The Sikhs follow the Guru Granth Sahib as their holy scripture. The Granth Sahib, unlike the holy Koran, is full of the Hindu ethos and Hindu cultural and religious traditions. Sikhism is a separate religion yet not inimical to Hinduism, in any sense of the word. Despite this there has emerged a very sharp conflict between the Hindus and Sikhs in Punjab. Bhindranwale had even begun to talk of a Sikh–Muslim united front in order to combat Hindu hegemonistic designs. Had religion been a causative factor, such a sharp conflict between two non-antagonistic religions (they can be described even as harmonious in their spiritual ethos) and their followers should not have arisen. The root of the conflict lay in socio-economic factors, as would be seen if the Akali demands are closely examined.

It would thus be absurd to maintain that the conflict between Hindus and Muslims would disappear if the latter give up the Koran and Hinduize themselves. Yet, despite its absurdity, the propaganda value of such slogans is very strong and invariably results in serious outbreaks of violence. Such propaganda evokes a highly emotive response from lower-middle-class Hindus and, what is more unfortunate, no serious attempt is made by the left and secular intellectuals to combat it systematically. The communal parties, on the other hand, are using highly emotive medieval symbolism to widen their emotional appeal. It would be seen in and around Bombay that the Shiv Sena has given all its offices the appearance of Shivaji forts. The extensive use of swords, Shivaji's weapon, in the recent riots was also symbolic.[9]

Communalism is a modern phenomenon with medieval trappings to enhance its emotional appeal. Use of medieval symbolism also ensures a relative autonomy to it. It also successfully creates the illusion in the minds of common people about the causative efficacy of religion in the whole conflict. The lower strata of society, in a developing socio-economic situation, are caught in a complex process of deprivation and dehumanization and are psychologically prone to ascribe their woes to the maliciousness of the rival religious community, especially if there has been such a historical tradition.

It was not accidental that both in Bhivandi and Bombay the main sufferers in the riots were the poorest of the poor. These victims had hardly anything to do with religion, let alone being aware of the theological and metaphysical doctrinal differences, except being conscious of belonging to Islam or Hinduism. All they knew was that they are being killed, injured and looted because they belong to a particular community. It was the most cynical exploitation of religion for its rich emotional value by the most irreligious politicians.

The pattern of communal violence in Bombay and its suburbs was slightly different. In Bhiwandi the main targets of attacks were the peripheral *bastis* (shanty towns), mostly inhabited by migrant Muslims and Hindus from UP and the south, and the assailants mainly came from the nearby villages who perceived these *bastis* as encroachments on their land by outsiders, among other things. There was no large-scale involvement of criminals in these attacks, although their role cannot be altogether denied. In Bombay and its suburbs, on the other hand, criminals and anti-social elements played the main role in the eruption of communal violence. The Shiv Sena in a planned and organized way mobilized local criminals to launch attacks on Muslims. Of course, local causes like rivalry over encroachments, water disputes, fight between owners of different gambling dens and similar other factors came in handy to incite and provoke. But it should not be forgotten that these were mere excuses. The Shiv Sena, it is clear from the evidence collected during our investigation, had carefully planned the riots.

Editors' Notes

1. First published in *Economic and Political Weekly*, 21 July 1984.
2. In about a week of communal violence in Bhiwandi, a power-loom centre on the outskirts of the city, and in Bombay itself and some of its suburbs, in May 1984, a total of 210 people were killed and 686 injured (according to official estimates). The events leading up to it included agitations by Hindu organizations to take out a religious procession, the hailing of the government's decision to permit the procession as a "triumph of militant Hinduism" in posters which appeared all over Bombay, and the anxieties and fears generated by these developments among Muslims (see *Economic*

and *Political Weekly*, editorials, vol. XIX, 19–26 May 1984, 20–1).

3. The relationships between the Congress leadership and Sikh extremism (of which Sant Jarnail Singh Bhindranwale was the most important leader), and the events leading up to the assault by the Indian army on the Golden Temple of the Sikhs at Amritsar, in 1984, are analysed in: M. J. Akbar, 1985; and M. Tully and S. Jacob, 1985.

4. The reference is to the assault by the Indian army on the Golden Temple; see note 3.

5. The BJP (the Bharatiya Janata Party) was formed from the Jana Sangh, a party which set forth a wide range of policy positions but had a decidedly communal character. Its primary social base has been the urban petty bourgeoisie. After it was first organized in 1951 the Jana Sangh was closely associated with the RSS (Rashtriya Swayam Sevak Sangh), founded as a paramilitary organization in 1925. The RSS has claimed to be a movement directed towards achieving the cultural and spiritual regeneration of the Hindu nation through a disciplined vanguard.

6. Violent rioting between middle- and upper-caste Hindus and members of Scheduled Castes took place in the Marathwada region of Maharashtra in 1978, following a decision by the state government to rename the Marathwada University after the Untouchable leader Dr Ambedkar (on whom see comments in the next chapter, by Barbara Joshi. See R. S. Morkhandikar, 1978, "Marathwada Riots: The Background", *Economic and Political Weekly* XIII, 34, 26 August.

7. The Shiv Sena movement was formally launched in Bombay in 1966 by Bal Thackeray, a well-known cartoonist. It is committed to a "Sons of the Soil" ideology and argues that native Maharashtrians are being deprived of jobs and opportunities in Bombay by non-Maharashtrian immigrants. The Sena has won considerable support in the city. See Dipankar Gupta, 1977, "The Causes and Constraints of an Urban Social Movement", *Contributions to Indian Sociology* (New Series) 11, 1.

8. See the ideas of Engineer and others in A. A. Engineeer (ed.) 1984.

9. Shivaji was the great Maratha leader of the seventeenth century.

Untouchable!
Voices of *Dalit* Liberation

Barbara Joshi

By the early 1980s there were more than 105 million untouchables distributed throughout peninsular India. The exact number is difficult to determine, because government statistics do not account for those who are converts to non-Hindu religions, even when they are demonstrably treated as untouchables by their neighbours. At the lowest estimate, the untouchables account for more than one out of every seven Indians.

Nearly 90 per cent live in India's rural villages, compared with approximately 80 per cent of the higher-caste population. Although untouchables are commonly clustered together in segregated hamlets at the edge of a village, they are a small and vulnerable minority in any given region, making resistance to exploitation and violence very difficult. Statistics from the 1971 census show that 52 per cent of the untouchable workforce were landless agricultural labourers, compared with 26 per cent of the non-untouchable workforce. The untouchable literacy rate was only 14.7 per cent compared with 29.5 per cent for the total population. There are new channels for mobility but the channels are narrow and hazardous, and the survivors few.

Most untouchable writers introduce themselves as "*dalit*", a term popularized by untouchable protest movements since the early 1970s. A literal translation of the word "dalit" is "the oppressed", but the term *dalit* has become a positive, assertive expression of pride in untouchable heritage and a rejection of oppression. Because *dalit* deliberately refers to all forms of social and economic oppression it can be, and often is, extended by untouchable writers and activists to other suppressed peoples – tribals, religious minorities, women, the economically oppressed of all castes. In other cases the term *dalit* is used to specify untouchables and the writer or speaker then makes separate but linked reference to other oppressed groups.

Other descriptive terms often appear in writing by or about untouchables. "*Harijan*" ("Children of God"), the term introduced by Mohandas (Mahatma) Gandhi, is most familiar to higher-caste Indians and foreigners, but is seldom used by today's untouchable activists, who dislike its patronizing tone and reject the strategy of reliance on higher-caste *noblesse oblige* with which it is associated. "Scheduled Caste" has a specific legal connotation and covers most, but by no means all, those who are socially treated as untouchables.

Accuracy often requires reference to separately named untouchable castes (or *jatis*) – Mahar, Madiga, Bhangi and so on – for "untouchable" is by no means a homogeneous category. There are many different hereditary untouchable castes and subcastes. Language has been one dividing line. Only recently has there been a substantial pool of untouchables with a command of several languages, including English, who could serve as human links between untouchable movements in different linguistic regions.

Each untouchable caste has also been defined by the same social rules of endogamy that shape the entire Indian caste system. The result has been the development of a variety of distinctive untouchable cultures, with significant differences in the direction and pace of mobilization for change. Frequently it also means social conflicts that make cooperative efforts difficult. The problem is all the more acute because the invidious hierarchic ranking of hereditary castes that permeates the dominant society does not stop at the social border of untouchability. Some untouchable castes long regarded themselves as superior to others, and even imposed their own internal touch-me-not-ism. One of the hallmarks of the contemporary *dalit* movement has been its explicit rejection of older divisive strategies by which a given untouchable caste would seek its own liberation by trying – usually unsuccessfully – to distance itself from other-untouchable castes. By now the goal is liberation of all *dalits* – and this means dismantling the burden of centuries.

Contemporary reality for untouchable is a world in which the basic substance of the past is sustained, even when the environment appears to change dramatically. Democracy has shifted political power from small high-caste urban élites to a variety of numerically large farming castes, including some that were once snubbed as "*shudra*" – castes that rank higher than untouchables but far below the "twice born" Hindu castes. Post-Independence land reforms supported by this new power bloc have stripped away a narrow strata of super-landed who once controlled vast populations, creating a new middle peasant élite but also blocking truly equal access to land. The "Green Revolution" of modern technology has further reinforced the status of the new peasant élite, who have had the capital to invest in hybrid seeds, fertilizer, irrigation pumps, tractors. In a number of areas, commercial and technological change has increased the demand for a large pool of labour that can be used intensively at peak periods, then shunted aside in slack seasons.

Regional patterns and details vary, but the subsistence agriculture and feudal relationships that once shaped the Indian village have increasingly given way to a world defined by capital, contract, cash crop – and economic conflict.

What has not changed is the linkage between land and power, the importance of caste-defined social ties in access to both, or the importance of untouchability in defining "where the bottom is". The pattern comes through with sickening clarity in a case that might be classified as "minor" – only one dead, an eight-year-old untouchable child. In late 1980, several untouchable huts in the village of Shankarpur in Bihar were set on fire. The homes were destroyed and a little girl burnt to death. A local district magistrate and a superintendent of police reported that the untouchables themselves had set the fires and had then tried to implicate higher-caste landlords. Journalists were less than impressed by this improbable tale, especially when they found that the landlords were trying to regain control of small sections of land that had been awarded to the untouchables by the government during a short burst of populist fervour a few years previously. A senior official was nudged into further enquiry but without result.

Urban India is hardly a Utopian escape – in the past few years, major cities from the south-east to the north-west have exploded in anti-untouchable riots. Even occasions for simple social invisibility prove less frequent and less useful than we have usually assumed. In any given job or neighbourhood in India, co-workers and neighbours are normally well informed about one another's social antecedents. Even highly educated and geographically mobile untouchables find to their cost that it is seldom possible to hide themselves and their extended kin networks from the curiosity of the potential employer or neighbour and his own kin network. This can lead to very overt touch-me-not-ism: refusal of jobs or apartment leases, the daily indignity of being excluded from a water tap. Invisibility is easiest in the least critical areas of life. It is indeed impossible physically to segregate inconspicuous untouchables in the bedlam of urban public transportation, and the patrons of cinema houses are inured to the presence of unidentifiable strangers. For untouchables who have lived with the constant strictures of village life this is a much prized relief, but it is important to avoid exaggerating its significance.

The more important element of urban life is that cities offer both facilities and organizational options that are not available in the villages. There are no village universities. Urban jobs may be in desperately short supply, but the city is where most of those few

jobs in India that are not dependent upon access to land exist, and
even the urban day-labourer is more likely to be able to escape a
master's constant surveillance than is his village counterpart. The
economics of concentrated numbers has made possible independent
literary magazines, small businesses, large-scale protest organizing.
Only 10 per cent of the untouchable population is urban, but this
means substantial absolute numbers (about 10 million) who have
begun to develop much-needed institutions.

Unfortunately, in the city also there is no escape from the basic
facts of Indian life: acute scarcity; the pervasive importance of social
networking in access to scarce goods and services; and the persistent
importance of hereditary status in these networks. The networks are
simply a normal part of life for those whose status makes them the
most frequent beneficiaries. The uninitiated may wish to consult
R. S. Khare's case study, complete with a bemused but accurate
flow chart, of one high-caste family's use of caste-kin networks in
obtaining a job for their son (Khare, 1970). It is an excellent
indirect commentary on the continuation of *de facto* "protective
discrimination" for upper-caste groups that is still far more effective
than any legislated "protective discrimination" for low-caste Indians.

Networks are critically important even at the level of the factory
floor. Although there have been serious efforts to develop official
employment exchanges, most job information and recruiting practices are still *ad hoc* and personalized (see Breman's "Particularism
and Scarcity" in Part V of this book). Below the level of prestige
positions, this routinized nepotism benefits a variety of castes, but
earlier patterns of industrial access sharply limit the areas in which
untouchables stand to benefit.

The untouchables' basic urban problem is that they cannot
simultaneously hide their identity and actively manipulate the only
social networks to which they have access. In the words of the *dalit*
poet, Daya Pawar:

> You say you want to flee
> this ghost-ridden town!
> Oh yes, but now can you run far enough?
> You may go anywhere, but wherever you step
> you will stumble over the ochre-coloured gods.

Increasing numbers will neither hide nor apologize for *dalit*
ancestry. This can be dangerous. It certainly has been in Agra, the
city of the Taj Mahal as well as an important regional commercial
centre. Here untouchables have some limited economic independence because their "polluting" leather craft is the basis for a cottage

industry and small-scale businesses. Many have also proclaimed cultural independence through conversion to their own autonomous form of Buddhism. An annual parade in honour of the late untouchable leader, Dr Ambedkar, symbolizes all that untouchables should *not* be in the eyes of many high-caste Hindus – proud, assertive, independent. The parade is deeply resented by the higher-caste population, and in 1978 conflict triggered a riot in which local police went on a rampage in untouchable residential areas. They killed nine untouchables, seriously injured more than 100 others, burned homes and left the walls of an untouchable Buddhist shrine riddled with bullet holes. As yet, no police have been brought to trial.

Three months of anti-untouchable riots in the state of Gujarat in 1981 brought the linkage between the cultural and economic underpinnings of untouchability into much sharper focus. The riots began in the industrial city of Ahmedabad, then spread to most other cities and many villages in the state. The initial incident was a protest by high-caste medical students about seven seats in Ahmedabad medical schools that had gone to untouchables and to other minority students under a special affirmative action pro-gramme. Anti-untouchable violence quickly spread to private sector factories, where there are neither affirmative action programmes nor simple anti-discrimination policies, and on out into the villages. Subsequent research showed a close correlation between levels and targets of violence and the relative degree of upward mobility among untouchables in different regions and among particular untouchable castes (Bose, 1981). The least mobile untouchable caste had generally been left in peace, as had all the non-untouchable minorities who were covered by the affirmative action programmes. On the other side, conflict was encouraged by high-caste dominated newspapers and professional associations, while mobs were recruited from industrial slum and university campus alike. The events in Gujarat are widely described as a caste war. It was – but it was a caste war over economic competition from people Indian society defines as beneath competition.

Although the professional middle class attracted most of the attention, the riot also underlined chronically destructive rifts in the Indian working class. The only significant labour union at the site of the fiercest fighting, Ahmedabad, is a textile union founded by Mahatma Gandhi in 1918 that still reflects his vision of cooperation between labour and paternalistic capital. Throughout the riots, the union refused to speak out on untouchable rights, and when one internationally-known woman organizer insisted on speaking out for both peace and affirmative action she was dismissed from the union. It is easy to see the union's role in the riots as a reflection of its leaders' ties to the economic establishment – better to let workers vent their frustration on a long-despised minority than on millowners. Unfortunately it is also true that the union's rank and file needed no coaching in its hostility to untouchables.

The Left has been a weak presence in Gujarat, but this has not always made a difference. There has been discouragingly little active leadership from the Left in developing a vision of working-class unity explicitly including untouchables as equal partners. Organizers of the Left, like those of the Centre and Right, find it easier to avoid confronting the bigotry of those who make up the largest pool of potential supporters. Organizational expediency is reinforced by the short-term pressures of electoral politics. Indian politics is open to the Left; a variety of socialist and communist parties have formed state governments and are routinely represented in Parliament. Their presence as active electoral competitors has kept alive critical issues and options, but the immediate search for votes has also discouraged attention to thorny minority issues. The one segment of the Left that is least interested in electoral strategies, the so-called "Naxalite" factions of the CPI–ML, is also the segment most committed to addressing untouchable and tribal issues directly.

Added to tactical problems are leadership attitudes that spread from Right to Left, and from medical professionals in western Gujarat to academics in eastern Bengal. Most of India's modern intelligentsia reject traditional theories of untouchable inferiority, just as their Western counterparts reject traditional theories of racial inferiority. It has also been just as adept at finding new rationalizations for maintaining old dominance.

Under these conditions it is inevitable that untouchable equality means untouchable pressure. The problem is that efficient pressure means resources; autonomous communication channels, the money and the skilled personnel to keep these channels alive, the audacity to challenge a society that demands daring and then rewards it with a combination of indifference and repression.

Most of the resources that untouchables now use as building blocks for change are the product of political manoeuvre before Indian Independence when unique political conditions gave untouchables unusual leverage.

By far the most influential of the untouchable leaders was Dr Bhimrao Ambedkar. Ambedkar regarded the British and high-caste Indian nationalists as competing forms of colonialism; neither could be trusted, but the competition itself could be used as a means to institutionalize access to resources untouchables would need for liberation. He eventually manoeuvred a floundering British empire into far more significant protective and developmental policies for untouchables than any the colonial empire had produced in its heyday. Gandhi and the Congress reversed course; an issue that had been politically untouchable had become politically imperative. Ambedkar lost a number of battles he considered critical, but by the time the British departed, the Congress as governing heir-apparent had committed itself to some policies that were subsequently written into the Indian Constitution, with Ambedkar serving as a member of the drafting committee.

The most visible feature of these policies is actually the single greatest source of frustration of the untouchables. Ambedkar sought, and the British finally awarded, separate untouchable electorates. Gandhi defeated the policy in a dramatic death fast. The compromise that emerged was a policy whereby a number of constituencies are "reserved"; only untouchables (or tribals in a separate set of constituencies) can stand for office, but non-untouchables make up the vast majority of the electorate within the constituencies. The result is still guaranteed proportional representation, in spite of a combination of geographic dispersion, social hostility and economic dependency that would normally block any significant access to the political system at a level above the occasional city council seat. Access, but not the autonomy that was sought. Dominant society voters and power-brokers determine the winning party in "reserved" constituencies as fully as they do elsewhere – rarely do untouchables compose as much as a third of the electorate – and dominant society élites determine distribution of party tickets and direction of party policy. Many untouchable legislators themselves, as well as untouchable activists, say the untouchable representatives are expected to be docile field hands.

Influence has been greater in policy areas where resistance is less overwhelming, including several that have been critical to untouchable development. Education is one of these areas. Untouchables had already used British support to move their children into common village schools, determined village resistance notwithstanding, and there has been no retreat to segregation. Government-supported education has broad support throughout Indian society, and has expanded rapidly since Independence. Special affirmative action programmes for untouchable and tribal students, pushed through by Ambedkar in the waning years of British rule, are profoundingly unpopular – witness the Gujarat riots – and yet these too have been expanded. Because of restrictions in the Constitution, central government schemes focus on the narrower field of college ("post matric") scholarships for untouchable and other minority students whose families fall below an income cut-off line. The results are unquestionably blunted by the incidence of parental poverty in the untouchable population. In 1977–8, only 75 per cent of untouchable children in the 6–11 age group were in school, compared with 88 per cent of non-untouchable children. For 11–14-year-olds the comparable figures were 25 per cent and 42 per cent. Nevertheless, the policies have pulled large blocks of students over the walls of poverty and caste and into school. In a recent national survey 60 per cent of all untouchable students at both the secondary and college levels proved to be the children of village servants and labourers. Survival is precarious for an impoverished pool of first-generation educated but there are specialists on economics and law whose parents were rural or urban labourers; college-educated sons of street-sweepers who are organizing a slum revolt; poets and dramatists from India's industrial slums who use their art to arouse their own people and challenge the dominant society.

The financial base for such action is still narrow. What there is has been built on the slow expansion of public sector affirmative action policies for untouchables that Ambedkar first pushed through in the years before Independence. Resistance from private employers and high-caste dominated labour unions has been intense. Not until the 1970s did these policies include most public sector industries. There are still no effective anti-discrimination policies in the private sector, including industries dependent on government contracts, or even an effective reporting system to monitor untouchable access to private sector jobs. Bureaucratic resistance continues to take a toll even when policies are in place; the reports of the independent Commissioner for Scheduled Castes and Tribes and those of a parliamentary watchdog committee formed at the insistence of untouchable representatives, routinely document harassment and overt job discrimination. Still, the numbers edge up. In 1947, untouchables accounted for 0.7 per cent of the most senior central government administrative posts; in 1979 it was 4.7 per cent, and at the level of skilled technical jobs in public sector industries the figure was 16.3 per cent. This bridgehead in the public sector is not the equal of private wealth, either in land or urban capital, but it has improved the untouchable resource base. One recent convention of public sector activists drew 5000 delegates from across the country to the capital in Delhi. Not all were untouchables – there were a number of tribals and other minority groups – but most of the leadership and membership were untouchable employees: railroad mechanics, lawyers, film technicians, doctors, printers. Public sector education plus public sector jobs have produced a swelling pool of skills, information and disposable income. Their own organization was already producing protest journalism in several different languages, running a small chain of medical and legal intervention centres in city slums, sending entertainer "Awakening Squads" to villages and provincial towns. Individual members provided funding for everything from literary magazines to young people organizing rural labourers.

Note

1. An extract from the book of the same title, published in London by Zed Press, 1986.

Politics of Ethnicity in India and Pakistan

Hamza Alavi

I

Ethnic issues have featured prominently in the politics of South Asian countries, as in most countries in the contemporary world. But forms and modalities of politics of ethnicity have differed from case to case. That poses large questions about the nature of ethnicity which we cannot pursue here. Our object here is rather more modest, namely to look at the social contexts and roots of ethnic politics in India and Pakistan.

Given the common history and shared cultural legacy of Pakistan and India it is remarkable to see how different are the forms that politics of ethnicity have taken in the two countries, given the fact that they are both multi-ethnic, multinational societies. The most striking difference is that ethnic movements in Pakistan take the form, primarily, of subnational movements, directed against the central power, demanding regional autonomy. The autocratic power of the central government is identified by disadvantaged regional groups as Punjabi domination. In India, no single ethnic group can be similarly identified as the dominant holder of state power at the centre. Politics of ethnicity in India have, by and large, been displaced on to local arenas, taking the form of "communalism". They revolve around demands of underprivileged or "backward" ethnic groups for positive action in their favour, for quotas in jobs and educational opportunities whereas privileged groups oppose quotas and favour their allocation on the basis of "merit". Local competition between ethnic groups often results in communal conflict and rioting. It must be said that localized communal conflict and the issue of quotas are not absent in Pakistan. But the political scene there is overshadowed by subnationalism of regional groups. Further, in India, the so-called "untouchables", or *dalits*, as they would prefer to call themselves, are a special category of underprivileged groups. Their oppressed status is qualitatively different from that of other disadvantaged groups and is analagous to that of the black people of South Africa under apartheid. Their condition invites separate consideration. Finally, we have in India one or two special cases, such as that of the militant Sikh movement for an independent Khalistan, that do not fall under the broad argument that will be presented here. The Sikh case falls into a category of its own and we shall consider it briefly.

Scholarly perceptions of ethnicity have, in recent years, tended to discount notions that treated it as a manifestation of primordial sentiments, a culturally predetermined social fact that exists *sui generis*. But, nevertheless, such a notion dies hard. While it is acknowledged that entry of an ethnic group into the political arena is contingent on a variety of contextual factors that precipitate subjective perceptions of the ethnic identity, it is held nevertheless that the boundaries of groups are pre-given and exist as culturally delineated objective facts. To take an example, we find that Ballard speaks of ethnicity as a *social category*, already existing by virtue of distribution of culturally defined attributes, that is transformed into a *social group* when it is mobilized for collective action in pursuit of material interests of those who are subsumed by the category. Emphasizing that ethnicity is a political phenomenon, he draws on Marx's distinction between a class-in-itself and a class-for-itself and suggests that "We must recognize at the outset the vital distinction between a social category, that is a set of people who share common attributes of one kind or another, and a social group, where people are organized into some form of collectivity" (Ballard, 1976). Brass makes an identical distinction (Brass, 1985, 49). I believe that this is a misleading analogy.

The category of class is delineated by a set of social relations of production in a structured social matrix dividing, say, industrial workers, peasants and capitalist entrepreneurs, respectively, into objectively determinate categories, independently of subjective perceptions. In the case of ethnicity, however, there are an indefinite number of competing criteria; not just those (say) of language, religion or region but in each case further divisible and divided, according to exigencies of ethnic politics and perceptions, into subcategories or even realigned, when one criterion (say religion) is dropped and another (say region) is taken up as the more relevant criterion for classification. There are no given ethnic categories defined by language or dialect, religion or sect, region or locality, or whatever else, that delineate groups of people independently of the line of division that is actually acknowledged and affirmed in the course of ethnic political competition.

The Pakistan experience suggests that boundaries of ethnic categories are not "objectively" pre-given for, with changes in contexts and perceptions of self-interest, radical realignments have occurred. One "objective" ethnic criterion (say religion) is abandoned in favour of another (say language or region) thus bringing together a quite different set of people into the category and community, alienating some and embracing others. The *ethnic community* therefore is not simply a politically mobilized condition of a pre-existing set of people, described as an *ethnic category*. The delineation of the "category" is itself contingent on the emergence of the "community". Our experience shows that both the ethnic category and the ethnic community are simultaneously constituted in a single movement. Soviet theorists, instead of taking ethnic categories as pre-given, go rather further and emphasize processual aspects of ethnicity and formation of ethnic categories and ethnic communities through "ethnogenesis" and "ethno-transformation". However, they perceive these as historical processes of long duration, whereby particular ethic communities make their appearance and others atrophy and disappear (Bromley and Kozlov, 1987). But such a conception does not help us to grasp and explain rapid transformations of ethnic identities when political circumstances undergo radical and far-reaching changes.

For example, in the context of Muslim Nationalism in India, the criterion "Muslim" aligned a section of the people of Bengal with Muslims of other parts of India. But they were also bearers of a different identity, namely "Bengali". That potentially separated them from other Muslims and aligned them instead with Hindus of Bengal, as joint bearers of Bengali nationalism. Choice between those two competing criteria of ethnic identity was not simply a question of objective differentiation on the basis of given ethnic criteria. We might recall that in May 1947 leaders of the Bengal Muslim League together with leading Bengal Congress leaders made a bid for a United Independent Bengal, independent of both Pakistan and India. The move, accepted by Jinnah, was unsuccessful because of the opposition of the central leadership of the Indian National Congress (Mansergh and Moon, 1981, document no. 229). The alternatives, therefore, did not turn simply on subjective perception of an already given ethnic identity. The choice was decided by the influence of powerful material interests, organized in the Indian National Congress that was able to impose its will and which kept the people of West Bengal within the framework of Indian national identity and separated them from Muslims of East Bengal. We cannot speculate about how Bengali ethnic identity might have turned out had that joint initiative of Bengali Hindus and Muslims fructified. But we would do violence to history if we were to take the Muslim identity of the people of East Bengal as pre-given, independently of the manner in which the balance of political forces actually worked out in those fateful months. With shifts in interests or circumstances, ethnic realignments take place and identities change.

The notion of ethnicity as a primordial social fact, however, serves as important political purpose by suggesting that boundaries of the ethnic community are deeply embedded, unquestionable and sacrosanct. That reinforces ideological bonds in the context of political struggles. It is therefore contended that such deeply embedded social bonds exist *sui generis*, that they transcend boundaries of class and have a prior claim to the loyalties of those who are subsumed thereunder. In Pakistan even Marxist vocabulary is brought into the ideological service of ethnic politics by the slogan that "the national contradiction is the primary contradiction" and that "class contradiction is secondary". The claims of ethnicity or "nationality", it is asserted, demand that class struggle must be put aside until the national question is resolved. Such a view, not surprisingly, is most attractive to those members of the economically dominant classes who stand to benefit most from demotion of class struggle and also to ambitious politicians who can hope to exploit emotive ethnic appeals. To evaluate such an assertion we need to examine the material factors and alignments of class interests that underlie ethnic and subnational movements.

An examination of the politics of ethnicity in South Asia suggests that there is one class or social group whose material interests have stood at the core of ethnic competition and conflict, although other class forces too play a role in it. That class was a product of the colonial transformation of Indian social structure in the nineteenth century and it consists of those who have received an education that equips them for employment in the state apparatus, at various levels, as scribes and functionaries. For the want of a better term I call them the "salariat", for the term "middle class" is too wide, the term "intelligentsia" unwarranted and the term "petty bourgeoisie" has connotations, especially in Marxist political discourse, that would not refer to this class. For our purposes we shall include within the term "salariat" not only those who are actually in white-collar employment, notably in the state apparatus, but also those who aspire to such jobs and seek to acquire the requisite credentials, if not the actual education itself, that entitle them to the jobs.

The "salariat" is an "auxiliary class", whose class role can be fully understood only with reference to "fundamental classes", the economically dominant classes, namely the indigenous and foreign bourgeoisies and the landowning classes on the one hand and the subordinate classes, the working class and the peasantry on the other. Nevertheless, it looms large in societies in which the production base and the bulk of the population is mainly rural and agricultural, for in them the educated urban population looks primarily to the government for employment and advancement. The salariat is not internally undifferentiated, for its upper echelons, the senior bureaucrats and military officers occupy positions of great power and prestige in the state apparatus, qualitatively different from the status of its lower-level functionaries. Nevertheless, they share a common struggle for access to a share of limited opportunities for state employment. In that struggle the salariat has a tendency to fracture (or align) along ethnic lines. Such cleavages occur because of the historical organization of division of labour and occupational specialization in India by communities, as well as uneven regional development.

Two factors affect the distribution of the salariat regionally and intercommunally. Regional disparities have much to do with early proximity to nodal points of colonial rule in India such as Calcutta, Madras and Bombay and later Delhi. Differential focus of missionary activities in the field of education has also contributed to regional and communal disparity. Hence some communities rather than others have traditionally provided cadres for service in the state apparatus, a communal specialization that has been breaking down in recent years. Communities that had traditionally provided cadres for state service had an edge over the late-comers. Under Muslim feudal rulers many Hindu communities had flourished in state employment and found themselves well-placed to exploit opportunities offered by the colonial state, such as Kayasthas and Kashmiri Brahmins of Northern India. In Sindh likewise, for example, Amils, a Hindu community, had traditionally provided cadres for state service under Muslim rulers and ethnic Sindhi Muslims were overwhelmingly rural. Members of communities that had not traditionally been employed in state service tended to be disadvantaged when they began to qualify for salariat jobs and started to look for state employment.

With the salariat, which plays a central role in ethnic politics, there are other classes which also have an interest in ethnic politics. Amongst these a class of considerable importance is the urban petty bourgeoisie, namely small traders and businessmen. Given the traditional communal division of labour, some communities tend to be already well entrenched in the respective fields when members of other ethnic communities begin to enter it. Faced with the power of those who are already well established they feel disgruntled when on entering these fields they find themselves unable to compete effectively with the old established communities. They are therefore drawn into politics of ethnicity, or communal politics. Sikh *bhapas*, who find it difficult to compete against Hindu traders, are a case in point (Singh, 1984, 46; and Bhushan, 1985, 7–8). These *bazaris* tend to take a stand shoulder-to-shoulder with the salariat in the politics of ethnicity and communal conflict.

These classes do not stand alone in the arena of ethnic or communal politics. Where prospective members of the salariat are sons of landowners or prospering peasants or, indeed, even of upper or skilled sections of the industrial working class, who work hard to give their sons an education for a better life as office workers, there is an organic link that ties members of these other classes to the salariat, and lines them up in ethnic politics. These bonds of kinship are "organic" bonds. But even beyond these, given the importance of access to officials and functionaries of government in our bureaucratized societies, politics of ethnicity attract not only kinsmen of the prospective salariats but also persons outside the kin group who have connections with them, such as fellow-villagers, inasmuch as installation of a member of an ethnic community in public office offers to the others a point of access to the bureaucratic machine. The salariat is therefore able to mobilize wide sections of the community behind itself.

In the case of subnational or regional movements, other factors enter into the equation, such as political ambitions of local-level power-holders who seek to profit from regional autonomy. Amongst these would be included powerful landlords and tribal leaders in various regions of Pakistan. They have much to gain from ethnic politics of the salariat because of the lure of political power in regional governments. They also gain when, in the rhetorical claims of ethnic solidarity, class struggle is demoted and delegitimized. Subordinate classes, the bulk of the working class and the impoverished peasantry, on the other hand, have the least to gain from politics of ethnicity. Conversely, members of a privileged ethnic group who are in control of state power to the exclusion of others, as Punjabis in Pakistan, denounce ethnicity as parochial and narrow and appeal to larger categories, such as the nation or the "brotherhood of Islam", in the name of which they seek to delegitimize ethnic demands.

Finally, we must consider the effects of the nature of the political system on the dynamics of politics of ethnicity. India and Pakistan provide contrasting cases of this. In India the plurality of salariat groups and the absence of dominance by any one of them has necessitated a political system through which those who hold positions of power in the state are obliged to operate a process of negotiation with a wide variety of local groups in the aggregation and exercise of state power. Such processes of negotiation operate either internally within the ruling Congress Party or between the Congress and other regionally powerful parties, so that there is some sense among regional groups of a degree of participation in the process of government. In Pakistan, by contrast, the dominance of a single salariat group, Punjabis, in the military and the bureaucracy has given rise to an authoritarian political system (even during periods when there was a semblance of representative "democracy" in the country). The absence of political negotiation, under authoritarian rule, compounds the sense of alienation of subordinate ethnic groups, the outsiders. Along with that difference we need to put into balance also the relatively greater weight of class organizations in the Indian political system which puts ethnic competition into perspective. In Pakistan this is absent.

II

The people who were first inducted into the colonial salariat were from communities that had traditionally provided state functionaries in pre-colonial India and who first came in contact with colonial rule as it spread regionally from its three nodal points, namely Calcutta, Madras, Bombay and later Delhi, to other parts of India. Members of communities that had not traditionally provided cadres for government service or who came from regions that were more distant from the nodal points of colonial rule and colonial education, began to enter this field much later and in smaller numbers. That applies also to differential capacities of various trading communities to take advantage of opportunities presented by the commercialization of Indian agriculture and growth of colonial trade during the nineteenth century and onwards. Both community-wise and inter-regionally, the distribution of membership of the salariat and the commercial petty bourgeosie has therefore been uneven. This unevenness is at the root of subsequent ethnic competition in South Asia, for access to education and jobs in the state apparatus and participation in commerce.

The salariat was at the heart of early Indian nationalism whose main slogan was not yet independence but "Indianization" of government service and "self-government"; within the Empire. Under conditions of colonial rule the salariats (we include in this concept not only those who are actually employed in government service but also those who acquire the necessary credentials and aspire to such jobs) from different parts of India were united in that common goal. Yet even at this early stage ethnic competition within the salariat was beginning to make its appearance.

In northern India, notably United Provinces (UP), Muslims who had held a lion's share of government jobs began to lose their predominance as more and more members of other communities were recruited. Their share in the highest ranks of government service declined from 64 per cent in 1857 to about 35 per cent by 1913, a remarkable decline of privilege, for Muslims were only about 13 to 15 per cent of the total population of the UP in that period. That provided the major thrust of Muslim Nationalism in India. In the Punjab the Muslim salariat was also quite sizeable for about 32 per cent of those who were educated in English in the Punjab were Muslims who numbered over 52 per cent of the total population of the province and felt that they were underrepresented. It is not surprising that it was in these two regions that the main base of "Muslim nationalism" in India was to be found. However, the salariat by itself was too narrow a base either for Muslim nationalism or the larger Indian nationalism, to achieve their respective goals. The latter extended itself, by virtue of being adopted by the Indian national bourgeoisie, anxious to shake off the yoke of the colonial regime that obstructed its development, and by incorporating the subordinate classes who were mobilized in a mass movement. In the case of Muslim nationalism, on the other hand, a mass mobilization of subordinate classes was absent and the requisite political weight was secured by virtue of a deal that was made by leaders of the Muslim League with Muslim landlords, especially of the Punjab and Sindh, as well as those of East Bengal. This had far-reaching consequences for the successor state in Pakistan (cf. Alavi, 1987).

Muslim nationalism was by no means the only movement of its kind. In South India the non-Brahmin salariat, disadvantaged *vis-à-vis* dominant Brahmins, generated the Dravidian movement. As in the case of Muslims, the early efforts of the Dravidian movement were directed at advancing education of non-Brahmins, to break Brahmin monopoly. E. V. Ramaswamy Naicker, the *Periyar*, (Great Sage) gave a call for the formation of a separate state of "Dravidisthan", a state of non-Brahmin people of the south – Tamils, Telugu, Malayalam and Kannada – that would be independent of the Brahmin-dominated northern India and free also of domination of local Brahmins denounced as agents of the north. Naicker's dream and also his failure to mobilize the different Dravidian people behind his call for an independent Dravidisthan, illustrate very well the character and the limits of politics of the salariat.

The Telugu, Malayali and Kannada non-Brahmin salariats, it seems, had no wish to exchange Brahmin domination for Tamil domination, for Tamils were relatively more advanced than the others. These others therefore preferred to remain within the ambit of wider Indian nationalism. In Tamil Nadu itself, the Tamil Language movement and the associated anti-Hindi Language movement, the anti-northerners movements, etc., continued with varying degrees of fervour, all variations on the original Dravidian anti-Brahmin movement responding to changing circumstances. There were other regionalist movements in militarily sensitive Nagaland and there was a movement for an independent Nagaland. There was, understandably, a great deal of anxiety in India during the 1950s about such regionalist and secessionist movements. By the early 1960s a National Integration Council went to work at the centre, setting up two Committees, one on "National Integration and Communalism" and other on "National Integration and Separatism". But the Nagaland movement lost steam when its demands were partially conceded by virtue of elevation of Nagaland as a state within the Indian Union. The Dravidisthan movement led by the DMK likewise settled down to wheeling and dealing with the central government when they won control of the state from the Congress Party. Indeed, much earlier, at the time of India's military conflict with China, the DMK even declared that it would not raise the separatist issue during the National Emergency at the time. Separatism was never a very serious issue for India, although for a time regionalist rhetoric existed.

More typical of ethnic movements that were to grow after independence was one that was launched in Bihar in the 1930s to reserve employment opportunities in the state for "sons of the soil" in opposition to the more advanced Bengali salariat that dominated the field of state employment there (Nirmal Bose, 1967, 47–50). There were to be similar movements of "sons of the soil" elsewhere in India, against immigrants, seeking to reserve opportunities within the respective states for locals (Weiner, 1978, *passim*).

The "Scheduled Castes Movement", or the *dalit* movement, was concerned initially mainly with demands of educated members of those castes. Problems concerning the bulk of the "untouchables", landless labourers, were pushed into the background. Later *dalit* movements were to become more broadly involved. Unlike Muslims or Dravidians, they did not have a regional focus so that their politics could not take the same form but emerged instead as pressure group politics for abolition of discrimination in all walks of life, against *dalits*, the "untouchables".

Given the relatively earlier and greater development of Bengali and Tamil (Brahmin) salariat classes, located at the principal centres of early colonial rule in India, they came to be preponderant in government employment. It became a part of the conventional wisdom of colonial rulers that these rather than other regional groups had a natural talent for administrative service. Bengalis were sent not only to the adjoining provinces but also to the UP and even Punjab. Urdu as well as Persian (the pre-colonial language of administration) were taught at the Fort William College in Calcutta so that Bengalis were able to learn not only English but also the languages that prepared them for work all over northern India. Likewise Tamils (Brahmins) were posted in various parts of southern India. However, other regional and linguistic groups soon began to establish themselves in state service. Educational, cultural and literary associations and movements sprang up everywhere to facilitate that process.

Early ethnic movements in India, apart from the Muslim, Dravidian, Bihari and *dalit* movements mentioned above, mobilized behind demands for realignment of state boundaries along linguistic lines. Even the Sikh movement had presented itself as a movement for creation of a Punjabi (language) state. Following a Report of the States Reorganization Commission (appointed in 1953), the demand for linguistic states was accepted in principle and, by and large, implemented by the 1960s. The movement of linguistic states was associated with demands against immigrant groups in each region, on behalf of "sons of the soil". They did not take the form of regional movements against the centre, as in Pakistan, for they did not perceive the centre itself to be dominated by any one ethnic group. When the principle of linguistic realignment of state boundaries was conceded there were inter-state disputes over the boundaries and such matters as division of river waters – for example that between Andhra, Mysore and Maharashtra or between Punjab and Rajasthan.

The Centre even took upon itself the role of a mediator and adjudicator in such inter-state disputes, for these movements were not for regional autonomy, much less for secession. The main ethnic conflicts in India have instead been between local communities and groups of states, against each other. Given the plurality of centres of colonial administration and colonial education, numerous well-developed regional salariat groups had emerged in India balancing each other in the Indian State, ruling out a sense of ethnic domination from the centre by any single one of them. Even the Dravidisthan rhetoric could not be more precise than a vague conception of domination by Brahmins and northerners in general. This is probably the main explanation for the difference in the form that politics of ethnicity have taken in India and Pakistan.

While movements on behalf of "sons of the soil" continue in several states of India (such as Assam) where immigrants have been a significant factor in the equation, by and large ethnic conflict in India is now mainly between local communities of each region, between those that are more advanced and others that are less privileged. These conflicts are fought out (often literally so) essentially in local political arenas. The objective is twofold – first, to achieve (larger) formally allocated quotas of jobs and places in institutions of higher education for particular communities and, second, to secure places in individual cases through patronage controlled by politicians who hold high office. Ministries of Education and of Health (which control admissions to medical colleges) are among the most prized political appointments because of the opportunities for patronage that go with them. Ethnic rhetoric is therefore important in electoral politics.

A Directive Principle of the Indian Constitution requires the Indian State to promote educational and economic interests of the weaker sections of the people, in particular "Scheduled Castes", i.e. *dalits* or untouchables, and "other socially and educationally Backward Classes" (the word "classes" as used here is meant to be a euphemism for "castes"). The state enforces "preferential policies", establishing quotas in education and jobs in favour of underprivileged communities. Unlike the concept of "Scheduled Castes" that of "Backward Classes" is vague and is interpreted differently in different regions and contexts. Broadly it refers to communities other than Brahmins, or Brahmins together with some more advanced non-Brahmins. The Backward Classes Commission, set up in 1953, identified no fewer than 2399 backward groups – about 32 per cent of India's population – but there are regional variations (Galanter, 1978, p. 1816). In practice the designation of Backward Classes and their quotas has been left to the states and local authorities to decide. This is another reason why politics of ethnicity in India are displaced onto the local level and not directed against the Centre, for the issues have to be resolved locally.

There are two reasons at least why ethnic conflict, or "communalism" has escalated in India over recent years. First is the fact that the Indian educational system is producing vast numbers of educated unemployed, persons who possess formal credentials for whom there are no realistic prospects of the jobs to which they aspire. Competition for scarce jobs (and for scarce places in institutions of higher education that provide access to jobs) is intense. Second, members of less privileged communities, the Backward Classes, look up to state employment as a major avenue for upward mobility and go to great lengths to give their children an education to qualify for it. This has fostered extreme right-wing politics that border on fascism. The Shiv Sena (God's Army) with a major base in Bombay is an example. It recruits its support from Maharashtrians, including better-off, skilled sections of the working class, who aspire for their sons to be educated and qualify for office jobs. South Indians are singled out by them as targets for vicious fascist attacks. All over India ethnic violence and communal riots have become a part of the everyday scene. Communal violence attracts and is reinforced by political opportunism, which seeks to exploit emotive slogans, and also by racketeers of all kinds who profit from it, for appeals to ethnicity can provide a cover for thuggery.

In recent years ethnic politics have moved to rural areas, with the growing prosperity of the better-off farmers who possess viable landholdings, labelled by the Rudolphs as "bullock capitalists" (Rudolph and Rudolph, 1987). These members of the "Backward Classes", having prospered economically in the 1960s, have emerged as a significant political force in the Indian countryside, having upset the traditional balance of political forces. They are vocal in their demands for quotas for admissions to institutions of higher education for their children and for jobs in government.

Once a system of ethnic quotas is in place, it becomes a self-reinforcing factor in politics. Politics of quotas are attacked by the better established groups in the name of merit and efficiency. But perhaps its more malign aspect is that by fostering narrow communal interpretations of social reality, it sows the seeds of fascist right-wing politics (even if they occasionally employ left-wing rhetoric) and it isolates the truly exploited sections of the community who, all too often, are dominated and oppressed by members of their own community.

The case of *dalits* or "untouchables" is qualitatively different from that of the aspiring salariats who have provided the main thrust of ethnic politics in India. It is true that the movement – the Scheduled Caste Federation – begun by Dr Ambedkar was mainly oriented towards the rising white-collar middle-class elements emerging from a *dalit* background. But nevertheless, the better-off *dalit* shares with his or her brothers and sisters in lower classes discrimination and oppression from higher castes. Indeed the upwardly mobile *dalit* is often the principal target of ethnic violence, whereas *dalits* at the bottom of the social heap may be ignored (Pradip Bose, 1981). It is not easy for upwardly mobile *dalits* to conceal their identity from potential employers, landlords or neighbours. Given the barriers of ritual pollution erected against them they find it difficult not only to get a suitable job that they merit but also to rent an apartment or to eat in public eating-houses and restaurants, although institutions of the city afford some anonymity and protection. *Dalits* are targets of constant indignities. This draws members of different *dalit* classes closer together than is the case with the others. Their problem is that of survival in a hostile environment, a total problem that encompasses all aspects of their life and not merely that of securing admission to an educational institution or a job, a once-for-all problem for the others. In recent decades therefore militant *dalit* movements have arisen to secure remedies that must go beyond quotas in university admissions and allocation of jobs, which draw in all sections of the *dalit* population.

On the face of it the Sikh movement for a Punjabi *suba* (state), and more recently for an independent Khalistan, may appear to fall outside the general pattern of ethnic politics in India. The militant Sikh movement, for an independent Khalistan has some special features that set it apart. Unlike regionalist movements in Pakistan, where dissident movements for regional autonomy and national self-determination are generated in underprivileged provinces, the Indian Punjab (and Sikhs) could well be described as being amongst the most privileged in India. From among Indan states, Punjab has the highest income per capita. Numbering only about 2 per cent of India's population, Sikhs have a massive presence in the Indian army and the police and not much less in civilian government jobs. Being the bread-basket of India, agriculture is the foundation of Punjab's prosperity. About 80 per cent of its cultivated area is irrigated. Its most productive agricultural economy is highly modernized and mechanized. Although Punjab does not have much by way of large-scale industries, it has flourishing small- and medium-sized industries. During the First Indian War of Independence (the so-called "Indian Mutiny") in 1857 Sikhs gave "loyal" support to the British and fought on behalf of the colonial regime. That "loyalty" was rewarded by grants of land and jobs in the colonial army and bureaucracy. It should be added parenthetically that Sikhs did later play a distinguished role in the national freedom movement and produced as many heroes and martyrs in the national cause as any other community of Indians. But the fact remains that under the colonial regime they, along with most Punjabis, were much favoured and their privileged position is undiminished.

Sikh Jats (powerful landowners) dominate Sikh politics through the communalist Akali Dal party which, in turn, is supported by the Shiromani Gurdwara Prabhandak Committee (SPGC) which controls the Sikh religious establishment. The SPGC has, since 1925, administered the several hundred Sikh shrines and places of worship with access to vast resources derived from control of religious property and offerings of devotees, estimated in 1985 to amount to over $12 million (Kapur, 1986, xv). It derives great power from patronage through the dispursement of these funds and appointments to jobs in the shrines and religious organizations.

As in the case of other salariat groups in India, educated Sikhs turned towards religious reform, notably through Singh Sabhas (Sikh Associations) whose object, *inter alia*, was to promote the Punjabi language and Sikh education (Barrier, 1970, xxiv–xxv). By 1902 the various Singh Sabhas came together in "an organisation known as the Chief Khalsa Diwan [which] was formed to serve as a centre for communication among educated Sikhs . . . From the outset [it] was dominated by prominent members of the Sikh gentry and large landowners" (Kapur, 1986, 18). The movement that resulted in the formation of the SPGC and its takeover of Sikh Gurdwaras, was a part of that Sikh reform movement. However, given the favoured position of Sikhs under the colonial regime and their disproportionate representation in the army and other branches of state employment, the Sikh movement did not need to make demands for quotas in education and employment, as in the case of other minority communities. Nevertheless the slogan of Sikhs being under the threat of being swamped by a Hindu majority was always exploited by Sikh communalist politicians as a rallying cry, though with less success than might be expected.

Their main demand was to secure a state within India, in which Sikhs would be in a majority. It is noteworthy that even this Sikh communal party couched that demand as one for a Punjabi (language) state. Punjabi was essentially a Sikh language in India, for Hindus of the region are Hindi-speaking and language was easily a surrogate for the religious community. After much pressure and agitation by the Akali Dal a new state of Punjab was finally constituted in 1966, after trifurcation of the old Punjab. But even here Sikhs numbered only 54 per cent of the population, Hindus numbering 44 per cent.

A substantial proportion of the Sikh population of the Punjab had always voted for the Indian National Congress and the Communist Party rather than the communal Akalis. "In the five elections to the Punjab Legislative Assembly held between 1967 and 1980, the . . . Akali Dal was unable to get more than 30 per cent of the total vote" (Kapur, 1986, 217). In other words the Congress Party got the last part of half the *Sikh* votes. On the occasions when the Congress was ousted from power in the province, that was on the basis of Akali alliances with the Hindu communalist Jana Sangh Party and Communists, which in today's circumstances is rather ironical. Even the Akali Dal, for all its rhetoric, has always been a moderate party that has believed in wheeling and dealing with the party in power at the Centre, the Congress or the Janata Party, and has not supported radical secessionist politics. The Akali party, after all, represents the Sikh establishment that has specific demands of its own but is not given to terrorism as a principal means to secure them. The rich and powerful *jat* clans of landowners, who dominate the SPGC and the Akali Party, have little to gain from extremist politics. Their concern is more with negotiable issues such as share of canal waters or prices of agricultural commodities, about which they can engage in wheeling and dealing with the central government. Even after the trauma of "Operation Blue Star" when the Indian army entered the Golden Temple in an attack on Sikh terrorists entrenched there (a very traumatic occasion for Sikhs) the Sikhs nevertheless voted for the moderate leadership of the Akali Dal under Sant Harchan Singh Longowal who had signed the Punjab Accord in December 1985 with Prime Minister Rajiv Gandhi. Gandhi's procrastination in honouring the Accord did much to undermine Longowal who was soon to be assassinated by Sikh extremists.

Within Punjab itself the militant terrorist movement for Khalistan rests on a very narrow class base. Its most fertile recruiting ground is the vast army of embittered unemployed and unemployable educated youth all over India. Sikh student organizations have been at the forefront of the struggle. Within the Punjab they get sympathy and support from *bhapas*, the not-so-successful Sikh small businessmen, who find it difficult to compete with Hindu businessmen (Singh, 1984, 46; and Bhushan, 1985, 7–8). A special feature of the Sikh situation is the very large size of the Sikh diaspora, spread not only all over India but also North America, Europe, South-east Asia and now the Middle East. In 1981 as many as 25 per cent of Sikhs were living outside the Punjab. Enormous funds flow by way of remittances from emigrants, into the Sikh economy in the Punjab.

Much financial support for Khalistan and supplies of arms come from Sikhs abroad notably those in Europe and North America, who fantasize about restoration of the "Kingdom of Lahore" – the Kingdom of Ranjit Singh, the last Sikh ruler of the Punjab, who was defeated by the advancing British.

Reasons for such fantasies lie in the conditions in which Sikhs (like other black immigrants) live abroad, rather than directly from conditions in India itself. Faced with racism and racial violence, treated as dirt, confined to menial and demeaning jobs well beneath their qualifications and experience, Asians in Britain and elsewhere, feel deeply alienated from the society in which they live. They compensate for that sense of alienation by fantasizing about the Utopia that awaits them at home. The dream of Khalistan is a part of that fantasy. The element of fantasy in the Khalistan movement is reflected in its wholly unrealistic demands, one of them being the idea of the Restoration of the Kingdom of Lahore. Another is that Sikh Punjab would not be a landlocked state because it would take in Rajasthan, Kathiawar and Cutch, the implication being that the Sikhs would subjugate these vast territories and their non-Sikh population and establish hegemony over them. Such ideas belong to a fools' paradise. But for all that the rich but alienated members of the Sikh diaspora in Britain and North America are quite prepared to finance terrorism by putting weapons of death into the hands of the bitter unemployed students and others in the Punjab who risk their lives by engaging in murderous activity, pathetic instruments of their deluded patrons. However, even in the diaspora the degree of support for the Khalistan cause can easily be overestimated. According to a Survey of Sikh opinion conducted by the Harris Research Centre, for British Independent Television, no more than 19 per cent of Sikhs in Britain (and probably far fewer in Punjab itself) supported Khalistan whereas 58 per cent were in favour of united India and no less than 69 per cent condemned killings by Sikh terrorists (Bandung File, Channel Four, 19 September 1986).

Violence and killing has its own tragic and vicious logic and one cannot speculate about the future of the Sikh extremist movement. One view is that the fantasies that were mentioned above are merely a part of a cynical mobilizatory ideology. It is suggested that there is a sinister practical purpose behind the terror and the killings, namely to turn Punjab into a wholly Sikh state by driving non-Sikh refugees out of the state and, by virtue of counter-violence provoked thereby against the Sikhs elsewhere in India, drive Sikh refugees into Punjab. There would thus be a massive "exchange" of population, following bloody massacres, which would parallel those that occurred at the time of the Partition of India and Pakistan in 1947. This is a grim prospect.

It is remarkable enough that in the aftermath of the Indian government's military action in the Golden Temple that so inflamed Sikh passions, moderate Akali leaders, themselves victims of separatist violence, nevertheless received the bulk of the Sikh vote and were elected. A more astute policy on the part of the central government in the circumstances might have isolated the terrorists. But Rajiv Gandhi and the Indian central government have shown extraordinary ineptitude in handling this very difficult and sensitive problem. Their failures are too numerous to catalogue here – the worst of them being their inability to prevent the organized massacre of thousands of Sikhs in Delhi following the assassination of Mrs Gandhi and then again their failure to bring the culprits to book. Moderate politics, understandably, have become more and more difficult among Sikhs. But it would be wholly misleading to view these developments simply as a purely ideological movement that involves all or even a majority of Sikhs, without taking into account both the forces that are at work in promoting terrorism in the Punjab and recognizing the degree to which moderate Sikh communal politics, as represented by the Akali Party, has resisted the worst of violent passions in that strife-torn state. By no means do all Sikhs share the delusions of the extremists among them. But in the absence of statesmanship from the Centre, life must be more and more difficult for moderate Akalis.

III

The pattern of politics of ethnicity in Pakistan has been radically different from that in India in two respects. First, ethnic movements in Pakistan have primarily taken the form of subnationalism although a secondary theme of localized ethnic conflict has not been absent. Second, there has been a succession of ethnic definitions and redefinitions as circumstances have changed. To begin with, the peoples of Pakistan were defined as Muslims by virtue of the claims of Muslim nationalism. However, the social roots of Muslim nationalism were quite shallow. Indeed it is quite remarkable that the Pakistan movement was weakest in Muslim majority provinces of India. In the Punjab political power lay in the hands not of the weak Punjabi urban Muslim salariat but rather in the hands of powerful landowners who were organized behind the secular right-wing landlord party, the Unionist Party, which brought together

Punjabi Muslim, Hindu and Sikh landowners into their class organization, and who despised (even when they patronized) the urban salariat groups.

In Sindh the pattern was virtually identical except for the fact that an ethnic Sindhi Muslim salariat was virtually non-existent, for Muslims in Sindh were either landowners or peasants. Sindhi urban society was overwhelmingly Hindu, consisting of Amils who traditionally provided cadres for the state apparatus of Muslim rulers of Sindh, and Bhaibands who were a community of traders. They were driven out of Sindh by deliberately organized urban riots in January 1948. Muslims in Sindh who were included in salariat occupations before the Partition were mostly migrants either from northern or western India. The position was similar in Sarhad (the land of the Pathans) and Baluchistan. In Bangladesh the party in power for a long time before independence was the secular Krishak Proja Party led by Fazlul Haq. It was only when Independence was in sight that an accommodation was made with the Muslim League which took office in the province. The region where the Muslim League was the strongest was in the UP and Bihar where the Muslim salariat was highly privileged in holding high-level government jobs more than in proportion to the Muslim population of the region, but was nevertheless insecure because the ratio of its privilege was rapidly declining as more and more Hindus were coming into salariat positions. "Muslim nationalism" was a movement that was aimed essentially to secure their positions (for an analysis of the Pakistan movement see Alavi, 1987).

By virtue of the claims of the Pakistan movement, the salariat groups, as above, adopted the ethnic identity of "Muslim" and proclaimed the "Two Nation" theory, that asserted that Indians were divided into two nations, Muslims and Hindus. The moment that Pakistan was established, Muslim nationalism in India had fulfilled itself and had outlived its purpose. Now there was a fresh equation of privilege and deprivation to be reckoned within the new state. Virtually overnight there were ethnic redefinitions. Punjabis, who were the most numerous, could boast of a greater percentage of people with higher education and were most firmly entrenched in both the army (being 85 per cent of the armed forces) and the bureaucracy. They were the new bearers of privilege, the true "Muslims" for whom Pakistan was created. The weaker salariats of Bengal, Sindh, Sarhad and Baluchistan did not share this and accordingly they redefined their identities, as Bengalis, Sindhis, Pathans and Baluch who now demanded fairer shares for themselves. Bengali, Sindhi, Pathan and Baluch nationalist movements exploded into view the day after Pakistan came into being, the state in Pakistan now being seen as an instrument of Punjabi domination.

Articulation of Bengali and Pathan identities, respectively, was relatively unproblematic. In Sindh and Baluchistan this was not quite so straightforward. In Baluchistan, if one were to interpret cultural and linguistic criteria very rigidly it would be possible to identify a number of different groups, namely Baluch proper, Brahuis (or Brohi), Lassis, Makranis and, in the north-east districts, Pushtuns who are Pathans rather than Baluch. The literature of Baluch nationalism repudiates attempts to differentiate amongst them and has produced historical accounts of convergent origins of the different sections of the Baluch people. The dominant Punjabi ideology, on the other hand, emphasizes the differences. More recently Makranis who inhabit the coast along the Persian Gulf are said to have found much favour with Americans who are reported to have sponsored large numbers of Makranis for study in the USA or for other types of programmes. Baluch nationalists fear that this may be a way to separate Makranis from Baluchistan to establish a client Makrani state which would entrench the USA in a strategically most valuable position on the Persian Gulf. The Baluch strongly repudiate attempts to divide them and stridently proclaim their unity. Such affirmations of Baluch unity are directed against Punjabis and other outsiders who dominate jobs and opportunities of all kinds in Baluchistan to the exclusion of the Baluch.

The situation in Sindh is much more complicated for Sindh is a multi-ethnic province. Hence contradictions of politics of ethnicity are concentrated there. That arises initially and principally from the pattern of settlement of refugees from India, known as Muhajirs. Forty years ago the Punjabi ruling oligarchy ensured that refugees from East Punjab (and only those) were settled in West Punjab so that Punjab in Pakistan remained ethnically homogeneous. All other refugees, mainly Urdu-speaking refugees from northern and central India, were settled in Sindh. They were kept out of the Punjab although Punjab is a much larger province and had a greater capacity to absorb the refugees. On the other hand, communal riots were deliberately instigated in Sindh to drive out Sindhi Hindus who were the overwhelming majority of the urban population. The population of Sindh was thus radically and irrevocably restructured.

Some of the Urdu-speaking refugees from India who were funnelled into Sindh settled on the land. But the bulk of them took the place of the urban Sindhi Hindus who were driven out of Pakistan, either as traders or professionals. Muhajirs also provided the bulk of the industrial working class in Sindh immediately after the

Partition. The ethnic Sindhi Muslim urban population, was minute. Whereas before Partition Sindh's cities were predominently *non-Muslim* (the Muslims that were there originated mostly from outside Sindh) now they are predominantly *non-Sindhi*. Initially overwhelmingly Muhajir in composition, the pattern of Sindh's urban population changed later as Pathan and Punjabi workers began to pour into the industrial cities of Sindh.

As a result only 52 per cent of the population of Sindh consists of those whose first language is Sindhi (census 1981). Urdu-speakers, the Muhajirs, are more than 22 per cent of the total population. But they predominate in the urban areas of Sindh where Urdu-speakers were reckoned to number over 50 per cent of the population. The disproportionate number of ethnic non-Sindhi population is less pronounced in smaller towns, which after all are mere extensions of the rural society. But non-ethnic Sindhis are in overwhelming majority in the three major industrial conurbations of Sindh, namely Karachi, Hyderabad and Sukkur.

In Karachi, the capital of Sindh and a metropolis of over 8 million people, 54.3 per cent of the population (in 1981) were Muhajirs, i.e. those whose first language is Urdu. 13.6 per cent were Punjabi speakers and 8.7 per cent Pushto-speaking Pathans. Those whose first language was Sindhi, were a mere 6.3 per cent. These census figures probably underestimate the numbers of Pathans and Punjabis in Karachi, many of whom live in slums or *katchi abadis* as they are called; experts believe that they have been underenumerated. An estimated 40 per cent of the population of the city live in the slums. Sindhis in Karachi, on the other hand, belong to the lower middle class and above, many of them being absentee landlords. Reliable figures are hard to come by but it is widely believed by informed persons that Pathans number far more than 8.7 per cent of the city's population as suggested by the Census data. Likewise in Hyderabad and Sukkur Sindhis are a small minority.

A different complication about the situation in Sindh arises from the influx of privileged groups from outside. These are mostly Punjabis. Large tracts of valuable land in Sindh, brought under irrigation since independence, have been allotted to Punjabis, members of the armed forces or senior bureaucrats or their relatives. They tend to be mostly absentee landlords and have brought with them Punjabi tenants or labourers whom they can better control (and rely upon) than local Sindhis. In urban areas, too, valuable land is allotted to persons in these categories. In the last decade or so a new trend has established itself. Because of the elaborate network of state control over business, members of the traditional business communities, mainly Gujerati-speaking, finding it increasingly difficult to cope with obstacles put in their way by the government, are moving out and their place is being taken by a new class of army related Punjabi capitalists. Their kinship connections are a vital element in negotiating bureaucratic hurdles which, in the past, were managed by simple bribery. Punjabis increasingly dominate most positions of wealth and power in society. The police force in Sindh is almost wholly Punjabi. Both Sindhis and Muhajirs have increasingly found themselves pushed into the background and resent it.

At the time of the Partition, Muhajirs were well-established in the bureaucracy, though not in the armed services which are about 85 per cent Punjabi, the rest being Pathans. The well-established Muhajir presence in the bureaucracy was a source of patronage and protection for them. They identified therefore with the Pakistan state and with Islamic ideology, and were hostile towards regional ethnic movements. They backed the fundamentalist Jamaat-e-Islami or the traditionalist Jamiat-e-Uleme-e-Pakistan (JUP). The bureaucracy, with its substantial Muhajir component, was presided over in Pakistan by the CSP (the Civil Service of Pakistan), successor to the colonial "Indian Civil Service", the so-called "Steel Frame" of the colonial regime. It was the senior partner in the military–bureaucratic oligarchy that has ruled Pakistan since its inception (cf. Alavi, 1983). It was powerful enough to keep the military at bay even during the Martial Law regimes of General Yahya Khan. The situation changed radically after Bhutto's reform of the bureaucracy which effectively broke its back. Ironically that removed the main barrier that had stood in the way of hegemony of the army which is now supreme. With it has come unchallenged Punjabi hegemony in the country. It has taken a little time for the effects of this shift in the ethnic balance of the state apparatus to manifest itself in the politics of ethnicity in the country, which crystallized in 1986.

Hitherto Muhajirs had agitated against the quota system for jobs and admission into institutions of higher education. As late as December 1986 a Jamaat-e-Islami-oriented Muhajir Urdu weekly carried an article entitled "Quota System: Denial of Justice and the Sword of Oppression" ("*Quota System: Adal ki nafi aur zulm ki Talwar*", *Takbeer*, 24 December 1986). The quota system dates back to the 1950s when it was introduced, in deference to Bengali demands. Unlike India where they are based on local communal criteria, quotas in Pakistan are regional, 10 per cent of the places being awarded "on merit", 50 per cent being for the Punjab, 19 per cent for Sind, of which 11.4 per cent for rural Sind and 7.6 per cent for urban Sind, 11.5 per cent for Sarhad, 3.5 per cent for Baluchistan and the rest for Azad Kashmir and Federally Administered Territories. In Sind it was calculated that the urban quota would be oriented towards Muhajirs and the rural quota towards ethnic Sindhis. The problem with the quota system, however, is that given Punjabi control of the administrative machinery in all provinces, it is not too difficult for a Punjabi to obtain a false "Certificate of Domicile" in say Quetta in Baluchistan or Hyderabad in Sindh, and poach quotas from other regions, depriving the locals.

With the collapse of bureaucratic power and consolidation of Punjabi-dominated army power, Muhajirs began to feel that they were losing out heavily under the existing system, and that they had little to gain from agitating for abolition of the quota system. In March 1984 a new movement called the Muhajir Qaumi Mahaz (MQM) (the Muhajir National Front) was set up, its initial impetus deriving from a students' organization. They demanded that Muhajirs should be recognized as the fifth nationality of Pakistan and that they should be allotted a 20 per cent quota at the Centre and between 50 per cent and 60 per cent in Sindh. They want quotas in Sindh to be reserved exclusively for Sindhis and Muhajirs, whom alone they consider to be the rightful communities of Sindh, so that the places should not be made available to any others.

The rise of the MQM on the national scene was quite sudden and dramatic, precipitated by certain events in September 1986. Only a few months earlier it would have been thought unbelievable that Muhajhirs would rally behind the slogan saying that *"Ham nain Pakistan aur Islam ka Theka nahin liya hai"* (i.e. "We have not signed contracts to uphold Pakistan and Islam"). Having for decades declared their identity as Pakistanis and Muslim, and opposed all ethnic movements in the name of Pakistan and Islam, they have now repudiated both of these criteria in favour of the notion of Muhajir nationality. There was an overnight ethnic redefinition. They abandoned the Islamic fundamentalist Jamaat-e-Islami and the traditionalist Jamait-e-Ulema-e-Pakistan and rallied massively behind the new MQM. Instead of moving towards an end to communalism, however, the rise of the MQM signifies a further consolidation of communalism in Pakistan.

Developments in Sind are still in a state of flux. In 1983 a powerful exclusively Sindhi (and therefore rural-based) militant movement arose in opposition to the military regime on a scale that fully stretched its repressive capacities. Nevertheless the movement was unsuccessful. Some Sindhi leaders and intellectuals recognize that this was so because of their inability to establish a united front with Muhajirs, the majority of the urban population, without whose participation a purely rural-based, non-revolutionary, movement can achieve little. They are sufficiently realistic in their grasp of the situation in Sindh to accept that Muhajirs are now part of the Sindhi people and must stand shoulder-to-shoulder with Sindhi speakers in Sindh. That recognition and a desire to establish solidarity with Muhajirs has led an influential section of the Sindhi leadership to redefine the Sindhi identity.

Sindhi identity has always been a little problematic in that multi-ethnic province, for many people from other regions have settled there, amongst them, notably the Baluch who speak Baluchi at home even though they consider themselves to be Sindhis and are acknowledged as such by other Sindhis. Indeed, some Baluch hold positions of leadership in the Sindhi movement. Now, in the aftermath of the failure of the 1983 movement, many Sindhi leaders, both on the right of the political spectrum and the left, extend the concept of Sindhi identity to other groups in the province whereas others would resist that.

The former argue that being Sindhi is not a matter of place of origin or language. If that were otherwise how could the Baluchis in Sindh have been accepted amongst them as Sindhis for so long and so many of them acknowledged as Sindhi leaders? The Baluch were Sindhis because they had roots in Sindh. They would extend that principle to Muhajirs. The Muhajirs, they say, were uprooted from India and deposited in Sindh "by fate and the forces of history". They have struck fresh roots in Sindhi soil. These Sindhi leaders repudiate paternalistic designation of Muhajirs as "New Sindhis", a term that has been widely used in the past but which, implicitly, denies Muhajirs full status as Sindhis. They are "Sindhis", they say, without qualification. Descent is no criterion of ethnicity they say, nor language nor religion. It is a question of roots.

In the eyes of these Sindhi leaders and intellectuals, Punjabis in Sindh, nevertheless, do not qualify for inclusion within the expanded notion of Sindhi identity. The Punjabis, mostly bureaucrats and members of the armed forces who have been allotted land in Sindh by the Government, have come into Sindh, they argue, on the strength of state power, as conquerors and usurpers. They do not have roots in Sindh for their roots lie in the Punjab. They should be expelled from Sindh and the lands that they have been given should be restored to Sindhi hands.

It is most significant that such ethnic redefinitions are taking place, impelled by the need for fresh political alignments, towards a united front with Muhajirs and away from a more narrow definition of Sindhi identity that isolates the predominantly rural Sindhi-speakers in Sindh. It takes into account the realities of political forces in Sindh and a recognition that without a united front of the peoples of Sindh, Sindhi-speakers on their own will get nowhere.

It is difficult to judge how widely accepted is this new orientation in the outlook of Sindhi leaders and intellectuals, amongst the Sindhi salariat itself. Certainly there are moves to outbid that leadership by more rabid and chauvinistic expressions of Sindhi nationalism that seem to be less calculated to serve the objective needs of the peoples of Sindh and more to foster personal ambitions of individual leaders who are trying to outbid the others, in one important case as it happens, in the name of "revolutionary Marxism". The problem of Sindh, however, does not involve only the contending claims of the rival ethnic salariat groups. It concerns also the complex mixture of people that make up the industrial working class in Sindh.

Industrial workers in Sindh are almost wholly non-Sindhi-speakers. Before independence the working class in Karachi were predominantly Baluch (Makrani) migrant workers. Immediately after the Partition Muhajirs made up the bulk of the working class in Sindh's expanding industrial cities, Karachi, Hyberbad and Sukkur. As industrialization progressed workers were pulled in from densely populated agricultural regions of Sarhad and Punjab (the Potwar area) where there was a "push effect", for the fragmented farm-holdings there could not provide subsistence for the peasant families living on them. Sindhis from the immediate hinterland were not drawn into working-class jobs because of the relatively favourable man–land ratio in Sindhi and therefore the absence of a "push effect". Sindhi peasants stayed on the land and it is only recently that Sindhi landlords have been evicting them in their thousands by taking over the land from share-croppers for mechanized cultivation. Extreme chauvinistic politics are pushing the non-Sindhi-speaking workers, notably Pathans, into the hands of reactionary right-wing political leaders and an organized drugs and arms mafia.

Karachi, the capital of Sindh, is a special case. Racist violence has been let loose there by Pathans against Muhajirs and the rioting has become endemic. But special factors are at work here. There is a well-organized Pathan mafia that is well-entrenched in trade in drugs, illegal arms and, not least, rackets in urban land. Vacant land is seized illegally by racketeers and developed and houses sold. The city administration is in the control of the mafia who also control agencies of law and order. It has a relatively free hand. They do not tolerate any developments that may interfere with their operations. Large-scale rioting was organized by them in the city after Bihari Muhajirs, brought over from Bangladesh, were settled on land in the Orangi district of Karachi on land that was coveted by them. These refugees became the prime victims of Pathan mafia violence which was conducted it is suggested in collusion with the authorities. There were attempts to explain away that violence as an ethnic conflict, an explanation that masks its organized nature and the interests that lie behind it. Ethnic solidarities were no doubt exploited in that, to some degree and with some effect. But the riots cannot be explained purely in terms of politics of ethnicity, without taking into account powerful organized interests that were at work. Here again Pathan leaders of the Left have failed dismally to give a positive lead and, if anything, have done much to give comfort and encouragement to some of the most despicable elements involved in racist violence and killings.

As for the future there is no simple answer to the problem of ethnic competition in Pakistan and India, though one would suggest that its narrow class bases and interests need to be recognized in order that it is handled as it deserves to be. An opposition to ethnic movements, without regard to the just demands of the underprivileged groups would play into the hands of the privileged who want a free hand for themselves in the name of merit and efficiency. On the other hand an unqualified line-up behind ethnic demands, under the slogan "the national contradiction takes precedence over class contradictions", means that the forces of the common people are not mobilized in the struggles against injustices but rather that the initiative is handed over to powerful landlords or political adventurers and opportunists or the way is left open for the issue to be exploited by gangsters. That means that politics in the country fail to generate forces that can take society forward towards an egalitarian and just society.

Ethnic Conflict in Sri Lanka: Perceptions and Solutions[1]

Newton Gunasinghe

The American sociologist, W. I. Thomas, once remarked that irrespective of a social situation being real or unreal, if people define it to be real, the social consequences of that definition are likely to be real. At the height of the anti-Tamil riots in Colombo in July, 1983, a cry went out: "The Tigers are coming." The masses, the rioters as well as the ordinary people at large – in the initial phase – responded by taking to their heels in a frenzied attempt to run away from the scene. The second phase resulted in a severe backlash of mass rioting reaching unprecedented levels of murderous mob action. Of course, not even a kitten was sighted, not to mention the "Tigers", the collective term applied by the Sinhala masses to the Tamil militant youth.

This however did not matter at all, as the social definition – or more accurately, the collective perception – constructed an imaginary reality, which anticipated a retaliatory assault from the "Tigers". Hence although the "Tigers" were absent from the scene of action, they were present in the mass consciousness, leading to real social consequences, frenzied flight at first and murderous mob violence later.

Constellations of perception, therefore, are of utmost importance and are not devoid of linkages with various social strata, factions and forces. Collective perceptions, especially in an emotionally tense and ideologically charged atmosphere, tend to reconstruct social reality. They add substance, colour and tonality obtained from the deeply-ingrained mytho-ideological currents associated with discourses that run parallel to various social interests.

Hardening Perception

The ethnic conflict in Sri Lanka has now almost reached an impasse. The maximum devolution which the government is ready to grant does not even approximate to what the Tamil moderates would be willing to accept. It has contributed to the crystallization and hardening of these ideological constellations of perceptions. President J. R. Jayewardene, even in early January 1985, had been toying with the idea of enhanced powers for the district councils and limited amalgamation of these bodies within the provinces, Now, he has apparently taken a step back and after all, provides the *raison d'être* for devolution of power to the areas mainly inhabited by Tamils. Tamil United Liberation Front (TULF) leaders, meanwhile, took time to comment on the government proposals on district councils and possible provincial councils. However, when their comments appeared in Sri Lankan newspapers, it seemed as if the leaders were determined to reject them, in spite of somewhat ambiguous and belated statements appearing in the Indian press. The President goes around saying that he withdrew the proposals because they were not acceptable to the TULF. Ironically, this fails to please the Sinhala extremists who would like to claim that the proposals were withdrawn not because of the TULF, but because of the pressure that they (the Sinhalese) mobilized and mounted. Some sections of Sri Lankans, both Sinhalese and Tamil, expected a transitional phase of de-escalation of violence, if not a lasting solution, from the proposals emanating from the political conference. To them, the withdrawal of the proposals and hardening of attitudes on both sides seem an unfortunate deadlock leading possibly to nothing but an undeclared state of civil war.

It is in this context that different constellations of perception, the social strata and layers associated with these, and the real or imaginary solutions that necessarily accompany these terrains of discourse should be investigated. The contours of a particular social structure are laid bare most lucidly, not when its constituent elements are in smooth articulation, but when it is in a crisis, when disarticulation pervades the entire social fabric. Although the following constellations of perception on the surface may appear to be those limited to the domain of the ethnic issue they are not really so, these in addition constitute indices to the texture of the social fabric in Sri Lanka.

1. *The "Nation Besieged" Perspective*   This is a fairly prevalent constellation of perception among different social strata of the Sinhalese. But its most articulate exponents are the middle-level mercantile elements engaged in trade competition, sections of the Buddhist monkhood, factions within the traditional intelligentsia who generally derive from a rural propertied background and cohorts of urban professionals who are generally self-employed and placed in highly

competitive situations. Large sections of the urban poor, including the lumpenproletariat whose perceptions are generally in a state of flux, gravitate towards this constellation of perception whenever ethnic tension mounts. The Sinhala mass media, whether state-controlled or not, have basically been active in propagating this perspective, although allowances have every now and then been made to alternative perspectives, especially in the state-controlled media, when it suits the regime. It is of interest to note that the privately owned Sinhala press, of course with the exception of the Communist-Party-controlled *Aththa*, has always taken a pronounced Sinhala chauvinist position far beyond the positions adopted by the government media.

This constellation of perception in mytho-ideological terms constructs a reality which has become real enough for the carriers of this "world-view". In a crystallized form it is articulated basically as follows: Sri Lanka is the country of the Sinhala, the descendants of the North Indian "Aryans" who are the original settlers of the island. Historically, they built a civilization not second to any in the world, under the influence of Buddhism. The Buddha himself visited Sri Lanka, drove away the demon hordes and made it suitable for later Sinhala colonization. The preservation of Buddhism is integrally connected with the preservation of the Sinhala nation. The country, although invaded frequently by the South Indians, was always a unitary state governed by an unbroken line of Sinhala kings. Today, the whole future of the Sinhala nation, the custodians of Buddhism, is in danger. The only solution to this problem is a military one; the Government should mobilize the armed forces and defeat the armed Tamil youth in battle. If necessary, military help should be obtained from whatever international sources are available. No further concessions should be granted to the Tamils or other minorities and the Sri Lankan State should continue as a unitary State with a pre-eminent position for Sinhala-Buddhists.

This constellation of perception, in spite of the sacking of its most vocal exponent, Cyril Mathew, still finds its strong adherents in Government circles; it is this social force that has become the principal obstacle to any rational negotiation leading to a political solution.

2. *"It Is Individuals, Not Ethnicity that Matters" Perspective*   The mytho-ideological crystallization of this perspective is not as clearly concrete as that of the former. It manifests itself as different but overlapping condensations and hence has a number of imaginary solutions attached to it. But the constellation as a whole could be outlined as

follows. "Sri Lanka is a multi-ethnic, multi-religious country. Sinhala, Tamil and various other communities have lived in Sri Lanka harmoniously for centuries. Every citizen should enjoy equality of opportunity in every field – education, employment and obtaining land. Every citizen should be able to live and work anywhere he chooses. But it is incorrect to consider certain areas as traditional Sinhala areas or traditional Tamil areas; the demand for devolution of power to the North and the East violates the unitary character of the republic and upholds the incorrect concept of ethnic homelands."

This perception too cuts across the different layers of Sinhala society but finds its articulate exponents among certain sections of the top entrepreneurs and Westernized business executives who are attempting to associate themselves with a cosmopolitan ethos. It is also by and large shared by the urban-oriented, educated young monks who come from a social background very different from that of the executives. The wide strata of the urban lower-middle-classes may give expression to this perspective, if this layer, at times of ethnic tension, does not succumb to the "Nation besieged" perspective. The peasantry, especially those not residing in tension-ridden areas, may agree with this view, even if they may not give clear expression to this view.

This constellation of perception is linked up with three parallel but distinct imagined solutions:

(a) The presence of the armed forces and combat should continue in the North and the East, while political negotiations with the TULF proceed. If the TULF gives up the demand for a separate State, accepts district councils, and perhaps a little more, and returns to Parliament, civil administrative organs can be restored. The armed youth groups could be socially isolated and a situation can be created where they will eventually be defeated.

(b) No political negotiations should be held with TULF or any other Tamil organization until armed violence of the Tamil militants is wiped out. On the strength of a military victory a political atmosphere will be created where parliamentary-oriented and peace-loving Tamil people can be persuaded to accept a solution close to the district council set-up.

(c) There is a "socialist–populist" version of an imagined solution which also runs parallel to this perspective. The real problem, the advocates of this line would argue is the conflict between the rich and the poor, the ethnic problem is a red herring, largely created by the rulers to mislead the masses. The masses, whether Sinhala or Tamil are equally oppressed by the ruling stratum. They should forget their ethnic differences and unite to overthrow the rulers. Then the questions of separatism or devolution will be automatically resolved.

Although the imagined solution (c) is specifically associated with political forces such as the proscribed JVP, whose membership is largely composed of small town and rural lower middle-class Sinhala youth, it is not possible to associate perspectives (a) and (b) with any specific and enduring social strata, generally the bulk of those who support this perspective tend to vacillate between these two imagined solutions as the political situation changes.

3. *"Recognition of Nationalities and Devolution of Power" Perspective*   The third constellation of perception, the one that I take to be the least mytho-ideolgoical one, proceeds from a concrete analysis of the concrete conditions. Although this perspective too commences with the recognition of the multi-ethnic, multi-religious character of Sri Lankan society, in common with the second perspective, it sharply differs from the former in a number of ways and above all, in the recognition of the concept of ethnic homelands.

To sum up: Sri Lanka is the home of a number of ethnic and religious communities which have lived harmoniously for centuries as communities in spite of the dynastic wars among various ruling houses; during British rule however, ethnic consciousness acquired pronounced expression and the major ethnic communities in Sri Lanka drifted apart from one another through the competitive economic and political processes. There was a widespread perception among educated middle-class Sinhala elements that the Tamils were being disproportionately recruited to the expanding government service under British rule. Ever since independence, within this context, amidst scarcity of economic resources and deepening under-development, the overwhelming Sinhala majority in the State legislature was used to divert resources primarily to the Sinhala community. This was reflected in the State-sponsored Sinhala colonization projects in traditional Tamil areas, standardization of university admissions, discrimination against Tamils in recruitment to the public service, etc. The relations between the Sinhala and Tamil ethnic communities deteriorated first with the enactment of the Sinhala Only Act, in 1956, eventually leading to the communal riots of 1958, then to the demand for a federal State by the major Tamil party and the total rejection of it by the government and finally to the open advocacy of a separate State by TULF at the general elections of 1977, the last election held in the country. The formation and the violent activities of the Tamil militant groups to create a separate State with the force of arms has also contributed significantly to the further worsening of relations between the two communities. All these processes culminated in the infamous anti-Tamil program of July 1983, which has made a return to the previous relative equilibrium virtually impossible. The increasing armed militancy of the Tamil youth is being confronted by the armed forces who in the absence of any serious battle experience have degenerated to the level of an indisciplined armed band, ready to run riot against the civilians. The only way out is a substantial devolution of power amounting to regional autonomy, which runs against the 1978 Constitution, designed to concentrate power in the presidential executive. A dialogue with the militants is needed as well as amnesty to those willing to accept a political solution. The entire political structure will have to be overhauled to democratize the system on an enduring basis within the context of a united Sri Lanka.

A most percpetive and lucid presentation of the third perspective was worked out collectively by the participants of the United Nations University's workshop on "Ethnic Relations and Nation Building in Sri Lanka," the full text of which was published in the *Lanka Guardian* of 15 July 1984.

Unlike the first and second perspectives, the third perspective, unfortunately does not cut across the different social strata of the Sinhala people. Its most vocal exponents are the radical and Left-oriented intelligentsia drawn from both the communities. The mainstream Left parties – Lanka Sama Samaja Party (LSSP) and Communist Party (CP) – whose electoral, as well as organized, working-class base has seriously eroded in the recent past, have basically adopted the "recognition of nationalities and devolution of power perspective" and have repeatedly condemned a military solution to a political problem. It can be assumed that the more class-conscious sections of the urban working class too adhere to this perspective as evidenced by various statements issued by the Left and independent trade unions on the ethnic issue. But it should not be forgotten that the bulk of the urban working class today is in the unions led by the UNP, with none other than the arch-chauvinist Cyril Mathew continuing to be the supreme boss of the "government union" despite the fact that he lost his Cabinet portfolio, with factions of the UNP hierarchy involved in an uphill struggle to dislodge him from his exceptionally important power base.

Other social forces which may support the third perspective can be found among the diverse social layers differentially located in the dimensions of ethnicity and class. The Colombo-based top Tamil entrepreneurs and senior executives with interlocking directorships in the old firms may favour the third perspective, as it would ensure their capitalist interests in Colombo within a united Sri Lanka while reducing ethnic tension. The plantation workers of Indian Tamil origin located mainly in the central hill country too are likely to prove to be another numerically large support group. The leader of their largest trade union, Thondaman, although continuing to hold a Cabinet portfolio in the Jayewardene Government, has always come out with an independent position on the ethnic question, emphasizing a political solution through devolution of power. Some sections of the Christian hierarchy and more enlightened sections of Muslim opinion have indicated a preference close to that of the third perspective.

But it is undeniable that the majority of the Sinhala masses is currently not oriented towards this perspective, and probably it will require a major political transformation to provide the material conditions and the ideological atmosphere for them to move in this direction.

4. *The "Eelam" Perspective* This constellation of perception, if anything, is even less precise and concise than perspective no. 2. To complicate the matter further, it has distinct condensations within it. A non-violent struggle to attain independent statehood, while negotiating with the Sri Lanka Government to achieve less than that, seems to be the TULF orientation. Even among the militant youth groups there are two discernible condensations, a view that primarily emphasizes nationalist aspirations with socialist undercurrents, and a view that primarily emphasizes socialist aspirations with nationalist undercurrents which naturally leads to two distinct lines on strategy and tactics.

Be that as it may, it is still possible to grasp the obvious contours of this constellation which is at least common to the armed militant groups. "Although the Sinhala and Tamil people have lived harmoniously for centuries, especially after independence the Tamil people have been discriminated against systematically by the Sinhala majority which has monopolized political power. All attempts to obtain a degree of devolution of power through non-violent and peaceful methods by the parliamentary Tamil leadership have utterly failed. The only way out for the Tamil people is to wage an armed struggle for independence where the right of self-determination amounting to the right of separation and sovereignty could be exercised. This cannot be attained through peaceful means, but through armed struggle where the twin objectives of national liberation and socialism may be combined."

In terms of social origins, the Tamil militants are not very different from the Sinhala youth who waged the unsuccessful insurrection of 1971; but since an element of national oppression was absent in the areas where the 1971 insurgency broke out, the level of spontaneous mass empathy that is definitely present in the north and the east today for the Tamil militants, was by and large absent for the Sinhala youth insurgents. Some people in the Opposition, who boast today about how they would have crushed the "Tigers" easily if they had been in power, should keep this crucial difference in mind.

The Tamil militants are young, basically in the 18 to 35 years age cohort, educated and mainly coming from non-propertied lower-middle-class backgrounds; traditionally, secure employment in the public sector kept them gainfully employed; the discriminative practices in the recruitment to the universities and the public sector closed the gates for many of them, compelling them to migrate abroad or to organize political protests. The open economic policy which removed the ban on essential agricultural products, flooding the market with cheap chillies, onions, and potatoes ruined the Jaffna middle peasantry, one of the most productive sections of the Lankan agricultural population. Military and police repression has brought the economy to a grinding halt, the fisher-folk cannot go to sea, the shopkeeper cannot keep his shop regularly open, the banks are closed, the government servant cannot go regularly to his office. As Professor K. Sivathamby, who led a delegation of Citizens Committees of the Northern province, emphasized to the Colombo press, owing to the frequent and consecutive imposition of curfew, people had to go hungry for a number of days. With the blowing up of the culverts and a Jaffna-bound train, the peninsula has become unreachable by road and rail transport. All this has resulted in a massive alienation of the people from the regime in Colombo and has strengthened the position of the militants.

But does it mean that the right to self-determination, an inalienable right of any community that has consolidated itself as a nation, should always be realized within the territorial boundaries of a sovereign independent state? Are there not many occasions in contemporary history, in the socialist countries as well as in India, where organizational forms were evolved to ensure the right of self-determination, in a federated State, a canton system, autonomous regions and so on? Sri Lanka should be able to learn from these international experiences in arriving at a political solution to the national problem which however, cannot be done in an atmosphere polluted with gunpowder and bomb smoke. A progressive de-escalation of violence from both sides is a *sine qua non* for a sane, democratic and humane solution.

Note

1. This article was written in March 1985. It first appeared in the 23 March–5 April 1985 issue of *Frontline*, a fortnightly magazine published in Madras, India; and subsequently in *South Asia Bulletin*, vol. vi, no. 2.

Part V

Classes and Popular Struggles

Editors' Introduction

A major feature of South Asian society, of fundamental importance for its political economy and social structure, and an organizing theme of this book, is the weakness of labour in relation to capital. In the Introduction to Part I we referred to historical research which shows how in the colonial period the possessors of capital acquired an increasingly dominant position in relation to direct producers, and that on the basis of this domination private Indian capital was able to expand enormously "by appropriating an ever larger share of resources from labour . . . without having to take the risk of reinvesting more than a tiny fraction of the profit". A central question in South Asian history is said to be that of "why it was that labour's position in relation to emergent capitalism proved so extremely weak" (Washbrook, 1988). But other historians, notably those of the so-called "Subaltern School" believe that this view underestimates the extent and significance of popular resistance throughout the colonial period, and that the history of popular struggles against hierarchy, patriarchy, exploitation and colonial rule provides the base for a vital critique of contemporary Indian society. In several volumes these historians have documented peasant and "tribal" struggles and, through the work of Dipesh Chakrabarty (see his chapter in Part IV) the development of resistance amongst industrial workers too (see Guha, ed., 1982, 1983, 1984, 1985; and Guha, 1983). Part of the avowed purpose of their work is to adopt the viewpoint of the subordinated classes (the "subalterns" of history) and to study, for example, "the peasant rebel's awareness of his own world and his will to change it" (Guha, 1983). This is an important enterprise, but it still seems that a key question remains *not* that of explaining the occurrence of resistance but rather of being able to say why it failed. Sarkar, to whose writing on twentieth-century Indian history we referred in the Introductions to Parts I and IV, has contributed to the "Subalterns" work. But a major theme of his book is precisely the containment of popular forces by the Congress, which as it "fought against the Raj . . . was also

progressively becoming the Raj" (Sarkar, 1983, 4) — with consequences for India's political economy which are considered by
Harriss in Part II.

The chapters in this final section pick up themes raised earlier
(by Byres in Part II, by Breman and notably by Omvedt in Part
III) concerning class consciousness and class political organization.
Chandavarkar is not a member of the "Subaltern" group but he
also takes the view that "historians have overlooked the extent to
which workers were active in the making of their own politics" —
and shows how the political culture of working-class neighbourhoods
in Bombay between the First and Second World Wars provided the
context for organized industrial action. But he also argues that "it
would be misleading to portray Bombay's workers as a 'revolutionary
proletariat'". His account is sympathetic to the workers' struggles
but also shows the obstacles that existed to the political realization
of class and consciousness, and the power of the structure of control
which workers confronted. In the next chapter Breman then analyses
contemporary conditions in the urban labour market which must
tend to "thwart any feeling of loyalty based on a common horizontal
solidarity".

Part of the problem of workers' struggles has been the nature of
India's trade unions. Waterman records the comments of B. T.
Ranadive, a veteran communist leader:

> Ranadive recognised the extent to which "rural poverty limits the
> urban wage", and the manner in which the existence of unorganised
> labour in small enterprises can be used to threaten the power of
> organised workers. He then accused the trade union movement of
> never having done anything to organise outside large-scale enterprise,
> of being "dominated by reformist economism", of being "a silent
> spectator" to repression and exploitation elsewhere, of failing to come
> to terms with the fact that "maybe 50 per cent of the workers have
> land". (Waterman, 1982, 466)

An academic account of Indian trade unions, sympathetically
critical, is by Holmström (1984, 287ff).

In his conversations with Waterman Ranadive accepted that the
charge of "economism" was properly laid at the door of unions of
the Communist Party of India (Marxist) too; and he is described as
"sober to the point of pessimism", as in his comments on the "failure
of the unions to present themselves as part of the democratic
movement, to take up civil rights issues, the right of peasants . . .
the rights of working women and tribals" (Waterman, 1982, 466).

But major changes are occurring in the labour and social movements in India, summarized by Waterman in his paper.

Kathleen Gough, in her influential chapter takes issue with the thesis associated with Alavi (1965) who, from his analysis of the respective roles of different strata of the peasantry at different stages of the revolutionary struggle in Russia and China, concluded that it was the middle peasant who was *initially* the most militant and that certain conditions had to arise or be created before the revolutionary energies of poor peasants were unleashed. Gough emphasizes the role of the poor peasantry in peasant resistance in South India. In his 1965 article Alavi in fact examines two of the most powerful peasant movements in India, the Tebhaga movement in Bengal and the Telengana movement in the Deccan which were both poor peasant movements and he proceeds to examine the conditions in which these arose and how they do fit in with his analysis of the Russian and the Chinese experience and the "Middle Peasant Thesis". Some of the criticism of Alavi therefore tends to be at cross purposes. The "middle peasant thesis" has also come to be associated with Eric Wolf, whose work refers to Alavi and has often been identified with it, but in fact is grounded in a subtly different theoretical argument although he appears to follow Alavi closely (Wolf, 1969).

The last paper here, by Gail Omvedt, documents the type of popular resistance to which Waterman refers in his article. Omvedt is critical of the communist parties (and of herself as a leftist intellectual, be it said) for their "purism", and the way, in consequence, in which they have failed to engage with peoples' struggles. Gough is also critical of the communist parties because they "have so far failed fully to utilize the militancy of poor peasants and landless labourers". And she argues that in pursuing the parliamentary road the welfare efforts of communists have fostered "dependency and helplessness rather than active self-organization amongst common people". The organized left has unquestionably failed to an important extent. But the task that Waterman specifies as essential for a new labour strategy – the task of "generating and linking the rich variety of complex mass struggles constantly occurring in the country" – is a formidable one in India, as elsewhere in the world.

Workers' Politics and the Mill Districts in Bombay between the Wars[1]

Rajnarayan Chandavarkar

Between the wars, the development of a labour movement in Bombay reflected a growing polarization in social and political relations in the city. This period, which saw an intensification of social conflict, also witnessed changes in the character of industrial action. Until 1914, strikes in the cotton textile industry were largely confined to particular departments and mills; increasingly after the war, they were coordinated across the industry as a whole. Yet even as strikes were coordinated across several mills, no stable trade union growth occurred until the mid-1920s; subsequently, the unions remained weak, vulnerable and often ineffective. It is perhaps by focusing too exclusively on the sphere of the workplace, by confining their model of social consciousness to what was reflected by trade-union development, that historians have overlooked the extent to which workers were active in the making of their own politics. The dynamic of labour politics in the inter-war years, in one view, was the struggle between politicians, attempting to mobilize labour, and their traditional leaders, the jobbers in the cotton mills.[2] The motive force behind labour militancy is thus located outside the realm which workers controlled: their political (and moral) choices, it would appear, were consistently being made by others. In such a view, the history of the working class becomes interchangeable with the history of their leaders, trade unions and political parties. As a result, the impact of labour militancy upon the development of labour politics in Bombay between the wars has been neglected; instead, the emphasis has rested upon the role of the nationalist and communist agitator and the role of the jobber, the agent of labour recruitment and control.

However, the weakness of trade union organizations did not prevent Bombay's workers from mounting an effective and sustained defence of their own interests. To understand the development of the perceptions and actions of Bombay's workers, therefore, we need to examine not only the social relationships of the workplace but particularly the context in which workers lived outside it. Customarily, the heterogeneity and cultural sectionalism of the working class is identified with the neighbourhood; yet in Bombay it provided an indispensable base for industrial action. Without organization and action in the neighbourhood, it is doubtful whether the general strikes could have been sustained. At the same time, the conduct of industrial action in the public arena of the street and the neighbourhood necessarily generalized the disputes of the workplace, at times brought workers into conflict with the state and created an explicitly political dimension for their struggle. While it would be misleading to portray Bombay's workers as a "revolutionary proletariat" or indeed to play down the important tensions and antagonisms between them, it is in terms of the political culture of the working-class neighbourhoods that the scale of industrial action and the ascendancy of the communists can be explained.

From the late nineteenth century, a distinctly working-class district began to emerge in Bombay. An overwhelming majority of the cotton mills came to be situated in the three wards to the north of the old "native town". Increasingly the working classes, fairly evenly dispersed in the native town of the mid-nineteenth century, crowded into this area. By 1925, 90 per cent of the mill workers lived within fifteen minutes' walking distance of their place of work. To its inhabitants, this area came to be known as Girangaon, literally the mill village. As the labour movement gathered momentum between the wars, Girangaon ceased to be a mere geographical entity; rather it came to represent an active political terrain.

Social relationships in the neighbourhood increasingly impinged upon industrial politics. This was partly because material conditions limited the possibility of organization at the workplace. In an overstocked labour market, employers were well placed to defeat workers' combinations and at times even exclude them from the workplace. Consequently, if workers were to demand better conditions, fight wage cuts or protect employment levels, it was imperative that they organize in the neighbourhood as well. The arcane procedures and legal niceties of collective bargaining were never far removed from the baser negotiations of the street.

In dealing with labour unrest, mill managements employed the usual forms of repression, as well as some novel ones. Workers who participated in trade-union activity were less likely to be promoted to more responsible and lucrative posts. They were obvious candidates for retrenchment after an industrial dispute or during a recession. They were also vulnerable to discrimination in the allocation of machinery or the distribution of raw materials. Trade unions – particularly those which did not meet with the employers' approval – could neither collect subscriptions nor hold their meetings in the vicinity of the workplace. By choosing with whom they would negotiate, by choosing between rival unions or factions, employers could deal with their most favoured workers and thus strengthen the organizations they approved while attempting to destroy those they considered dangerous. Such action was by no means confined to the textile industry; however, both within and outside it, these measures were most effective when the conditions of employment were casual and the level of skill low.

Significantly, although the millowners failed to combine across the industry in order to control production when their markets slumped, they were able to coordinate impressively in dealing with industrial action. As early as 1893, the millowners had circulated the names of strikers among themselves. As conflict in the textile industry intensified between the wars, their efforts grew more vigorous. By the mid-1920s the Sassoon group, for instance, was employing agents to spy upon the meetings and organization of their workers as well as to take down and translate such speeches as were made. Each mill had in its "Watch and Ward" department its own organized force for coercion. By the mid-1930s, they had become more systematic in keeping an eye on trade-union activities, reporting on workers' meetings and sharing information with each other.

In addition, the millowners were increasingly able to call upon the assistance of the state. Fearful of the infiltration of class struggle into nationalist agitation and concerned at the spread of support for the communists among Bombay's workers in the late 1920s, the provincial government government grew increasingly ready to intervene in industrial disputes. From the late 1920s, the government constructed a legal framework for the conduct and settlement of disputes, sent more police to the mill gates during strikes to restrict picketing and control "intimidation", and prosecuted the communist leaders of the labour movement more readily for incitement or conspiracy. The presence of the state was most evident, however, in the form of the police when they supervised pickets or escorted blacklegs to work.

This structure of dominance within industrial relations, ranging from the economic sanctions available to employers at the workplace to the political means of repression outside, was often sufficient to smother any sustained resistance from the workers. For one thing, industrial action necessarily placed jobs in jeopardy. Moreover, unless workers were able to effect a fairly complete strike, they stood little chance of negotiating their demands with management, let alone achieving any concessions. When the state intervened, workers were placed under greater pressure to devise means by which they could prevent their jobs being usurped by "blackleg" labour. It shifted the focus of action to the neighbourhood where social pressure as well as force could be deployed to maintain an offensive. Workers' combinations, excluded from the workplace, were forces to act in the social arena outside. The disputes of the workplace were brought into the street. Patterns of association developed in the neighbourhood were integrated into the conduct of industrial action. Managements were, at times, also active in forging anti-strike alliances in the neighbourhood, but unless workers had been able to constrain and immobilize these alliances, they would have been able to offer little effective resistance. As the neighbourhood itself became an arena of industrial conflict, workers used their social connections outside the workplace in two ways: first, as a material base and second, for varying degrees of direct action.

Neighbourhood social connections, indispensable to the daily life of workers, influenced the possibilities of their collective action. How long workers could remain on strike was governed by the extent to which they could draw upon the material resources of the neighbourhood and especially upon the credit they were able to mobilize. If through participation in a strike a worker risked his job, his willingness to strike would to some extent be influenced by his chances of finding another job, and for this he depended upon his neighbourhood connections. Industrial action sometimes even brought into play the rural connections of the workers. M. S. Bhumgara, formerly manager of the Khatau Makanji Mills, explained in 1931 that it was upon workers who had lost all connections with the land that "the millowners generally depend to break the strike as these people have no home to return to and hence they are the worst sufferers at such times." Those workers who could fall back upon their village connections were often the most resilient in industrial action. Migrants with strong rural connections were expected to be less concerned, perhaps even less conscious of their economic interests in the city than urban proletarians with nowhere else to turn. In this case, however, it would appear that migrants with the strongest rural connections could also be the most conscious of their "urban" interests and most active in their defence.

Strikers, trade unions and the political parties also had to rely upon the pressure which they could bring to bear upon the community as a whole in confronting strike breakers. Their actions were based partly on their own strength of numbers, partly on the alliances which they could effect within the structure of neighbourhood power and partly on their ability to publicize and thereby discredit workers and jobbers, *dadas* and gymnasiums involved in strike-breaking.[3] It was sometimes said of the communist-led Girni Kamgar Union that it hired *"mavalis* and *badmashes"*, literally "roughs" to stop workers crossing the picket lines or to "intimidate" blacklegs in their chawls.[4] But most unions did not have money for such enterprises.

One of the achievements of organization – especially the extensive organization which the communists were able to build up after 1928 – was that unions could deal with *dadas* in an attempt to contain their hostility or negotiate their support. From 1928, the Girni Kamgar Union maintained a list of *dadas* in the mill district and invited workers to contribute to it. *Kranti*, the union's official organ, published the names of "loyal" workers, which meant their jobbers and escorts as well. Workers, too, were involved in making the identities of strike breakers public, and, indeed, moral outrage was repeatedly expressed at their deeds at meetings and through leaflets. For instances, the residents of a *wadi* sometimes held public meetings at which local *dadas* were forced to explain and justify their actions. Blacklegs were often brought to strike meetings and humiliated. Often, strike breakers suffered social boycotts. Their names, particularly those of collaborationist head jobbers, were read out at strike meetings. That moral pressure could be effective emphasizes the ambiguity inherent in the behaviour of some "blacklegs". Although the effect of working during a strike was clearly to contribute to its defeat, it would be misleading to assume that when workers crossed the picket lines they simply signified total opposition to industrial action, or revealed thereby an undeveloped social consciousness. Several contradictory pressures, both moral and material, for as well as against action, operated throughout the conduct of a strike and governed workers' options. Indeed, it was for this reason that moral pressure, which often entailed some degree of physical coercion as well, could be effective at all: it found an ideological resonance in the public morality of the neighbourhood.

At the same time, moral pressure and public embarrassment, however effective, were not always enough. Throughout the 1930s, communist leaflets highlighted the causes of unemployment and argued the case for an identity of interest in the long term between the jobless and the workers in an attempt to deter "blacklegs", while maintaining a steady, moralizing attack against "blacklegging". Notions of morality and justice – or more clearly injustice – infused the most direct and physical forms of public pressure. At a meeting called to propagate the one-day strike of 1938, Lalji Pendse said that "some *goondas* have beaten our volunteers" and called upon those children of workers who trained at gymnasiums to "teach a good lesson to these *dadas*".

It was sometimes necessary as well as possible for strikers actively to picket particular neighbourhoods, road junctions and even inside their *chawls*. For instance, during the 1938 strikes Madanpura was picketed so effectively that the Simplex Mill reported that its "jobbers complained that they were not allowed to leave the *moholla*". The experience of the Simplex Mill was by no means exceptional. The efficacy of such action depended upon the particular political circumstances of each neighbourhood. The fact (for example) that several mills of the Sassoon group continued to work on 7 November 1938 was attributed to perhaps the most significant *dada* in Bombay between the wars, and a Congressman, Kashav Borkar. "The peculiarity about those mills" said Deputy Commissioner of Police, U'ren:

> is that they are in the area which is looked after by Keshav Borkar. He was naturally against the strike . . . It is quite obvious that by virtue of the fact that he holds sway in that area, the Red Flag Union did not think that they could get much success there . . . The mere fact that he was the headman of that area, I think, was sufficient for the Red Flag volunteers not to bother with that area.

The balance of power on the streets was clearly a crucial factor in determining the geography, and sometimes even the possibility, of political action.

Another common response to the structure of control which workers had to face was to impose pressure at the most vulnerable point of most strikes: the jobber. In 1928, strike breaking jobbers were hounded out of their neighbourhoods. In one case reported in 1938, Jaysingrao Bajirao, a head jobber of the winding department related how during the one-day strike of 7 November, workers waited in batches of ten to twenty until 11 p.m. at night "in order to assault me if I ventured to go out of the mill gate".

It was because workers were often most effective in political action beyond the workplace that the millowners preferred the state to intervene in the conduct rather than the settlement of strikes, for instance, by deploying the police to prevent picketing not only at the mill gates but also in the neighbourhood. They were particularly emphatic that picketing at the workers' "place of residence" should be made a criminal offence, for "it is precisely this type of picketing that is most desirable to prevent".

The intimidation of "ordinary workers" by "strikers" often

explained to the millowners as well as the Home Department why political agitators and their allies were able to shut down their mills. Clearly, intimidation by itself did not explain the solidarity of a strike, as, for instance, the Bombay Millowners' Association believed it did; at the same time without "intimidation" it was impossible at times to conduct a strike. In public discourse, intimidation simply meant that union bullies threatened to beat those who went to work. Undoubtedly, the sanction of physical force lay behind most forms of "political" pressure in the neighbourhood. But intimidation was not conducted only by such "professional" groups. It was more usual for workers who favoured a strike to act in their own *chawls* to prevent their fellow-residents from going to work. Since their own jobs were in the balance, it is unlikely that their actions needed to be instigated or organized for them.

The permanent social relations of the workplace, and of the industry, pushed strikes which began within the limits of the workplace into the wider arena of the neighbourhood. As workers attempted to cope with the limits which this structure of control imposed upon them, paradoxically their actions acquired an important political edge. Conventionally, we should consider a strike, as a form of industrial or even political action, as an event which related directly to the workplace and concerned particular groups of workers. However, as industrial action was forced into the public sphere, into the streets and neighbourhoods, the effects of industrial disputes were generalized. In this wider context, the parochial disputes of a mill or a group of mills were placed before the mill district as a whole. By being placed in the wider arena of the working-class neighbourhood, each individual strike became an essential part of the collective experience of Bombay's workers. As a result, the apparently limited nature of industrial disputes became essential to the process by which the social experience and the social consciousness of the working class as a whole was forged.

It is difficult to estimate the impact of class consciousness upon other competing social identities amongst Bombay's workers. It would be misleading to suggest that the response of Bombay's workers to the growth of industrial action and the communist ascendancy in labour politics was in any sense uniform. The possibilities of action varied with their village connections, their position in the neighbourhood and their bargaining power in the workplace. For instance, weavers, working in the most profitable and rapidly growing sector of the industry, and protected by their level of skill, formed the most militant section of the workforce; while Mahars who manned the unskilled jobs in spinning departments or north Indian workers, whose lines of supply from their villages were weak, were more easily contained.

Many of these cultural differences were developed into political conflicts and sectarian rivalries by the actions of the employers and the state. As we have seen, the jobber system operated along the lines of these cultural divisions; it not only facilitated strike-breaking but also could, if necessary, enable employers to replace one group of workers with those of another caste or religion. Indeed, the communal riots of 1929 began during a strike when Hindu workers tried to stop Muslims from going to work. It is probable that industrialization, far from dissolving caste, strengthened its bonds. The cotton textile industry did not depend upon the perpetuation of these bonds, but it profited greatly from their use. Caste should, therefore, be seen less as a cultural condition whose primacy was being challenged by the emergence of "class" than another important tension embedded within a class context.

Editors' Notes

1. Abridged version of paper which first appeared in *Modern Asian Studies*, vol. 15, no. 3 (1981).
2. The recruitment, discipline, supervision and training of workers in Indian factories was (and to an extent still is) in the hands of "jobbers", described thus by the Royal Commission on Labour in India of 1931: "The jobber . . . is almost ubiquitous in the Indian factory system and usually combines in one person a formidable series of functions. Promoted from the ranks after full experience of the factory, he is responsible for the supervision of labour while at work. In a large factory there may be a hierarchy of jobbers, including women overseers in departments staffed by women . . . So far as the worker is given technical teaching, the jobber is expected to provide it. He is not, however, merely responsible for the worker once he has obtained work; the worker has generally to approach him to secure a job."
3. "*Dada*" is a term for a neighbourhood gang leader in Bombay. Gymnasiums were an important focus of working-class culture in the city: "Young men, brought together at a gymnasium, skilled at fighting and training in the use of *lathis*, had considerable potential for political mobilisation, and frequently provided a basis for neighbourhood action" (Chandavarkar, 1981, 619).
4. A *chawl* is a block of small tenements with shared lavatories and washing places, built by private landlords, mill managements or the pre-war Bombay Development Department.

Particularism and Scarcity:
Urban Labour Markets and Social Classes[1]

Jan Breman

Particularism and Scarcity

Lack of work is the predominant characteristic of the local economy in Gujarat, also in the urban sector. This naturally has its effects on the structure of the labour market. To start with, there is no question of equal chances for all in the search for work, in terms of acceptability for employment. Many kinds of work have only minimal requirements as regards education and experience, but not all those who meet these requirements have equal access. The extremely skewed distribution of economic opportunity among the various population groups is in no way a new phenomenon. In the past, an important dimension of the social system was the linkage of labour division with particular social categories. The fact that membership of a certain caste, region, ethnic group, tribal unit or religious community is still an important factor in the search for employment, causes many people to conclude that the traditional system is still in force, though with some modifications.

I would maintain, however, that the persistence of primordial sentiments is principally due to the situation of scarcity of work and not due to "force of tradition", constancy, and margins for accommodation of a social system that is involved in a process of modernization. The durability of tested loyalties is linked to the advantages offered by such ties under highly unfavourable economic conditions. If employment opportunities are slow to expand and population growth is rapid, the sources of existence will be under pressure, and people are likely to fall back on familiar social mechanisms and make use of them to exert influence and to promote their own interests.

In view of the situation of extreme scarcity, however, it would be a fallacy to think that competition for work on the labour market is absolute. Some economic functions are linked so much to particular groups that penetration by outsiders is almost inconceivable. This closed-shop character of some activities is naturally connected to income, level of education, etc., but it also makes itself felt in other

268

respects. It is too simple to seek the reason for evident cases of self-restraint in cultural inhibition. Apart from the unfamiliarity with the type of work and insufficient knowledge of opportunities, lack of access is one of the most important structurally determined impediments. The linkage between supply and demand originates in a particularistic fashion, and is part of the reason why the number of applicants for some activities is found to be insufficient even though labour is available in abundance. But it would be rash to conclude that labour market behaviour becomes irrational or imperfect once universalistic norms no longer form the guiding rule.

The particularistic orientation of the labour market does not automatically mean that the higher social classes succeeded in monopolizing the most attractive jobs. It is true that their members have the advantage following from their education and contacts, but as other social categories gain access to formal education they are gradually able to penetrate to those jobs that are allocated on the basis of primordial group cohesion. In many countries, some shift in the social distribution is definitely perceptible, although this tendency is hardly likely to be very pronounced in a tight labour market. Nevertheless, it may happen nowadays that younger members of the lower middle classes are educationally equipped for relatively well-paid and highly-qualified jobs. They literally try to buy their way into the modern sector in an attempt to compensate their lack of influence and protection. In this way, they obtain access to greatly coveted jobs in formal organizations with the prospect of greater security and higher social prestige. These intruders create an outpost through which they try to bring in relatives and other social equals.

Particularistic loyalties are not only found within the same social class. Job allocation is also coloured by patronage relationships, particularly those jobs over which people of high rank have some say. These people then use their rank to benefit clients in the lower rankings of the social hierarchy. Control over a number of jobs or over licences which are required for certain economic activities can be used to political advantage, economic profit and social prestige. Personal intervention, through the use of protection, occurs both horizontally and vertically on every level of employment and is not tied to favouritism by social élites alone.

Mobility

Scarcity not only has its repercussions on the question of who should be considered for which type of work and in what way; it also has its effect on labour mobility. Todaro, in a model that is as simple as it is naive, assumes that the unskilled workers who migrate to the town first drift into what he calls the urban traditional sector, and subsequently move on to jobs in the modern sector. This model is a striking example of the assumption that small-scale, labour-intensive activities act as a buffer zone and are carried out by a floating labour force. This way of thinking has various shortcomings. In the first place the rural migrant is elevated to a uniform type, whose mobility is laid down in a completely mechanistic pattern. In practice, however, access to employment occurs at different levels, dependent on the socio-economic background, education, availability or lack of protection, etc. Under otherwise equal conditions, determinants of a high ranking in the rural system are converted into advantages over other categories of migrants who, conversely, see their former backward position within the village continued in the urban environment.[2]

In the second place, the idea that in the town it is possible to progress to better-paid and more highly qualified work is largely fictional. Those who join the lower ranks of the urban labour system usually remain there,[3] and even horizontal mobility is limited. Shortage of work and limited chances to accumulate any capital or to invest in any formal education, can lead to a position of defensiveness in which one's accustomed sphere of activity is protected as much as possible and entrance to it is restricted to those who can appeal to particularistic loyalties – although the success in doing so may vary.

The frequently heard view, that small-scale and non-institutionalized activities are capable of almost unlimited expansion and that newcomers can set themselves up as self-employed with almost no money or without too much trouble and with few tools, because those already present obligingly make room for them, is a dangerous and misplaced romanticization of the hard fight for existence at the bottom of the urban economy.

Even the shoeshine-boy, the common example of work which, although it might not provide an opulent standard of living would at least appear to be within reach of any resourceful youngster is in fact not an open trade at all and working conditions are also more constricted than might be assumed. In an interesting description of this type of street-work in the Indian town of Patna, Bhattacharya (1969) distinguishes between two categories of shoeshiners. Members of the first group have a fixed place of work for which they sometimes have to pay rent to an intermediary who has leased this right from the municipal authorities. These people form a more or less cohesive group, are equipped with proper tools (box with accessories), and demanded a fixed sum for their work. The "non-standardised" itinerant shoeshiners, on the other hand, are not organized in a group, have few or only very poor tools, and do not have standard prices. Almost all of them are of the same social class, a low-ranking Moslem community. To gain access, a candidate needs to have connections with a working shoeshiner and sometimes to have been apprenticed to him without payment for a certain period. Only then is the newcomer given the opportunity to rent a shoeshine box, for which he then has to pay the owner a sum equal to half his daily takings. Bonds of this sort often continue almost indefinitely because many younger shoeshiners cannot afford to buy their own material and are, therefore, compelled to rent their boxes from older colleagues or from outsiders.

Examination of the social context of the informal sector shows clearly that access to it is not so easy as is usually assumed. In other respects, too, activities in the sector are closed in character and are typified by dependency relationships which give the concept of "self-employed" a rather dubious meaning.

The difficulty in capturing a place on the labour market and the necessity of doing it within the restricted socio-economic network of which one forms part, does not mean that there is no vertical mobility. Although the road upwards is often blocked, the road downwards is all too easy to traverse. As the inflow of the labour market continues, pressure on the sources of livelihood increases, thus accentuating the competition for work. From one generation to the next, more and more families have to face the problem of consolidating their position in society. Inequality then seems to increase rather than decrease. For example, a particular job nowadays requires a higher level of education than was formerly the case, the access threshold to all levels of employment having been raised during the last few years. This has a socially depressive effect. It is discouraging to have to accept employment of a lower level than one's educational attainments. The consequences for the lower working classes are even more serious. Jobs, which formerly required little if any formal education, now only go to those who have a school-leaving certificate, but many households lack the material resources which would enable them to make such a lengthy and ultimately hazardous investment. It is reasonable to assume, therefore, that although more people participate in the education process their actual performance cannot keep up with the higher demands which are set as a result of the surplus on the labour market. This process of marginalization denies the younger generation access to jobs which are still filled by older, less-educated members of the same family. In these circumstances, we can only conclude that the lower socio-economic groups are mobilized in the urban economy under increasing tensions and under conditions which clearly illustrate the worsening of their overall social and economic position.

Social Classes

It is not difficult to consider the minority, who are employed on the basis of regular employment and standardised working conditions and are thus able to lead a relatively secure existence, as a labour élite. This includes the employees of private enterprises and government institutions, workers in large factories, and other groups who in view too of their social standing comply more with the image of a salariat than of a proletariat. The principal characteristics of such employment, linked to major enterprises and government offices, have already been discussed, but it is important to note that this favoured part of the labour force can also be recognized by its living standard. At the household level, this is expressed in the type of house, in its furnishings, in the use of food (both quality and quantity), clothing and other symbols of relative material affluence. The style of housekeeping shows evidence of regularity, the rhythm being attuned to fixed working hours, holidays, etc. Considerable value is attached to formal education. The women rarely work outside the home, and they give a great deal of attention to the care and socialization of their children. People are well-informed as to what goes on outside their locality, show great interest in non-routine events, and evince signs of a long-term perspective with regard to the future. But can the multitude of small self-employed and casual labourers be classified as a peripheral mass and absorbed under the concept "lumpenproletariat", which has the reverse characteristics?

In agreement with the content originally given to it by Marx, it seems wiser to reserve the term "lumpenproletariat" for the urban residue with criminal tendencies whose presence is appreciated by no one. These are the declassed, who have broken all ties with their original environment, who have nowhere to live, and who have no proper or regular contact with others in their immediate surroundings. Having fallen into a state of pauperization, they form a beaten and apathetic muster of lone men, women with children, children without parents, the maimed and the aged. Prepared to do anything that will earn them a penny, the majority roam the streets begging, collecting old paper and bottles, and scavenging through the city's garbage for anything edible or usable. These are the genuinely uprooted, and it is quite inconceivable that they could ever act as a revolutionary force.

The working élite and the lumpenproletariat – the latter concept taken in its original meaning of a residue of impoverished elements – can be regarded as the extremes of the social hierarchy of the labour force. The dynamics of the two social classes are very different. While employment in the formal, large-scale, organizations shows little sign of expansion and even appears to be at a standstill, the dregs of society gradually increase because the production process is unable to absorb the inflow of rural migrants. However, these two categories are not the only, or even the most important, social classes.

The petit bourgeoisie includes the owners of small-scale enter-prises, certain categories of one-man firms such as self-employed craftsmen, retail traders, shopkeepers, and those who earn their daily bread by economic brokerage, such as moneylenders, labour recruiters, contractors of piece-work or house industry, rent collec-tors, etc. Their incomes are often quite high when compared with those of people in protected employment, and they are given pride of place in those reports which praise the informal sector as a nursery and training ground for entrepreneurs. All such groups cling strongly to their comparative autonomy – guarding against subordination to others – while as individuals they show signs of wanting to improve their position within the existing social system by such bourgeois characteristics as hard work, thrift, and deferred gratification. In Lloyd's opinion (1974), these tactics characterize the behaviour of all populations of urban slums in the Third World as a whole. In other words, like penny capitalists they have a great urge towards self-achievement, confident in the openness of the system, appreciative of the value of education, and realizing that to climb the social ladder they have to depend on favourable contacts with those of higher status.

Without going to the extreme of an antithetical stereotype of a culture of poverty, I cannot agree with a concept that attributes bourgeois habits to all layers of the urban poor. The differences in style of living which they show are, in my opinion, far too great.

The urban labour force is primarily made up of the subproletariat. This social class – the victims of urbanization without industrialization – forms the largest section of the working popu-lation. In my view, it includes not only the casual and unskilled labourers, but also those employed by small-scale workshops and labour reserve of large enterprises; they are split up in small groups, gangs of labour, which are continuously changing in composition and which are rarely tied to a permanent place of work. It further includes those who are condemned to self-employment such as the ambulant craftsmen who each morning tender their labour and (paltry) tools in the urban market-place, the houseworkers, street-vendors, and a long list of others, including the inevitable shoeshine. The earnings of this subproletariat are half or even less than half of the earnings of the labour élite, and their earnings are also subject to great fluctuation. Bose (1974) quotes figures which show that the expenditures of households in this category regularly exceed their incomes, a fact that can only be explained if debt mechanisms are included as an important feature in determining the price of labour. Such groups are pitiably housed, and although a family may manage to keep together, their housekeeping is very makeshift. Members of the subproletariat are often better educated than might be assumed, and their attitude towards education is not necessarily negative. They put forward many excuses for not sending their children to school regularly – no money for clothing and books, the school is too far away, the older children have to care for the younger, or they have to contribute to the income of the household; on the other hand they question the usefulness of education that does not lead to any obvious social or economic improvement. Nevertheless, the opinion prevails that those who cannot read or write are ineffectual and shiftless members of society. It is all too usual for them to seek to escape their daily misery with the aid of alcohol. Their day-to-day existence precludes any long-term orientation. Major and minor crises – lack of employment and the inability to work due to illness – are chronic and consequently power of resistance is very limited. The consciousness that they lack dignity, that they are stigmatized in the eyes of others, makes them feel powerless. However, their consciousness should not be underestimated. Their perception of their situation and the social determinants which cause it, is frequently quite accurate; but equally accurate is their awareness that they are unlikely to find a way out.

The fragmentation of the labour market is not combined with any form of poverty-sharing, but is more indicative of a search for security within limited group linkages. The necessity to fence off one's own domain and simultaneously to penetrate into other areas of work causes a rivalry which must detract from any common feelings of belonging to the same social class. The need for protection along vertical lines, the contracting of obligations in patronage and brokerage relationships with privileged kin or social superiors, must thwart any feeling of loyalty based on a common horizontal solidarity.

Even though the urban dweller usually shows greater understanding of the social conditions which are responsible for his continued poverty, factors which are due to a mixture of internal dissension and external dependency force us to the conclusion that the urban subproletariat lacks the required level of consciousness of forming one class on the basis of which action can be taken, and also that any efforts in that direction are systematically undermined from the outside. However, it is impossible to predict the future on the basis of conditions which apply for a particular class at a particular moment in time.

The nature of interaction with other classes and the forces to which this may give rise are of crucial significance. The increasing tendency shown by the employers of urban labour to organize themselves on a class basis in an attempt to bundle their own interests more systematically and to promote them on a collective basis will need to be given particular attention. The polarizing effect of this tendency may help to defuse the antagonisms among the various categories within the working classes and thus increase their commonality and solidarity. However it should be emphasized, once again, that the nature of the state system will be of decisive significance for the outcome of this process.

Editors' Notes

1. A slightly abridged version of a paper which first appeared in *Economic and Political Weekly*, December 1976.
2. This is shown in the large-scale study of the Bombay labour market undertaken by Deshpande, and reported on by Holmström (1984, 183–95).
3. See the Bombay labour market study again: "The casual worker continues to be employed at the lowest rung of the socio-economic ladder in Bombay . . ." (Holmström, 1984, 188).

Peasant Resistance and Revolt in South India[1]

Kathleen Gough

With a third of the world socialist, and guerilla movements active in more than a dozen countries, some social scientists in the West have turned their attention to the role of peasants in revolution. This chapter stems from work by Hamza Alavi and Eric Wolf.[2] It tries to supplement Alavi's analysis of peasant revolts in two areas of India – Telengana (in the old princely state of Hyderabad, now part of Andhra Pradesh) and Bengal – with an account of some peasant actions in the northern part of the state of Kerala, with references (for purposes of comparison) to Thanjavur, a district in south-east Madras, now in the state of Tamil Nadu.[3]

The questions of principal concern are, first: is rural class struggle endemic in these South Indian regions, or is it engendered by self-interested political parties, especially the communists? Second: in modern peasant insurrections, what have been the respective roles of landlords, rich peasants, middle and poor peasants, and landless labourers? Third: what is the potential for future peasant revolt?

Kerala has a large number of types of land tenure, which vary, moreover, as between Malabar, Cochin, and Travancore. The most common traditional tenure has been *kānam*, in which the tenant surrenders a fixed rent, often about a third of the crop, to the landlord, in addition to a cash renewal fee every twelve years. In pre-British times this "superior" tenure was confined to Nayars and other high caste Hindus of similar rank and to relatively high-ranking Muslims and Christians. The most common "inferior" tenure is *verumpāṭṭam*, in which the tenant pays a fixed rent, usually amounting to about two-thirds of the net produce, to the landlord or the *kānam* tenant, whichever is immediately above him. *Verumpāṭṭam* and similar tenures have traditionally been accorded mainly to members of the large, relatively low-ranking cultivating caste of Tiyyars or Iravas; very seldom to the lowest, "Untouchable" castes such as Pulayas and Parayas, almost all of whom are landless labourers.

In Thanjavur the most common types of tenure have been *kuthakai*, in which the tenant traditionally paid a fixed rent usually amounting to about three- to four-fifths of his net produce, and *vāram*, an older, share-cropping tenure in which the tenant retained one-fifth of his net produce each year, regardless of the size of his crop.[4]

Alavi distinguishes three sectors of the rural economy in India. In the first sector, land is owned by landlords who do not themselves undertake cultivation. They rent land to poor peasants, mainly share-croppers. In the second sector are independent smallholders or middle peasants, who own the land they cultivate and do not exploit the labour of others. In the third sector, land is owned by capitalist farmers or rich peasants, who manage the land themselves and employ hired labour. Alavi's argument is that it was the independent middle peasant who, in Russia and China, played the most active role in the early stages of revolution; the poor peasants, both more backward and potentially more militant, were drawn in along with the middle peasants in later stages. In India, he sees the poor peasants as having been most active in the Bengal and Telengana movements of 1946–8; he attributes their failure in part to a failure to draw the middle peasant into the struggle.

This analysis differs from Alavi's on two counts. First, the situations in Kerala and Thanjavur do not allow a clear distinction between the "landlord" and the "capitalist" sectors, nor can either of them be separated from the sector of the middle peasant. In both regions there has been, over the past hundred years, a gradual increase in the proportions of landlords and rich peasants who employ hired labour, and in the proportions of hired labourers to poor and middle peasants. This tendency has not declined, and may even have been stepped up, with the land reforms of the past decade. At least since the late nineteenth century, however, it has been common for both landlords and rich peasants to lease out portions of their lands to poor peasants and to have other portions cultivated by labourers. It is, moreover, common in these regions for both rich and middle peasants to lease at least part of their land from landlords, a fact which makes it virtually impossible to separate Alavi's three 'sectors". The attempt to do so probably stems from a "dual economy" (in this case "triple economy") thesis which sees the capitalist and pre-capitalist (sometimes called "feudal") sectors of the economy as existing side by side, with the former gradually overtaking the latter. But while some features of pre-capitalist relations (payments in kind, debt-labour, special levies, etc.) may undoubtedly continue to exist here and there in rural India, the system as a whole has been a colonial capitalist system, incorporated into, and affected by, the fluctuations of world markets, since at least the last third of the nineteenth century.

The distinction between landlords and rich peasants rests, therefore, not on whether tenants or hired labourers are engaged, although it is true that rich peasants tend to have most of their land cultivated by labourers, and that big landlords rent out substantial amounts of land. Instead, the distinction is made in terms of whether or not the owner or holder actively engages in management of his lands and contributes some of his own manual labour to their cultivation.

In Kerala and Thanjavur, a landlord is thus a land owner (*janmi* in Kerala, *mirasdar* in Thanjavur) who himself does no cultivation, who almost always rents out part of his land, but who in addition often employs hired labourers; the latter are usually managed by overseers. A landlord may own anything from about eight to several thousand acres; if he owns less than eight acres, he is likely to have clerical, professional, or mercantile work in addition, and will thus not be primarily a landlord. A rich peasant is likely to own or to lease from about eight to thirty acres of land. He manages most of it himself, usually does some manual labour, and regularly hires a number of labourers; he may also rent out small plots to tenants. Rich peasants in Kerala are likely to be either *kānam* tenants or to own some acres and to lease more on *kānam*. In Thanjavur they are usually small *mirasdars* who may in addition lease land on *kuthakai*. Middle peasants in Kerala and Thanjavur may own a little land of their own, but almost all lease some from landlords, on *kānam* or *verumpāṭṭam* in Kerala and on *kuthakai* in Thanjavur. "Pure" middle peasants who hire no landless labourers are actually almost non-existent at peak seasons. They are thus somewhat hard to separate from the rich peasants and are involved in both of Alavi's first and third sectors – as tenants and as hirers of labour. Poor peasants in Kerala lease all their lands, usually on *verumpāṭṭam* or one of the less favourable variants of *kānam*; in Thanjavur they may be *kuthakai* or *vāram* tenants. They are too poor to survive on these lands and work either half-time or seasonally for landlords, or for rich or even middle peasants. Most poor peasants come from relatively low or "backward" castes (in Kerala, Iravas or low-ranking Muslims or Christians; in Thanjavur, Kōnar, Nādar or relatively low-ranking subcastes of Kallar or Vanniyar) whose ancestors have traditionally served as tied labourers or semi-serfs of landlords. Substantial numbers of high caste people such as Vellālas and Naidus in Thanjavur, or Nāyars and Syrian Christians in Kerala, have, however, become middle or poor peasants in recent decades. Landless labourers, finally, include almost all members of the Harijan or "Untouchable" castes of former agricultural slaves: Pallas and Parayas in Thanjavur; Pulayas, Cherumas, and Parayas in Kerala. Many Muslims and Christians in Kerala, and many "clean" caste Hindus in both Kerala and Thanjavur, have, however, become landless labourers during this century. Landless labourers possess no land, and lease at best only a minute plot as a house-site. They work full time for wages, either in cash or kind, and either for long periods or casually by the day.

A second difference from Alavi's analysis derives from the different course taken by the revolts in Bengal and Andhra as described by Alavi, and those in Kerala and Thanjavur. In the latter, while poor peasants and also landless labourers were drawn into the struggle, there was still a tendency on the part of the communists to rely on the middle peasants for local leadership. It is true that it has always been difficult to combine middle and poor peasants and landless labourers in a united struggle. Nevertheless, in these regions, the failure of the revolts of the late 1940s was due more to vacillations of policy on the part of the communist leadership, and to the fact that only isolated sectors of India were at that time ripe for agrarian revolt, than to a "sectarian" preference for poor peasants and landless labourers on the part of the communists. If anything, it would seem that the communists have so far failed fully to utilize the militancy of poor peasants and landless labourers in Southern India. Today, the increasing proportions and restlessness of these agrarian classes are causing some communist groups and leaders to reconsider their policies in this regard.

The period of the late 1930s, together with the post-war period of 1947–50, saw the most intense politically sponsored activity among middle and poor peasants that has occurred in South India. Most of it was organized by communists, although socialist, Congress and independent peasant unions sponsored some peasant boycotts and strikes. Communist peasant actions were inspired not only by immediate economic goals but also by a belief in revolutionary class struggle. Peasants came to hope and expect that it would eventually culminate in seizure of the land by its cultivators and of the country by the Communists.

The communist leaders in Telengana were influenced by the Chinese theory and practice of peasant guerrilla warfare. This differed both from the path of proletarian uprising and from that of United Front constitutional opposition which the Indian communists had hitherto alternately pursued. Chinese influence also affected the leadership of Thanjavur and Kerala. In these regions the struggle never attained the proportions seen in Bengal and Telengana. Nevertheless, communist-organized groups of middle and poor peasants did drive out the landlords and take over a block of villages in eastern Thanjavur for several weeks early in 1948. In many other villages, unions of tenants and labourers struck during the harvest season until they had compelled the landlords to halve rents and double wages. The Thanjavur revolt was put down by armed police in the course of 1949. In Kerala, too, there were strikes of tenants and labourers for lower rents and higher wages, large demonstrations, and organized seizures of black-market grain-stocks from rich landlords and merchants. Both in Thanjavur and Kerala, landless labourers as well as poor peasants were now drawn into the struggles and played a militant role. Many of them came from the lowest castes of Harijans, hitherto ostracized and exploited by the somewhat higher Hindu castes of middle and poor tenants. In Thanjavur, Harijans (called Ādi Drāvidas) form about one-quarter of the population and live in segregated streets on the outskirts of villages. The communists organized these streets into unions on the basis of their existing caste-assemblies. The Ādi Drāvidas acted separately, although in alliance, with the unions of higher ranking middle and poor peasants, thus raising the struggle to new heights of militancy. In Kerala, thousands of Harijan and Backward Caste landless labourers struck for the first time on the cash-crop farming estates of big village landlords in 1947. Both men and women came out. Their discipline and militancy were remarkable. In one North Malabar village sprawling over four square miles of mountains and valleys only one labourer went to work on the first day of the strike. He had heard of it but did not really think the people would be united. His caste members approached him before the second day and he stayed away thereafter.

The peasant revolts of 1947 took place without support from the central leadership of the Communist Party. In 1948, however, as in 1940, the CPI line changed to one of revolutionary upsurge led by the urban proletariat. In theory, the peasants were still neglected. B. T. Ranadive, the Party's general secretary, in fact described Mao's theories as "horrifying", "reactionary," and "counterrevolutionary." In practice, however, communist revolutionary action in this period was more successful in the countryside than in the cities, and South Indian rural leaders clung to the Chinese line. Finally, in mid-1950, a reconstituted central committee briefly adopted the Maoist approach of armed revolution based primarily on guerrilla warfare. By this time, however, the main revolts had been crushed. The Congress government was firmly in control and most villagers appear to have been made hopeful by the prospect of universal franchise under the new constitution. In 1951 the communists changed their approach to one of parliamentary opposition. They renewed their attempts to unite the workers, all classes of peasants, and the "patriotic" bourgeoisie to bring about a mixed economy under government regulation, with a democratic parliamentary structure. Beginning with the all-India elections of 1952, the communists have followed the parliamentary road up to the present time, in spite of the party-split of 1964 and a variety of fundamental disagreements on international and national problems.

During the period of parliamentary democracy, many communist peasant unions have been allowed to lapse. In 1964 I found that local communist leaders in Kerala, absorbed in electioneering, legal work, and ideological meetings and conflicts, often had little time for day-to-day organization in their villages. Union meetings were infrequent and in many villages peasants had ceased to pay their dues. Some militant struggles *had* been waged by the communists, however, and also by a new Christian Peasants and Workers' Party which has since joined a United Front with the communists. These struggles were especially prominent among some 30,000 peasants in hill areas, who had occupied government and private forest lands and whom the Congress government of 1960–64 had tried to evict. It is important to notice that even in the absence of their communist leaders, peasants often revert to their traditional forms of joint action and resistance in crises.

In Kerala, as is well known, the Communist Party came to power in the state government in 1957 with 41 per cent of the vote. It was ousted by the Central government in 1959 on grounds of inability to maintain law and order. Through its policies of land ceilings, minimum wages, rural debt-cancellations, and welfare provisions, the Party increased its support among the poor tenants and the propertyless classes. Even while pursuing the parliamentary road, the communists deepened the class struggle by encouraging the poor to put forward their claims. In the sixteen years of parliamentary struggle the communists have continued to help tenants and landless labourers by filing suits on their behalf, leading strikes and boycotts within the constitutional framework, and counselling them on their rights under the various land reform laws.[5]

In 1964, Left and Right communists split on the fundamental question of approaches to the Congress Party. These were in turn, of course, linked with Rightist support of the Soviet Union, which gives aid to the Congress government and hopes for a peaceful transition to socialism. The Left communists (CPI–M) oppose Soviet revisionism and any compromise with the Congress Party, and give critical support to China. They foresee the possibility of armed revolution if the Indian government succumbs to American penetration and closes all avenues to constitutional and parliamentary struggle. At the same time, the CPI–M continues to participate in elections. In Kerala, the Right communists have rather weak support from the urban lower middle classes and the industrial unions; the Left communists have much stronger support from middle and poor peasants and from landless labourers in villages and export crop plantations. While bitterly opposing each others' ideology, the two parties have forced electoral or post-electoral alliances in a number of states. Communist-led United Front governments came to power in Kerala and Bengal in the Indian elections of early 1967.

Subsequently, further serious divisions of policy have appeared among Left communists. In May 1967 a revolt broke out among share-croppers and landless labourers in the mountainous district of Naxalbari in West Bengal. It arose because landlords refused to cede land taken from them by the government under the land-ceiling laws, and sent police and armed bands against the cultivators when they tried to occupy the lands. Many of the cultivators were Santal tribespeople who countered the landlords' attacks with bows and arrows. Plantation workers on nearby foreign tea plantations struck in sympathy. The revolt was led, or at least supported, by local Left communists. It appears to have followed traditional patterns: expropriation of the land, driving out of the landlords, attempts to set up peasant soviets and to immobilize local government officials. One policeman and ten peasants were killed. The West Bengal Minister of Land and Land Revenue, a Left communist, tried to bring about a compromise but it was foiled by police who continued to attack and by local Left communists and peasants who continued to defend themselves. The revolt at one point affected some 42,000 people in seventy villages over an area of 80 square miles. It appears to have been temporarily put down by the police, although rebel Left communists claim that a revolutionary framework has been maintained. The United Front government condemned the revolt as adventurist, and the Left Communist Party expelled the rebels. The United Front Government was, however, ousted by the Central Government in November 1967.

The rebel policy has since triumphed in the Left Communist Party plenum in Delhi, and spread to a number of Left communist district and village committees in Bengal, Orissa, Bihar, Punjab, Uttar Pradesh, Maharashtra, Andhra, Mysore, Madras, and Kerala.

The rebel approach includes the following: the organization of peasant-based guerrilla warfare as the main path to revolution in India, with the assistance of the urban working class; rejection of parliamentary participation as revisionist; and an analysis of Indian society which sees the Congress Central Government as the captive of American imperialism, and India as already a neo-colonial state. This last contrasts with the orthodox Left communist view of India as under the class-rule of the landlords and the bourgeoisie, led by the big bourgeoisie which, so far, is only "increasingly collaborating" with imperialism.

The rebels accept the Left communist distinction between a "feudal" sector of the economy dominated by the landlords, an "imperial" sector dominated by foreign monopoly capital with the assistance of an Indian comprador bourgeoisie, and a "national capitalist" sector led by an independent national bourgeoisie, at least part of which is seen as a potential revolutionary ally. I would question such distinctions, arguing instead that the various sectors of the economy are fully integrated with one another in a colonial-style capitalism which is itself part of world capitalism and whose main features of underdevelopment derive from its satellite relationships with the metropolitan powers. Correspondingly, it is questionable whether there is, or is any longer, a sizeable independent national bourgeoisie in India, for the increasing penetration of the economy by American and European capital since the Second World War has co-opted to the imperialists' side virtually the whole Indian bourgeoisie, whether mercantile, farming, or industrial.

The rebel analysis does, however, give greater weight to foreign penetration of the Indian economy than does the orthodox Left communist analysis. Thus the rebels, like the Chinese Communist Party, argue that substantial elements of the Indian industrial bourgeoisie are part of the comprador bourgeoisie as a result of American, British, and other foreign penetration of Indian industry.

It seems probable that much of the rebel Left communist analysis will appeal to poor peasants and landless labourers in Kerala. In 1964 I found on the one hand that support for the communists, especially the Left communists, had become virtually universal among landless labourers and had increased among poor and middle peasants. This resulted from the deterioration of food supplies and real wages in these classes in the 1960s and from the communists' record of 1957–9. On the other hand, there was a growing impatience and a wish to return to the militant actions of the late 1930s and 1947.

What conclusions can be drawn from this analysis? In Kerala and Thanjavur peasant revolts occurred frequently during British rule. These revolts appear to have been responses to increased exactions from poor and middle peasants brought about by colonial capitalist relations. When they achieved scope and intensity the revolts aimed at throwing off the authority of the state and of landlords, and at setting up a local government drawn from the peasantry.

When modern reform or radical parties have coordinated the peasants without constricting them, peasants have tended to follow the same pattern of overthrow of landlords, seizure of the land, and removal or neutralization of officials of the existing state. The difference has been that radical parties, especially the communists, have been able sometimes to link these revolts over wider areas and to infuse them with a revolutionary ideology and a new conception of the state.

In relatively traditional villages, peasants have ready-made bases of organization in their caste assemblies, composed of the heads of households of one caste within each village or group of villages. These assemblies were traditionally organized for the settlement of internal disputes; in addition, the assembly of the dominant high-ranking caste usually governed the village as a whole. During British rule, the assemblies of middle or low castes of tenants or labourers often provided a framework for revolt or resistance. The communists have appreciated the value of caste assemblies and, especially in Thanjavur, have managed to unite the assemblies of several middle- and low-ranking castes in groups of villages to form labour unions capable of either organized revolt or constitutional agitation. Caste assemblies have their greatest strength and unity on large village estates where a majority of poor tenants or landless labourers fill the same roles and are exposed to the same forms of oppression. Such assemblies are especially strong, egalitarian, internally democratic, and militant among Untouchable landless labourers. On foreign export crop plantations, in spite of caste, linguistic, religious, and kinship diversity, workers of the same street or barracks tend to form assemblies to settle their internal disputes along lines similar to their old caste assemblies. Such multi-caste, local assemblies also provide a ready basis for union organizing by left-wing parties.

Communist Party cadres operating in villages have come mainly from families of less successful landlords and rich peasants, from the children of priests and *literati* whose authority had been challenged by new bureaucratic and market-oriented institutions, and from such local and low-paid intellectual workers as schoolteachers and village clerks.

The communists were first able to recruit tenant cultivators of middle-peasant rank into their peasant unions, and have hitherto tended to rely on the village leadership of this class. In Kerala and Thanjavur, middle peasants come mainly from the middle to high castes of Hindus, Christians, and Muslims. Their early responsiveness to socialist ideas can probably be attributed to various factors mentioned by Eric R. Wolf. These include their comparative literacy and knowledge of the wider society, their enjoyment of relatively greater security and autonomy than the poorest share-cropping tenants or landless labourers, yet their experience of uncertainty and of new kinds of exploitation in the market economy. In the agitations of the 1930s, as apparently during Malabar's nineteenth century peasant revolts, Kerala's middle peasants were able to organize large numbers of poor peasants to throw off some of the more traditional exactions of landlords. From about 1947, landless labourers were also, apparently for the first time, drawn into political struggles and organized into unions on a large scale. Difficulties exist because middle peasants themselves often exploit landless labourers. In many contexts, the interests of the two classes are opposed, and landlords have used every opportunity to keep them at enmity. In South India the extremely deep social and ritual barriers between middle or poor peasants of middle to low Hindu caste on the one hand, and those landless labourers who are of the lowest, untouchable castes on the other, made the rapprochement between tenant and landless labourer peculiarly difficult. By the late 1950s, however, both in Kerala and Thanjavur, the two were beginning to amalgamate within the same peasant unions and thus to reinforce each other's demands.

It is noteworthy, moreover, that the communists (and since 1964, the Left communists) have drawn their greatest support from states and districts where landless labourers are numerically most prominent, for example Bengal, Kerala, Andhra, and Thanjavur. In Thanjavur and Kerala, further, it is to my knowledge the landless labourers who, once they are aroused, most completely and consistently vote for the communists.[6] In Thanjavur, landless labourers, chiefly untouchables, formed about one quarter of the total population in 1952. In Kerala, landless labourers and their families increased from 12.5 per cent of the total population in 1931 to 21.6 per cent in 1951. In Malabar (North Kerala), the proportion of landless labourers to the total agriculturally dependent population increased from 38 per cent in 1931 to 44 per cent in 1951 and 47 per cent in 1961. In contrast to Alavi, I would argue that the Indian communists have never accorded sufficient weight to the poor peasants and landless labourers in their organizational and revolutionary efforts. A change may, however, be underway among both rebel and orthodox Left communists. In a recent speech to the All-India Left Communist Kisan Sabha (Peasant Association) A. K. Gopalan stated that agricultural labourers now form 25–40 per cent of the population in most of the states of India. Gopalan's conclusion seems warranted, namely, "We have to make them [the landless labourers] the hub of our activity. Reluctance to take up their specific demands, fearing that this will drive the rich and middle peasant away from us, will have to be given up."

Over the past sixteen years, the communists' pursuit of the parliamentary path has allowed them to increase the numbers of their supporters in several states. At the same time, it has placed serious difficulties in the way of organizing peasants and workers "from below." Concern with canvassing for national, state, and village elections takes village communist workers away from day-to-day organizational work among the propertyless. It causes even village communists, let alone national leaders, to focus on budgetary problems, short-term reforms, and the arithmetic of seats and votes. As a result, they tend to neglect socialist education and the deeper political and ethical problems of class struggle. The policy of "unity from above" through electoral alliances and adjustments with non-revolutionary social democratic or non-socialist ethnic parties seriously damages the potential for class unity, with clear ideological direction, from below. It makes many peasants cynical about the sincerity of communist analyses of class struggle and suspicious that the communists, after all, are interested less in revolution than in power. When communists have actually attained power at the state level, as in Kerala in 1957–9 and, in 1967, their efforts to protect and to redistribute benefits to the poorest classes have brought them the gratitude of poor and middle peasants, landless labourers, and urban workers. These efforts are, however, too meagre to make a substantial difference. Confined within the provisions of the Indian constitution, it is impossible for the communists to transform property relations, allocate resources, and plan production. This means that they can compensate the propertyless only at the expense of the petty bourgeoisie, the rich peasants, and even some of the middle peasants, without increasing production. Further, their welfare-state efforts foster dependence and helplessness rather than active self-organization among the common people.[7]

Editors' Notes

1. Abridged version of a paper which was first published in *Pacific Affairs*, vol. XLI, no. 4.
2. Hamza Alavi, "Peasants and Revolution", in Miliband, R. and Saville, J. (eds) *Socialist Register, 1965*, reprinted in Gough, K. and Sharma, H.

(eds) *Imperialism and Revolution in South Asia* (New York: Monthly Review Press, 1969); Eric Wolf, *Peasant Wars of the Twentieth Century* (London: Faber, 1969).

3. Kathleen Gough's *Rural Society in South-east India* (Cambridge: Cambridge University Press, 1981) is a rich account of agrarian production relations in Thanjavur, based mainly on her fieldwork there in the late 1940s and early 1950s. Other analyses of agrarian politics in this region are: André Beteille, "Agrarian Relations in Tanjore District" in *Studies in Agrarian Social Structure* (New Delhi: Oxford University Press, 1974); Marshall Bouton, *Agrarian Radicalism in South India* (Princeton: Princeton University Press, 1985) and Saraswathi Menon, "Responses to Caste and Class Oppression in Thanjavur District, 1940–1952", *Social Scientist*, vol. 7. Beteille and Bouton both emphasize the role of landless agricultural labourers in radical agrarian political movements in Thanjavur, and show the importance of local conditions in which there is a high proportion of Schedule Caste landless labourers, in accounting for the occurrence of radical mobilization. A more recent account of agrarian politics in Kerala is T. K. Oommen, *From Mobilization to Institutionalization: The Dynamics of Agrarian Movement in Twentieth Century Kerala* (Bombay: Popular Prakashan, 1985).

4. Accounts of the impact of post-Independence land reforms on these tenurial systems are found in Bouton; *Agrarian Radicalism in South India* on Thanjavur; and in R. J. Herring, *Land to the Tiller* (New Haven: Yale University Press, 1983) on Kerala.

5. Herring, *Land to the Tiller*, gives a comprehensive analysis of land reforms in Kerala.

6. Beteille, "Agrarian Relations", and Bouton, *Agrarian Radicalism*, amplify this conclusion of Gough's.

7. The stance of both the main communist parties remains ambiguous on this point, however. The *Political Resolution* of the Communist Party of India (Marxist) of 1978 stated "the need for peasant unity, not the old peasant unity based on middle and rich peasants based on the agricultural labourers and poor peasants". For the Communist Party of India, too, "The main tactic of establishing peasant unity is to rely firmly on agricultural labourers and poor peasants, to unite solidly with middle peasants and to try to win over rich peasants . . ." (*Party Life*, Journal of the Communist Party of India, 7 August 1978, p. 6). Gough's point that "Indian communists have never accorded sufficient weight to the poor peasants and landless labourers in their organizational and revolutionary efforts", arguably, still stands.

Ecology and Social Movements[1]

Gail Omvedt

It has become fashionable in India among established Marxists of the big communist parties to characterize ecology movements as "petty bourgeois". This kind of stamping has also been done in Europe and North America. But the conception is wrong. Ecology movements from the beginning have had their social base in peasant or farming communities and among tribal peoples. Even in the "advanced" capitalist countries it has not been middle class vacationers longing for nice scenery but the people who live in the mountains and forests and whose whole materially-based cultural tradition gives them a living relation to the land who have fought the hardest, from German and French farmers opposing nuclear power to American Indians who have fought the devastation of their reservation lands. Middle-class intellectuals, joining these movements, have helped to articulate their ideologies, though sometimes giving them a reformist and anti-socialist direction. Factory workers, alienated from the land as from all means of production, have been slower to move on these issues – partly also from being under the leadership of unions and parties who are almost invariably more economistic than the workers themselves – but as they begin fighting on issues of health and safety on the job and against the total degradation of their own urban environment, their linkage with the ecology-oriented movements gives these a new thrust. This sequence can be seen both in Europe and North America and in the Third World, though it may take very different forms – from the emergence of the Green Party as the first viable radical socialist party in West Germany to the Philippines where tribal resistance to the destruction of their lands is now taking the form of armed struggle led by the New People's Army against a World Bank-financed dam in Luzon.

In India, the final shape of movements on ecology and environmental issues and the nature of the leadership emerging remains to be seen. But here also it is clear that these are most strongly based among peasants and *adivasis*, and that their fight for livelihood on the issues of forests, famine and fishing not only confronts the state and imperialist penetration, but also raises new issues about the nature of economic development itself and the very meaning of socialism.

Forests for People or Profit?

The most well-known of ecology movements is undoubtedly the Chipko movement. From 1973 its base has been among the low-caste Himalayan peasantry and especially the women – for these have been the closest to the forests, the gatherers of fodder, fuel and water, while men have often been away seeking jobs in the plains or getting minor rake-offs from the commercialization of "development". But the wider connections of its Gandhian leadership, have helped to make its principles, like those of the "5 Fs" (food, fodder, fuel, fertilizer and fibre), quite widely known.

The Gandhism of the leaders is undoubtedly related to a certain element of reformism. It can be seen in Sunderlal Bahuguna's tendency to see the state as good and only the local forest officials as the enemy, a tendency also reflected in the recent effort of Sarvodaya leader Baba Amte to take up a *jungle bachao* movement in Gadchiroli district of Maharashtra; in this case not only Amte's personal appeals to Indira Gandhi but even more his unwillingness to work with local tribal leaders or CPI(ML) activists in the area has resulted in the movement fading out. It does not mean that the movement as such is a reformist movement. There is a radicalizing process involved in fighting on these issues. Most recently this seems to be expressed in the emergence of the Uttarkhand Sangarsh Vahini (USV) as a new element in the Chipko movement, a militant youth section moving towards a synthesis of Gandhism and Marxism. The Vahini-led anti-alcohol movement has recently become famous, but the main thrust of its efforts is to link together issues – mining, tree-cutting, alcoholism – as related to a single process of exploitation which destroys both the environment and the cultural traditions of the people. "It is the relationship among human beings which determines the relationship between humans and the forests" – that is the theme of Vahini activists. They are also firmly opposed to the leadership principle, that is to movement bureaucracy, a feature which links them to the ecology and feminist movements in the West in contrast to traditional Gandhism in India.

In any event, the class-struggle orientation of the USV is not in contradiction with but rather helps to confirm the basic themes of the Chipko movement: that control over forests should rest not with the state but with the local community, which is more capable of responsible management; that scientists and experts, who up to now have mainly legitimized the state's decisions as "scientific forestry" while the real ecology issues have been raised by peoples' movements, should learn to serve the people; that an alternative form of development must be sought, which unlike the destructive role of the market is based on technology which allows for ecological harmony and local self-reliance.

The Red and Green Flag

Most forest dwellers and tribal peasants in India do not have a surplus of intellectual leadership to articulate their principles. Their own educated sections have tended to become co-opted and Brahmanized, while outside left leadership very often tells the local people their problems rather than asks them. However there are striking similarities between these Chipko themes and some of the issues raised in practice by the other famous forest movement in India.

This is of course the Jharkhand movement.[2] Its biggest radical organization, the Jharkhand Mukti Morcha, was founded in 1973, about the same time as Chipko started, but the demand for a separate province within the Indian union goes back to the 1930s (and the tradition of tribal and peasant resistance, of course, much farther than that, in both areas) when it was first raised by educated *adivasis*. The reasoning is simple: stopping the ongoing drain of resources from the Jharkhand area, which continues to provide steel, and valuable minerals for all-India use and for export, while its factories and mines are only enclaves totally controlled by outsiders and the local people remain impoverished and subject to *goonda*ism[3] and extreme forms of economic and social–sexual exploitation.

There has been little scope in this tumultuous area for a tradition of Gandhian non-violence, and with the emergence of new struggles in the late 1960s and the birth of the Jharkhand Mukti Morcha tribal militancy and police repression reached greater heights than in the Chipko area. In contrast to *satyagrahas* the movement has been characterized by militant rallies, direct action and from the other side, *goonda*ism and police firing. Issues have also ranged from opposition to moneylending and alcoholism to fighting exploitative dam and development projects which only threatened to deprive the people of more land and forests. In 1978–9 a campaign was undertaken against a World Bank-sponsored "social forestry" project, in which the *adivasis* cut down teak trees which had been planted at the expense of the *sal* tree, centre of their economic and cultural life. Here as well militant clashes with the police occurred, and much of the resulting "jungle *khatao*" movement climaxed in the brutal firing and repression in Singbhum in 1980.

What does tree-cutting have to do with tree-hugging? The same issue of local human needs *versus* commercial needs underlies it. The "social forestry" of the Indian government and international agencies involves the planting of commercial trees like eucalyptus and teak, which provide only lumber and profits for rich farmers (eucalyptus in fact sucks up excessive water from the land, according to most peasants), while local people prefer mixed forests and trees whose leaves, roots, bark, fruit and nuts may be as useful to them as the lumber itself. "Teak is Bihar, *sal* is Jharkhand", say the *adivasis*. Their trees are for profit, ours are for people. And their campaign resulted in, for the first time, a World Bank project being called to a halt.

The political articulation of the Jharkhand movement is significant. The Jharkhand Mukti Morcha was born with a green and red flag, and with the concrete practice of the alliance that this symbolized – Dhanbad mine-workers, lower-caste peasants, *adivasis*. "Lalkhand–Jharkhand" was the slogan of early marches. But the Congress(I), while on one hand collaborating with the ferocious repression of the state, has also sought to chip away at the alliance, wooing the middle-class section of *adivasis* with the theme of "only green" and stigmatizing the red flag as that of outsiders. Their game has been immensely helped by the economistic tendency (and the predominantly outside leadership) of the CPI and CPI(M) and especially by the CPI(M)'s ongoing opposition to the movement. The CPI(M)'s propaganda lumps together Khalistan, Kolhan, Jharkhand, and Chattisgarh Mukti Morcha, and the Assam movement as all "splittist" and "separatist" and calls instead for "pure" class struggle. Which means in practice struggle for wages, and expansion of the party. This rhetorical posing of the "pure red flag" in fact drives people away from it, for it is extremely difficult for *adivasis*, *dalits*, women or other sections of toilers to understand that Marxism might be something other than what the most powerful Marxists around them say it is. And they have been saying for a very long time that Marxism means class struggle only – in a narrow sense that excludes the issues of national, sexual and other forms of oppression. So, in spite of the fact that ML groups have supported the Jharkhand movement, that the CPI has wavered, and that a section of the ex-MLs has worked in it to develop a theory of Jharkhandi nationality, it has been hard for the *adivasis* to resist the

propaganda that the red flag is the flag of the outsiders, the Dikus.
With some of the leadership won over to a Congress(I) position, the
conference of the Jharkhand Mukti Morcha in 1983 decided to adopt
only a green flag. But the red–green flag lives on in the area, as the
flag of the Singhbum contract labourers' struggle, of many Dhanbad
coal miners of the Chattisgarh Mukti Morcha and now of the textile
workers in Rajnandgaon, the flag of unity and struggle.

Dams and Development

Opposition to dams itself raises crucial issues about the form of
capitalist development in India. Major river valley control projects,
along with high yielding seeds and fertilizer and provision of bank
capital have been central to efforts to create capitalist agricultural
development. But, while big dam projects have certainly provided
electricity and have helped raise India's irrigated area from 18 per
cent to about 30 per cent, they have often resulted in localized
problems of waterlogging and salination, they have failed in significant cases at flood control (south-west Bengal has been plagued
with floods for several years in spite of the much heralded Damodar
Valley project) and they have often intensified uneven development
since surrounding dry areas remain untouched.

A good example is south Maharashtra state. Here in the apparently
lush irrigated river valleys of Satara, Sangli and Kolhapur districts,
sugarcane and other cash crops have provided a base for one of the
most powerful sections of *kulak* farmers in India, using their
control over "cooperative" sugar factories and other institutions of
development to accumulate political power as well as capital. The
factory controlled by Chief Minister Vasantdada Patil, for instance,
is said to be the largest in Asia with 7500 ton per day crushing
capacity. But even in the central areas, thousands of acres are being
lost to waterlogging, while crop productivity is falling – sugarcane
yields, for instance which used to be 60 to 80 tons per acre in some
parts, have been sinking to 30 to 40 tons. And the dry *talukas* of the
same districts, especially in Satara and Sangali, have become steadily
worse off, with steadily declining rainfall due partly to the near-
complete deforestation of the coastal Sahyadris. "Development"
itself seems to be systematically unequal, since in the last two years –
in spite of governmental proclamations of spreading the benefits of
development – new cane-crushing tonnage licensed for the factories
in the "advanced" areas is more than that licensed for new factories
in the backward areas. Local activists of the backward *talukas* have

even argued that this is a deliberate conspiracy, motivated by the interests of the *kulaks* and capitalists in keeping large areas as labour reserves. In fact, while some areas are providing the *lakhs* of migrant sugarcane harvest-workers, the drought-ridden *talukas* of the southern Maharashtra region are the main source of the workers in the Bombay textile industry, whose real wages and living standards have risen little in the hundred years of this industry.

These interlinked dry/irrigated regions of agricultural capitalism have been much more difficult to organize than the tribal or Himalayan peasantry. Caste divisons are much more acute, and the existence of a single large community whose traditions are also traditions of resistance is lacking. The division between agricultural labourers and the toiling middle peasantry is also a serious one, and the local ruling classes are both strong and shrewd enough to utilize these caste and class splits. Nor is ecology an immediately visible issue; here the forests have been long gone, and "development" seems the only way out. Thus the sporadic left-led struggles of agricultural labourers and peasants have generally implicitly accepted the capitalist developmental framework. Every major dam project in India has been accompanied by peasant struggles, but these have nearly all focused on issues of "rehabilitation", i.e. demand for fair resettlement. They have not questioned the nature of the projects. Similarly, famine and drought conditions have led to massive struggles of the rural poor, especially in Maharashtra, but these have focused on demanding government relief works (EGS projects) and other forms of immediate famine relief. Until fairly recently, the entire Marxist left has looked on development primarily as a distributional issue. The critique has been: there has not been enough of it (the "bourgeois-landlord state" or the "semi-feudal state" cannot provide *real* capitalist development), its benefits do not go to the toiling people ("capitalist development is like that").

This includes the writer of this article; and if some "petty bourgeois" intellectuals and activists have begun to change in the last few years, the impetus for all of us has come from outside, from the movements of the people themselves.

A new trend can be seen in the past few years. While forest area tribal peasants are moving towards struggles to oppose big dam construction entirely, the rural poor in parts of Sangli district and elsewhere have begun to demand that EGS projects should be not simply makework road-building, but should focus on small irrigation projects that will help the land. Unlike big dams, such small bunding and percolation tanks are much more susceptible to local control and planning. Such a demand also unites the interest of the landless and very poor peasants on the projects with the majority of peasants in the area.

These struggles in part grew out of the textile workers' strike of 1982–3.[4] Workers, returning to their villages, often went on the EGS schemes as a way of supporting themselves, and took part in organizing struggles. Their rural strike/struggles helped them to understand the connection between the textile owners, state, and Congress(I)-based rural *kulaks*. They also laid a basis for seeing something of the inherently unequal nature of capitalist development, the connections between rural wealth, rural poverty and factory-level exploitation. In fact, textile workers have always been less "economistic" than their unions in the sense that they have always been concerned about the "development" of their villages; only previously this was reformist and linked to Congress(I) village leadership. Now it began to be linked to struggles for a different kind of development. In Khanapur, the most perennially drought-ridden area of Sengali district in the past decades, textile workers led the formation of a rural labourer–peasants' organization, the Shoshit Shetkari, Kashtakari, Kamgar Mukti Sangarsh (Mukti Sangarsh for short), which took up the leadership of rural struggles.

On 30 July, after only eight inches of rain during the entire monsoon resulted in failures of several crops, over 5000 peasants and labourers organized by Mukti Sangarsh brought their bullocks and cows onto the road, demanding that the police either arrest them along with all the animals, or else provide free fodder and a long-term scientific alternative to drought conditions. The free fodder was won, but as it is apparent that the bourgeois state has no real answer to uneven development and drought, Mukti Sangarsh has gone ahead with its own plans for a 10-day 'science fair' in which activists of the Peoples' Science Movement (PSM) will join local peasants and labourers, students and teachers in exhibitions and programmes dealing with water, health and superstition – with the hope eventually of developing an alternative "peoples' plan" for the entire district.

In this way PSM, which in the four-to-five years of its existence has been involved in numerous rural tours, anti-superstition campaigns, and poster exhibits on issues ranging from women's health to Hiroshima Day, is getting linked to rural struggles. In the process, they are not simply providing some needed skills and resources, but also learning from the people. In an initial Khanapur meeting it was older peasants who argued vigorously that in the days of their childhood there had been abundant rainfall and extensive forests, and the younger scientists who were sceptical. Government records, in fact, show that droughts in areas like Khanapur have been on the increase in the twentieth century.

It seems that the "natural" and therefore inevitable character of droughts and floods has become as much a part of bourgeois ideology, at least relating to the Third World, as it presumably was of pre-capitalist modes in which people were supposed to have stood helpless before natural onslaughts. However, historical research confirms that the irrigation and development projects of the colonial period were accompanied from the beginning not only by inherent problems of waterlogging and salination, but also by disruption of the environment and increased incidence of malaria. In the post-colonial period also big dam projects have often meant destruction of local cultures, increased disease problems, and even occasional failures in the irrigation which they promised. As for rainfall, it is undoubtedly a natural fact that some regions have less and others more, that periods of floods and aridity have been constant phenomena. This does not by itself mean drought, famine, and destructive flash floods. A recent book by the Allchins, two of the most reputed archeologists of South Asia, notes, "The impression of rapidly increasing aridity at the present time, frequently referred to in the current literature, is considered by more informed sources and authority on climate and agriculture to be due to human activity" – and they go on to discuss the theory that "over-exploitation" of the environment, more than attacks by invading Aryans, was responsible for the collapse of the Harappan civilization. The assault on the environment which began with the advent of class society 5000 years ago is today being pushed to its limits by capital, with the danger of even graver consequences.

Today, the balance of nature can only be achieved by a conscious balancing of human society and nature – something that requires a revolutionary movement. The taking up of environmental issues requires the coming together of intellectuals who have the resources of scientific training and access to knowledge with the rural toilers and tribals fighting for the lands and forests so much a part of their lives – as well as the working class with its still untapped ability to transform the world. It also has the potential of uniting these sections. It can bring together the two great exploited classes of the rural areas, agricultural labourers and toiling peasants. It can also unite the urban working class, as they become conscious of the link of their increasingly devastated urban environment and the ongoing oppression of their kin elsewhere with the whole system of capitalist exploitation. It is perhaps not accidental that some of the most ecologically conscious revolutionary poetry in the USA today is coming from black writers, whose identity stretches from the completely proletarianized black working class of city slums to the revolutionaries of rural Africa – such as Jayne Cortez, who can almost never write a poem without a call to resistance, who describes "the lifeblood of the earth almost dead in the greedy mouth of imperialism", and depicts the graphic wreckages of disease and pollution but ends with a simple version,

> To breath clean air
> to drink pure water to plant new crops
> to soak up the rain to wash off the stink
> to hold body and soul together in peace
> That's it
> Push back the catastrophes.

Editors' Notes

1. First published in Economic and Political Weekly, 3 November 1984.
2. Jharkhand is a region of the eastern state of Bihar with a large "tribal" population. On this region and its politics see N. Sengupta (ed.) *Fourth World Dynamics: Jharkhand* (New Delhi: Authors Guild Publications, 1982).
3. "*Goonda*ism" is violence organized by local bosses.
4. The reference here is to the protracted strike of workers in the Bombay textile mills.

Bibliography

Guides to further reading are found in various chapters of this book. The Introduction to Part I introduces the literature on the impact of colonialism and colonial capitalist development; the Introduction to Part II introduces further reading on the political economy of South Asia; Chapter 6 gives a guide to the literature on the state and on the industrial economy of India; Chapter 10 introduces reading on South Asian society; the Introduction to Part IV, and Chapter 19 introduce literature on ethnicity, regionalism and South Asian politics. To this should be added Hardgrave's textbook on *India: Government and Politics in a Developing Nation* (1971 and later editions), which is a useful basic text, containing much information and a good guide to the politics literature.

Key reading on Bangladesh is given in the Introduction to Part II and amongst the references in Chapter 8.

The Introduction to Part IV introduces some literature on Sri Lanka. In addition there is a useful general collection of articles edited by K. M. de Silva (1977); vol. III of the University of Ceylon's *History of Ceylon* (de Silva (ed.), 1973) contains key articles on the colonial period; Morrison *et al.* (eds) 1979 contains a recent collection of sociological field studies on rural Sri Lanka; Jupp (1978) and Wilson (1979) introduce Sri Lankan politics, and Manor (ed.) 1984, surveys more recent trends; Herring (1983) illuminates Sri Lankan agrarian politics; the same author has also surveyed the political economy of Sri Lanka's recent development (1987), while Richards and Gooneratne (1980) give a good account of earlier patterns of development. Quite outstanding is Moore's *The State and Peasant Politics in Sri Lanka* (1985), which ranges much more widely than its title might suggest, and has something authoritative and interesting to say about many aspects of contemporary Sri Lankan economy and society.

Agarwal, B. 1984. "Rural Women and High Yielding Variety Rice Technology", *Economic and Political Weekly* Review of Agriculture, March.
— —. 1986. "Women, Poverty and Agricultural Growth in India", *Journal of Peasant Studies*, 13, 4.
Ahluwalia, I. J. 1985. *Industrial Growth in India; Stagnation since the mid-Sixties.* Delhi: Oxford University Press.
Ahmed, I., ed. 1973. *Caste and Social Stratification among Muslims.* New Delhi: Manohar.
Akbar, M. J. 1985. *India: The Siege Within.* Harmondsworth: Penguin Books.
Alavi, H. 1964. "Imperialism, Old and New" in R. Miliband and J. Saville eds. *Socialist Register 1964.*
— —. 1965. "Peasants and Revolution", in Miliband, R. and Saville, J.

Socialist Register 1965, reprinted in Gough, K. and Sharma, H. eds. *Imperialism and Revolution in South Asia*. New York: Monthly Review Press.

— —. 1972. "The State in Post-Colonial Societies", *New Left Review*.

— —. 1973a. "Elite Farmer Strategy and Regional Disparities in Pakistan", *Economic and Political Weekly* VIII, 13, March 1973, reprinted in H. N. Gardezi and J. Rashid eds. 1983, *Pakistan: The Roots of Dictatorship*. London: Zed Books.

— —. 1973b. "Peasant Classes and Primordial Loyalties", *Journal of Peasant Studies*, 1, 1.

— —. 1975. "India and the Colonial Mode of Production", *Economic and Political Weekly* Special Number. August.

— —. 1982. "India: The Transition to Colonial Capitalism", in H. Alavi *et al. Capitalism and Colonial Production*. London: Croom Helm.

— —. 1983. "Class and State in Pakistan" in H. Gardezi and J. Rashid eds. *Pakistan: The Roots of Dictatorship*. London: Zed Books.

— —. 1987. "Pakistan and Islam: Ethnicity and Ideology", in Fred Halliday and Hamza Alavi eds. *State and Ideology in the Middle East*. London: Macmillan.

Amjad, R. 1984. *The Impact of Return Migration on Domestic Employment in Pakistan*. Islamabad: ILO–ARTEP.

Baden-Powell, B. H. 1892. *The Land Systems of British India*, 3 vols. Oxford: Clarendon Press.

Bagchi, A. K. 1972. *Private Investment in India, 1900–1939*. Cambridge: Cambridge University Press.

— —. 1976. "De-industrialisation in India in the Nineteenth Century: Some Theoretical Implications", *Journal of Development Studies* 12, 2.

— —. 1975. "Some Characteristics of Industrial Growth in India", *Economic and Political Weekly* Annual Number February.

— —. 1983. "Review of A. K. Banerji", *Economic and Political Weekly* 5 March 1983.

Bailey, F. G. 1957. *Caste and the Economic Frontier*. Manchester: Manchester University Press.

— —. 1963. *Politics and Social Change: Orissa in 1959*. Bombay: Oxford University Press.

Baines, E. 1966. *History of the Cotton Manufactures in Great Britain*. London: Cass. (originally published in 1835).

Baker, C. J. 1976. *The Politics of South India 1919–1937*. Cambridge: Cambridge University Press.

— —. 1984. *An Indian Rural Economy 1880–1955: The Tamilnad Countryside*. Delhi: Oxford University Press.

Balasubramanyam, V. 1984. *The Indian Economy*. London: Weidenfeld & Nicolson.

Ballard, R. 1976. "Ethnicity: Theory and Experience", *New Community* V, 3.

— —. 1983. "The Context and Consequences of Migration: Jullundur and Mirpur Compared", *New Community* XI, 117–36.

— —. 1987. The Political Economy of Migration: Pakistan, Britain and the

Middle East, in J. S. Eades ed. *Migration and the Social Order*. London: Tavistock.

Banerji, A. K. 1982. *Aspects of Indo-British Economic Relations, 1858–1898*. Bombay: Oxford University Press.

Bapna, S. L. 1973. *Economic and Social Implications of Green Revolution: A Case Study of the Kota District*, Vallabh Vidyanagar: Agro Economic Research Centre, Sardar Patel University.

Baran, P. 1957. *The Political Economy of Growth*. New York: Monthly Review Press.

Bardhan, K. 1977. "Rural Employment, Wages and Labour Markets in India. A Survey of Research. – I. Size and Composition of Rural Working Force", *Economic and Political Weekly* Review of Agriculture, 25 June, XII, 26.

——. 1983. "Economic Growth, Poverty and Rural Labour Markets in India". International Labour Office, World Employment Programme, *Working Paper* WEP 10–6/WP 54.

Bardhan, P. 1974. "On Life and Death Questions", *Economic and Political Weekly*, vol. 9, August.

——. 1984. *The Political Economy of Development in India*. Oxford: Blackwell.

Barnett, M. R. 1977. *The Politics of Cultural Nationalism*. Princeton: Princeton University Press.

Barnett, S. A. 1975. "Approaches to Changes in Caste Ideology in South India", in B. Stein ed. *Essays on South India*, University of Hawaii Press.

——. 1977. "Identity Choice and Caste Ideology in Contemporary South Asia", in K. David ed. *The New Wind: Changing Identities in South Asia*. The Hague: Mouton & Co.

Barnett, S. A., Fruzzetti, L. and Ostor, A. 1976. "Hierarchy Purified: Notes on Dumont and his Critics", *Journal of Asian Studies*, XXXV, 4.

Barrier, N. G. 1970. *The Sikhs and their Literature*. Delhi: Manohar Book Service.

Baru, S. 1982. "The IMF Loan, Facts and Issues", *Social Scientist*, 104.

Basu, Aparna. 1974. *The Growth of Education and Political Development in India, 1898–1920*. Delhi: Oxford University Press.

Beck, B. 1972. *Peasant Society in Konku: A Study of Right and Left Sub-castes in South India*. Vancouver: University of British Columbia Press.

Beidelman, T. 1959. *A Comparative Analysis of the Jajmani System*. Locust Valley (NY): Monographs of the Association for Asian Studies, VIII.

Beteille, A. 1963. *Caste, Class and Power: Changing Patterns of Stratification in a Tanjore village*. Berkeley: University of California Press.

——. 1974. *Studies in Agrarian Social Structure*. Delhi: Oxford University Press.

Bhaduri, Amit. 1973. "A Study in Agricultural Backwardness under Semi-Feudalism", *Economic Journal*, March, 83, 329.

——. *et al.* 1986. "Persistence and Polarisation: A Study in the Dynamics of Agrarian Contradiction", *Journal of Peasant Studies* 13, 3.

Bhalla, Sheila. 1976. "New Relations of Production in Harvana Agriculture", *Economic and Political Weekly* Review of Agriculture, 27 March, XI, 13.

— —. 1977a. "Changes in Acreage and Tenure Structure of Land Holdings in Haryana, 1962–72", *Economic and Political Weekly* Review of Agriculture, 26 March, XII, 13.

— —. 1977b. "Agricultural Growth: Role of Institutional and Infrastructural Factors", *Economic and Political Weekly* 5 and 12 November, XII, 45 and 46.

Bhattacharya, S. 1969. "The Shoe-Shiners of Patna", *Sociological Bulletin*, XVIII: 167–74.

Bushan, Bharat. 1985. "The Origins of Rebellion in the Punjab", *Capital and Class*, 24, Winter.

Billings, M. H. and Singh, A. 1971. "The Effect of Technology on Farm Employment in India", *Development Digest*.

Blair, H. W. 1980. "Mrs Gandhi's Emergency, The Indian Elections of 1977, Pluralism and Marxism: Problems with Paradigms", *Modern Asian Studies* 14, 2.

Bondurant, J. 1958. *Regionalism vs. Provincialism*. Berkeley: University of California Press.

Bose, A. B. and Jodha, N. S. 1965. "The Jajmani System in a Desert Village", *Man in India*, 45: 105–26.

Bose, A. N. 1974. *The Informal Sector in the Calcutta Metropolitan Economy*. Geneva: International Labour Office.

Bose, N. K. 1967. *Problems of National Integration*. Simla: Institute of Advanced Study.

Bose, Pradip K. 1981. "Social Mobility and Caste Violence", *Economic and Political Weekly*, 18 April 1981.

Brass, Paul. 1974. *Language, Religion and Politics in Northern India*. Cambridge: Cambridge University Press.

— —. 1982. "Pluralism, Regionalism and Decentralising Tendencies in Contemporary Indian Politics", in A. J. Wilson and D. Dalton eds *The States of South Asia: Problems of National Integration*. London: Hurst.

— —. 1985. *Ethnic Groups and the State*. London: Croom Helm.

Breman, J. 1985. *Of Peasants, Migrants and Paupers: Rural Labour Circulation and Capitalist Production in West India*. Delhi: Oxford University Press.

Bromley, Yuri and Kozlov, V. I. 1987. "The Theory of Ethnos and Ethnic Processes in the Soviet Sciences", *Comparative Studies in Society and History* (forthcoming).

Byres, T. J. 1974. "Land Reform, Industrialisation and the Marketed Surplus in India: An Essay on the Power of Rural Bias", in David Lehmann ed. *Agrarian Reform and Agrarian Reformism*. London: Faber & Faber.

— —. 1979. "Of Neo-Populist Pipe Dreams: Daedalus in the Third World and the Myth of Urban Bias", *Journal of Peasant Studies*, January, 6, 2.

Cain, M. 1981. "Risk and Insurance: Perspectives on Fertility and Agrarian Change in India and Bangladesh", *Population and Development Review* 7, 3.

Caldwell, J. *et al.* 1982. "The Causes of Demographic Change in South India: A Micro-approach", *Population and Development Review* 8, 4.

Chandra, B. 1966. *The Rise and Growth of Economic Nationalism in India*. New Delhi: People's Publishing House.

Chandra, Bipan *et al.* 1969. *Indian Economy in the 19th Century: A Symposium.* Delhi: Indian Economic and Social History Association.

Chandrasekhar, C. P. 1978. "Growth and Technical Change in a Stagnant Industry: The Case of Textiles", Working Paper, Centre for Development Studies, Trivandrum.

Charlesworth, N. 1980. "The 'Middle Peasant Thesis' and the Roots of Rural Agitation in India, 1914–1947", *Journal of Peasant Studies* 7, 3.

— —. 1982. *British Rule and the Indian Economy 1800–1914.* London: Macmillan.

Cohn, B. S. 1962. "Political Systems in Eighteenth Century India: The Benares Region", *Journal of the American Oriental Society* 82: 312–20.

— —. 1970. "Society and Social Change under the Raj", *South Asian Review* 4: 27–49.

Commander, S. 1983. "The Jajmani System in North India: An Examination of its Logic and Status across Two Centuries", *Modern Asian Studies,* 17.

Correspondent, Special. 1973. "Government May Propose, But . . .", *Economic and Political Weekly* 9 June.

Correspondent, Special. 1975. "Arrested Green Revolution", *Economic and Political Weekly* 21 and 28 June.

Crouzet, F. 1972. *Capital Formation in the Industrial Revolution.* London: Methuen.

Dahya, B. 1974. "Pakistani Ethnicity in Industrial Cities in Britain" in A. Cohen ed. *Urban Ethnicity.* London: Tavistock.

Dasgupta, Biplab. 1977. *Agrarian Change and the New Technology in India.* Geneva: United Nations Research Institute for Social Development.

Desai, A. R. ed. 1978. *Peasant Movements in India.* Bombay: Oxford University Press.

Devylder, S. and Asplund, D. 1979. "Contradictions and Distortion in a Rural Economy: The Case of Bangladesh" (report by Policy Development and Evaluation Division, SIDA, Stockholm, May; mimeo).

Djurfeldt, G. and Lindberg, S. 1975. *Behind Poverty: the Social Formation in a Tamil Village.* Scandinavian Institute of Asian Studies Monograph Series, no. 22. London: Curzon Press.

Dumont, L. 1970a. *Homo Hierarchicus.* London: Weidenfeld & Nicolson.

— —. 1970b. *Religion, Politics and History in India.* Paris: Mouton.

— —. 1980. *Homo Hierarchicus: The Caste System and its Implications.* Chicago: Chicago University Press. (This is the complete Revised English Edition of the work first published in French in 1966, and in English translation in 1970.)

Dumont, L. and Pocock, D. 1957. "For a Sociology of India", *Contributions to Indian Sociology,* 1.

— —. 1957. "Village Studies", *Contributions to Indian Sociology,* 1.

Dutt, R. C. 1956. *The Economic History of India Vol. 1: Under Early British Rule.* London: Routledge.

— —. 1956. *The Economic History of India, Vol. 2: In the Victorian Age.* London: Routledge.

Dutt, R. Palme. 1940. *India Today.* London: Left Book Club (Unabridged edition, New Delhi, 1972, Peoples' Publishing House).

Dyson, T. and Moore, M. 1983. "Kinship Structure, Female Autonomy and Demographic Behaviour", *Population and Development Review*, 9, 1.

Emmanuel, A. 1972. *Unequal Exchange: A Study of the Imperialism of Trade.* New York: Monthly Review Press.

Engineer, A. A., ed. 1984. *Communal Riots in Post-Independence India.* Hyderabad: Sangam Books.

———. 1987. "Meerut: The Nation's Shame", *Economic and Political Weekly* XXII, 25.

Epstein, T. S. 1962. *Economic Development and Social Change in South India.* Bombay: Oxford University Press.

———. 1967. "Productive Efficiency and Customary Systems of Rewards in South India", in Firth, R., ed. *Themes in Economic Anthropology.* London: Tavistock Press.

Farmer, B. H., ed. 1977. *Green Revolution? Technology and Change in Rice-growing Areas of Tamil Nadu and Sri Lanka.* London: Macmillan.

Fox, R. G. 1971. *Kin, Clan, Raja and Rule.* Berkeley: University of California Press.

Frankel, F. 1978. *India's Political Economy 1947–1977.* Princeton: University Press.

Frykenberg, R. E., ed. 1969. *Land Control and Social Structure in Indian History.* Madison: University of Wisconsin Press.

Gadgil, D. R. 1973. *The Industrial Evolution of India in Recent Times, 1860–1939.* Delhi: Oxford University Press.

Galanter, Marc. 1978. "Who Are the Backward Classes?", *Economic and Political Weekly*, 28 October.

Gallagher, J. 1973. "Congress in Decline", in J. Gallagher, *et al.* eds. *Locality, Province and Nation.* Cambridge: Cambridge University Press.

Gankovsky, Yu. (n.d.). *The People of Pakistan: An Ethnic History.* Lahore: People's Publishing House.

Gardezi, H. and Rashid, J. eds. 1983. *Pakistan: The Roots of Dictatorship.* London: Zed Books.

Gellner, E. 1964. *Thought and Change.* London: Weidenfeld & Nicolson.

Gilani, I., Khan, M. F. and Iqbal, M. 1979. *Labour Migration from Pakistan to the Middle East.* Islamabad: Pakistan Institute of Development Economics.

Good, A. 1982. "The Actor and the Act: Categories of Prestation in South India", *Man* (N.S.) 17.

Gordon, L. 1974. *Bengal: the Nationalist Movement 1876–1940.* New York: Columbia University Press.

Gough, K. 1960. "The Hindu Jajmani System", *Economic Development and Cultural Change* 9: 83–91.

———. 1981. *Rural Society in South East India.* Cambridge: Cambridge University Press.

Gould, H. A. 1967. "Priest and Contrapriest: A Structural Analysis of Jajmani Relations", *Contributions to Indian Sociology* New Series, 1.

Government of Bangladesh. 1980. *Second Five-Year Plan 1980–85.* Dacca, Planning Commission, May.

Government of India, Planning Commission. 1961. *Third Five Year Plan*. Delhi: Government Publications.

Greenough, P. 1982. *Prosperity and Misery in Modern Bengal*. New York: Oxford University Press.

Guha, R., ed. 1982. *Subaltern Studies I: Writings on South Asian History and Society*. Delhi: Oxford University Press.

——, ed. 1983. *Subaltern Studies II*. Delhi: Oxford University Press.

——, ed. 1984. *Subaltern Studies III*. Delhi: Oxford University Press.

——, ed. 1985. *Subaltern Studies IV*. Delhi: Oxford University Press.

——. 1983. *Elementary Aspects of Peasant Insurgency in Colonial India*. Delhi: Oxford University Press.

Guisinger, S. E. 1984. "The Impact of Temporary Worker Migration on Pakistan", in S. Burki and R. Laporte eds. *Pakistan's Development Priorities*. Karachi: Oxford University Press.

Habib, I. 1963. *The Agrarian System of Mughal India (1556–1707)*. Bombay: Asia.

——. 1969. "Potentialities of Capitalist Development in Mughal India", *Journal of Economic History* XXIX.

Hale, S. M. 1973. *Barriers to Free Choice in Development*, typescript.

Hanson, A. H. 1966. *The Process of Planning*. Oxford: Oxford University Press.

Hardgrave, R. L. 1971 and later editions. *India: Government and Politics in a Developing Nation*. New York, etc.: Harcourt Brace and World.

Hardiman, D. 1981. *Peasant Nationalists of Gujarat: Kheda District 1917–1934*. Delhi: Oxford University Press.

Harrison, S. S. 1960. *India: The Most Dangerous Decades*. Princeton: Princeton University Press.

Harriss, B. 1984. *State and Market*. New Delhi: Concept.

Harriss, B. and Watson, E. 1987. "The Sex Ratio in South Asia", in J. Momsen and J. Townsend eds. *Geography of Gender in the Third World*. London: Hutchinson Education.

Harriss, J. 1982. *Capitalism and Peasant Farming; Agrarian Structure and Ideology in Northern Tamil Nadu*. Bombay: Oxford University Press.

——. 1986. "The Working Poor and the Labour Aristocracy in a South Indian City: A Descriptive and Analytical Account", *Modern Asian Studies*, 20, 2.

——. 1987. "Capitalism and Peasant Production: The 'Green Revolution' in India", in T. Shanin, ed. *Peasants and Peasant Societies* (new edn). Oxford: Blackwell.

——. 1988. "A Review of South Asian Studies", *Modern Asian Studies*, 22, 1.

Hartman, B. and Boyce, J. 1983. *A Quiet Violence: View from a Bangladesh Village*. London: Zed Books.

Hawthorn, G. 1982. "Caste and Politics in India since 1947" in D. B. McGilvray (ed.) *Caste Ideology and Interaction*. Cambridge: Cambridge University Press.

Herring, R. J. 1983. *Land to the Tiller: The Political Economy of Agrarian Reform in South Asia*. New Haven, Connecticut: Yale University Press.

—— —. 1984. "Economic Consequences of Local Power Configurations in Rural South Asia", in M. Desai *et al.* eds. *Agrarian Power and Agricultural Productivity in South Asia.* Delhi: Oxford University Press.

—— —. 1987. "Economic Liberalisation Policies in Sri Lanka: International Pressures, Constraints and Supports", *Economic and Political Weekly* 21 February.

Hiro, D. 1976. *Inside India.* London: Routledge & Kegan Paul.

Holmström, M. 1971. "Religious Change in an Industrial City of South India", *Journal of the Royal Asiatic Society* 1971, 1.

—— —. 1984. *Industry and Inequality: The Social Anthropology of Indian Labour.* Cambridge: Cambridge University Press.

Hussain, A. 1980. *The Impact of Agricultural Growth on Changes in the Agrarian Structure of Pakistan.* University of Sussex, D.Phil. thesis.

—— —. 1982. "Technical Change and Social Polarisation in Rural Punjab", in Karamat Ali ed. *The Political Economy of Rural Development.* Lahore: Vanguard Publications.

ISI. 1975. "Structural Causes of the Economic Crisis", *Economic and Political Weekly* 18 January.

Jayawardena, K. 1984. "Class Formation and Communalism", *Race and Class* XXVI: 1.

Jeffrey, P. 1979. *Frogs in a Well: Indian Women in Purdah.* London: Zed Books.

Jupp, J. 1978. *Sri Lanka: Third World Democracy.* London: Frank Cass.

Kahlon, A. S. and Singh, Gurbachan. 1973a. *Social and Economic Implications of Large Scale Introduction of High-Yielding Varieties of Wheat in the Punjab with Special Reference to the Ferozepur District.* Ludhiana: Department of Economics and Rural Sociology, Punjab Agricultural University.

—— and —— —. 1973b. *Social and Economic Implications of Large Scale Introduction of High-Yielding Varieties of Rice in the Punjab with Special Reference to the Gurdaspur District.* Ludhiana: Department of Economics and Rural Sociology, Punjab Agricultural University.

Kapur, Rajiv. 1986. *Sikh Separatism: The Politics of Faith.* London: Allen & Unwin.

Kautsky, Karl (forthcoming, 1988). *The Agrarian Question.* London: Swan Publishers (originally published in 1899).

Keith, A. B. 1922. *Speeches and Documents on Indian Policy: 1750–1921.* London.

Kessinger, T. 1974. *Vilyatpur 1848–1968: Social and Economic Change in a North Indian Village.* Berkeley: University of California Press.

Khan, M. H. 1981. *Underdevelopment and Agrarian Structure in Pakistan.* Lahore: Vanguard Publications.

Khan, V. S. 1977. "The Pakistanis" in J. L. Watson ed. *Between Two Cultures.* Oxford: Blackwell.

Khare, R. S. 1970. *The Changing Brahmin: Association and Elites among the Kanya Kubjas of North India.* Chicago: University of Chicago Press.

Kidron, Michael. 1965. *Foreign Investments in India.* Oxford: Oxford University Press.

Kochanek, S. 1974. *Business and Politics in India.* Berkeley: University of California Press.

— —. 1983. *Interest Groups and Development: Business and Politics in Pakistan.* Karachi/Delhi: Oxford University Press.

Kohli, A. 1987. *The State and Poverty in India.* Cambridge: Cambridge University Press.

Kothari, R. 1970a. *Politics in India.* Boston: Little, Brown.

— —, ed. 1970b. *Caste in Indian Politics.* Delhi: Orient Longman.

— —. 1983. "The Crisis of the Moderate State and the Decline of Democracy" in P. Lyon and J. Manor eds. *Transfer and Transformation: Political Institutions in the New Commonwealth.* Leicester: Leicester University Press.

Kumar, D., ed. 1982. *The Cambridge Economic History of India*, vol. 2, 1757–c.1970. Cambridge: Cambridge University Press.

Kurien, C. T. 1982. "The Budget and the Economy", *Economic and Political Weekly* 20 March.

Landes, David. 1970. *The Unbound Prometheus.* Cambridge: Cambridge University Press.

Lewis, S. R. Jr. 1969. *Economic Policy and Industrial Growth in Pakistan.* London: Allen & Unwin.

Lifschultz, L. 1979. *Bangladesh: The Unfinished Revolution.* London: Zed Press.

Lipton, M. 1977. *Why Poor People Stay Poor: Urban Bias in World Development.* London: Temple Smith.

Lloyd, P. 1974. "Class Consciousness in the Third World", *New Society* XXX, 348–50.

Lukes, S. 1974. *Power: A Radical View.* London: Macmillan.

Mahmood, Raisul Awal. 1980. "Structure of Imports under the Bangladesh Wage Farmer's Scheme". Dacca: BIDS, September, mimeo.

Maine, H. S. 1871. *Village-Communities in the East and West.* London: John Murray.

Mandelbaum, D. G. 1970. *Society in India*, 2 vols. Berkeley: University of California Press.

Manor, J. 1983. "The Electoral Process amid Awakening and Decay: reflections on the Indian General Election of 1980", in P. Lyon and J. Manor eds. *Transfer and Transformation: Political Institutions in the New Commonwealth.* Leicester: Leicester University Press.

Manor, J., ed. 1984. *Sri Lanka in Change and Crisis.* London: Croom Helm.

Mansergh, N. and Moon, P., eds. 1981. *Constitutional Relations Between Britain and India: The Transfer of Power 1942–47*, vol. X. London: HMSO.

Markovits, C. 1984. *Indian Business and Nationalist Politics, 1931–1939: The Indigenous Capitalist Class and the Rise of the Congress Party.* Cambridge: Cambridge University Press.

Marriott, M., ed. 1955. *Village India.* Chicago: University of Chicago Press.

Marriott, M. and Inden, R. 1974. "Caste Systems", *Encyclopaedia Britannica*, 15th edition, vol. III.

Marshall, P. J. 1976. *East Indian Fortunes.* Oxford: Oxford University Press.

Marx, K. 1959. "The British Rule in India" (1853) in Marx and Engels, *The First Indian War of Independence.* Moscow: Progress Publishers.

— —. 1960. "On the Future Results of British Rule in India" in *On Colonialism*. Moscow: Progress Publishers.

Mayer, A. 1960. *Caste and Kinship in Central India*. London: Routledge.

Mellor, J. 1976. *The New Economics of Growth*. Ithaca, New York: Cornell University Press.

Mencher, J. 1974. "The caste system upside down . . .", *Current Anthropology*, 15.

— —. 1978. *Agriculture and Social Structure in Tamil Nadu*. New Delhi: Allied Publishers.

Metcalf, T. R. 1969a. From Raja to Landlord: The Oudh talukdars, 1850– 1870 in Frykenberg ed. 1969.

— —. 1969b. Social Effects of British Land Policy in Oudh, in Frykenberg ed. 1969.

Mies, M. 1981. *Lacemakers of Narsipur*. London: Zed Books.

Miller, B. 1981. *The Endangered Sex: Neglect of Female Children in Rural North India*. Ithaca, New York: Cornell University Press.

Ministry of Finance. 1986. *Pakistan Economic Survey 1984–5*. Islamabad: Government of Pakistan.

Misra, B. B. 1961. *The Indian Middle Classes*. Oxford: Oxford University Press.

— —. 1977. *The Bureaucracy in India:* Delhi: Oxford University Press.

Mitra, A. 1977. *Terms of Trade and Class Relations*. London: Frank Cass.

Moffatt, M. 1979. *An Untouchable Community in South India: Structure and Consensus*. Princeton: Princeton University Press.

Moore, M. 1985. *The State and Peasant Politics in Sri Lanka*. Cambridge: Cambridge University Press.

Morrison, B. *et al.*, eds. 1979. *The Disintegrating Village: Social Change in Rural Sri Lanka*. Colombo: Lake House Investments.

Mukherjee, R. 1974. *The Rise and Fall of the East Indian Company*. New York: Monthly Review Press.

Mumtaz, K. and Shaheed, F., eds. 1987. *Women of Pakistan*. London: Zed Books.

Naoroji, D. 1871. *Poverty and Un-British Rule in India*. Reprinted by Government of India, New Delhi, 1962.

Naqvi, Hameeda. 1968. *Urban Centres and Industries in Upper India: 1556–1803*. London: Asia Publishing House.

Naqvi, S. N. H. 1984. *Pakistan's Economy Through the Seventies*. Islamabad: Pakistan Institute for Development Economics.

Nations, R. 1975. "The Economic Structure of Pakistan and Bangladesh" in R. Blackburn ed. *Explosion in the Subcontinent*. London: Pelican Books.

Neale, W. C. 1957. "Reciprocity and Redistribution in the Indian Village" in K. Polanyi, C. M. Arensberg and H. W. Pearson eds. *Trade and Markets in the Early Empires*. Glencoe: Free Press.

— —. 1962. *Economic Change in Rural India*. New Haven: Yale University Press.

— —. 1969. "Land is to Rule", in Frykenberg ed. 1969.

Nicholas, R. 1968. "Factions: A Comparative Analysis", in M. Banton ed. *Political Systems and the Distribution of Power*. ASA monograph, London: Tavistock.

Omvedt, G. 1978. "Women and Rural Revolt in India", *Journal of Peasant Studies*, 5, 3.

—— ——. 1980. *We Will Smash this Prison! Indian Women in Struggle*. London: Zed Books.

—— ——. 1980. "Agrarian Economy and Rural Classes", *Frontier*, vol. 13; 18 October, 1, 8, 15, 22, 29 November.

Pacey, A. and Payne; P. 1985. *Agricultural Development and Nutrition*. London: Hutchinson Education.

Pandey, G. 1982. "Peasant Revolt and Indian Nationalism: The Peasant Movement in Awadh 1919–22", in R. Guha ed. *Subaltern Studies* I, 1982. Delhi: Oxford University Press.

Patnaik, P. 1972. "Imperialism and the Growth of Indian Capitalism", in R. Owen and R. B. Sutcliffe eds. *Theories of Imperialism*. London: Longman.

—— ——. 1979. "Industrial Development in India since Independence", *Social Scientist* 83.

—— ——. 1986. "New Turn in Economic Policy: Context and Prospects", *Economic and Political Weekly* XXI: 23. 7 June.

Patnaik, P. and Rao, S. K. 1977. "1975–76: Beginning of the End of Stagnation?", *Social Scientist* 54–5.

Patnaik, U. 1972. "Capitalism in Agriculture", *Social Scientist*, 2 and 3.

—— ——. 1986. "The Agrarian Question and the Development of Capitalism in India", *Economic and Political Weekly* XXI: 18.

Pavlov, V. I. 1964. *The Indian Capitalist Class*. New Delhi: People's Publishing House.

—— ——. 1978. *Historical Premises for India's Transition to Capitalism*. Moscow: Nauka Publishing House.

Perlin, F. 1983. "Proto-Industrialisation and Pre-Colonial South Asia", *Past and Present* XCVIII.

Planning Commission. 1984. *The Sixth Five Year Plan 1983–88*. Islamabad: Government of Pakistan.

Ponnambalam, S. 1983. *Sri Lanka: The Tamil Liberation Struggle*. London: Zed Books.

Pouchpedass, J. 1980. "Peasant Classes in Twentieth Century Agrarian Movements in India" in E. Hobsbawm *et al.* eds. *Peasants in History: Essays in Honour of Daniel Thorner*. Delhi: Oxford University Press.

Prinsep, G. A. 1971. "Remarks on the External Commerce and Exchanges of Bengal" (1823) in K. N. Chaudhuri ed. *The Economic Development of India Under the East India Company, 1814–1858*, Cambridge: Cambridge University Press.

Radhakrishnan, S. 1927. *The Hindu Way of Life*. Oxford: Oxford University Press.

Raj, K. N. 1976. "Growth and Stagnation in Indian Industrial Development", *Economic and Political Weekly* Annual Number, February.

Ramanujam, A. K. 1973. *Speaking of Siva*. Harmondsworth: Penguin.

Ramaswamy, E. A. 1977. *The Worker and His Union: A Study in South India.* Delhi: Oxford University Press.

Ramaswamy, E. A. and U. 1981. *Industry and Labour: An Introduction.* Delhi: Oxford University Press.

Rao, C. H. Hanumantha. 1975. *Technological Change and Distribution of Gains in Indian Agriculture.* Delhi: Macmillan of India.

Richards, P. J. and Gooneratne, W. 1980. *Basic Needs, Poverty and Government Policies in Sri Lanka.* Geneva: ILO.

Roberts, M., ed. 1979. *Collective Identities, Nationalism and Protest in Modern Sri Lanka.* Colombo: Marga Institute.

Robinson, F. C. R. 1974. *Separatism among Indian Muslims.* Cambridge: Cambridge University Press.

Rubin, B. 1985. "Economic Liberalisation and the Indian State", *Third World Quarterly* 7, 4, October.

Rudolph, L. I. and Rudolph, S. H. 1967. *The Modernity of Tradition: Political Development in India.* Chicago: Chicago University Press.

—— and ——. 1984. "Determinants and Varieties of Agrarian Mobilisation" in M. Desai *et al.* eds. *Agrarian Power and Agricultural Productivity in South Asia.* Delhi: Oxford University Press.

—— and ——. 1987. *In Pursuit of Lakshmi: The Political Economy of the Indian State.* Chicago: The University of Chicago Press.

Rudra, Ashok. 1971. "Employment Patterns in Large Farms of Punjab", *Economic and Political Weekly* Review of Agriculture, 26 June.

Saberwal, S. 1979. "Inequality in Colonial India", *Contributions to Indian Sociology* (New Series) 13, 2.

Sarkar, S. 1983. *Modern India 1885–1947.* Delhi: Macmillan.

Sau, R. 1972. "Indian Economic Growth: Constraints and Prospects", *Economic and Political Weekly* Annual Number, February.

Sau, R. 1977. "Indian Political Economy, 1967–77: Marriage of Wheat and Whisky", *Economic and Political Weekly* 9 April.

Scott, J. C. 1976. *The Moral Economy of the Peasantry: Rebellion and Subsistence in South East Asia.* New Haven: Yale University Press.

Sen, A. K. 1977. "Starvation and Exchange Entitlement: A General Approach and its Application to the Great Bengal Famine", *Cambridge Journal of Economics* 1, 1.

——. 1981. *Poverty and Famines: An Essay on Entitlement and Deprivation.* Oxford: Oxford University Press.

Sen, A. 1982. *The State, Industrialisation and Class Formations in India: A neo-Marxist Perspective on Colonialism, Underdevelopment and Development.* London: Routledge.

Shah, A. M. 1982. "Division and Hierarchy: An Overview of Caste in Gujarat", *Contributions to Indian Sociology* (New Series) 16, 1.

Shetty, S. L. 1978. "Structural Retrogression in the Indian Economy since the Mid-Sixties", *Economic and Political Weekly* Annual Number, February.

Shrivastava, G. N. 1970. *The Language Controversy and the Minorities.* Delhi: Atmaram Publishers.

Siddiqi, A. 1973. *Agrarian Change in a Northern Indian State.* Oxford: Clarendon Press.

de Silva, C. R. 1982. "The Sinhalese–Tamil Rift in Sri Lanka", in A. Jeyaratnam Wilson and D. Dalton (eds) *The States of South Asia: Problems of National Integration*. London: Hurst.

de Silva, K. M., ed. 1973. *History of Ceylon, Volume III: From the Beginning of the Nineteenth Century to 1948*. Peradeniya: University of Ceylon.

——, ed. 1977. *Sri Lanka: A Survey*. London: Hurst.

Singh, Gopal. 1984. "Social-Economic Bases of the Punjab Crisis", *Economic and Political Weekly* 7 January.

Sobhan, R. 1979. "Politics of Food and Famine", *Economic and Political Weekly* 1 December.

——. 1980. "Growth and Contradictions within the Bangladesh Bourgeoisie", *Journal of Social Studies* 9 (Dacca).

Sobhan, R. and Ahmad, M. 1980. *Public Enterprise in an Intermediate Regime: A Study in the Political Economy of Bangladesh*. Dacca: Bangladesh Institute of Development.

Srinivas, M. 1959. "The Dominant Caste in Rampura", *American Anthropologist* 61.

——. 1966. *Social Change in Modern India*. Berkeley: University of California Press.

——. 1975. "The Indian Village: Myth and Reality" in J. H. M. Beattie and R. G. Lienhardt eds. *Studies in Social Anthropology*. Oxford: Clarendon Press.

Stein, B. 1983. "Idiom and Ideology in Early Nineteenth Century India" in P. Robb ed. *Rural India: Land, Power and Society under British Rule*. London: Curzon Press (collected papers on South Asia, no. 6).

Stokes, E. 1959. *The English Utilitarians and India*. Oxford: Clarendon Press.

——. 1973. "The First Century of British Colonial Rule: Social Revolution or Social Stagnation?", *Past and Present* 58. Also in *The Peasant and the Raj: Studies in Agrarian Society and Peasant Rebellion in Colonial India*. Cambridge: Cambridge University Press, 1978.

Thorner, A. 1982. "Semi-Feudalism or Capitalism: Contemporary Debate on Classes and Modes of Production in India", *Economic and Political Weekly* 4, 11 and 18 December.

Thorner, Daniel and Thorner, Alice. 1962. "Employer–Labourer Relationships in Agriculture" in their *Land and Labour in India*. London: Asia Publishing House.

Times Literary Supplement. 1969. Anonymous review of E. H. Carr and R. W. Davies, *Foundations of a Planned Economy, 1926–1929*. 4 December.

Toye, J. 1981. *Public Expenditure and Indian Development Policy 1960–1970*. Cambridge: Cambridge University Press.

——. 1988. "Political Economy and the Analysis of Indian Development", *Modern Asian Studies* 22, 1.

Tripathi, D. 1984. *Business Communities of India*. New Delhi: Manohar.

Tsakok, I. 1984. "The Export of Manpower from Pakistan to the Middle East" in S. Burki and R. Laporte eds. *Pakistan's Development Priorities*. Karachi: Oxford University Press.

Tully, M. and Jacob, S. 1985. *Amritsar*. London: Jonathan Cape.

Twomey, M. J. 1983. "Employment in Nineteenth Century Indian Textiles", *Explorations in Economic History*, vol. 20.

Tyagi, D. S. 1979. "Farm Prices and Class Bias in India", *Economic and Political Weekly* Review of Agriculture, September.

Van Schendel, W. 1981. *Peasant Mobility: The Odds of Life in Rural Bangladesh*. Assen: Van Gorcum.

Vashistha, P. 1975. *An Economic Study of the Effect of Tractorisation on Farm Output and Employment*, mimeo.

Vicziany, M. 1979. "The De-Industrialisation of India in the Nineteenth Century: A Methodological Critique of Amiya Kumar Bagchi", *Indian Economic and Social History Review* 16, 2.

Wade, R. 1982. "The System of Administrative and Political Corruption: Canal Irrigation in South India", *Journal of Development Studies*, 18: 287ff.

Washbrook, D. 1981. "Law, State and Agrarian Society in Colonial India", *Modern Asian Studies* 15, 3.

———. 1988. "South Asian Economic and Social History c. 1720–1860", *Modern Asian Studies* 22.

Waterman, P. 1982. "Seeing the Straws: Riding the Whirlwind: Reflections on Unions and Popular Movements in India", *Journal of Contemporary Asia* 12, 4.

Weiner, M. 1962. *The Politics of Scarcity: Public Pressure and Political Response in India:* Chicago: Chicago University Press.

———. 1978. *Sons of the Soil: Migration and Ethnic Conflict in India*. Princeton: Princeton University Press.

Weiner, M. and Katzenstein, M. 1981. *India's Preferential Policies*. Chicago: Chicago University Press.

Westergaard, K. 1985. *State and Rural Society in Bangladesh*. Scandinavian Institute of Asian Studies. Monograph Series No. 49. London: Curzon Press.

Whitcombe, E. 1972. *Agrarian Conditions in Northern India*, vol. I. Berkeley: University of California Press.

Williams, Eric. 1964. *Capitalism and Slavery*. London: Deutsch.

Wilson, A. J. 1979. *Policies in Sri Lanka, 1947–1979*. London: Macmillan.

Wolf, E. 1982. *Europe and the People Without History*. Berkeley: University of California Press.

Wood, G. 1981. "Rural Class Formation in Bangladesh – 1940–1980", *Bulletin of Concerned Asian Scholars* 13, 4.

World Bank. 1973. *The World Jute Economy*.

Zahir, S. and Kamal, A. 1981. "Urban Rationing System in Bangladesh". Dacca: BIDS; draft.

Index